8th International Workshop on Tree Adjoining Grammar and Related Formalisms 2006

(TAG+8)

Held in conjunction with COLING/ACL 2006

Sydney, Australia
15-16 July 2006

ISBN: 978-1-61738-497-4

Printed from e-media with permission by:

Curran Associates, Inc.
57 Morehouse Lane
Red Hook, NY 12571
www.proceedings.com

Some format issues inherent in the e-media version may also appear in this print version.

Printed by Curran Associates, Inc. (2010)

Association for Computational Linguistics
209 N. Eighth Street
Stroudsburg, Pennsylvania 18360

Phone: 1-570-476-8006
Fax: 1-570-476-0860

acl@aclweb.org

Table of Contents

Preface

It is with great pleasure that we present the current volume of papers accepted for presentation at the Eighth International Workshop on Tree Adjoining Grammar and Related Formalisms (TAG+8). We are indebted to the paper authors and the members of our program committee, both of whom contributed to making this a collection of high quality research papers. Furthermore, we also thank our invited speakers, Mark Johnson and Mark Steedman, for their participation in the workshop. Finally, our thanks go to Mark Dras as the local organizer who also helped in numerous ways in preparing the workshop and the proceedings.

As at previous TAG+ conferences, the topics addressed by the presentations belong to diverse areas of research, namely the mathematics of grammar formalisms and parsing, the syntax and semantics of natural languages, compact grammar representations and grammar engineering, the relation between TAG and other grammar formalisms, and applications to computational biology. By bringing together these different topics under the common theme of Tree Adjoining Grammars, the workshop promises to be an inspiring and fruitful event.

The volume contains 24 research papers that will be presented at TAG+8. They are divided into two parts; the first one covering the 11 papers that are to be deliverd in oral presentations and the second one covering the 13 papers that are to be presented as posters.

Tilman Becker and Laura Kallmeyer
Program Co-Chairs

Organizers

Local Organizer:

Mark Dras, Macquarie University

Program Committee:

Tilman Becker (co-chair), DFKI
Laura Kallmeyer (co-chair), University of Tuebingen
Srinivas Bangalore, AT&T Research
Eric de la Clergerie, INRIA
Dan Flickinger, CSLI, Stanford University
Robert Frank, Johns Hopkins University
Akio Fujiyoshi, Ibaraki University
Claire Gardent, LORIA
Chung-Hye Han, Simon Fraser University
Karin Harbusch, University of Koblenz
Geert-Jan Kruijff, Language Technology Lab, DFKI
Vincenzo Lombardo, University of Turin
David McDonald, BBN Technologies
Martha Palmer, University of Colorado
Owen Rambow, Columbia University
Frank Richter, University of Tuebingen
James Rogers, Earlham College
Maribel Romero, University of Pennsylvania
Anoop Sarkar, Simon Fraser University
Giorgio Satta, University of Padua
Stuart Shieber, Harvard College
Mark Steedman, University of Edinburgh
Matthew Stone, Rutgers University
Yuka Tateisi, Kogakuin University
David Weir, University of Sussex
Vijay K. Shanker, University of Delaware
Naoki Yoshinaga, Japan Society for the Promotion of Science

Invited Speakers:

Mark Steedman, University of Edinburgh
Mark Johnson, Brown University

Workshop Program

Saturday, 15 July 2006

9:00–9:10 Opening Remarks

9:10–9:50 *The Hidden TAG Model: Synchronous Grammars for Parsing Resource-Poor Languages*
David Chiang and Owen Rambow

9:50–10:30 *A Constraint Driven Metagrammar*
Joseph Le Roux, Benoît Crabbé and Yannick Parmentier

10:30–11:00 Coffee Break

11:00–11:40 *The Metagrammar Goes Multilingual: A Cross-Linguistic Look at the V2-Phenomenon*
Alexandra Kinyon, Owen Rambow, Tatjana Scheffler, SinWon Yoon and Aravind K. Joshi

11:40–12:20 *The Weak Generative Capacity of Linear Tree-Adjoining Grammars*
David Chiang

12:20–13:40 Lunch Break

13:40–14:40 Poster Session I

14:40–15:20 *A Tree Adjoining Grammar Analysis of the Syntax and Semantics of It-Clefts*
Chung-hye Han and Nancy Hedberg

15:20–15:50 Coffee Break

15:50–16:50 Invited Talk: Mark Steedman

16:50–17:30 *Pied-Piping in Relative Clauses: Syntax and Compositional Semantics Based on Synchronous Tree Adjoining Grammar*
Chung-hye Han

19:00 Conference Dinner

Sunday, 16 July 2006

9:30–10:30 Invited Talk: Mark Johnson

10:30–11:00 Coffee Break

11:00–11:40 *Negative Concord and Restructuring in Palestinian Arabic: A Comparison of TAG and CCG Analyses*
Frederick M. Hoyt

11:40–12:20 *Stochastic Multiple Context-Free Grammar for RNA Pseudoknot Modeling*
Yuki Kato, Hiroyuki Seki and Tadao Kasami

12:20–13:40 Lunch Break

13:40–14:40 Poster Session II

14:40–15:20 *Binding of Anaphors in LTAG*
Neville Ryant and Tatjana Scheffler

15:20–15:50 Coffee Break

15:50–16:30 *Quantifier Scope in German: An MCTAG Analysis*
Laura Kallmeyer and Maribel Romero

16:30–17:10 *Licensing German Negative Polarity Items in LTAG*
Timm Lichte and Laura Kallmeyer

17:10–17:30 Closing Remarks

Poster Presentations

The Hidden TAG Model: Synchronous Grammars for Parsing Resource-Poor Languages

David Chiang[*]
Information Sciences Institute
University of Southern California
4676 Admiralty Way, Suite 1001
Marina del Rey, CA 90292, USA
chiang@isi.edu

Owen Rambow
Center for Computational Learning Systems
Columbia University
475 Riverside Dr., Suite 850
New York, NY, USA
rambow@cs.columbia.edu

Abstract

This paper discusses a novel probabilistic synchronous TAG formalism, synchronous Tree Substitution Grammar with sister adjunction (TSG+SA). We use it to parse a language for which there is no training data, by leveraging off a second, related language for which there is abundant training data. The grammar for the resource-rich side is automatically extracted from a treebank; the grammar on the resource-poor side and the synchronization are created by handwritten rules. Our approach thus represents a combination of grammar-based and empirical natural language processing. We discuss the approach using the example of Levantine Arabic and Standard Arabic.

1 Parsing Arabic Dialects and Tree Adjoining Grammar

The Arabic language is a collection of spoken dialects and a standard written language. The standard written language is the same throughout the Arab world, Modern Standard Arabic (MSA), which is also used in some scripted spoken communication (news casts, parliamentary debates). It is based on Classical Arabic and is not a native language of any Arabic speaking people, i.e., children do not learn it from their parents but in school. Thus most native speakers of Arabic are unable to produce sustained spontaneous MSA. The dialects show phonological, morphological, lexical, and syntactic differences comparable to those among the Romance languages. They vary not only along a geographical continuum but also with other sociolinguistic variables such as the urban/rural/Bedouin dimension.

The multidialectal situation has important negative consequences for Arabic natural language processing (NLP): since the spoken dialects are not officially written and do not have standard orthography, it is very costly to obtain adequate corpora, even unannotated corpora, to use for training NLP tools such as parsers. Furthermore, there are almost no parallel corpora involving one dialect and MSA.

The question thus arises how to create a statistical parser for an Arabic dialect, when statistical parsers are typically trained on large corpora of parse trees. We present one solution to this problem, based on the assumption that it is easier to manually create new resources that relate a dialect to MSA (lexicon and grammar) than it is to manually create syntactically annotated corpora in the dialect. In this paper, we deal with Levantine Arabic (LA). Our approach does not assume the existence of any annotated LA corpus (except for development and testing), nor of a parallel LA-MSA corpus.

The approach described in this paper uses a special parameterization of stochastic synchronous TAG (Shieber, 1994) which we call a "hidden TAG model." This model couples a model of MSA trees, learned from the Arabic Treebank, with a model of MSA-LA translation, which is initialized by hand and then trained in an unsupervised fashion. Parsing new LA sentences then entails simultaneously building a forest of MSA trees and the corresponding forest of LA trees. Our implementation uses an extension of our monolingual parser (Chiang, 2000) based on tree-substitution

[*]This work was primarily carried out while the first author was at the University of Maryland Institute for Advanced Computer Studies.

Proceedings of the 8th International Workshop on Tree Adjoining Grammar and Related Formalisms, pages 1–8, Sydney, July 2006.

grammar with sister adjunction (TSG+SA).

The main contributions of this paper are as follows:

1. We introduce the novel concept of a hidden TAG model.
2. We use this model to combine statistical approaches with grammar engineering (specifically motivated from the linguistic facts). Our approach thus exemplifies the specific strength of a grammar-based approach.
3. We present an implementation of stochastic synchronous TAG that incorporates various facilities useful for training on real-world data: sister-adjunction (needed for generating the flat structures found in most treebanks), smoothing, and Inside-Outside reestimation.

This paper is structured as follows. We first briefly discuss related work (Section 2) and some of the linguistic facts that motivate this work (Section 3). We then present the formalism, probabilistic model, and parsing algorithm (Section 4). Finally, we discuss the manual grammar engineering (Section 5) and evaluation (Section 6).

2 Related Work

This paper is part of a larger investigation into parsing Arabic dialects (Rambow et al., 2005; Chiang et al., 2006). In that investigation, we examined three different approaches:

- Sentence transduction, in which a dialect sentence is roughly translated into one or more MSA sentences and then parsed by an MSA parser.
- Treebank transduction, in which the MSA treebank is transduced into an approximation of a LA treebank, on which a LA parer is then trained.
- Grammar transduction, which is the name given in the overview papers to the approach discussed in this paper. The present paper provides for the first time a complete technical presentation of this approach.

Overall, grammar transduction outperformed the other two approaches.

In other work, there has been a fair amount of interest in parsing one language using another language, see for example (Smith and Smith, 2004; Hwa et al., 2004). Much of this work, like ours, relies on synchronous grammars (CFGs). However, these approaches rely on parallel corpora. For MSA and its dialects, there are no naturally occurring parallel corpora. It is this fact that has led us to investigate the use of explicit linguistic knowledge to complement machine learning.

3 Linguistic Facts

We illustrate the differences between LA and MSA using an example:

(1) a. الرجال بيحبو ش الشغل هدا (LA)

AlrjAl byHbw $ Al$gl hdA
the-men like not the-work this

the men do not like this work

b. لا يحب الرجال هذا العمل (MSA)

lA yHb AlrjAl h*A AlEml
not like the-men this the-work

the men do not like this work

Lexically, we observe that the word for 'work' is الشغل *Al$gl* in LA but العمل *AlEml* in MSA. In contrast, the word for 'men' is the same in both LA and MSA: الرجال *AlrjAl*. There are typically also differences in function words, in our example ش *$* (LA) and لا *lA* (MSA) for 'not'. Morphologically, we see that LA بيحبو *byHbw* has the same stem as MA يحب *yHb*, but with two additional morphemes: the present aspect marker *b-* which does not exist in MSA, and the agreement marker *-w*, which is used in MSA only in subject-initial sentences, while in LA it is always used.

Syntactically, we observe three differences. First, the subject precedes the verb in LA (SVO order), but follows in MSA (VSO order). This is in fact not a strict requirement, but a strong preference: both varieties allow both orders, but in the dialects, the SVO order is more common, while in MSA, the VSO order is more common. Second, we see that the demonstrative determiner follows the noun in LA, but precedes it in MSA. Finally, we see that the negation marker follows the verb in LA, while it precedes the verb in MSA. (Levantine also has other negation markers that precede the verb, as well as the circumfix *m- -$*.) The two phrase structure trees are shown in Figure 1 in the convention of the Linguistic Data Consortium (Maamouri et al., 2004). Unlike the phrase

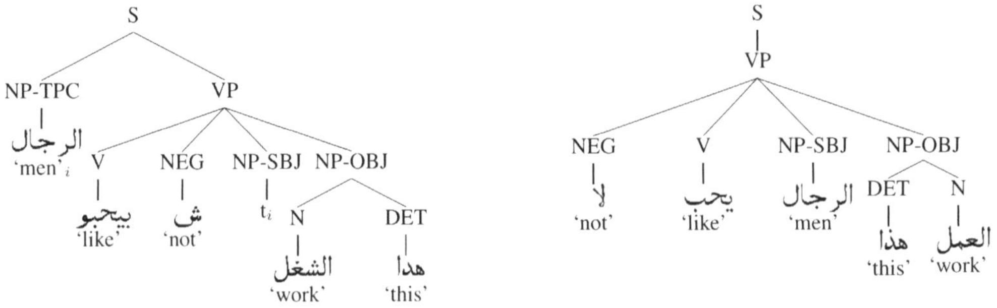

Figure 1: LDC-style left-to-right phrase structure trees for LA (left) and MSA (right) for sentence (1)

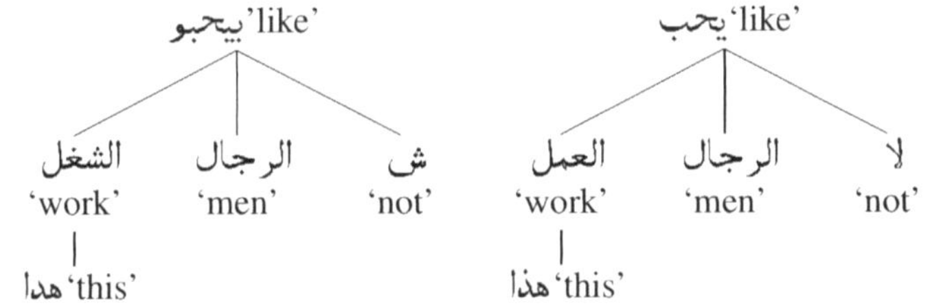

Figure 2: Unordered dependency trees for LA (left) and MSA (right) for sentence (1)

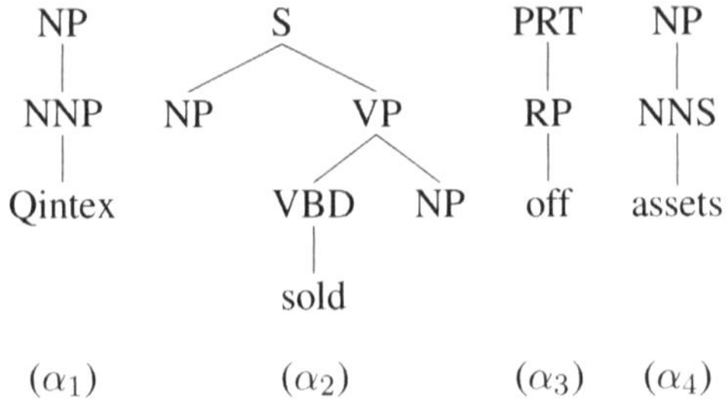

Figure 3: Example elementary trees.

structure trees, the (unordered) dependency trees for the MSA and LA sentences are isomorphic, as shown in Figure 2. They differ only in the node labels.

4 Model

4.1 The synchronous TSG+SA formalism

Our parser (Chiang, 2000) is based on synchronous tree-substitution grammar with sister-adjunction (TSG+SA). Tree-substitution grammar (Schabes, 1990) is TAG without auxiliary trees or adjunction; instead we include a weaker composition operation, *sister-adjunction* (Rambow et al., 2001), in which an initial tree is inserted between two sister nodes (see Figure 4). We allow multiple sister-adjunctions at the same site, similar to how Schabes and Shieber (1994) allow multiple adjunctions of modifier auxiliary trees.

A *synchronous* TSG+SA is a set of pairs of elementary trees. In each pair, there is a one-to-one correspondence between the substitution/sister-adjunction sites of the two trees, which we represent using boxed indices (Figure 5). A derivation then starts with a pair of initial trees and proceeds by substituting or sister-adjoining elementary tree pairs at coindexed sites. In this way a set of string pairs $\langle S, S' \rangle$ is generated.

Sister-adjunction presents a special problem for synchronization: if multiple tree pairs sister-adjoin at the same site, how should their order on the source side relate to the order on the target side? Shieber's solution (Shieber, 1994) is to allow any ordering. We adopt a stricter solution: for each pair of sites, fix a permutation (either identity or reversal) for the tree pairs that sister-adjoin there. Owing to the way we extract trees from the Treebank, the simplest choice of permutations is: if the two sites are both to the left of the anchor or both to the right of the anchor, then multiple sister-adjoined tree pairs will appear in the same order on both sides; otherwise, they will appear in the opposite order. In other words, multiple sister-adjunction always adds trees from the anchor outward.

A *stochastic* synchronous TSG+SA adds probabilities to the substitution and sister-adjunction operations: the probability of substituting an elementary tree pair $\langle \alpha, \alpha' \rangle$ at a substitution site pair

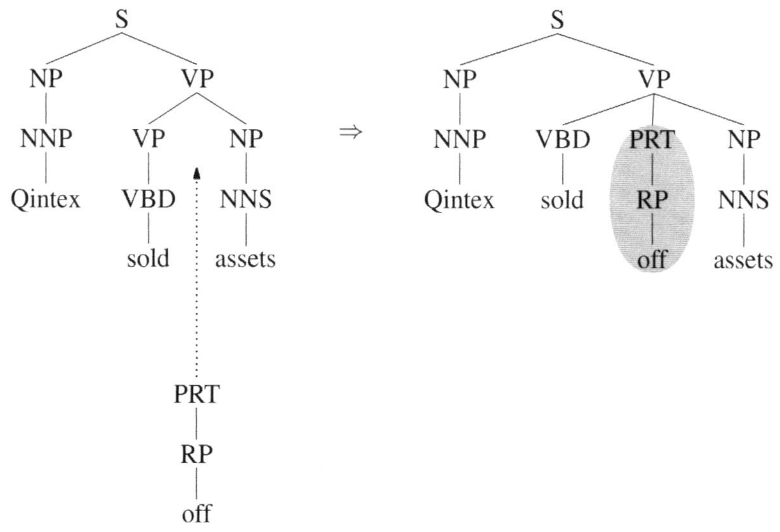

Figure 4: Sister-adjunction, with inserted material shown with shaded background

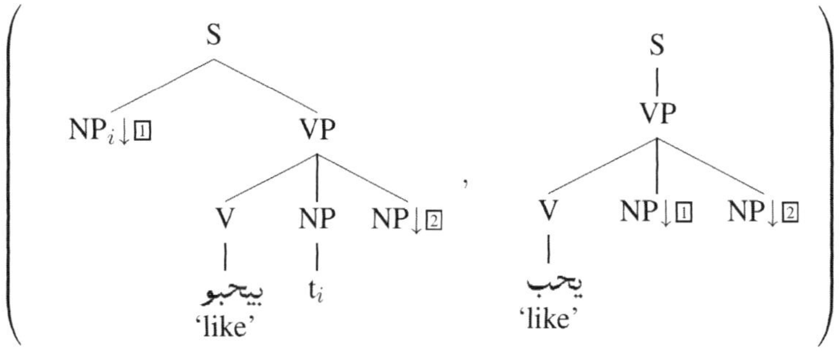

Figure 5: Example elementary tree pair of a synchronous TSG: the **SVO** transformation (LA on left, MSA on right)

$\langle \eta, \eta' \rangle$ is $P_{\mathbf{s}}(\alpha, \alpha' \mid \eta, \eta')$, and the probability of sister-adjoining $\langle \alpha, \alpha' \rangle$ at a sister-adjunction site pair $\langle \eta, i, \eta', i' \rangle$ is $P_{\mathbf{sa}}(\alpha, \alpha' \mid \eta, i, \eta', i')$, where i and i' indicate that the sister-adjunction occurs between the i and $(i+1)$st (or i' and $(i'+1)$st) sisters. These parameters must satisfy the normalization conditions

$$\sum_{\alpha,\alpha'} P_{\mathbf{s}}(\alpha, \alpha' \mid \eta, \eta') = 1 \quad (1)$$

$$\sum_{\alpha,\alpha'} P_{\mathbf{sa}}(\alpha, \alpha' \mid \eta, i, \eta', i') + P_{\mathbf{sa}}(\mathbf{STOP} \mid \eta, i, \eta', i') = 1 \quad (2)$$

4.2 Parsing by translation

We intend to apply a stochastic synchronous TSG+SA to input sentences S'. This requires projecting any constraints from the unprimed side of the synchronous grammar over to the primed side, and then parsing the sentences S' using the projected grammar, using a straightforward generalization of the CKY and Viterbi algorithms. This gives the highest-probability derivation of the synchronous grammar that generates S' on the primed side, which includes a parse for S' and, as a by-product, a parsed translation of S'.

Suppose that S' is a sentence of LA. For the present task we are not actually interested in the MSA translation of S', or the parse of the MSA translation; we are only interested in the parse of S'. The purpose of the MSA side of the grammar is to provide reliable statistics. Thus, we approximate the synchronous rewriting probabilities as:

$$P_{\mathbf{s}}(\alpha, \alpha' \mid \eta, \eta') \approx P_s(\alpha \mid \eta) P_t(\alpha' \mid \alpha) \quad (3)$$

$$P_{\mathbf{sa}}(\alpha, \alpha' \mid \eta, i, \eta', i') \approx P_{sa}(\alpha \mid \eta, i) P_t(\alpha' \mid \alpha) \quad (4)$$

These factors, as we will see shortly, are much easier to estimate given the available resources.

This factorization is analogous to a hidden Markov model: the primed derivation is the observation, the unprimed derivation is the hidden state sequence (except it is a branching process instead of a chain); the P_s and P_{sa} are like the transition probabilities and the P_t are like the observation probabilities. Hence, we call this model a "hidden TAG model."

4.3 Parameter estimation and smoothing

P_s and P_{sa} are the parameters of a monolingual TSG+SA and can be learned from a monolingual Treebank (Chiang, 2000); the details are not important here.

As for P_t, in order to obtain better probability estimates, we further decompose P_t into P_{t1} and P_{t2} so they can be estimated separately (as in the monolingual parsing model):

$$P_t(\alpha' \mid \alpha) \approx P_{t1}(\bar{\alpha}' \mid \bar{\alpha}, w', t', w, t) \times P_{t2}(w', t' \mid w, t) \quad (5)$$

where w and t are the lexical anchor of α and its POS tag, and $\bar{\alpha}$ is the equivalence class of α modulo lexical anchors and their POS tags. P_{t2} represents the lexical transfer model, and P_{t1} the syntactic transfer model. P_{t1} and P_{t2} are initially assigned by hand; P_{t1} is then reestimated by EM.

Because the full probability table for P_{t1} would be too large to write by hand, and because our training data might be too sparse to reestimate it well, we smooth it by approximating it as a linear combination of backoff models:

$$\begin{aligned} P_{t1}(\bar{\alpha}' \mid \bar{\alpha}, w', t', w, t) \approx{} & \lambda_1 P_{t11}(\bar{\alpha}' \mid \bar{\alpha}, w', t', w, t) + \\ & (1-\lambda_1)(\lambda_2 P_{t12}(\bar{\alpha}' \mid \bar{\alpha}, w', t') + \\ & (1-\lambda_2) P_{t13}(\bar{\alpha}' \mid \bar{\alpha})) \end{aligned} \quad (6)$$

where each λ_i, unlike in the monolingual parser, is simply set to 1 if an estimate is available for that level, so that it completely overrides the further backed-off models.

The initial estimates for the P_{t1i} are set by hand. The availability of three backoff models makes it easy to specify the initial guesses at an appropriate level of detail: for example, one might give a general probability of some $\bar{\alpha}$ mapping to $\bar{\alpha}'$ using P_{t13}, but then make special exceptions for particular lexical anchors using P_{t11} or P_{t12}.

Finally P_{t2} is reestimated by EM on some held-out unannotated sentences of L', using the same method as Chiang and Bikel (2002) but on the syntactic transfer probabilities instead of the monolingual parsing model. Another difference is that, following Bikel (2004), we do not recalculate the λ_i at each iteration, but use the initial values throughout.

5 A Synchronous TSG-SA for Dialectal Arabic

Just as the probability model discussed in the preceding section factored the rewriting probabilities into three parts, we create a synchronous TSG-SA and the probabilities of a hidden TAG model in three steps:

- P_s and P_{sa} are the parameters of a monolingual TSG+SA for MSA. We extract a grammar for the resource-rich language (MSA) from the Penn Arabic Treebank in a process described by Chiang and others (Chiang, 2000; Xia et al., 2000; Chen, 2001).
- For the lexical transfer model P_{t2}, we create by hand a probabilistic mapping between (word, POS tag) pairs in the two languages.
- For the syntactic transfer model P_{t1}, we created by hand a grammar for the resource-poor language and a mapping between elementary trees in the two grammars, along with initial guesses for the mapping probabilities.

We discuss the hand-crafted lexicon and synchronous grammar in the following subsections.

5.1 Lexical Mapping

We used a small, hand-crafted lexicon of 100 words which mapped all LA function words and some of the most common open-class words to MSA. We assigned uniform probabilities to the mapping. All other MSA words were assumed to also be LA words. Unknown LA words were handled using the standard unknown word mechanism.

5.2 Syntactic Mapping

Because of the underlying syntactic similarity between the two varieties of Arabic, we assume that every tree in the MSA grammar extracted from the MSA treebank is also a LA tree. In addition, we define tree transformations in the Tsurgeon package (Levy and Andrew, 2006). These consist of a pattern which matches MSA elementary trees in the extracted grammar, and a transformation which produces a LA elementary tree. We perform the following tree transformations on all elementary trees which match the underlying MSA pattern. Thus, each MSA tree corresponds to at least two LA trees: the original one and the transformed one. If several transformations apply, we obtain multiple transformed trees.

- Negation (**NEG**): we insert a *$* negation marker immediately following each verb. The preverbal marker is generated by a lexical translation of an MSA elementary tree.
- VSO-SVO Ordering (**SVO**): Both Verb-Subject-Object (VSO) and Subject-Verb-Object (SVO) constructions occur in MSA and LA treebanks. But pure VSO constructions (without pro-drop) occur in the LA corpus only 10ordering in MSA. Hence, the goal is to skew the distributions of the SVO constructions in the MSA data. Therefore, VSO constructions are replicated and converted to SVO constructions. One possible resulting pair of trees is shown in Figure 5.
- The *bd* construction (**BD**): *bd* is a LA noun that means 'want'. It acts like a verb in verbal constructions yielding VP constructions headed by NN. It is typically followed by an enclitic possessive pronoun. Accordingly, we defined a transformation that translated all the verbs meaning 'want'/'need' into the noun *bd* and changed their respective POS tag to NN. The subject clitic is transformed into a possessive pronoun clitic. Note that this construction is a combination lexical and syntactic transformation, and thus specifically exploits the extended domain of locality of TAG-like formalisms. One possible resulting pair of trees is shown in Figure 6.

6 Experimental Results

While our approach does not rely on any annotated corpus for LA, nor on a parallel corpus MSA-LA, we use a small treebank of LA (Maamouri et al., 2006) to analyze and test our approach. The LA treebank is divided into a development corpus and a test corpus, each about 11,000 tokens (using the same tokenization scheme as employed in the MSA treebank).

We first use the development corpus to determine which of the transformations are useful. We use two conditions. In the first, the input text is not tagged, and the parser hypothesizes tags. In the second, the input text is tagged with the gold (correct) tag. The results are shown in Table 1. The baseline is simply the application of a pure MSA Chiang parser to LA. We see that important improvements are obtained using the lexical mapping. Adding the **SVO** transformation does not improve the results, but the **NEG** and **BD** transformations help slightly, and their effect is (partly)

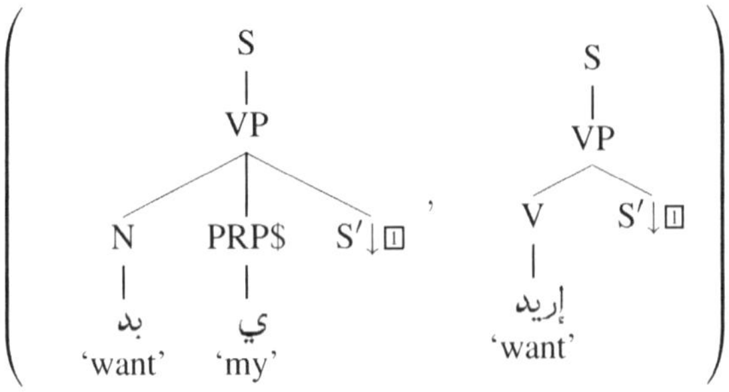

Figure 6: Example elementary tree pair of a synchronous TSG: the **BD** transformation (LA on left, MSA on right)

cumulative. (We did not perform these tuning experiments on input without POS tags.)

The evaluation on the test corpus confirms these results. Using the **NEG** and **BD** transformations and the small lexicon, we obtain a 17.3% error reduction relative to the baseline parser (Figure 2).

These results show that the translation lexicon can be integrated effectively into our synchronous grammar framework. In addition, some syntactic transformations are useful. The **SVO** transformation, we assume, turns out not to be useful because the **SVO** word order is also possible in MSA, so that the new trees were not needed and needlessly introduced new derivations. The **BD** transformation shows the importance not of general syntactic transformations, but rather of lexically specific syntactic transformations: varieties within one language family may differ more in terms of the lexico-syntactic constructions used for a specific (semantic or pragmatic) purpose than in their basic syntactic inventory. Note that our tree-based synchronous formalism is ideally suited for expressing such transformations since it is lexicalized, and has an extended domain of locality. Given the impact of the **BD** transformation, in future work we intend to determine more lexico-structural transformations, rather than pure syntactic transformations. However, one major impediment to obtaining better results is the disparity in genre and domain which affects the overall performance.

7 Conclusion

We have presented a new probabilistic synchronous TAG formalism, synchronous Tree Substitution Grammar with sister adjunction (TSG+SA). We have introduced the concept of a hidden TAG model, analogous to a Hidden Markov Model. It allows us to parse a resource-poor language using a treebank-extracted probabilistic grammar for a resource-rich language, along with a hand-crafted synchronous grammar for the resource-poor language. Thus, our model combines statistical approaches with grammar engineering (specifically motivated from the linguistic facts). Our approach thus exemplifies the specific strength of a grammar-based approach. While we have applied this approach to two closely related languages, it would be interesting to apply this approach to more distantly related languages in the future.

Acknowledgments

This paper is based on work done at the 2005 Johns Hopkins Summer Workshop, which was partially supported by the National Science Foundation under grant 0121285. The first author was additionally supported by ONR MURI contract FCPO.810548265 and Department of Defense contract RD-02-5700. The second author was additionally supported by contract HR0011-06-C-0023 under the GALE program. We wish to thank the other members of our JHU team (our co-authors on (Rambow et al., 2005)), especially Nizar Habash and Mona Diab for their help with the Arabic examples, and audiences at JHU for their useful feedback.

References

Daniel M. Bikel. 2004. *On the Parameter Space of Generative Lexicalized Parsing Models*. Ph.D. thesis, University of Pennsylvania.

John Chen. 2001. *Towards Efficient Statistical Parsing Using Lexicalized Grammatical Information*. Ph.D. thesis, University of Delaware.

	no tags			gold tags		
	LP	LR	F1	LP	LR	F1
Baseline	59.4	51.9	55.4	64.0	58.3	61.0
Lexical	63.0	60.8	61.9	66.9	67.0	66.9
+ SVO				66.9	66.7	66.8
+ NEG				67.0	67.0	67.0
+ BD				67.4	67.0	67.2
+ NEG + BD				67.4	67.1	67.3

Table 1: Results on development corpus: LP = labeled precision, LR = labeled recall, F1 = balanced F-measure

	no tags	gold tags
	F1	F1
Baseline	53.5	60.2
Lexical + NEG + BD	60.2	67.1

Table 2: Results on the test corpus: F1 = balanced F-measure

David Chiang and Daniel M. Bikel. 2002. Recovering latent information in treebanks. In *Proceedings of the Nineteenth International Conference on Computational Linguistics (COLING)*, pages 183–189.

David Chiang, Mona Diab, Nizar Habash, Owen Rambow, and Safiullah Shareef. 2006. Parsing Arabic dialects. In *Proceedings of EACL*.

David Chiang. 2000. Statistical parsing with an automatically-extracted tree adjoining grammar. In *38th Meeting of the Association for Computational Linguistics (ACL'00)*, pages 456–463, Hong Kong, China.

Rebecca Hwa, Philip Resnik, Amy Weinberg, Clara Cabezas, and Okan Kolak. 2004. Bootstrapping parsers via syntactic projection across parallel texts. *Natural Language Engineering*.

Roger Levy and Galen Andrew. 2006. Tregex and Tsurgeon: tools for querying and manipulating tree data structures. In *Proceedings of LREC*.

Mohamed Maamouri, Ann Bies, and Tim Buckwalter. 2004. The Penn Arabic Treebank: Building a large-scale annotated Arabic corpus. In *NEMLAR Conference on Arabic Language Resources and Tools*, Cairo, Egypt.

Mohamed Maamouri, Ann Bies, Tim Buckwalter, Mona Diab, Nizar Habash, Owen Rambow, and Dalila Tabessi. 2006. Developing and using a pilot dialectal Arabic treebank. In *Proceedings of LREC*, Genoa, Italy.

Owen Rambow, K. Vijay-Shanker, and David Weir. 2001. D-Tree Substitution Grammars. *Computational Linguistics*, 27(1).

Owen Rambow, David Chiang, Mona Diab, Nizar Habash, Rebecca Hwa, Khalil Sima'an, Vincent Lacey, Roger Levy, Carol Nichols, and Safiullah Shareef. 2005. Parsing Arabic dialects. Final Report, 2005 JHU Summer Workshop.

Yves Schabes and Stuart Shieber. 1994. An alternative conception of tree-adjoining derivation. *Computational Linguistics*, 1(20):91–124.

Yves Schabes. 1990. *Mathematical and Computational Aspects of Lexicalized Grammars*. Ph.D. thesis, Department of Computer and Information Science, University of Pennsylvania.

Stuart B. Shieber. 1994. Restricting the weak generative capacity of Synchronous Tree Adjoining Grammar. *Computational Intelligence*, 10(4):371–385.

David A. Smith and Noah A. Smith. 2004. Bilingual parsing with factored estimation: Using English to parse Korean. In *Proceedings of the 2004 Conference on Empirical Methods in Natural Language Processing (EMNLP04)*.

Fei Xia, Martha Palmer, and Aravind Joshi. 2000. A uniform method of grammar extraction and its applications. In *Proceedings of the 2000 Conference on Empirical Methods in Natural Language Processing (EMNLP00)*, Hong Kong.

A constraint driven metagrammar

Joseph Le Roux
LORIA
Institut National
Polytechnique de Lorraine
615, Rue du Jardin Botanique
54 600 Villers-Lès-Nancy
France
leroux@loria.fr

Benoît Crabbé
HCRC / ICCS
University of Edinburgh
2 Buccleuch Place
EH8 9LW,
Edinburgh, Scotland
bcrabbe@inf.ed.ac.uk

Yannick Parmentier
INRIA / LORIA
Université Henri Poincaré
615, Rue du Jardin Botanique
54 600 Villers-Lès-Nancy
France
parmenti@loria.fr

Abstract

We present an operational framework allowing to express a large scale Tree Adjoining Grammar (TAG) by using higher level operational constraints on tree descriptions. These constraints first meant to guarantee the well formedness of the grammatical units may also be viewed as a way to put model theoretic syntax at work through an efficient offline grammatical compilation process. Our strategy preserves TAG formal properties, hence ensures a reasonable processing efficiency.

1 Introduction

This paper is concerned with the semi-automatic grammar development of real-scale grammars. For natural language syntax, lexicalised TAGs are made of thousands of trees, carrying an extreme structural redundancy. Their development and their maintenance is known to be cumbersome as the size of the grammar raises significantly.

To counter the lack of generalisations inherent to strong lexicalisation, various proposals for semi-automatic grammar development have been carried out: lexical rules or meta-rules (Becker, 2000) and metagrammars: (Candito, 1999; Gaiffe et al., 2002; Xia, 2001). The aim of these frameworks is twofold: expressing general facts about the grammar of a language and factorising the information to avoid redundancy.

The metagrammar path adopts a different perspective from the lexical rule based grammar development: instead of describing how a derived tree is different from a canonical one, grammatical description mainly consists of combining fragmentary tree descriptions or building blocks.

The paper is structured as follows. We start in section 2 by providing motivations and background information on the framework we are using. Section 3 shows that the metagrammar framework may be viewed as an offline system allowing to express high level well-formedness constraints on elementary grammatical structures while preserving TAG computational and formal properties. Section 4 shows how to implement efficiently this constraint-based approach with logic programming techniques and finally section 5 provides an idea of the performance of the implemented system.

2 eXtensible MetaGrammar (XMG)

By opposition to other metagrammatical frameworks, XMG (Duchier et al., 2004) uses an expressive though simple language, enabling a monotonic description of a real scale grammar. Monotonicity is important because it means that the order of application of the different operations does not matter. This is the major drawback of lexical-rule systems. Moreover, (Crabb´e, 2005b) shows that it is sufficiently expressive to implement conveniently a core TAG for French.

XMG allows the grammar writer to manipulate tree descriptions through a control language. The intuition behind is that a metagrammatical language needs to provide means to describe syntactic information along two methodological axis (Crabb´e, 2005b): *structure sharing* and *alternatives*. Structure sharing is the axis dedicated to express factorisation in the grammar, whereas alternatives allow to express regular alternation relationships such as alternatives between the representation of a canonical nominal subject and its interrogative representation, or between an active

Proceedings of the 8th International Workshop on Tree Adjoining Grammar and Related Formalisms, pages 9–16,
Sydney, July 2006. ©2006 Association for Computational Linguistics

and a passive verb form[1].

Building on this intuition the XMG language allows the user to name partial tree descriptions within classes. The name of the class can be manipulated afterwards. For instance the following tree descriptions on the right of the arrow are associated with the names stated on the left of the arrow[2]:

(1) a. *CanonicalSubject* $\rightarrow$ 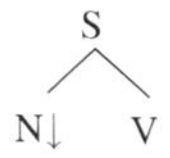

b. *RelativisedSubject* $\rightarrow$ 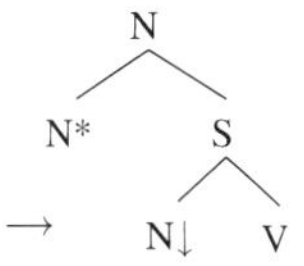

c. *VerbalForm* $\rightarrow$ 

Naming is the main device that allows the grammar writer to express and to take advantage of the structure sharing axis mentioned above. Indeed class names can be reused in other descriptions. Thus names can also be used to describe alternatives. To express, in our simplified example, that a *Subject* is an abstract way to name a *RelativisedSubject* or a *CanonicalSubject*, we use a choice operator ($\vee$) as illustrated below:

(2) Subject $\rightarrow$ CanonicalSubject
$\vee$ RelativisedSubject

Disjunction (non-deterministic choice) is the device provided by the language to express the methodological axis of alternatives.

Finally, names can be given to class combinations. To express the composition of two tree descriptions in the language, we use the $\wedge$ operator. Thus we can say that an *IntransitiveVerb* is made by the composition of a *Subject* and a *VerbalForm* as follows:

(3) IntransitiveVerb $\rightarrow$ Subject $\wedge$ VerbalForm

Given these 3 primitives, the control language is naturally interpreted as a context free grammar whose terminals are tree descriptions and where our composition plays the role of concatenation. This abstract grammar or metagrammar is further restricted to be non recursive in order to ensure that the generated TAG is finite.

Provided the axiom *IntransitiveVerb*, an interpreter for this language generates non deterministically all the sentences of the grammar[3] underlying a grammatical description. Thus in our current example the two sentences generated are those depicted on the left hand side of the arrows in Figure 1. On the right hand side of the arrow is depicted the result of the composition of the tree descriptions.

It remains to make clear what is actually this composition. The grammatical classes may contain information on tree descriptions and/or express composition of descriptions stated in other classes. Tree descriptions take their inspiration from the logic described in (Rogers and Vijay-Shanker, 1994). Its syntax is the following:

$$\begin{array}{lll} \textit{Description} & ::= & x \rightarrow y \mid x \rightarrow^* y \mid \\ & & x \prec y \mid x \prec^* y \mid \\ & & x[f{:}E] \end{array}$$

where x, y are node variables, $\rightarrow$ the dominance relation, $\prec$ the precedence relation, * denoting the reflexive transitive closure of a relation. The last line associates x with a feature f whose value is the result of evaluating expression E.

Tree descriptions are interpreted as finite linear ordered trees being the minimal models of the description.

Using tree descriptions, the above mentioned operation of tree "composition" breaks down to a conjunction of formulas where variables of each conjunct are in first approximation renamed to avoid name collisions. Renaming is a crucial difference with previous approaches to metagrammar (Candito, 1999; Xia, 2001) where the user had to manage explicitly a "global namespace". Here a specific attention is given to namespace management, because this was a bottleneck for real scale

[1]The passive is a semi-regular alternation, many transitive verbs do not passivise. Our system presupposes a classical architecture for the computational representation of Tree Adjoining Grammars such as XTAG, where means to express such exceptions during the anchoring process are well-known. In what follows, we therefore consider only tree templates (or tree schematas) as our working units. Finally the trees depicted in this paper take their inspiration from the grammar described by (Abeill´e, 2002).

[2]To represent the tree descriptions mentioned in this paper, we use a graphical notation. Immediate dominance is depicted with a straight line and precedence follows the graphical order. Note that nodes are decorated with their labels only, ignoring the names of the variables denoting them. Note also that we use only the reflexive transitive closure of precedence between sibling nodes and it is explicitly stated with the symbol $\prec^*$.

[3]Understood as compositions of tree fragments.

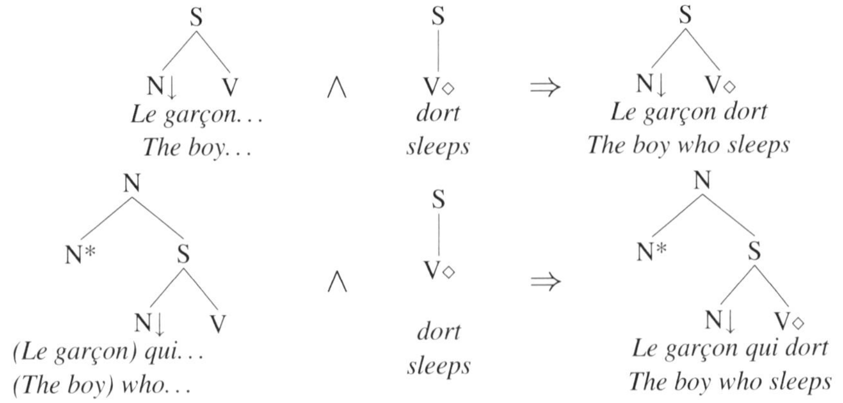

Figure 1: Interpretation of a grammatical description

grammar design. More precisely each class has its own namespace of identifiers and namespace merging can be triggered when a class combination occurs. This merging relies on a fine-grained import/export mechanism.

In addition to conjunction and disjunction, XMG is augmented with syntactic sugar to offer some of the features other metagrammatical formalisms propose. For instance, inheritance of classes is not built-in in the core language but is realised through conjunction and namespace import. Of course, this restricts users to monotonic inheritance (specialisation) but it seems to be sufficient for most linguists.

3 Constraining admissible structures

XMG has been tested against the development of a large scale French Grammar (Crabb´e, 2005a). To ease practical grammatical development we have added several augmentations to the common tree description language presented so far in order to further restrict the class of admissible structures generated by the metagrammar.

Further constraining the structures generated by a grammar is a common practice in computational linguistics. For instance a Lexical Functional Grammar (Bresnan and Kaplan, 1982) further restricts the structures generated by the grammar by means of a functional uniqueness and a functional completeness principles. These constraints further restricts the class of admissible structures generated by an LFG grammar to verify valency conditions.

For TAG and in a theoretical context, (Frank, 2002) states a set of such well formedness principles that contribute to formulate a TAG theory within a minimalist framework. In what remains we describe operational constraints of this kind that further restrict the admissibility of the structure generated by the metagrammar. By contrast with the principles stated by (Frank, 2002), we do not make any theoretical claim, instead we are stating operational constraints that have been found useful in practical grammar development.

However as already noted by (Frank, 2002) and by opposition to an LFG framework where constraints apply to the syntactic structure of a sentence as a whole, we formulate here constraints on the well-formedness of TAG elementary trees. In other words these constraints apply to units that define themselves their own global domain of locality. In this case, it means that we can safely ignore locality issues while formulating our constraints. This is theoretically weaker than formulating constraints on the whole sentential structure but this framework allows us to generate common TAG units, preserving the formal and computational properties of TAG.

We formulate this constraint driven framework by specifying conditions on model admissibility. Methodologically the constraints used in the development of the French TAG can be classified in four categories: formal constraints, operational constraints, language dependent constraints and theoretical principles.

First the *formal constraints* are those constraining the trees generated by the model builder to be regular TAG trees. These constraints require the trees to be linear ordered trees with appropriate decorations : each node has a category label, leaf nodes are either terminal, foot or substitution, there is at most one foot node, the category of the foot note is identical to that of the root node, each tree has at least one leaf node which is an anchor.

It is worth noting here that using a different set of formal constraints may change the target formalism. Indeed XMG provides a different set of formal constraints (not detailed here) that allow to generate elementary units for another formalism, namely Interaction Grammars.

The second kind of constraint is a single *operational constraint* dubbed the colouration constraint. We found it convenient in the course of grammar development. It consists of associating colour-based polarities to the nodes to ensure a proper combination of the fragmentary tree descriptions stated within classes. Since in our framework descriptions stated in two different classes are renamed before being conjoined, given a formula being the conjunction of the two following tree descriptions :

(4) 

both the following trees are valid models of that formula:

(5) (a) 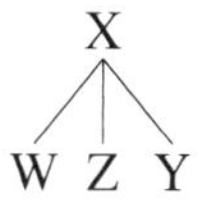

(b) 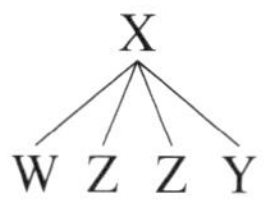

In the context of grammar development, however, only (a) is regarded as a desired model. To rule out (b) (Candito, 1999; Xia, 2001) use a naming convention that can be viewed as follows[4]: they assign a name to every node of the tree description. Both further constrain model admissibility by enforcing the identity of the interpretation of two variables associated to the same name. Thus the description stated in their systems can be exemplified as follows:

(6) 

Though solving the initial formal problem, this design choice creates two additional complications: (1) it constrains the grammar writer to manually manage a global naming, entailing obvious problems as the size of the grammatical description grows and (2) it prevents the user to reuse several times the same class in a composition. This case is a real issue in the context of grammatical development since a grammar writer willing to describe a ditransitive context with two prepositional phrases cannot reuse two times a fragment describing such a PP since the naming constraint will identify them.

To solve these problems we use a colouration constraint. This constraint associates unary properties, colours, to every node of the descriptions. A colour is taken among the set *red*($\bullet_R$), *black*($\bullet_B$), *white* ($\circ_W$). A valid model is a model in which every node is coloured either in red or black. Two variables in the description interpreted by the same node have their colours merged following the table given in Figure 2.

	$\bullet_B$	$\bullet_R$	$\circ_W$	$\perp$
$\bullet_B$	$\perp$	$\perp$	$\bullet_B$	$\perp$
$\bullet_R$	$\perp$	$\perp$	$\perp$	$\perp$
$\circ_W$	$\bullet_B$	$\perp$	$\circ_W$	$\perp$
$\perp$	$\perp$	$\perp$	$\perp$	$\perp$

Figure 2: Colour identification rules.

The table indicates the resulting colour after a merge. The $\perp$ symbol indicates that this two colours cannot be merged and hence two nodes labelled with these colours cannot be merged. Note that the table is designed to ensure that merging is not a procedural operation.

The idea behind colouration is that of saturating the tree description. The colour white represents the non saturation or the *need* of a node to be combined with a *resource*, represented by the colour black. Black nodes need not necessarily be combined with other nodes. Red is the colour used to label nodes that cannot be merged with any other node. A sample tree description with coloured node is as follows:

(7) 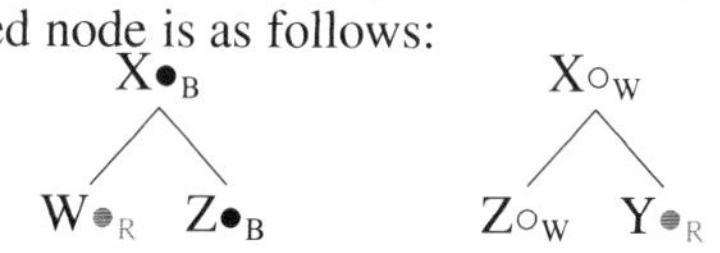

Colours contribute to rule out the (b) case and remove the grammar writer the burden of managing manually a "global namespace".

The third category of constraints are *language dependent constraints*. In the case of French, such constraints are clitic ordering, islands constraints, etc. We illustrate these constraints with clitic ordering in French. In French clitics are non tonic particles with two specific properties already identified by (Perlmutter, 1970): first they appear in front of the verb in a fixed order according to their rank (8a-8b) and second two different clitics in front of the verb cannot have the same rank (8c). For instance the clitics *le, la* have the rank 3 and *lui* the rank *4*.

[4] They actually use a different formal representation that does not affect the present discussion.

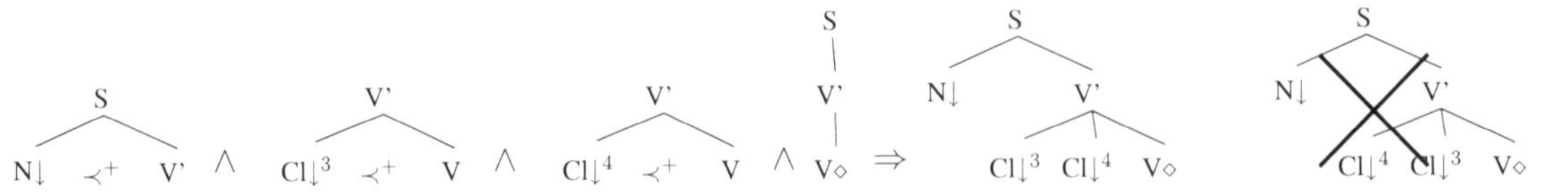

Figure 3: Clitic ordering

(8) a. Jean le_3 lui_4 donne
John gives it to him

b. *Jean lui_4 le_3 donne
*John gives to him it

c. *Jean le_3 la_3 donne
*John gives it it

In the French grammar of (Crabb´e, 2005a) trees with clitics are generated with the fragments illustrated on the left of the arrow in Figure 3[5]. As illustrated on the right of the arrow, the composition may generate ill-formed trees. To rule them out we formulate a clitic ordering constraint. Each variable labelled with a clitic category is also labelled with a property, an integer representing its rank. The constraint stipulates that sibling nodes labelled with a rank have to be linearly ordered according to the order defined over integers.

Overall language dependent constraints handle cases where the information independently specified in different fragments may interact. These interactions are a counterpart in a metagrammar to the interactions between independently described lexical rules in a lexical rule based system. Assuming independent lexical rules moving canonical arguments (NP or PP) to their clitic position, lexical rules fall short for capturing the relative ordering among clitics[6].

A fourth category of constraints, not implemented in our system so far are obviously the *language independent principles* defining the theory underlying the grammar. Such constraints could involve for instance a Principle of Predicate Argument Coocurrency (PPAC) or even the set of minimalist principles described by (Frank, 2002).

4 Efficient implementation

We describe now the implementation of our metagrammatical framework. In particular, we will focus on the implementation of the constraints discussed above within XMG.

As mentioned above, a metagrammar corresponds to a reduced description of the grammar. In our case, this description consists of tree fragments combined either conjunctively or disjunctively. These combinations are expressed using a language close to the *Definite Clause Grammar* formalism (Pereira and Warren, 1980), except that partial tree descriptions are used as terminal symbols. In this context, a metagrammar can be reduced to a logic program whose execution will lead to the computation of the trees of the grammar.

To perform this execution, a compiler for our metagrammatical language has been implemented. This compilation is a 3-step process as shown in Figure 4.

First, the metagrammar is compiled into instructions for a specific virtual machine inspired by the Warren's Abstract Machine (Ait-Kaci, 1991). These instructions correspond to the unfolding of the relations[7] contained in the tree descriptions of the metagrammar.

Then, the virtual machine performs unifications of structures meant to refer to corresponding information within fragments (*e.g.* two nodes, two feature structures ...). Note that the XMG's virtual machine uses the *structure sharing* technique for memory management, *i.e.* data are represented by a pair *pattern – environment* in which to interpret it. The consequences are that (a) we save memory when compiling the metagrammar, and (b) we have to perform pointer dereferencing during unification. Even if the latter is time-consuming, it remains more efficient than *structure copying* as we have to possibly deal with a certain amount of tree descriptions.

Eventually, as a result of this instruction processing by the virtual machine, we obtain poten-

[5]Colours are omitted.

[6]This observation was already made by (Perlmutter, 1970) in a generative grammar framework where clitics where assumed to be moved by transformations.

[7]These relations are either dominance or precedence between node variables, or their reflexive transitive closure, or the labelling of node variable with feature structures.

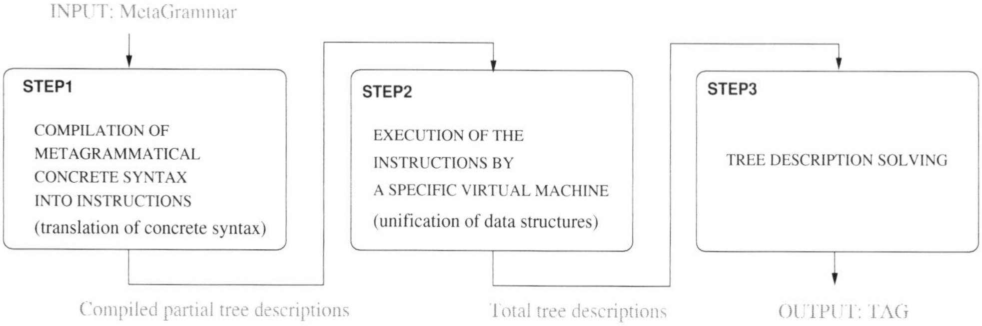

Figure 4: Metagrammar compilation.

tially total tree descriptions, that have to be solved in order to produce the expected TAG.

Now, we will introduce XMG's tree description solver and show that it is naturally designed to process efficiently the higher level constraints mentioned above. In particular, we will see that the description solver has been designed to be easily extended with additional parametric admissibility constraints.

4.1 Tree descriptions solving

To find the minimal models corresponding to the total tree descriptions obtained by accumulating fragmentary tree descriptions, we use a tree description solver. This solver has been developed in the *Constraint Programming* paradigm using the constraint satisfaction approach of (Duchier and Niehren, 2000). The idea is to translate relations between node variables into constraints over sets of integers.

Basically, we refer to a node of the input description in terms of the nodes being equals, above, below, or on its side (see Figure 5). More precisely, we associate each node of the description with an integer, then our reference to a node corresponds to a tuple containing sets of nodes (*i.e.* sets of integers).

As a first approximation, let us imagine that we refer to a node x in a model by means of a 5-tuple $N^i_x = (Eq, Up, Down, Left, Right)$ where i is an integer associated with x and *Eq* (respectively *Up*, *Down*, *Left*, *Right*) denotes the set of nodes[8] in the description which are equal, (respectively above, below, left, and right) of x.

Then we can convert the relations between nodes of our description language into constraints on sets of integer.

[8] *I.e. integers.*

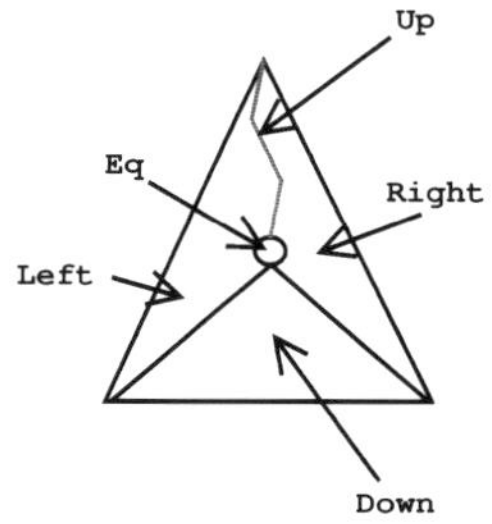

Figure 5: Node representation.

For instance, if we consider 2 nodes x and y of the description. Assuming we associate x with the integer i and y with j, we can translate the dominance relation $x \rightarrow y$ the following way[9]:

$$N^i_x \rightarrow N^j_y \equiv \begin{array}{l} [N^i_{x.EqUp} \subseteq N^j_{y.Up} \wedge N^i_{x.Down} \supseteq N^j_{y.EqDown} \\ \wedge N^i_{x.Left} \subseteq N^j_{y.Left} \wedge N^i_{x.Right} \subseteq N^j_{y.Right}] \end{array}$$

This means that if the node[10] x strictly dominates y in the input description, then (i) the set of nodes that are above or equal x in a valid model is included in the set of those that are strictly above y *and* (ii) the dual holds for the nodes that are above *and* (iii) the set of nodes that are on the left of y is included in the set of those that are on the left of x *and* (iv) similarly for the right part.

Once the constraints framework is settled, we can search for the solutions to our problem, *i.e.* the variable assignments for each of the sets of integers used to refer to the nodes of the input description. This search is performed by associating with each pair of nodes (x, y) of the input description a choice variable denoting the mutually exclusive relations[11] between these two nodes. Then

[9] $N^i_{x.EqUp}$ corresponds to the disjoint union of $N^i_{x.Eq}$ and $N^i_{x.Up}$, similarly for $N^j_{x.EqDown}$ with $N^i_{x.Eq}$ and $N^i_{x.Down}$.

[10] One should read the node denoted by the variable x.

[11] Either x equals y, x dominates y, y dominates x, x precedes y or y precedes x.

we use a search strategy to explore the consistent assignments to these choices variables (and the associated assignments for sets of integers referring to nodes)[12]. Note that the strategy used in XMG is a *first-fail* strategy which leads to very good results (see section 5 below). The implementation of this solver has been done using the constraint programming support of the Mozart Programming System (The Oz-Mozart Board, 2005).

4.2 Extension to higher-level constraints solving

An important feature of our approach is that this system of constraints over integer sets can be extended so that we not only ensure tree well-formedness of the outputted trees, but also the respect of linguistic properties such as the uniqueness of clitics in French, etc.

The idea is that if we extend adequately our node representation, we can find additional constraints that reflects the syntactic constraints we want to express.

Clitic uniqueness For instance, let us consider the *clitic uniqueness* constraint introduced above. We want to express the fact that in a valid model ϕ, there is only one node having a given property p (*i.e.* a parameter of the constraint, here the category *clitic*[13]). This can be done by introducing, for each node x *of the description*, a boolean variable p_x indicating whether the node denoting x *in the model* has this property or not. Then, if we call $\mathcal{V}_p^\phi$ the set of integers referring to nodes having the property p *in a model*, we have:

$$p_x \equiv (N^i_{x.Eq} \cap \mathcal{V}_p^\phi) \neq \emptyset$$

Finally, if we represent the true value with the integer 1 and false with 0, we can sum the p_x for each x *in the model*. When this sum gets greater than 1, we can consider that we are not building a valid model.

Colouration constraint Another example of the constraints introduced in section 3 is colouration. Colouration represents operational constraints whose effect is to control tree fragment combination. The idea is to label nodes with a colour between red, black and white. Then, during description solving, nodes are identified according to the rules given previously (see Figure 2).

That is, red nodes are not identified with any other node, white nodes can be identified with a black one. Black nodes are not identified with each other. A valid model in this context is a saturated tree, *i.e.* where nodes are either black (possibly resulting from identifications) or red. In other words, for every node in the model, there is at most one red or black node with which it has been identified. The implementation of such a constraint is done the following way. First, the tuples representing nodes are extended by adding a integer field *RB* referring to the red or black node with which the node has been identified. Then, considering the following sets of integers: $\mathcal{V}_\mathrm{R}$, $\mathcal{V}_\mathrm{B}$, $\mathcal{V}_\mathrm{W}$ respectively containing the integers referring to red, black and white nodes in the input description, the following constraints hold:

$$\begin{aligned} x \in \mathcal{V}_\mathrm{R} &\Rightarrow N^i_{x.RB} = i \wedge N^i_{x.Eq} = \{i\} && (a) \\ x \in \mathcal{V}_\mathrm{B} &\Rightarrow N^i_{x.RB} = i && (b) \\ x \in \mathcal{V}_\mathrm{W} &\Rightarrow N^i_{x.RB} \in \mathcal{V}_\mathrm{B}^\phi && (c) \end{aligned}$$

where $\mathcal{V}_\mathrm{B}^\phi$ represents the black nodes in a model, *i.e.* $\mathcal{V}_\mathrm{B}^\phi = \mathcal{V}^\phi \cap \mathcal{V}_\mathrm{B}$. (a) expresses the fact that for red nodes, $N^i_{x.RB}$ is the integer i associated with x itself, and $N^i_{x.Eq}$ is a set only containing i. (b) means that for black nodes, we have that $N^i_{x.RB}$ is also the integer i denoting x itself, but we cannot say anything about $N^i_{x.Eq}$. Eventually (c) means that whites nodes have to be identified with a black one.

Thus, we have seen that *Constraint Programming* offers an efficient and relatively natural way of representing syntactic constraints, as "all" that has to be done is to find an adequate node representation in terms of sets of nodes, then declare the constraints associated with these sets, and finally use a search strategy to compute the solutions.

5 Some features

There are two points worth considering here: (i) the usability of the formalism to describe a real scale grammar with a high factorisation, and (ii) the efficiency of the implementation in terms of time and memory use.

Concerning the first point, XMG has been used successfully to compute a TAG having more than 6,000 trees from a description containing 293

[12]More information about the use of such choice variables is given in (Duchier, 1999)

[13]In fact, the uniqueness concerns the rank of the clitics, see (Crabb´e, 2005b), §9.6.3.

classes[14]. Moreover, this description has been designed relatively quickly as the description language is intuitive as advocated in (Crabb´e, 2005a).

Concerning the efficiency of the system, the compilation of this TAG with more than 6,000 trees takes about 15 min with a P4 processor 2.6 GHz and 1 GB RAM. Note that compared with the compilation time of previous approaches (Candito, 1999; Gaiffe et al., 2002) (with the latter, a TAG of 3,000 trees was compiled in about an hour), these results are quite encouraging.

Eventually, XMG is released under the terms of the GPL-like CeCILL license[15] and can be freely downloaded at `http://sourcesup.cru.fr/xmg`.

6 Conclusion

Unlike previous approaches, the description language implemented by XMG is fully declarative, hence allowing to reuse efficient techniques borrowed to Logic Programming. The system has been used successfully to produce core TAG (Crabb´e, 2005b) and *Interaction Grammar* (Perrier, 2003) for French along with a core French TAG augmented with semantics (Gardent, 2006).

This paper shows that the metagrammar can be used to put model theoretic syntax at work while preserving reasonably efficient processing properties. The strategy used here builds on constraining offline a TAG whose units are elementary trees The other option is to formulate constraints applied on-line, in the course of parsing, applying on the whole syntactic structure. In a dependency framework, XDG followed this path (Debusmann et al., 2004), however it remains unknown to us whether this approach remains computationally tractable for parsing with real scale grammars.

References

A. Abeill´e. 2002. Une grammaire ´electronique du franais. CNRS Editions, Paris.

H. Ait-Kaci. 1991. Warren's abstract machine: A tutorial reconstruction. In K. Furukawa, editor, *Proc. of the Eighth International Conference of Logic Programming*. MIT Press, Cambridge, MA.

T. Becker. 2000. Patterns in metarules. In A. Abeille and O. Rambow, editors, *Tree Adjoining Grammars: formal, computational and linguistic aspects*. CSLI publications, Stanford.

[14]I.e. tree fragments or conjunction / disjunction of fragments

[15]More information about this license at `http://www.cecill.info/index.en.html`.

Joan Bresnan and Ronal M. Kaplan. 1982. *The Mental Representation of Grammatical Relations*. The MIT Press, Cambridge MA.

M.H. Candito. 1999. *Représentation modulaire et paramétrable de grammaires électroniques lexicalisées : application au franç ais et à l'italien*. Ph.D. thesis, Universit´e Paris 7.

B. Crabb´e. 2005a. Grammatical development with XMG. Proceedings of the Fifth International Conference on Logical Aspects of Computational Linguistics (LACL05).

B. Crabb´e. 2005b. *Représentation informatique de grammaires fortement lexicalisées : Application à la grammaire d'arbres adjoints*. Ph.D. thesis, Universit´e Nancy 2.

R. Debusmann, D. Duchier, and G.-J. M. Kruijff. 2004. Extensible dependency grammar: A new methodology. In *Proceedings of the COLING 2004 Workshop on Recent Advances in Dependency Grammar*, Geneva/SUI.

D. Duchier and J. Niehren. 2000. Dominance constraints with set operators. In *Proceedings of CL2000*, volume 1861 of *Lecture Notes in Computer Science*, pages 326–341. Springer.

D. Duchier, J. Le Roux, and Y. Parmentier. 2004. The Metagrammar Compiler: An NLP Application with a Multi-paradigm Architecture. In *2nd International Mozart/Oz Conference (MOZ'2004)*, Charleroi.

D. Duchier. 1999. Set constraints in computational linguistics - solving tree descriptions. In *Workshop on Declarative Programming with Sets (DPS'99), Paris, pp. 91 - 98.*

Robert Frank. 2002. *Phrase Structure Composition and Syntactic Dependencies*. MIT Press, Boston.

B. Gaiffe, B. Crabb´e, and A. Roussanaly. 2002. A new metagrammar compiler. In *Proceedings of TAG+6, Venice*.

C. Gardent. 2006. Int´egration d'une dimension s´emantique dans les grammaires d'arbres adjoints. In *Actes de La 13ème édition de la conférence sur le TALN (TALN 2006)*.

F. Pereira and D. Warren. 1980. Defi nite clause grammars for language analysis —a survey of the formalism and a comparison to augmented transition networks. *Artifi cial Intelligence*, 13:231–278.

David Perlmutter. 1970. Surface structure constraints in syntax. *Linguistic Inquiry*, 1:187–255.

Guy Perrier. 2003. Les grammaires d'interaction. HDR en informatique, Universit´e Nancy 2.

J. Rogers and K. Vijay-Shanker. 1994. Obtaining trees from their descriptions: An application to tree-adjoining grammars. *Computational Intelligence, 10:401–421*.

The Oz-Mozart Board. 2005. The Oz-Mozart Programming System. http://www.mozart-oz.org.

Fei Xia. 2001. *Automatic Grammar Generation from two Different Perspectives*. Ph.D. thesis, University of Pennsylvania.

The Metagrammar Goes Multilingual: A Cross-Linguistic Look at the V2-Phenomenon

Alexandra Kinyon
Department of CIS
University of Pennsylvania
kinyon@linc.cis.upenn.edu

Owen Rambow
CCLS
Columbia University
rambow@cs.columbia.edu

Tatjana Scheffler
Department of Linguistics
University of Pennsylvania
tatjana@ling.upenn.edu

SinWon Yoon
UFRL
Université Paris 7
swyoon@linguist.jussieu.fr

Aravind K. Joshi
Department of CIS
University of Pennsylvania
joshi@linc.cis.upenn.edu

Abstract

We present an initial investigation into the use of a metagrammar for explicitly sharing abstract grammatical specifications among languages. We define a single class hierarchy for a metagrammar which allows us to automatically generate grammars for different languages from a single compact metagrammar hierarchy. We use as our linguistic example the verb-second phenomenon, which shows considerable variation while retaining a basic property, namely the fact that the verb can appear in one of two positions in the clause.

1 An Overview of Metagrammars

A metagrammar (MG) factors common properties of TAG elementary trees to avoid redundancy, ease grammar development, and expand coverage with minimal effort: typically, from a compact manually encoded MG of a few dozen classes, one or more TAGs with several hundreds of elementary trees are automatically generated. This is appealing from a grammar engineering point of view, and also from a linguistic point of view: cross-linguistic generalizations are expressed directly in the MG. In this paper, we extend some earlier work on multilingual MGs (Candito, 1998; Kinyon and Rambow, 2003) by proposing cross-linguistic and framework-neutral syntactic invariants, which we apply to TAG. We focus on the verb-second phenomenon as a prototypical example of cross-language variation.

The notion of Metagrammar Metagrammars were first introduced by Candito (1996) to manually encode syntactic knowledge in a compact and abstract class hierarchy which supports multiple inheritance, and from which a TAG is automatically generated offline. Candito's class hierarchy imposes a general organization of syntax into three dimensions:

- Dimension 1: to encode initial subcategorization frames i.e. TAG tree families
- Dimension 2: to encode valency alternations / redistribution of syntactic functions
- Dimension 3: to encode the surface realization of arguments.

Each class in the MG hierarchy is associated with a partial tree description The tool computes a set of well-formed classes by combining exactly one terminal class from dimension 1, one terminal class from dimension 2, and n terminal classes from dimensions 3 (n being the number of arguments subcategorized by the lexical head anchoring the elementary tree(s) generated). The conjunction of the tree descriptions associated with each well-formed class in the set yields a minimal satisfying description, which results in the generation of one or more elementary trees. Candito's tool was used to develop a large TAG for French as well as a medium-size TAG for Italian Candito (1999), so multilinguality was addressed from the start, but each language had its dedicated hierarchy, with no sharing of classes despite the obvious similarities between Italian and French. A related approach was proposed by (Xia, 2001); the work of Evans, Gazdar, and Weir (2000) also has some common elements with MG.

Framework- and language-neutral syntactic invariants Using a MG, and following Candito, we can postulate cross-linguistic and cross-framework syntactic invariants such as:

Proceedings of the 8th International Workshop on Tree Adjoining Grammar and Related Formalisms, pages 17–24,
Sydney, July 2006.

- The notion of subcategorization
- The existence of a finite number of syntactic functions (subject, object etc.)
- The existence of a finite number of syntactic categories (NP, PP, etc.)
- The existence of valency alternations (Candito's dimension 2)
- The existence, orthogonal to valency alternations, of syntactic phenomena which do not alter valency, such as *wh*-movement (Candito's dimension 3).

These invariants — unlike other framework-specific syntactic assumptions such as the existence of "movement" or "*wh*-traces" — are accepted by most if not all existing frameworks, even though the machinery of a given framework may not necessarily account explicitly for each invariant. For instance, TAG does not have an explicit notion of syntactic function: although by convention node indices tend to reflect a function, it is not enforced by the framework's machinery.[1]

Hypertags Based on such framework- and language-neutral syntactic properties, Kinyon (2000) defined the notion of **Hypertag** (HT), a combination of Supertags (ST) Srinivas (1997) and of the MG. A ST is a TAG elementary tree, which provides richer information than standard POS tagging, but in a framework-specific manner (TAG), and also in a grammar-specific manner since a ST tagset can't be ported from one TAG to another TAG. A HT is an abstraction of STs, where the main syntactic properties of any given ST is encoded in a general readable Feature Structure (FS), by recording which MG classes a ST inherited from when it was generated. Figure 1 illustrates the <ST, HT> pair for *Par qui sera accompagnée Marie* 'By whom will Mary be accompanied'. We see that a HT feature structure directly reflects the MG organization, by having 3 features "Dimension 1", "Dimension 2" and "Dimension 3", where each feature takes its value from the MG terminal classes used to generate a given ST.

The XMG Tool Candito's tool brought a significant linguistic insight, therefore we essentially retain the above-mentioned syntactic invariants. However, more recent MG implementations have been developed since, each adding its significant contribution to the underlying metagrammatical hypothesis.

In this paper, we use the eXtensible MetaGrammar (XMG) tool which was developed by Crabbé

[1]But several attempts have been made to explicitly add functions to TAG, e.g. by Kameyama (1986) to retain the benefits of both TAG and LFG, or by Prolo (2006) to account for the coordination of constituents of different categories, yet sharing the same function.

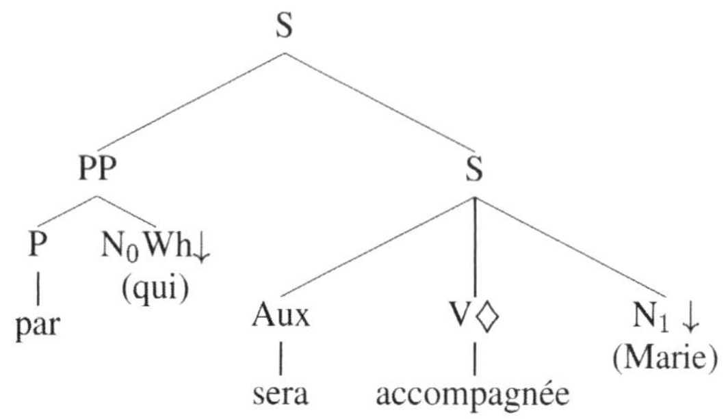

[DIMENSION1 STRICTTRANSITIVE
DIMENSION2 PERSONALFULLPASSIVE
DIMENSION3 [SUBJECT INVERTEDSUBJECT
COMPLEMENT WHQUESTIONEDBYCOMPLEMENT]]

Figure 1: A <SuperTag, HyperTag> pair for *accompagnée* ('accompanied') obtained with Candito's MetaGrammar compiler

(2005). In XMG, an MG consists of a set of *classes* similar to those in object-oriented programming, which are structured into a multiple inheritance hierarchy. Each class specifies a partial tree description (expressed by dominance and precedence constraints). The nodes of these tree fragment descriptions may be annotated with features. Classes may instantiate each other, and they may be parametrized (e.g., to hand down features like the grammatical function of a substitution node). The compiler unifies the instantiations of tree descriptions that are called. This unification is additionally guided by *node colors*, constraints that specify that a node must not be unified with any other node (red), must be unified (white), or may be unified, but only with a white node (black). XMG allows us to implement a hierarchy similar to that of Candito, but it also allows us to modify and extend it, as no structural assumptions about the class hierarchy are hard-coded.

2 The V2 Phenomenon

The Verb-Second (V2) phenomenon is a well-known set of data that demonstrates small-scale cross-linguistic variation. The examples in (1) show German, a language with a V2-constraint: (1a) is completely grammatical, while (1b) is not. This is considered to be due to the fact that the finite verb is required to be located in "second position" (V2) in German. Other languages with a V2 constraint include Dutch, Yiddish, Frisian, Icelandic, Mainland Scandinavian, and Kashmiri.

(1) a. Auf dem Weg sieht der Junge eine Ente.
on the path sees the boy a duck
'On the path, the boy sees a duck.'

b. *Auf dem Weg der Junge sieht eine Ente.
on the path the boy sees a duck
Int.: 'On the path, the boy sees a duck.'

Interestingly, these languages differ with respect to how exactly the constraint is realized. Rambow and Santorini (1995) present data from the mentioned languages and provide a set of parameters that account for the exhibited variation. In the following, for the sake of brevity, we will confine the discussion to two languages: German, and Yiddish. The German data is as follows (we do not repeat (1a) from above):

(2) a. Der Junge sieht eine Ente auf dem Weg.
the boy sees a duck on the path
'On the path, the boy sees a duck.'
b. ..., dass der Junge auf dem Weg eine Ente sieht.
..., that the boy on the path a duck sees
'..., that the boy sees a duck on the path.'
c. Eine Ente sieht der Junge.
a duck sees the boy
'The boy sees a duck.'

The Yiddish data:

(3) a. Dos yingl zet oyfn veg a katshke.
the boy sees on-the path a duck
'On the path, the boy sees a duck.'
b. Oyfn veg zet dos yingl a katshke.
on-the path sees the boy a duck.
'On the path, the boy sees a duck.'
c. ..., az dos yingl zet a katshke
..., that the boy sees a duck
'..., that the boy sees a duck.'

While main clauses exhibit V2 in German, embedded clauses with complementizers are verb-final (2b). In contrast, Yiddish embedded clauses must also be V2 (3c).

3 Handling V2 in the Metagrammar

It is striking that the basic V2 phenomenon is the same in all of these languages: the verb can appear in either its underlying position, or in second position (or, in some cases, third). We claim that what governs the appearance of the verb in these different positions (and thus the cross-linguistic differences) is that the heads—the verbal head and functional heads such as auxiliaries and complementizers—interact in specific ways. For example, in German a complementizer is not compatible with a verbal V2 head, while in Yiddish it is. We express the interaction among heads by assigning the heads different values for a set of features. Which heads can carry which feature values is a language-specific parameter. Our implementation is based on the previous pen-and-pencil analysis of Rambow and Santorini (1995), which we have modified and extended.

The work we present in this paper thus has a threefold interest: (1) we show how to handle an important syntactic phenomenon cross-linguistically in a MG framework; (2) we partially validate, correct, and extend a previously proposed linguistically-motivated analysis; and (3) we provide an initial fragment of a MG implementation from which we generate TAGs for languages which are relatively less-studied and for which no TAG currently exists (Yiddish).

4 Elements of Our Implementation

In this paper, we only address verbal elementary trees. We define a verbal realization to be a combination of three classes (or "dimensions" in Candito's terminology): a *subcategorization frame*, a *redistribution of arguments/valency alternation* (in our case, voice, which we do not further discuss), and a *topology*, which encodes the position and characteristics of the verbal head. Thus, we reinterpret Candito's "Dimension 3" to concentrate on the position of the verbal heads, with the different argument realizations (topicalized, base position) depending on the available heads, rather than defined as first-class citizens. The subcat and argument redistributions result in a set of structures for *arguments* which are left- or right-branching (depending on language and grammatical function). Figure 2 shows some argument structures for German. The topology reflects the basic clause structure, that is, the distribution of arguments and adjuncts, and the position of the verb (initial, V2, final, etc.). Our notion of sentence topology is thus similar to the notion formalized by Gerdes (2002). Specifically, we see positions of arguments and adjuncts as defined by the positions of their verbal heads. However, while Gerdes (2002) assumes as basic underlying notions the fields created by the heads (the traditional *Vorfeld* for the topicalized element and the *Mittelfeld* between the verb in second position and the verb in clause-final position), we only use properties of the heads. The fields are epiphenomenal for us.As mentioned above, we use the following set of features to define our MG topology:

- I (finite tense and subject-verb agreement): creates a specifier position for agreement which must be filled in a derivation, but allows recursion (i.e., adjunction at IP).
- Top (topic): a feature which creates a specifier position for the topic (semantically represented in a lambda abstraction) which must be filled in a derivation, and which does not allow recursion.
- M (mood): a feature with semantic content (to be defined), but no specifier.
- C (complementizer): a lexical feature introduced only by complementizers.

We can now define our topology in more detail. It consists of two main parts:

German:

	What	Features Introduced	Directionality
1	Verb (clause-final)	+I	head-final
2	Verb (V2, subject-inital)	+M, +Top, +I	head-initial
3	Verb (V2, non-subject-initial)	+M, +Top	head-initial
4	Complementizer	+C, +M	head-initial

Yiddish:

	What	Features Introduced	Directionality
1	Verb	+I	head-initial
2	Verb (V2, subject-inital)	+M, +Top, +I	head-initial
3	Verb (V2, non-subject-initial)	+M, +Top	head-initial
4	Complementizer	+C	head-initial

Figure 4: Head inventories for German and Yiddish.

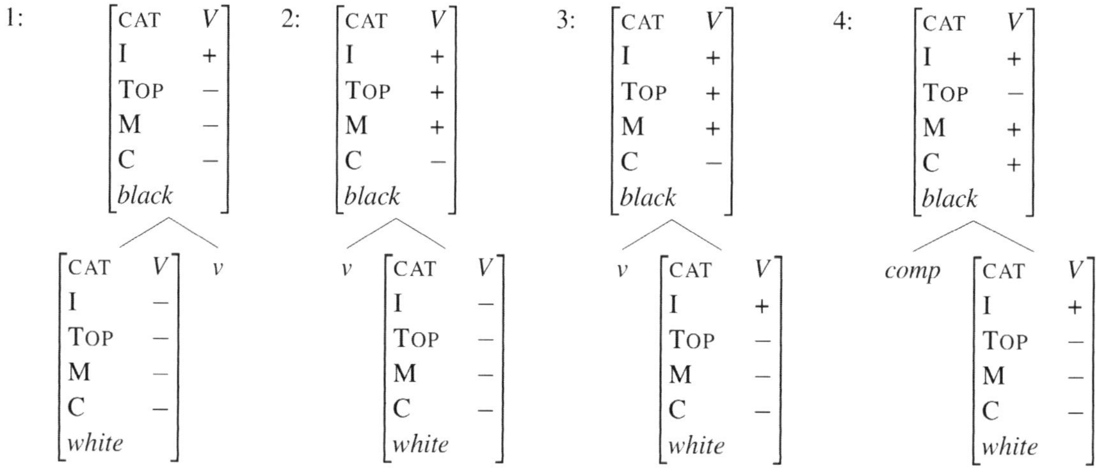

Figure 5: Head structures for German corresponding to the table in Figure 4 (above)

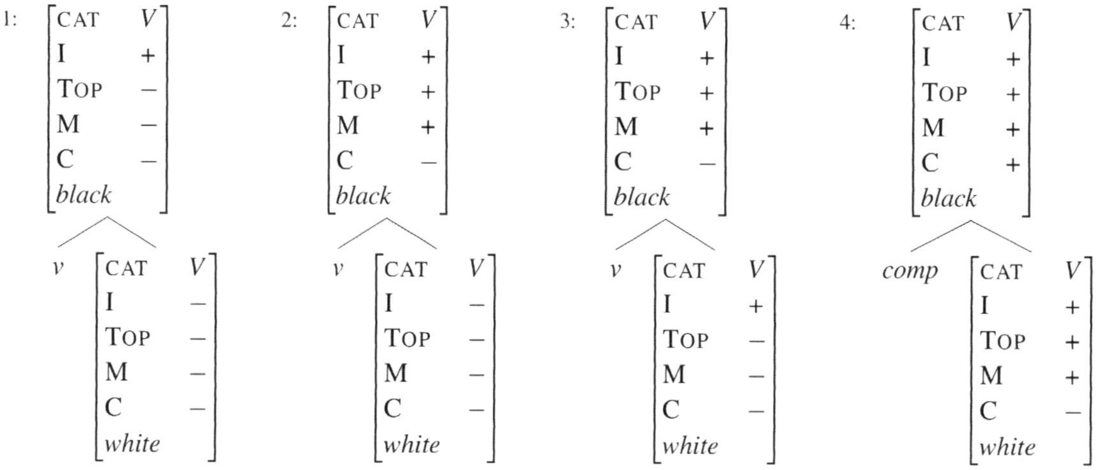

Figure 6: Head structures for Yiddish corresponding to the table in Figure 4 (below)

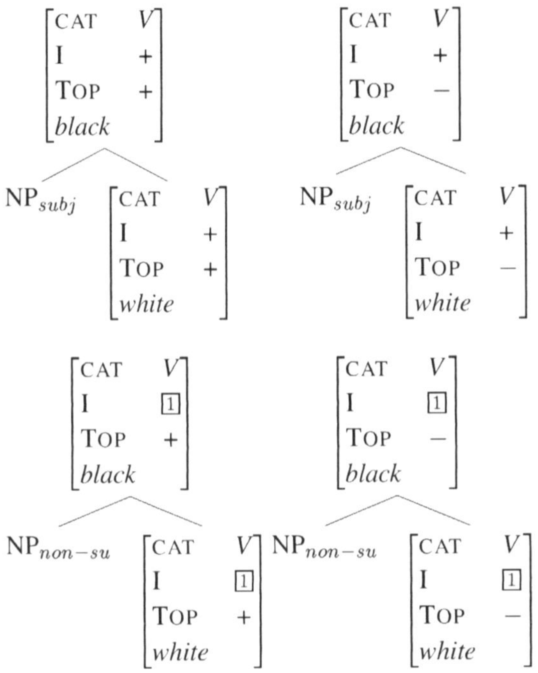

Figure 2: The argument structures

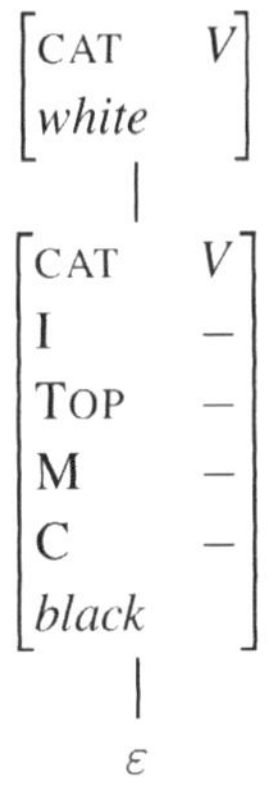

Figure 3: The projection structure; feature values can be filled in at the top feature structure to control the derivation.

- The **projection** includes the origin of the verb in the phrase structure (with an empty head since we assume it is no longer there) and its maximal projection. It is shown in Figure 3. The maximal projection expresses the expected feature content. For example, if we want to model non-finite clauses, the maximal projection will have [−I], while root V2 clauses will have [+Top], and embedded finite clauses with complementizers will have [+I,+C].
- Structures for **heads**, which can be head-initial or head-final. They introduce categorial features. Languages differ in what sort of heads they have. Which heads are available for a given language is captured in a **head inventory**, i.e., a list of possible heads for that language (which use the head structure just mentioned). Two such lists are shown in Figure 4, for German and Yiddish. The corresponding head structures are shown in Figures 5 and 6.

A topology is a combination of the projection and any combination of heads allowed by the language-specific head inventory. This is hard to express in XMG, so instead we list the specific combinations allowed. One might ask how we derive trees for language without the V2 phenomenon. Languages without V2 will usually have a smaller set of possible heads. We are working on a metagrammar for Korean in parallel with our work on the V2 languages. Korean is very much like German without the V2 phenomenon: the verbal head can only be in clause-final position (i.e., head 1 from Figure 5. However, passivization and scrambling can be treated the same way in Korean and German, since these phenomena are independent of V2.

5 Sample Derivation

Given a feature ordering (C > M > Top > I) and language-specific head inventories as in Figure 4, we compile out MGs for German (Figure 5) and Yiddish (Figure 6).[2] The projection and the argument realizations do not differ between the two languages: thus, these parts of the MG can be reused. The features, which were introduced for descriptive reasons, now guide the TAG compilation: only certain heads can be combined. Furthermore, subjects and non-subjects are distinguished, as well as topicalized and non-topicalized NPs (producing 4 kinds of arguments so far). The compiler picks out any number of compatible elements from the Metagrammar and performs the unifications of nodes that are permitted (or required) by

[2]All terminal nodes are "red"; spine nodes have been annotated with their color.

the node descriptions and the colors. By way of example, the derivations of elementary trees which can be used in a TAG analysis of German (2c) and Yiddish (3c) are shown in Figures 7 and 8, respectively.

6 Conclusion and Future work

This paper showed how cross-linguistic generalizations (in this case, V2) can be incorporated into a multilingual MG. This allows not only the reuse of MG parts for new (often, not well-studied) languages, but it also enables us to study small-scale parametric variation between languages in a controlled and formal way. We are currently modifying and extending our implementation in several ways.

The Notion of Projection In our current approach, the verb is never at the basis of the projection, it has always been removed into a new location. This may seem unmotivated in certain cases, such as German verb-final sentences. We are looking into using the XMG unification to actually place the verb at the bottom of the projection in these cases.

Generating Top and Bottom Features The generated TAG grammar currently does not have top and bottom feature sets, as one would expect in a feature-based TAG. These are important for us so we can force adjunction in adjunct-initial V2 sentences (where the element in clause-initial position is not an argument of the verb). We intend to follow the approach laid out in Crabbé (2005) in order to generate top and bottom feature structures on the nodes of the TAG grammar.

Generating test-suites to document our grammars Since XMG offers more complex object-oriented functionalities, including instances, and therefore recursion, it is now straightforward to directly generate parallel multilingual sentences directly from XMG, without any intermediate grammar generation step. The only obstacle remains the explicit encoding of Hypertags into XMG.

Acknowledgments

We thank Yannick Parmentier, Joseph Leroux, Bertrand Gaiffe, Benoit Crabbé, the LORIA XMG team, and Julia Hockenmaier for their invaluable help; Eric de la Clergerie, Carlos Prolo and the Xtag group for their helpful feedback, comments and suggestions on different aspects of this work; and Marie-Hélène Candito for her insights. This work was supported by NSF Grant 0414409 to the University of Pennsylvania.

References

Candito, M. H. 1998. Building parallel LTAG for French and Italian. In *Proc. ACL-98*. Montreal.

Candito, M.H. 1996. A principle-based hierarchical representation of LTAGs. In *Proc. COLING-96*. Copenhagen.

Candito, M.H. 1999. Représentation modulaire et paramétrable de grammaires électroniques lexicalisées. Doctoral Dissertation, Univ. Paris 7.

Clément, L., and A. Kinyon. 2003. Generating parallel multilingual LFG-TAG grammars using a MetaGrammar. In *Proc. ACL-03*. Sapporo.

Clergerie, E. De La. 2005. From metagrammars to factorized TAG/TIG parsers. In *IWPT-05*. Trento.

Crabbé, B. 2005. Représentation informatique de grammaires fortement lexicalisées. Doctoral Dissertation, Univ. Nancy 2.

Evans, R., G. Gazdar, and D. Weir. 2000. Lexical rules are just lexical rules. In *Tree Adjoining Grammars*, ed. A. Abeillé and O. Rambow. CSLI.

Gerdes, K. 2002. DTAG. attempt to generate a useful TAG for German using a metagrammar. In *Proc. TAG+6*. Venice.

Kameyama, M. 1986. Characterising LFG in terms of TAG. In *Unpublished report*. Univ. of Pennsylvania.

Kinyon, A. 2000. Hypertags. In *Proc. COLING-00*. Sarrebrucken.

Kinyon, A., and O. Rambow. 2003. Generating cross-language and cross-framework annotated test-suites using a MetaGrammar. In *Proc. LINC-EACL-03*. Budapest.

Prolo, C. 2006. Handling unlike coordinated phrases in TAG by mixing Syntactic Category and Grammatical Function. In *Proc. TAG+8*. Sidney.

Rambow, Owen, and Beatrice Santorini. 1995. Incremental phrase structure generation and a universal theory of V2. In *Proceedings of NELS 25*, ed. J.N. Beckman, 373–387. Amherst, MA: GSLA.

Srinivas, B. 1997. Complexity of lexical descriptions and its relevance for partial parsing. Doctoral Dissertation, Univ. of Pennsylvania.

Xia, F. 2001. Automatic grammar generation from two perspectives. Doctoral Dissertation, Univ. of Pennsylvania.

XTAG Research Group. 2001. A lexicalized tree adjoining grammar for English. Technical Report IRCS-01-03, IRCS, University of Pennsylvania.

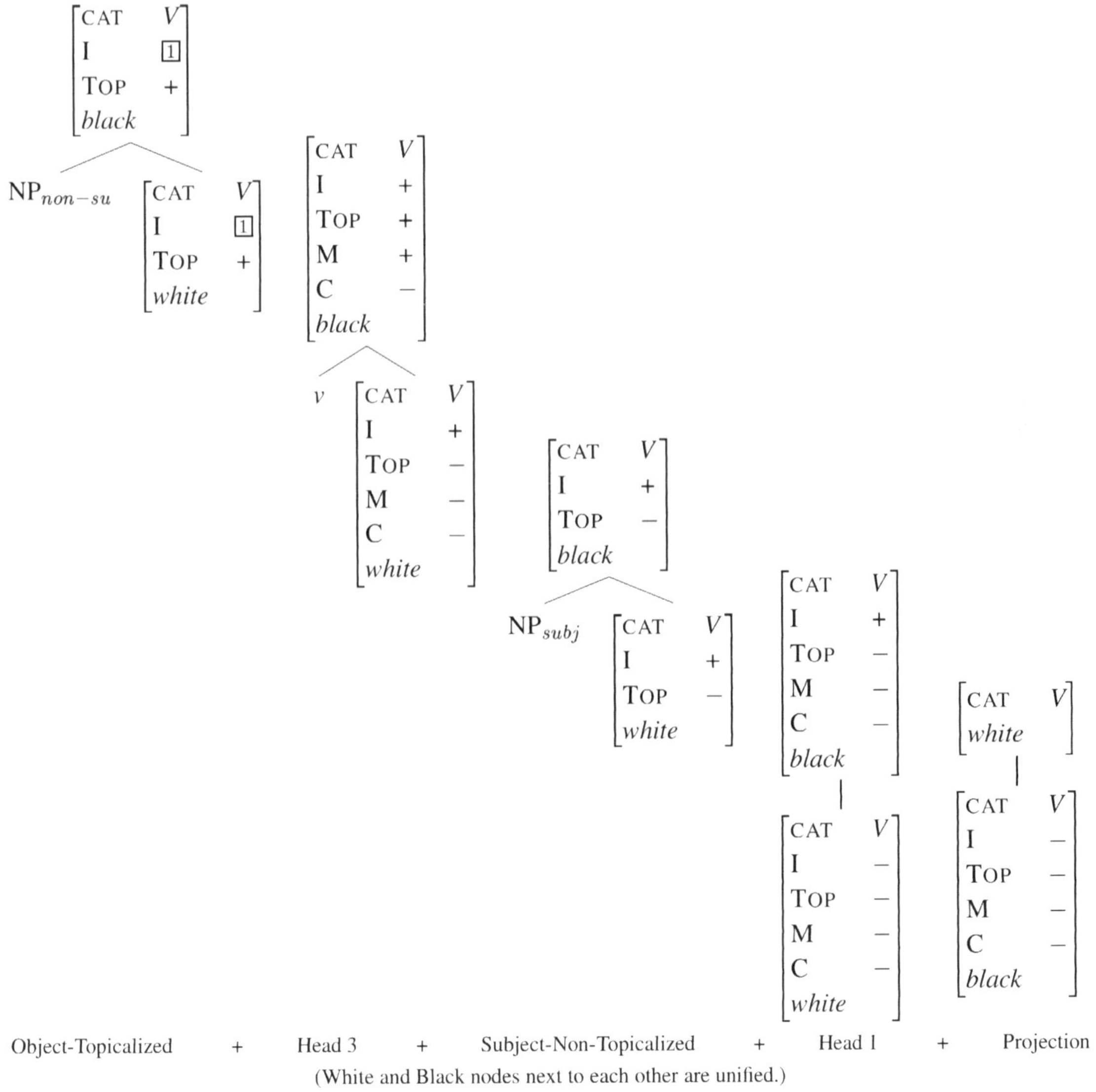

Figure 7: Derivation of the German elementary tree NP$_{obj}$ V NP$_{subj}$ (2d).

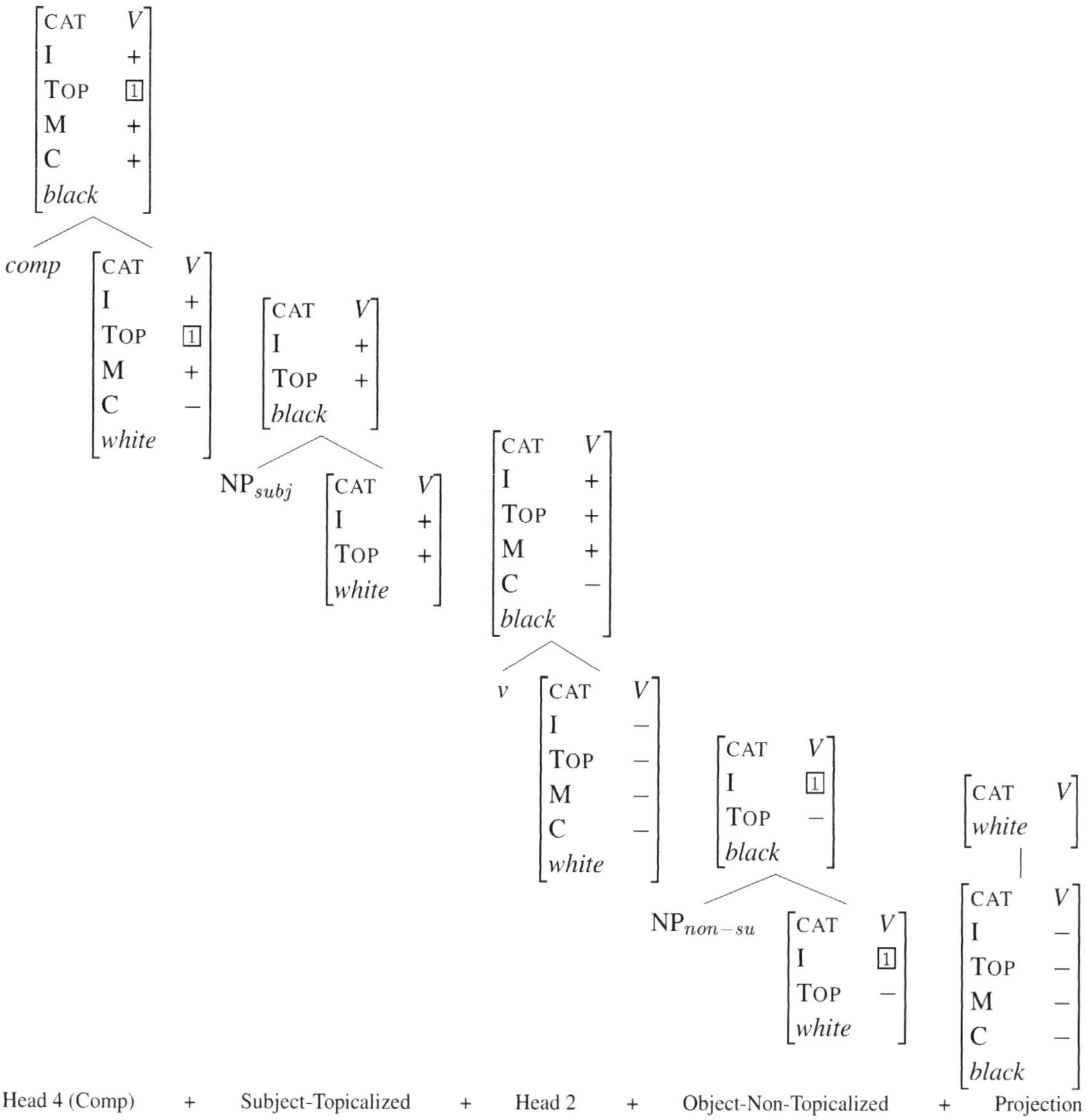

Figure 8: Derivation of the Yiddish elementary tree Comp NP_{subj} V NP_{obj} (3c).

The weak generative capacity of linear tree-adjoining grammars

David Chiang*
Information Sciences Institute
University of Southern California
4676 Admiralty Way, Suite 1001
Marina del Rey, CA 90292, USA
chiang@isi.edu

1 Introduction

Linear tree-adjoining grammars (TAGs), by analogy with linear context-free grammars, are tree-adjoining grammars in which at most one symbol in each elementary tree can be rewritten (adjoined or substituted at). Uemura et al. (1999), calling these grammars *simple linear TAGs* (SL-TAGs), show that they generate a class of languages incommensurate with the context-free languages, and can be recognized in $\mathcal{O}(n^4)$ time.

Working within the application domain of modeling of RNA secondary structures, they find that SL-TAGs are too restrictive—they can model RNA pseudoknots but because they cannot generate all the context-free languages, they cannot model even some very simple RNA secondary structures. Therefore they propose a more powerful version of linear TAGs, *extended simple linear TAGs* (ESL-TAGs), which generate a class of languages that include the context-free languages and can be recognized in $\mathcal{O}(n^5)$ time.

Satta and Schuler (1998), working within the application domain of natural language syntax, define another restriction on TAG which is also recognizable in $\mathcal{O}(n^5)$ time. Despite being less powerful than full TAG, it is still able to generate languages like the copy language $\{ww\}$ and Dutch cross-serial dependencies (Joshi, 1985). Kato et al. (2004) conjecture that this restricted TAG is in fact equivalent to ESL-TAG.

In this paper we prove their conjecture, and also prove that adding substitution to ESL-TAG does not increase its weak generative capacity, whereas adding substitution to SL-TAG makes it weakly equivalent to ESL-TAG. Thus these four formalisms converge to the same weak-equivalence class, the intuition being that the "hardest" operation in TAG, namely, adjunction of a wrapping auxiliary tree in the middle of the spine of another wrapping auxiliary tree, is subjected to the linearity constraint, but most other operations are unrestricted.[1] Kato et al. (2004) show that these formalisms are more powerful than SL-TAG or general CFG or their union and conjecture, on the other hand, that they are less powerful than TAG. We prove this conjecture as well.

2 Definitions

We assume a standard definition of TAG, with or without substitution, in which adjunction is not allowed at foot nodes, and other nodes can have no-adjunction (NA) constraints, obligatory-adjunction (OA), or selective-adjunction constraints. We use the symbols η, η_1, η_2, etc. to range over nodes of elementary trees or derived trees, although sometimes we use the label of a node to refer to the node itself. The *spine* of an auxiliary tree is the path from its root node to its foot node, inclusive. The *subtree* of a node η is the set of all nodes dominated by η, including η itself. The *segment* of a tree from η_1 to η_2 (where η_1 dominates η_2) is the set of all nodes in the subtree of η_1 but not in the subtree of η_2. A segment can be *excised*, which means removing the nodes of the segment and making η_2 replace η_1 as the child of its parent.

We also assume a standard definition of TAG derivation trees. We use the symbols h, h_1, h_2, etc. to range over nodes of derivation trees. The *sub-*

*This research was primarily carried out while the author was at the University of Pennsylvania.

[1] Adjunction at root and foot nodes is another operation that by itself will not take a formalism beyond context-free power, a fact which is exploited in Rogers' regular-form TAG (Rogers, 1994). But allowing this in a linear TAG would circumvent the linearity constraint.

Proceedings of the 8th International Workshop on Tree Adjoining Grammar and Related Formalisms, pages 25–32,
Sydney, July 2006.

derivation of h is the subtree of h in the derivation tree. When we cut up derivations into subderivations or segments and recombine them, the edge labels (indicating addresses of adjunctions and substitutions) stay with the node above, not the node below.

Now we define various versions of linear TAG.

Definition 1. A *right (left) auxiliary tree* is one in which the leftmost (rightmost) frontier node is the foot node, and the spine contains only the root and foot nodes. A *wrapping auxiliary tree* is one which is neither a left or a right auxiliary tree.

Definition 2. We say that a node of an elementary tree is *active* if adjunction is allowed to occur at it, and that a node is *w-active* if adjunction of a wrapping auxiliary tree is allowed to occur at it.

Definition 3. A *Satta-Schuler linear tree-adjoining grammar* (SSL-TAG) is a TAG with substitution in which:

1. In the spine of each wrapping auxiliary tree, there is at most one w-active node.
2. In the spine of each left or right auxiliary tree, there are no w-active nodes, nor are there any other adjoining constraints.

Definition 4. A *simple linear tree-adjoining grammar* (SL-TAG), with or without substitution, is a TAG, with or without substitution, respectively, in which every initial tree has exactly one active node, and every auxiliary tree has exactly one active node on its spine and no active nodes elsewhere.

Definition 5. An *extended simple linear tree-adjoining grammar* (ESL-TAG), with or without substitution, is a TAG, with or without substitution, respectively, in which every initial tree has exactly one active node, and every auxiliary tree has exactly one active node on its spine and at most one active node elsewhere.

3 Properties

We now review several old results and prove a few new results relating the weak generative capacity of these formalisms to one another and to (linear) CFG and TAG. These results are summarized in Figure 1.

3.1 Previous results

Proposition 1 (Uemura et al. 1999).

$$\textit{Linear CFL} \subsetneq \textit{SL-TAL}$$

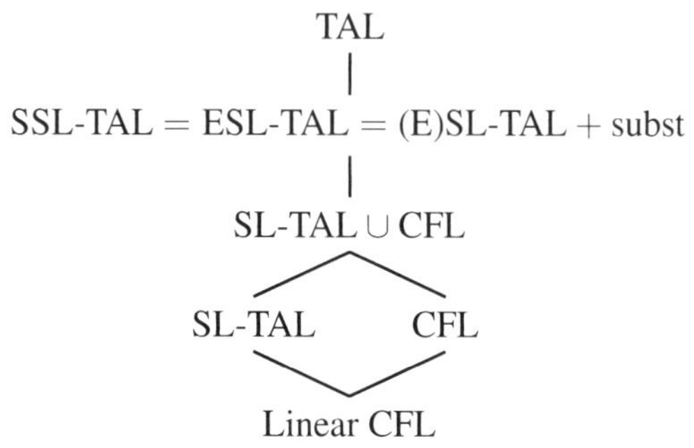

Figure 1: Summary of results: an edge indicates that the higher formalism has strictly greater weak generative capacity than the lower.

Proposition 2 (Uemura et al. 1999).

$$\textit{CFL} \subsetneq \textit{ESL-TAL}$$

Proposition 3 (Kato et al. 2004).

$$\textit{CFL} \cup \textit{SL-TAL} \subsetneq \textit{ESL-TAL}$$

Proposition 4 (Satta and Schuler 1998; Uemura et al. 1999). *SSL-TAG and ESL-TAG can be parsed in* $\mathcal{O}(n^5)$ *time.*

3.2 Weak equivalence

Proposition 5. *The following formalisms are weakly equivalent:*

(i) ESL-TAG

(ii) SL-TAG with substitution

(iii) ESL-TAG with substitution

(iv) SSL-TAG

Proof. We prove this by proving four inclusions.

$\mathcal{L}$(ESL-TAG) $\subseteq \mathcal{L}$(ESL-TAG + substitution): Trivial.

$\mathcal{L}$(ESL-TAG + substitution) $\subseteq \mathcal{L}$(SSL-TAG): Trivial.

$\mathcal{L}$(SSL-TAG) $\subseteq \mathcal{L}$(SL-TAG + substitution): We deal first with the left and right auxiliary trees, and then with off-spine adjunction.

First, we eliminate the left and right auxiliary trees. Since these only insert material to the left or right of a node, just as in tree-insertion grammars (TIGs), we may apply the conversion from TIGs to tree-substitution grammars (Schabes and Waters, 1995), used in the proof of the context-freeness of

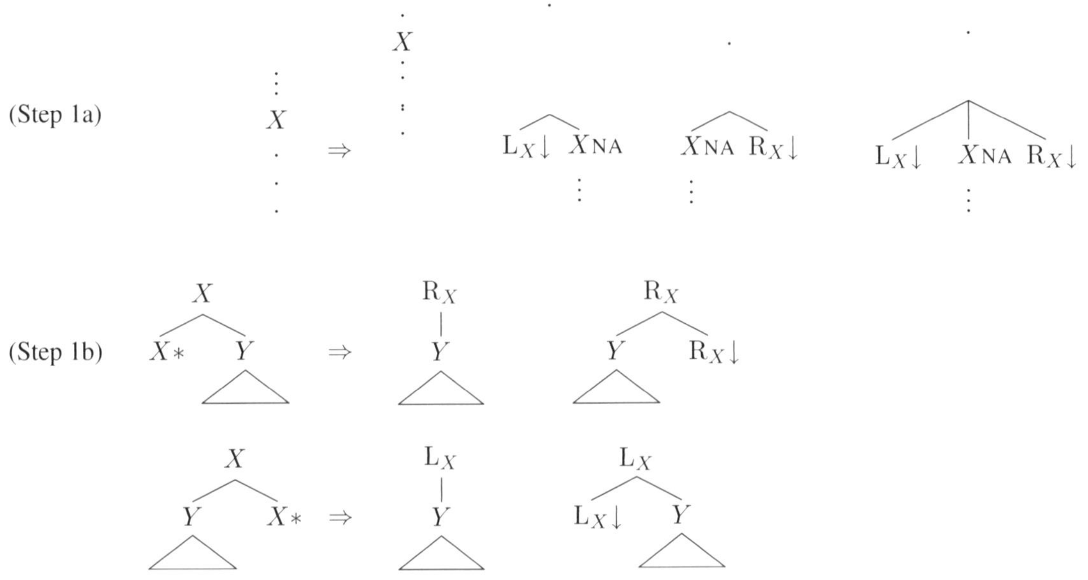

Figure 2: Elimination of left/right auxiliary trees.

TIG.[2] (Step 1a) For each active node X that is not the root of a left or right auxiliary tree, we create four copies of the containing elementary tree with X altered in the following ways: first, leave X unchanged; then, add a copy of X above it, making both nodes no-adjunction nodes, and add a new left sister substitution node labeled L_X or a new right sister substitution node labeled R_X, or both. See Figure 2. (Step 1b) For each β that was originally a left (right) auxiliary tree with root/foot label X, relabel the root node as L_X (R_X) and delete the foot node, and create two copies of the containing elementary tree, one unchanged, and one with a new left (right) sister substitution node. See Figure 2. When the modified β substitutes at one of the new children of an η, the substitution clearly results in the same string that would have resulted from adjoining the original β to η.

This construction might appear incorrect in two ways. First, the new grammar has trees with both an L_X and an R_X node corresponding to the same original node, which would correspond to adjunction of two auxiliary trees β_L and β_R at the same node X in the original grammar. But this new derivation generates a string that was generable in the original grammar, namely by adjoining β_L at X, then adjoining β_R at the root of β_L, which is allowed because the definition of SSL-TAG prohibits adjunction constraints at the root of β_L.

Thus the first apparent problem is really the solution to the second problem: in the original grammar, a left auxiliary tree β_L could adjoin at the root of a right auxiliary tree β_R, which in turn adjoined at a node η, whereas in the new grammar, β_R does not have an L_X substitution node to allow this possibility. But the same string can be generated by substituting both trees under η in the new grammar. In the case of a whole chain of adjunctions of left/right auxiliary trees at the root of left/right auxiliary trees, we can generate the same string by rearranging the chain into a chain of left auxiliary trees and a chain of right auxiliary trees (which is allowed because adjunction constraints are prohibited at all the roots), and substituting both at η.

(Step 2) Next, we eliminate the case of a wrapping auxiliary tree β that can adjoin at an off-spine node η. (Step 2a) For each active off-spine node η, we relabel η with a unique identifier $\hat{\eta}$ and split the containing elementary tree at η:

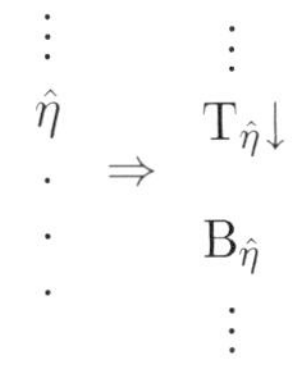

[2] This corresponds to Steps 1–4 of that proof (Schabes and Waters, 1995, p. 486). Since that proof uses a more relaxed definition of left and right auxiliary trees, it is probable that SSL-TAG could also be relaxed in the same way.

(Step 2b) After step 2a has been completed for all nodes η, we revisit each η, and for every wrapping β that could adjoin at η, create a copy of β with root relabeled to $\mathrm{T}_{\hat{\eta}}$ and foot relabeled to $\mathrm{B}_{\hat{\eta}}$.

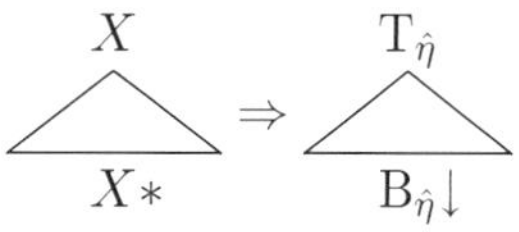

Then the original β is discarded. Substituting one of these copies of β at a $\mathrm{T}_{\hat{\eta}}$ node and then substituting a $\mathrm{B}_{\hat{\eta}}$ tree at the former foot node has the same effect as adjoining β at η. Finally, unless η had an obligatory-adjunction constraint, simulate the lack of adjunction at η by adding the initial tree

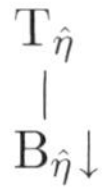

$\mathcal{L}(\text{SL-TAG} + \text{substitution}) \subseteq \mathcal{L}(\text{ESL-TAG})$: This construction is related to Lang's normal form which ensures binary-branching derivation trees (Lang, 1994), but guarantees that one adjunction site is on the spine and one is off the spine.

(Step 0a) Ensure that the elementary trees are binary-branching. (Step 0b) Add a new root and foot node to every elementary tree:

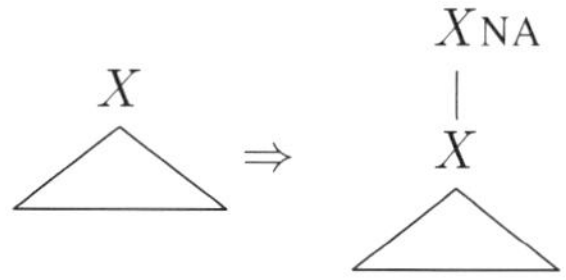

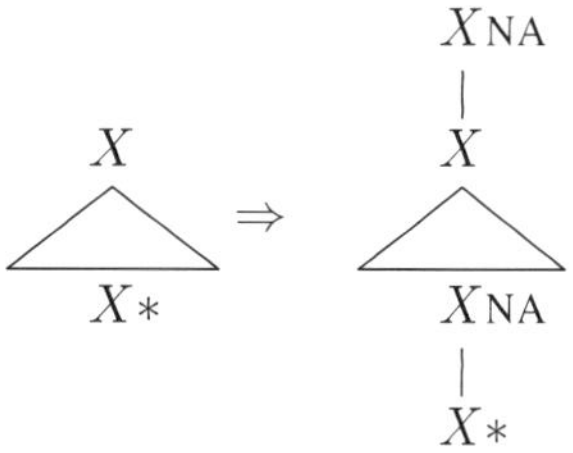

(Step 1) We transform the grammar so that no auxiliary tree has more than one substitution node. For any auxiliary tree with spine longer than four nodes, we apply the following transformation: target either the active node or its parent, and call it Y. Let Z_1 be the child that dominates the foot node; let V_1 be a fresh nonterminal symbol and insert V_1 nodes above Y and below Z_1, and excise the segment between the two V nodes, leaving behind an active obligatory-adjunction node. If Y has another child, call it Z_2; let V_2 be a fresh nonterminal symbol and insert a V_2 node above Z_2, and break off the subtree rooted in V_2, leaving behind a substitution node. See Figure 3. This transformation reduces the spine of the auxiliary tree by one node, and creates two new trees that satisfy the desired form. We repeat this until the entire grammar is in the desired form.

(Step 2) Next, we transform the grammar so that no initial tree has more than one substitution node, while maintaining the form acquired in step 1. For any initial tree with height greater than three nodes, we apply the same transformation as in step 1, except that Y is the child of the root node, Z_1 is its left child, and Z_2 is its other child if it exists and is not already a substitution node. See Figure 3. This transformation replaces an initial tree with at most two shorter initial trees, and one auxiliary tree in the desired form. Again we repeat this until the entire grammar is in the desired form.

(Step 3) Finally, we convert each substitution node into an adjunction node (Schabes, 1990). For each substitution node η, let X be the label of η. Relabel η to S_X with obligatory adjunction and place an empty terminal beneath η.

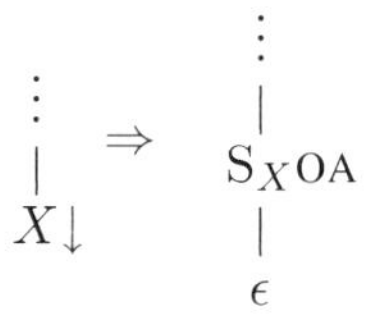

For each initial tree with root label X, convert it into an auxiliary tree by adding a new root node labeled S_X whose children are the old root node and a new foot node.

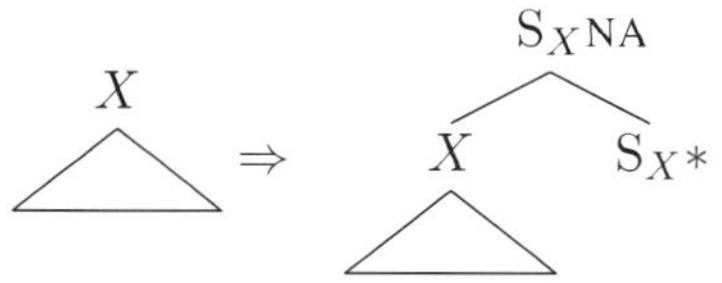

□

3.3 Relation to tree-adjoining languages

Our second result, also conjectured by Kato et al., is that the weak equivalence class established above is a proper subset of TAL.

Proposition 6. *The language*

$$L = \{a_1^r b_1^p b_2^p c_1^q c_2^q a_2^r a_3^r c_3^q c_4^q b_3^p b_4^p a_4^r\}$$

is in TAL but not ESL-TAL.

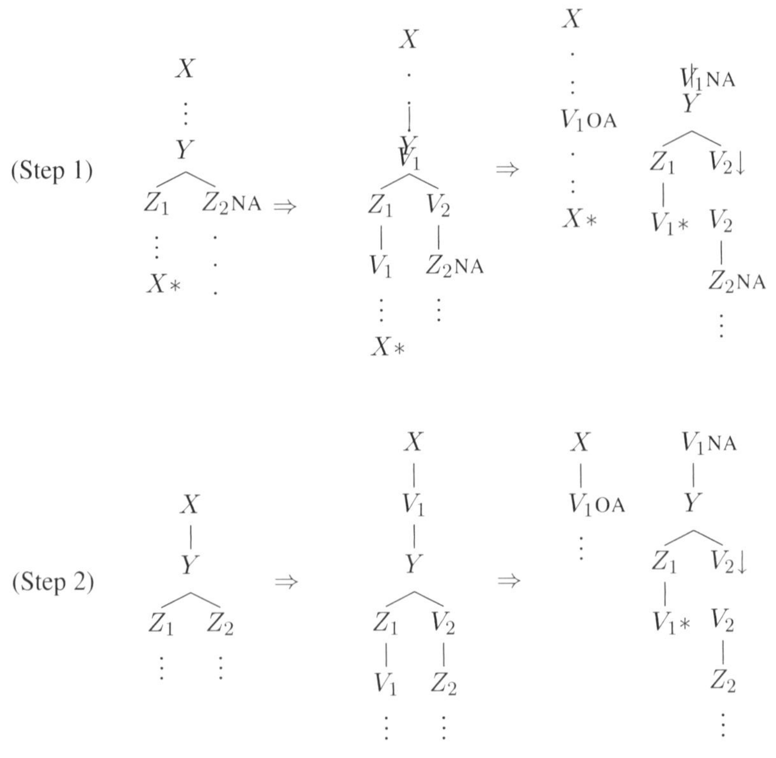

Figure 3: Separation of substitution nodes. Some adjunction constraints are omitted to avoid clutter.

Proof ($L \in TAL$). The language is generated by the following TAG:

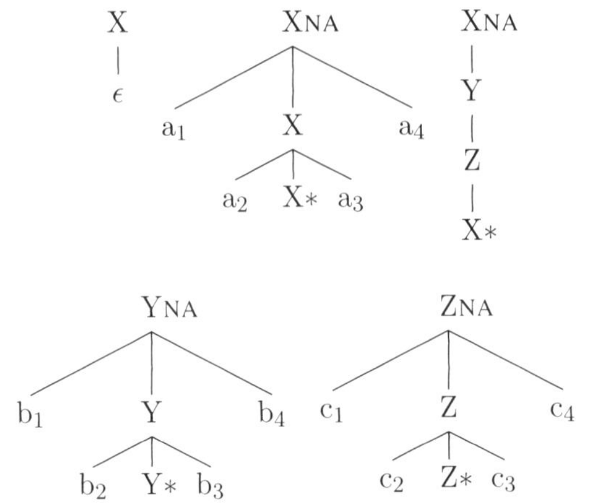

□

Before proceeding to the other half of the proof, we define a few useful notions. A *marked string* (as in Ogden's Lemma) over an alphabet Σ is a string over $\Sigma \times \{0, 1\}$, where a symbol $\langle \sigma, 1 \rangle$ is *marked* and a symbol $\langle \sigma, 0 \rangle$ is not. Marked strings over Σ can be projected into Σ^* in the obvious way and we will talk about marked strings and their projections interchangeably.

A *decomposed string* over Σ is a sequence of strings over Σ, which can be projected into Σ^* by concatenating their members in order, and again we will talk about decomposed strings and their projections interchangeably. In particular, we will often simply write a decomposed string $\langle w_1, \ldots, w_n \rangle$ as $w_1 \cdots w_n$. Moreover, we may use the symbol w_i to refer to the occurrence of the ith member of the decomposition in w; for example, if w is a marked string, we may say that a symbol in w_i is marked, or if w is generated by a TAG derivation, we may say that w_i is generated by some set of nodes in the derivation tree.

The second half of the proof requires a double-decker pumping lemma.

Condition 1 (cf. Vijay-Shanker (1987), Theorem 4.7). Given a language L and a decomposed string $x_1 z x_2 \in L$ with some symbols in z marked, there exists a decomposition of z into $u_1 v_1 w_1 v_2 u_2 v_3 w_2 v_4 u_3$ such that one of the v_i contains a mark, and L contains, for all $k \geq 1$,

$$x_1(u_1 v_1^k w_1 v_2^k u_2 v_3^k w_2 v_4^k u_3)x_2$$

Condition 2 (cf. Uemura et al. (1999), Lemma

1). Given a language L and a decomposed string $x_1 z_1 z_2 x_2 z_3 z_4 x_3 \in L$ with some symbols in one of the z_i marked, there exist decompositions of the z_i into $u_i v_i w_i$ such that one of the v_i contains a mark, and L contains, for all $k \geq 1$,

$$x_1(u_1 v_1^k w_1)(u_2 v_2^k w_2)x_2(u_3 v_3^k w_3)(u_4 v_4^k w_4)x_3$$

Lemma 7. *If L is an ESL-TAL, then there exists a constant n such that for any $z \in L$ with n symbols marked, Condition 1 holds of $\epsilon \cdot z \cdot \epsilon$. Moreover, it holds such that the w_1 and w_2 it provides can be further decomposed into $z_1 z_2$ and $z_3 z_4$, respectively, such that for any marking of n symbols of any of the z_j, either Condition 1 holds of $z = x_1 z_j x_2$ (where x_1 and x_2 are the surrounding context of z_j) or Condition 2 holds of $z = x_1 z_1 z_2 x_2 z_3 z_4 x_3$ (where x_1, x_2, and x_3 are the surrounding context of $z_1 z_2$ and $z_3 z_4$).*

Proof. Since L is an ESL-TAL, it is generated by some ESL-TAG G. Let k be the number of elementary trees in G and t be the maximum number of terminal symbols in any elementary tree of G. Then set $n = 2^{k+1}t$.

The first invocation of Condition 1 is the TAG version of Ogden's lemma (Hopcroft and Ullman, 1979). To show that it holds, we need to find a path P in the derivation tree of z that has a cycle that generates at least one marked symbol. Define a *branch point* to be a node h in the derivation tree such that the marked nodes generated by the subderivation of h are not all generated by the subderivation of a single child of h. We seek a P that has at least $k+1$ branch points. Start by adding the root of the derivation tree to P. Thereafter let h be the last node in P. If h is a leaf, stop; otherwise, add to P the child of h whose subderivation generates the most marked symbols. Note that if a branch point in P generates m marked symbols, the next branch point generates at least $\frac{m-t}{2}$. Our choice of n then guarantees that P has at least $k+1$ branch points, at least two of which must correspond to the same auxiliary tree. Call these nodes h_1 and h_2.

These two nodes divide the derivation up into three phases: first, the derivation segment from the root to h_1, which we call α (because it can be thought of as the derived initial tree it generates); then the segment from h_1 to h_2, which we call β_1 (because it can be thought of as the derived auxiliary tree it generates); then subderivation of h_2, which we call β_2. Note that we can form new valid derivations of G by repeating β_2: that is, in terms of derivation trees, stacking α on top of one or more copies of β_1, on top of β_2—or in terms of derived trees, repeatedly adjoining β_1 into α and then adjoining β_2.

If β_2 adjoins into the spine of β_1, then let $\langle u_1, u_2, u_3 \rangle$ be the parts of z generated by α, $\langle v_1, v_2, v_3, v_4 \rangle$ the parts generated by β_1, and $\langle w_1, w_2 \rangle$ the parts generated by β_2 (see Figure 4a). Then these new derivations generate the strings $u_1 v_1^k w_1 v_2^k u_2 v_3^k w_2 v_4^k u_3$.

But if β_2 adjoins at a node to the left of the spine of β_1, then let $\langle u_1, v_{42}, u_3 \rangle$ be the parts of the z generated by α, $\langle v_1, u_2, v_{41}, v_{43} \rangle$ the parts generated by β_1, and $\langle w_1, w_2 \rangle$ the parts generated by β_2 (see Figure 4b). Then let $v_2 = v_3 = \epsilon$ and $v_4 = v_{41} v_{42} v_{43}$; the new derivations will generate the strings $u_1 v_1^k w_1 v_2^k u_2 v_3^k w_2 v_4^k u_3$. The case where β_2 adjoins to the right of the spine.

Now we focus attention on β_2. Let S be the longest path of the derivation of β_2 containing the root of the derivation and auxiliary trees adjoined at spine nodes. This S is unique because each spine can only have one active node. Let h_3 be the last node in S, which divides the derivation of β_2 into two phases: the segment from the root to h_3, which we call β_{21}, and the subderivation of h_3, which we call β_{22}. This gives a decomposition $\langle w_1, w_2 \rangle = \langle z_1 z_{21} z_{22}, z_{31} z_{32} z_4 \rangle$, where β_{22} generates z_{21} and z_{32} (see Figure 5). Note that the derivation nodes in S are the only ones that can generate symbols in z_1, z_{22}, z_{31}, and z_4 at once; the other derivation nodes only generate symbols in a single z_i. We let $z_2 = z_{21} z_{22}$ and $z_3 = z_{31} z_{32}$ and hand off the decomposition $\langle w_1, w_2 \rangle = \langle z_1 z_2, z_3 z_4 \rangle$ to our adversary, who may choose a z_j and mark n symbols in it.

Then we recapitulate the reasoning above to get a path P' starting from the root of the derivation of β_2 and containing at least $k+1$ branch points, two of which correspond to the same auxiliary tree. Call these nodes h_4 and h_5 and the segment between them β_3, and let $\langle v_1, v_2, v_3, v_4 \rangle$ now stand for the parts of $\langle w_1, w_2 \rangle$ generated by β_3. Once again, we are going to repeat β_3 to generate new derivations, pumping copies of the v_i into $\langle w_1, w_2 \rangle$. But the location of the v_i depends on h_5: if h_5 is in S, then the v_i will appear inside each of the z_i, satisfying Condition 2. Otherwise, they will all appear inside z_j. □

(a)

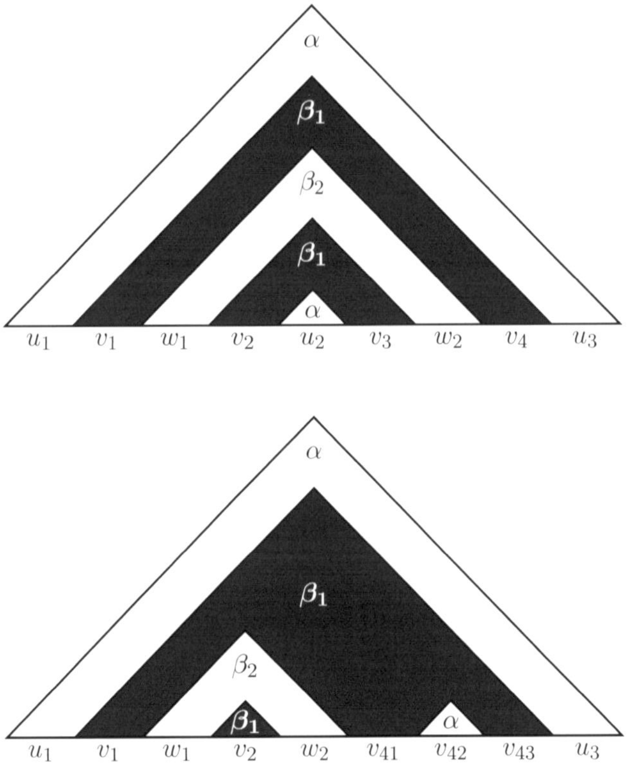

Figure 4: Anatomy of derived tree in proof of Lemma 7.

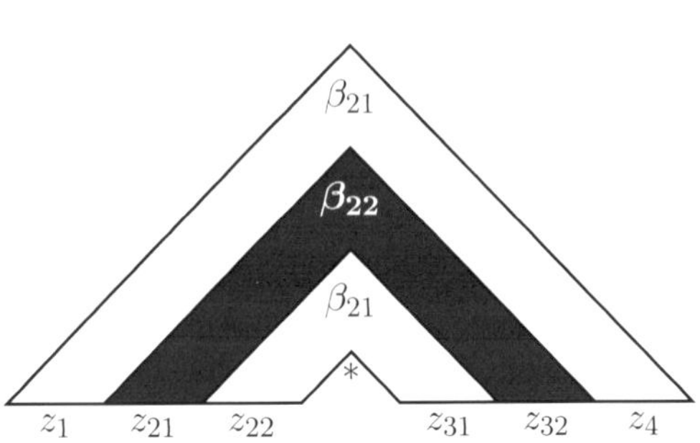

Figure 5: Anatomy of β_2 in proof of Lemma 7.

Finally, we complete the proof of Proposition 6.

Proof of Proposition 6 ($L \notin$ ESL-TAL). Suppose L is an ESL-TAL. Let z be the string obtained by setting $p = q = r = s = n$ and mark the a_1s. Then Lemma 7 must hold. The first invocation of Condition 1 must give a w_1 of the form $a^* b^n_1 \ldots$ Lemma 7 must further decompose w_1 into $z_1 z_2$. Obviously, either z_1 contains all the b_js or z_2 contains all the c_js. Supposing the former, we can obtain a contradiction by marking the b_1s: Condition 2 is impossible because it would give unequal numbers of b_1s and b_2s; Condition 1 is impossible because it would give unequal numbers of b_1s and b_3s. On the other hand, if z_2 contains all the c_js, we mark the c_1s, and both Conditions are again rendered impossible.

□

4 Conclusion

The weak equivalence of the previously proposed ESL-TAG and SSL-TAG, along with the fact that SL-TAG with substitution and ESL-TAG with substitution belong to the same class, suggests that they represent a useful compromise between CFGs and TAGs. In the two-dimensional language hierarchy of Rambow and Satta (1999), where the two dimensions are *rank* (how many substructures does a rule combine) and *fanout* (how many discontinuous spans of the input does a substructure cover), CFGs comprise the fanout-1 grammars and TAGs are a subset of the the fanout-2 grammars; both have arbitrary rank, whereas linear CFGs and linear TAGs are rank-1. The grammars discussed here are mixed: a rule can combine one fanout-2 substructure and an arbitrary number of fanout-1 substructures. A related example would be a version of synchronous CFG that allows only one pair of linked nonterminals and any number of unlinked nonterminals, which could be bitext-parsed in $\mathcal{O}(n^5)$ time, whereas inversion transduction grammar (Wu, 1997) takes $\mathcal{O}(n^6)$. It may be of interest to make a more general exploration of other formalisms that are mixed in this sense.

Acknowledgements

Thanks to Hiroyuki Seki for discussions that led to this paper, and to Anoop Sarkar, Giorgio Satta, and William Schuler. This research was partially supported by NSF grant ITR EIA-02-05456. *S. D. G.*

References

John E. Hopcroft and Jeffrey D. Ullman. 1979. *Introduction to Automata Theory, Languages, and Computation*. Addison-Wesley, Reading, MA.

Aravind K. Joshi. 1985. Tree adjoining grammars: How much context-sensitivity is necessary for assigning structural descriptions? In David Dowty, Lauri Karttunen, and Arnold Zwicky, editors, *Natural Language Parsing*, pages 206–250. Cambridge University Press, Cambridge.

Yuki Kato, Hiroyuki Seki, and Tadao Kasami. 2004. Subclasses of tree adjoining grammar for RNA secondary structure. In *Proc. Seventh International Workshop on TAG and Related Formalisms (TAG+)*, pages 48–55.

Bernard Lang. 1994. Recognition can be harder than parsing. *Computational Intelligence*, 10(4):484–494. Special Issue on Tree Adjoining Grammars.

Owen Rambow and Giorgio Satta. 1999. Independent parallelism in finite copying parallel rewriting systems. *Theoretical Computer Science*, 223:87–120.

James Rogers. 1994. Capturing CFLs with tree adjoining grammars. In *Proc. 32nd Annual Meeting of the ACL*, pages 155–162.

Giorgio Satta and William Schuler. 1998. Restrictions on tree adjoining languages. In *Proc. COLING-ACL*, pages 1176–1182.

Yves Schabes and Richard C. Waters. 1995. Tree insertion grammar: a cubic-time parsable formalism that lexicalizes context-free grammar without changing the trees produced. *Computational Linguistics*, 21:479–513.

Yves Schabes. 1990. *Mathematical and Computational Aspects of Lexicalized Grammars*. Ph.D. thesis, University of Pennsylvania. Available as technical report MS-CIS-90-48.

Yasuo Uemura, Aki Hasegawa, Satoshi Kobayashi, and Takashi Yokomori. 1999. Tree adjoining grammars for RNA structure prediction. *Theoretical Computer Science*, 210:277–303.

K Vijayashanker. 1987. *A study of tree adjoining grammars*. Ph.D. thesis, University of Pennsylvania. Available as technical report MS-CIS-88-03.

Dekai Wu. 1997. Stochastic inversion transduction grammars and bilingual parsing of parallel corpora. *Computational Linguistics*, 23:377–404.

A Tree Adjoining Grammar Analysis of the Syntax and Semantics of *It*-Clefts

Chung-hye Han
Department of Linguistics
Simon Fraser University
chunghye@sfu.ca

Nancy Hedberg
Department of Linguistics
Simon Fraser University
hedberg@sfu.ca

Abstract

In this paper, we argue that in *it*-clefts as in *It was Ohno who won*, the cleft pronoun (*it*) and the cleft clause (*who won*) form a discontinuous syntactic constituent, and a semantic unit as a definite description, presenting arguments from Percus (1997) and Hedberg (2000). We propose a syntax of *it*-clefts using Tree-Local Multi-Component Tree Adjoining Grammar and a compositional semantics on the proposed syntax using Synchronous Tree Adjoining Grammar.

1 Introduction

The extant literature on the syntax of *it*-clefts, as in (1), can be classified into two main approaches. First, the cleft pronoun *it* is an expletive, and the cleft clause bears a direct syntactic or semantic relation to the clefted constituent, such as one of predication (Jesperson, 1937; Chomsky, 1977; Williams, 1980; Delin, 1989; Delahunty, 1982; Rochemont, 1986; Heggie, 1988; É. Kiss, 1998). Second, the cleft clause bears a direct syntactic or semantic relation to the cleft pronoun and is spelled-out after the clefted constituent through extraposition or by forming a discontinuous constituent with the cleft pronoun from the base-generated position at the end of the sentence (Jesperson, 1927; Akmajian, 1970; Emonds, 1976; Gundel, 1977; Wirth, 1978; Percus, 1997; Hedberg, 2000). Under this second approach, the cleft pronoun is not necessarily expletive but rather has a semantic function such as that of a definite article.

(1) It was OHNO [who won].
cleft pronoun + copula + clefted constituent + cleft clause

In this paper, we argue for a particular version of the second approach, in which the cleft pronoun and the cleft clause form a discontinuous syntactic constituent, and a semantic unit as a definite description. We propose a syntax of *it*-clefts using Tree-Local Multi-Component Tree Adjoining Grammar (MCTAG), and a compositional semantics on the proposed syntax using Synchronous Tree Adjoining Grammar (STAG). In section 2, we present arguments against the expletive approach, and in section 3, we provide arguments supporting the discontinuous constituent analysis. We present our TAG analysis in section 4 and extend our proposal to grammatical variations on *it*-clefts in section 5.

2 Arguments against the expletive approach

It has been shown in Hedberg (2000) that the cleft pronoun can be replaced with *this* or *that*, as in (2), depending on the discourse contextual interpretation of the cleft clause. The fact that the choice of the cleft pronoun is subject to pragmatic constraints indicates that the cleft pronoun cannot simply be an expletive element devoid of any semantic content.

(2) a. This is not Iowa we're talking about. (Hedberg 2000, ex. 17)
b. That's the French flag you see flying over there. (Hedberg 2000, ex. 20)

Although the details are different, many expletive analyses advocate for the position that the clefted constituent is syntactically associated with the gap in the cleft clause either directly through movement, or indirectly through co-indexation with an operator in the cleft clause. One thing that is common in all these analyses is that the cleft clause is not considered to have the internal structure of a restrictive relative clause. We point out

Proceedings of the 8th International Workshop on Tree Adjoining Grammar and Related Formalisms, pages 33–40,
Sydney, July 2006.

that the initial element in the cleft clause may be realized either as a *wh*-word (1) or as *that* (3a), or it may be absent altogether when the gap is not in the subject position (2, 3b). It may even be in the form of a genitive *wh*-word as in (3c). The cleft clause is thus a restrictive relative clause.

(3) a. It was Ohno that won.
b. It was Ohno Ahn beat.
c. It was Ohno whose Dad cheered.

The cleft clause, however, does not relate to the clefted constituent in the way that a restrictive relative clause relates to its head noun, as first noted in Jespersen (1927). This is because the clefted constituent can be a proper noun, unlike a head noun modified by a restrictive relative clause, as illustrated in (4). This suggests that there is no syntactic link between the clefted constituent and the gap in the cleft clause.

(4) * Ohno that won is an American.

3 A discontinuous constituent analysis

As pointed out in Percus (1997) and Hedberg (2000), *it*-clefts have existential and exhaustive presuppositions, just as definite descriptions do. The inference in (5c) associated with (5a) survives in the negative counterpart in (5b). This is exactly the way the presupposition associated with the definite description *the king of France* behaves: the presupposition spelled-out in (6c) survives in both the affirmative (6a) and the negative counterpart in (6b). Both authors argue that this parallelism between definite descriptions and *it*-clefts can be accounted for if the cleft pronoun and the cleft clause form a semantic unit, with *it* playing the role of the definite article and the cleft clause the descriptive component. What this translates to syntactically is that the cleft clause is a restrictive relative clause which is situated at the end of the sentence, forming a discontinuous constituent with the cleft pronoun.

(5) a. It was Ohno who won.
b. It was not Ohno who won.
c. Someone won, and only one person won.

(6) a. The king of France is bald.
b. The king of France is not bald.
c. There is one and only one king of France.

Percus (1997) further points out that *it*-clefts pattern with copular sentences containing definite description subjects with regard to anaphor binding. In the absence of c-command, an anaphor in the clefted constituent position can be bound by an antecedent inside the cleft clause, as shown in (7a). While we don't yet have an explanation for how this type of binding takes place, we follow Percus in noting that since copular sentences with definite description subjects also exhibit this pattern of binding, as shown in (7b), a uniform explanation for the two cases can be sought if the cleft pronoun and the cleft clause together form a definite description.

(7) a. It was herself that Mary saw first.
b. The one that Mary saw first was herself.

Under the discontinuous constituent analysis, *it*-clefts reduce to copular sentences, and therefore the observation that they can have equative and predicational interpretations (Ball 1978, DeClerck 1988, Hedberg 2000), the readings attested in copular sentences, follows. For instance, (5a) (repeated as (8a)) can be paraphrased as (8b), and corresponds to a typical equative sentence. And (9a) can be paraphrased as (9b), and corresponds to a typical predicational sentence. According to our analysis, (8a) will be assigned the semantic representation in (8c), and (9a) will be assigned the semantic representation in (9c).

(8) a. It was Ohno who won.
b. The one who won was Ohno.
c. THEz [won(z)] [z = Ohno$'$]

(9) a. It was a kid who beat John.
b. The one who beat John was a kid.
c. THEz [beat(z, John$'$)] [kid(z)]

4 Our TAG analysis

Inspired by work of Kroch and Joshi (1987) and Abeillé (1994) on discontinuous constituents resulting from extraposition, we propose a tree-local MCTAG analysis for the syntax of *it*-clefts. Crucially, we propose that the elementary trees for cleft pronoun and the cleft clause form a multi-component set, as in $\{(\alpha\text{it}), (\beta\text{who\_won})\}$ in Figure 1 and $\{(\alpha\text{it}), (\beta\text{who\_beat})\}$ in Figure 4.

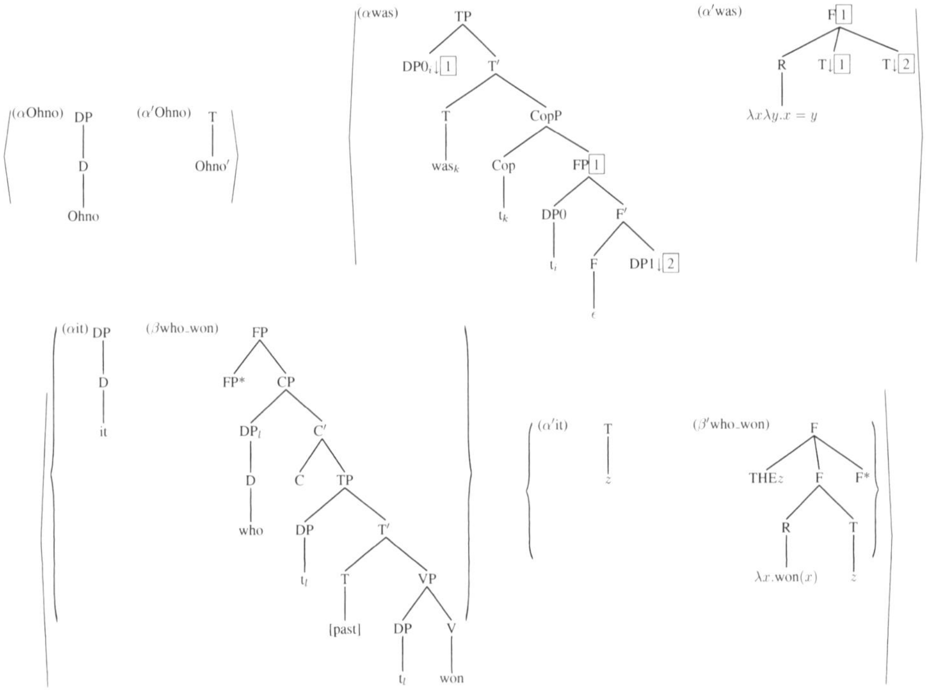

Figure 1: Syntactic and semantic elementary trees for *It was Ohno who won*

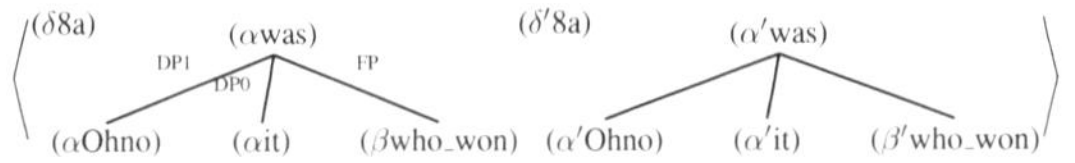

Figure 2: Syntactic and semantic derivation trees for *It was Ohno who won*

For the derivation of equative *it*-clefts as in (8a), we adopt the copular tree in ($\alpha$was), a tree similar to the one proposed in Frank (2002) for copular sentences. In this tree, FP is a small clause of the copula from which the two DPs being equated originate. (8a) is derived by substituting (αit) into DP0 in ($\alpha$was), adjoining (βwho_won) into FP in ($\alpha$was), and substituting (αOhno) into DP1 in ($\alpha$was). The syntactic derivation tree and the derived tree for (8a) are given in (δ8a) in Figure 2 and (γ8a) in Figure 3 respectively.

Postulating separate projections for the copula and the small clause can account for the fact that the clefted constituent and the cleft clause seem to form a constituent, as in (10ab) (from Hedberg 2000), and yet they can be separated by an adverbial phrase, as in (10c). In our analysis, (10ab) are possible because the bracketed parts are FPs. (10c) is possible because an adverbial phrase can adjoin onto FP or F′, separating the clefted constituent and the cleft clause.

(10) a. I said it should have been [Bill who negotiated the new contract], and it should have been.

b. It must have been [Fred that kissed Mary] but [Bill that left with her].

c. It was Kim, in my opinion, who won the race.

We propose to do compositional semantics using STAG as defined in Shieber (1994). In STAG, each syntactic elementary tree is paired with one or more semantic tree with links between matching nodes. A synchronous derivation proceeds by mapping a derivation tree from the syntax side to an isomorphic derivation tree in the semantics side, and is synchronized by the links specified in the elementary tree pairs. In the tree pairs given in Figure 1, the trees on the left side are syntactic elementary trees and the ones on the right side are semantic trees. In the semantic trees, F stands for formulas, R for predicates and T for terms. (α'it) and (β'who_won) in the multi-component set in Figure 1 together define semantics of quantification, where the former contributes the argument variable and the latter the restriction and scope, and ($\alpha'$was) represents the semantics of equative sentences. The derivation tree for the semantics of (8a) is given in (δ'8a) in Figure 2, and the seman-

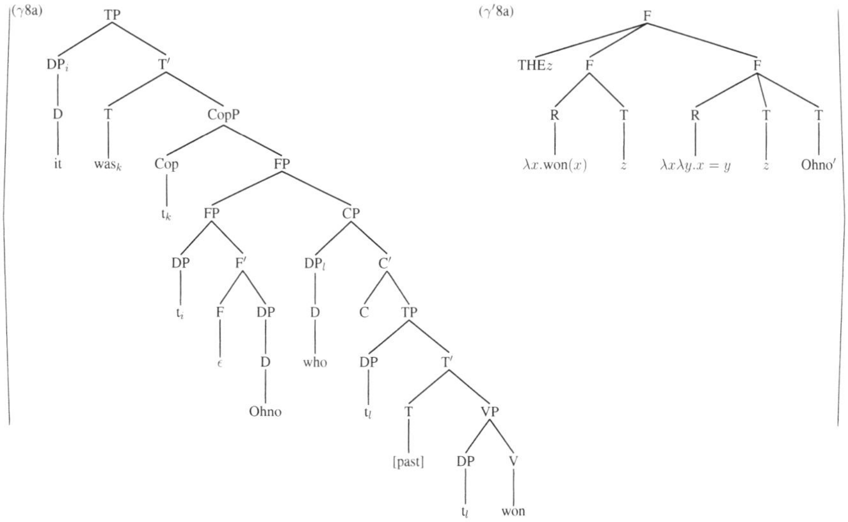

Figure 3: Syntactic and semantic derived trees for *It was Ohno who won*

tic derived tree is given in (γ'8a) in Figure 3. Note that the semantic derivation tree in (δ'8a) is isomorphic to the syntactic one in (δ8a). The semantic derived tree in (γ'8a) can be reduced to the formula in (11) after the application of λ-conversion.

(11) THEz [won(z)] [z = Ohno′]

For the derivation of predicational *it*-clefts as in (9a), we use the tree pairs in <(αwas_kid), (α'was_kid)>, <(αJohn), (α'John)>, and <{(αit), (βwho_beat)}, {(α'it), (β'who_beat)}> in Figure 4. The elementary tree in (αwas_kid) which represents a predicational copular sentence is similar to the one in ($\alpha$was) in that in both trees, the copula combines with a small clause FP. The important difference is that in (αwas_kid) the subject DP is an argument substitution site and the predicative DP (*a kid*) is lexicalized, whereas in ($\alpha$was) both the subject and the non-subject DPs are argument substitution sites. This difference is reflected in the semantic trees, as seen in ($\alpha'$was) in Figure 1 with two term nodes and (α'was_kid) in Figure 4 with one term node. The syntactic and semantic derivation trees, which are isomorphic, are given in <(δ9a), (δ'9a)> in Figure 5, and the corresponding derived trees are given in <(γ9a), (γ'9a)> in Figure 6. The semantic derived tree in (γ'9a) can be reduced to the formula in (12) after the application of λ-conversion.

(12) THEz [beat(z, John′)] [kid(z)]

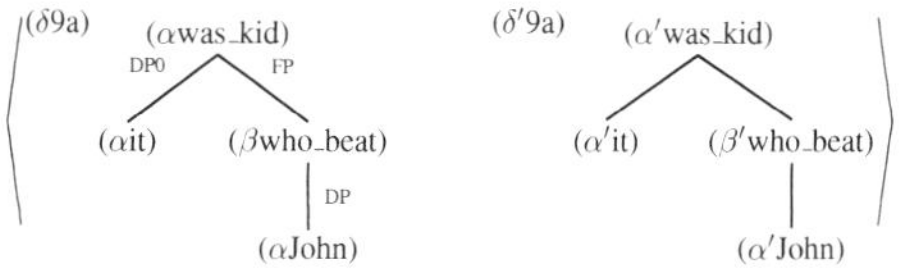

Figure 5: Syntactic and semantic derivation trees for *It was a kid who beat John*

5 Extensions

In this section, we extend the proposed syntactic analysis to grammatical variations on *it*-clefts: *wh*-extraction of the clefted constituent as in (13), unbounded dependency between the relative pronoun and its gap in the cleft clause as in (14), and coordination of the constituent containing the clefted constituent and the cleft clause as in (15).

(13) Who$_j$ was it t$_j$ who won?

(14) It was Ohno who$_l$ the judges said t$_l$ won.

(15) It was [Ohno who won] and [Kim who lost].

For the derivation of (13), the elementary trees in Figure 7 are required in addition to {(αit), (βwho_won)} in Figure 1. (αwho_was) represents the structure with the *wh*-extraction of the clefted constituent. Substituting (αwho) into DP1 and (αit) into DP0, and adjoining (βwho_won) onto FP in (αwho_was), as in the derivation tree in (δ13), produces the derived tree in (γ13) in Figure 8.

For the derivation of (14), the elementary trees in Figure 9 are required in addition to {(αit),

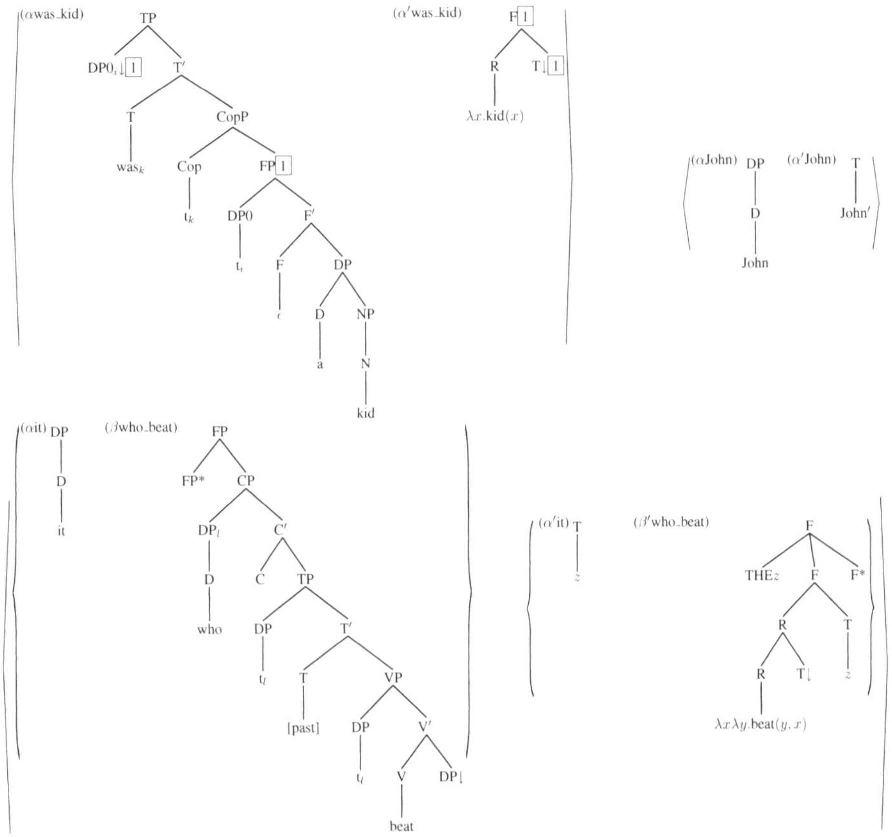

Figure 4: Syntactic and semantic elementary trees for *It was a kid who beat John*

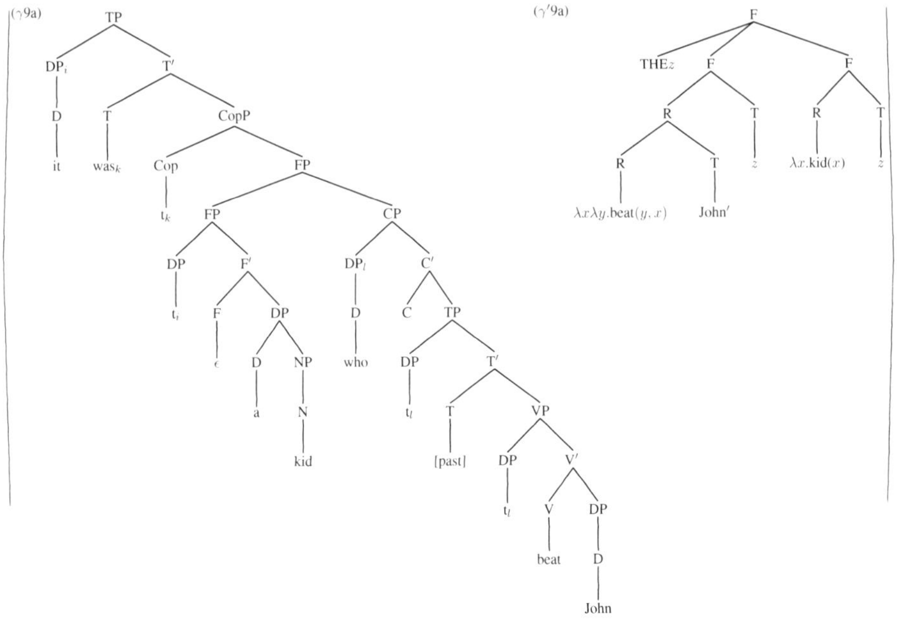

Figure 6: Syntactic and semantic derived trees for *It was a kid who beat John*

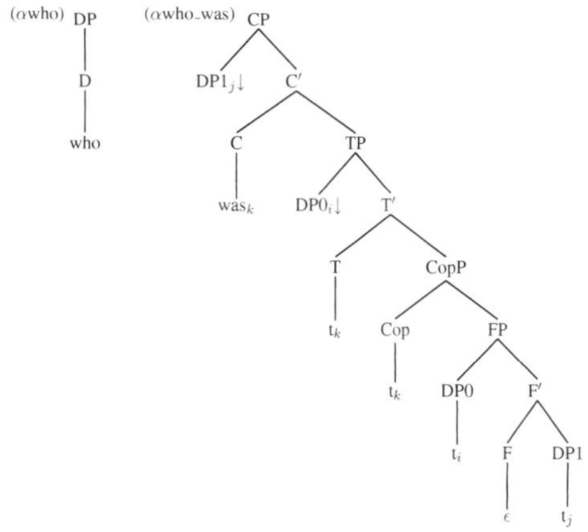

Figure 7: Syntactic elementary trees for *Who was it who won?*

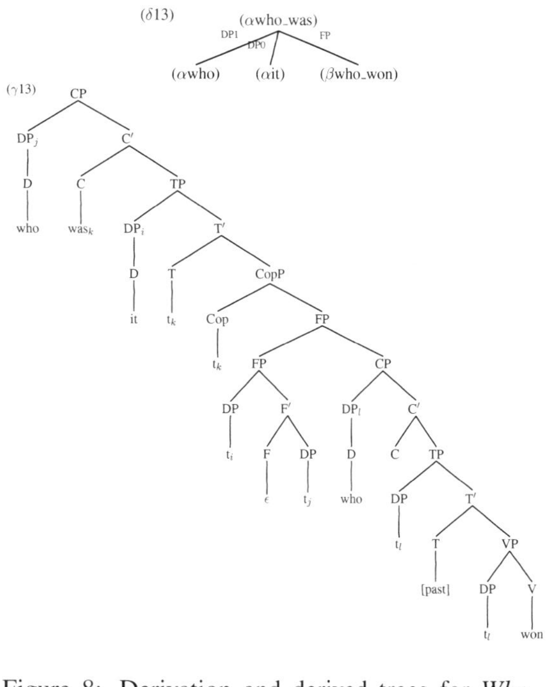

Figure 8: Derivation and derived trees for *Who was it who won?*

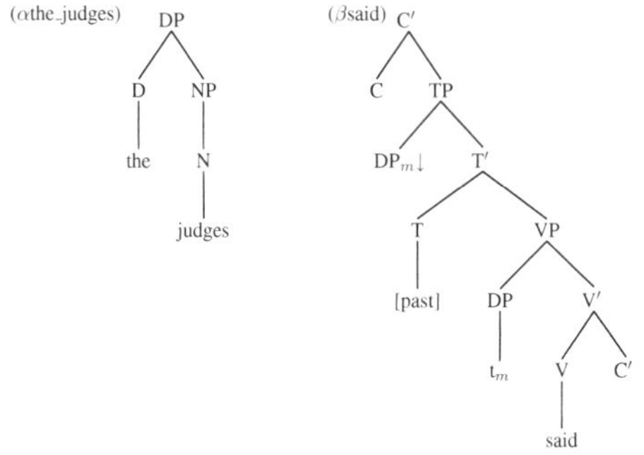

Figure 9: Syntactic elementary trees for *It was Ohno who the judges said won*

(βwho_won)} in Figure 1. Adjoining (βsaid) onto the C′ node in (βwho_won) has the effect of stretching the dependency between the relative pronoun *who* and its gap in the cleft clause. The derivation and the derived trees for (14) are given in Figure 10.

To handle the coordination of the constituent containing the clefted constituent and the cleft clause, as illustrated in (15), we propose to use Node Contraction and Conjoin proposed in Sarkar and Joshi (1996). Informally, Node Contraction takes two nodes of like categories and collapses them into a single node, and Conjoin coordinates the least nodes dominating the two contiguous strings. We use the conjunction tree in Figure 11 to apply Conjoin at FP.

Figure 12 contains the elementary tree anchoring equative *was*. We mark the nodes to be contracted with a box, and augment the name of the elementary tree with a set listing these contraction nodes. Thus, $(\alpha\text{was})_{\{DP_i,T,Cop\}}$ means that DP_i, T and Cop nodes are marked for contraction in (αwas) elementary tree.

Composition of $(\alpha\text{was})_{\{DP_i,T,Cop\}}$ tree in Figure 12 and another $(\alpha\text{was})_{\{DP_i,T,Cop\}}$ tree with the conjunction tree in Figure 11, along with the substitution and adjoining of (αOhno) and an equivalent tree (αKim) anchoring *Kim*, (βwho_won) and an equivalent tree (βwho_lost) anchoring *lost*, and (αit) in appropriate places, yields the derived structure in Figure 13, where the contracted nodes get identified. In this structure, the DP hosting *it* is dominated by two TP nodes, T is dominated by two T′ nodes and Cop is dominated by two CopP nodes. Thus, the derived structure produced by Conjoin and Node Contraction is a directed graph, not a tree.

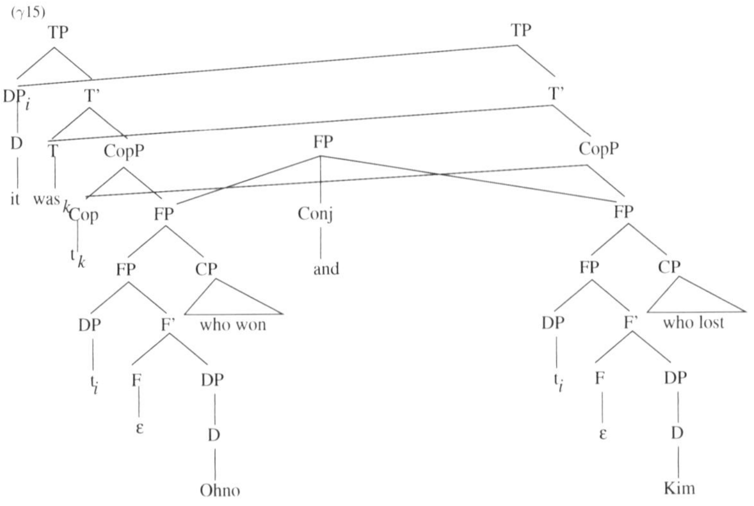

Figure 13: Derived structure for *It was Ohno who won and Kim who lost*

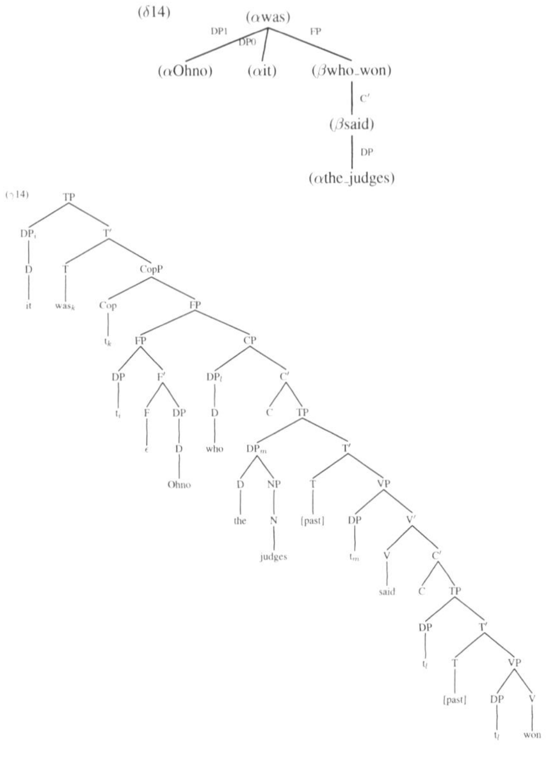

Figure 10: Derivation and derived trees for *It was Ohno who the judges said won*

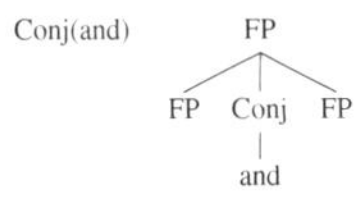

Figure 11: Elementary tree for conjunction

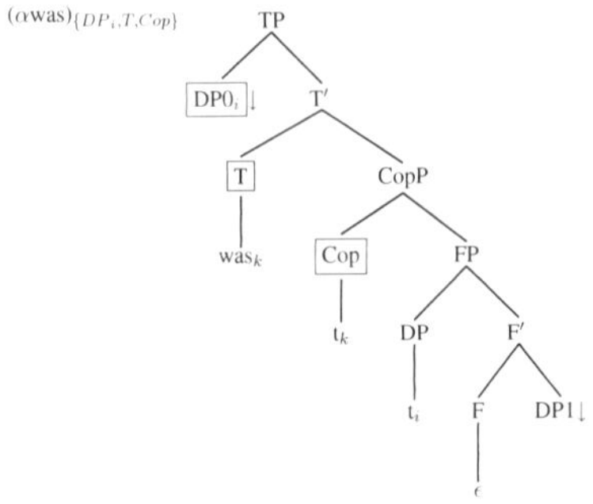

Figure 12: Elementary tree anchoring equative *was* with contraction nodes

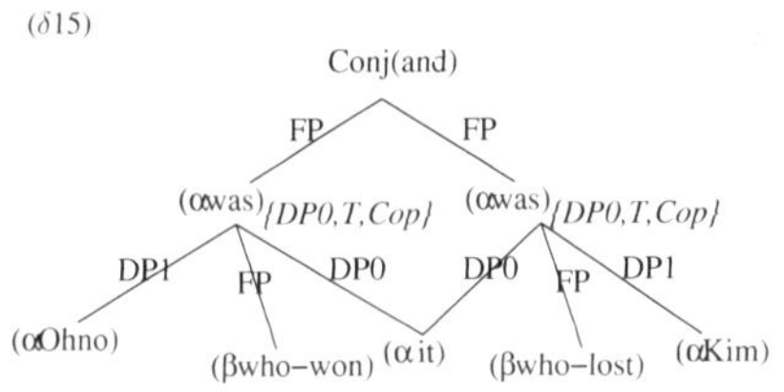

Figure 14: Derivation structure for *It was Ohno who won and Kim who lost*

The derivation structure for (15) is also a directed graph, as shown in Figure 14. (αit) is dominated by two $(\alpha\text{was})_{\{DP_i,T,Cop\}}$ trees, indicating that it is being shared by the two $(\alpha\text{was})_{\{DP_i,T,Cop\}}$ trees.

6 Conclusion

We have proposed a syntax and semantics of *it*-clefts, using tree-local MCTAG and STAG, and shown that the proposed syntactic analysis is extendable to handle various grammatical variations on *it*-clefts such as *wh*-extraction of the clefted constituent, unbounded dependency between the relative pronoun and its gap in the cleft clause and coordination of the constituent containing the clefted constituent and the cleft clause. In our TAG analysis of *it*-clefts, the cleft pronoun and the cleft clause bear a direct syntactic relation because the elementary trees for the two parts belong to a single multi-component set. They do not actually form a syntactic constituent in the derived tree, but as the elementary trees for the two belong to the same multi-component set, the intuition that they form a discontinuous constituent is captured. Further, the semantics of the two trees is defined as a definite quantified phrase, capturing the intuition that they form a semantic unit as a definite description.

Acknowledgment

We thank Anoop Sarkar and the three anonymous reviewers for their insightful comments.

References

Ann Abeillé. 1994. Syntax or semantics? handling nonlocal dependencies with MCTAGs or Synchronous tags. *Computational Intelligence*, 10:471–485.

Adrian Akmajian. 1970. On deriving cleft sentences from pseudo-cleft sentences. *Linguistic Inquiry*, 1:149–168.

Noam Chomsky. 1977. On wh-movement. In P. W. Culicover, T. Wasow, and A. Akmajian, editors, *Formal Syntax*, pages 71–132. Academic Press, New York.

Gerald P. Delahunty. 1982. *Topics in the syntax and semantics of English cleft sentences*. Indiana University Linguistics Club, Bloomington.

Judy L. Delin. 1989. *Cleft constructions in discourse*. Ph.D. thesis, University of Edinburgh.

Katalin É. Kiss. 1998. Identificatinoal focus versus information focus. *Language*, 74(245-273).

Joseph E. Emonds. 1976. *A Transformational Approach to English Syntax*. Academic Press, New York.

Robert Frank. 2002. *Phrase Structure Composition and Syntactic Dependencies*. MIT Press, Cambridge, MA.

Jeanette K. Gundel. 1977. Where do cleft sentences come from? *Language*, 53:53–59.

Nancy Hedberg. 2000. The referential status of clefts. *Language*, 76(4):891–920.

Lorie A. Heggie. 1988. *The syntax of copular structures*. Ph.D. thesis, University of Southern California, Los Angeles.

Otto Jesperson. 1927. *A Modern English Grammar*, volume 3. Allen and Unwin, London.

Otto Jesperson. 1937. *Analytic Syntax*. Allen and Unwin, London.

Anthony S. Kroch and Aravind K. Joshi. 1987. Analyzing extraposition in a Tree Adjoining Grammar. In G. Huck and A. Ojeda, editors, *Discontinuous Constituents*, volume 20 of *Syntax and Semantics*. Academic Press.

Orin Percus. 1997. Prying open the cleft. In K. Kusumoto, editor, *Proceedings of the 27th Annual Meeting of the North East Linguistics Society*, pages 337–351. GLSA.

Michael Rochemont. 1986. *Focus in Generative Grammar*. John Benjamins, Amsterdam.

Anoop Sarkar and Aravind Joshi. 1996. Coordination in tree adjoining grammars: formalization and implementation. In *Proceedings of COLING'96*, pages 610–615, Copenhagen.

Stuart Shieber. 1994. Restricting the weak-generative capacity of synchronous tree-adjoining grammars. *Computational Intelligence*, 10(4).

Edwin Williams. 1980. Predication. *Linguistic Inquiry*, 11:203–238.

Jessica R. Wirth. 1978. The derivation of cleft sentences in English. *Glossa*, 12(58-81).

Pied-Piping in Relative Clauses: Syntax and Compositional Semantics based on Synchronous Tree Adjoining Grammar

Chung-hye Han
Department of Linguistics
Simon Fraser University
chunghye@sfu.ca

Abstract

In relative clauses, the *wh* relative pronoun can be embedded in a larger phrase, as in *a boy [whose brother] Mary hit*. In such examples, we say that the larger phrase has pied-piped along with the *wh*-word. In this paper, using a similar syntactic analysis for *wh* pied-piping as in Han (2002) and further developed in Kallmeyer and Scheffler (2004), I propose a compositional semantics for relative clauses based on Synchronous Tree Adjoining Grammar. It will be shown that (i) the elementary tree representing the logical form of a *wh*-word provides a generalized quantifier, and (ii) the semantic composition of the pied-piped material and the *wh*-word is achieved through adjoining in the semantics of the former onto the latter.

1 Introduction

In relative clauses, the *wh* relative pronoun can be embedded in a larger phrase, as in (1) and (2). In such examples, we say that the larger phrase containing the *wh*-word has PIED-PIPED along with the *wh*-word.

(1) a boy [[whose brother]$_i$ Mary hit t$_i$]

(2) a boy [[whose brother's friend]$_i$ Mary hit t$_i$]

In this paper, using a similar syntactic analysis for *wh* pied-piping as in Han (2002) and further developed in Kallmeyer and Scheffler (2004), I propose a compositional semantics for relative clauses of the sort illustrated in (1) and (2), based on Synchronous Tree Adjoining Grammar (STAG). The two main components of my proposal are that (i) the semantic tree representing the logical form of a *wh* relative pronoun provides a generalized quantifier, and (ii) the semantic composition of the pied-piped material and the *wh*-word is achieved through adjoining of the former onto the latter in the semantics. Although TAG semantics for relative clauses based on flat semantics have been proposed before (Han, 2002; Kallmeyer, 2003), no STAG-based analysis exists, as far as I know.

In section 2, I introduce the framework of STAG and STAG-based compositional semantics and clarify my assumptions. In section 3, I present my analysis of relative clauses and pied-piping. I extend the proposed analysis to relative clauses in which *wh*-word is in a PP and those in which no pied-piping has taken place in section 4.

2 STAG-based Compositional Semantics

Before presenting my analysis of relative clauses, I first illustrate the framework of STAG-based compositional semantics and clarify my assumptions, using a simple sentence that contains an existential quantifier and an attributive adjective in (3).

(3) John saw a good movie.

I use STAG as defined in Shieber (1994). In an STAG, each syntactic elementary tree is paired with one or more semantic trees that represent its logical form with links between matching nodes. A synchronous derivation proceeds by mapping a derivation tree from the syntax side to an isomorphic derivation tree in the semantics side, and is synchronized by the links specified in the elementary tree pairs. In the tree pairs given in Figure 1, the trees in the left side are syntactic elementary trees and the ones in the right side are semantic trees. In the semantic trees, F stands for formulas, R for predicates and T for terms. I assume that these nodes are typed and I represent predicates as unreduced λ-expressions. The linked nodes are shown with boxed numbers. For sake of simplicity, in the elementary tree pairs, I only include links that are relevant for the derivation of given examples.

Figure 1 contains elementary trees required to generate the syntactic structure and the logical

Proceedings of the 8th International Workshop on Tree Adjoining Grammar and Related Formalisms, pages 41–48,
Sydney, July 2006.

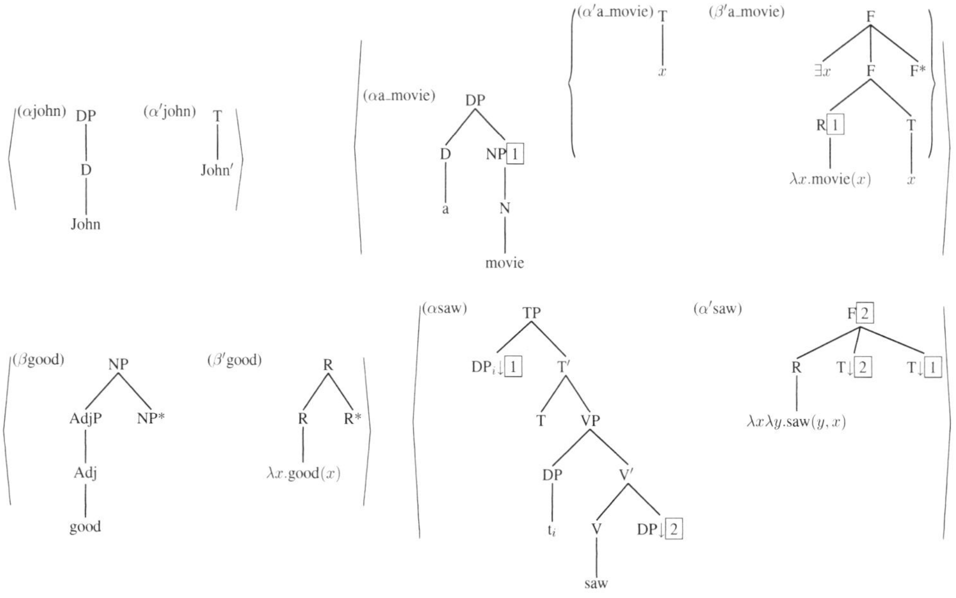

Figure 1: Elementary trees for *John saw a good movie.*

form of (3). All the syntactic elementary trees satisfy Frank's (2002) Condition on Elementary Tree Minimality (CETM), which states that "the syntactic heads in an elementary tree and their projections must form an extended projection of a single lexical head" (Frank 2002, p. 54). Particularly, (αa_movie) is a valid elementary tree, as a noun can form an extended projection with a DP, in line with the DP Hypothesis. The proper name tree in (αJohn) is paired with a tree representing a term in the semantics, and the attributive adjective tree in (βgood) is paired with an auxiliary tree in the semantics that represents a one-place predicate to be adjoined to another one-place predicate. As for the syntax-semantics pairing of elementary trees for quantified DPs, I follow Shieber and Schabes (1990), and use Tree Local Multi-Component TAG (as defined in Weir (1988)) in the semantics. Thus, the DP in (αa_movie) is paired with a multi-component set {(α′a_movie), (β′a_movie)} in the semantics: (α′a_movie) provides an argument variable, and (β′a_movie) provides the existential quantifier with the restriction and scope. The transitive tree in (αsaw) is paired with a semantic tree representing a formula that consists of a two-place predicate and two term nodes. The links, shown with boxed numbers, guarantee that whatever substitutes into DP_i, the corresponding semantic tree will substitute into the term node marked with [1], and whatever substitutes into DP is paired up with a multi-component set in the semantics where one of the components will substitute into the term node marked with [2] and the other will adjoin onto the F node marked with [2]. The syntactic and semantic derivation trees are given in Figure 2, and the derived trees are given in Figure 3. I leave out the tree addresses in the semantic derivation tree, as these are determined by the links between the syntactic and semantic elementary trees.[1]

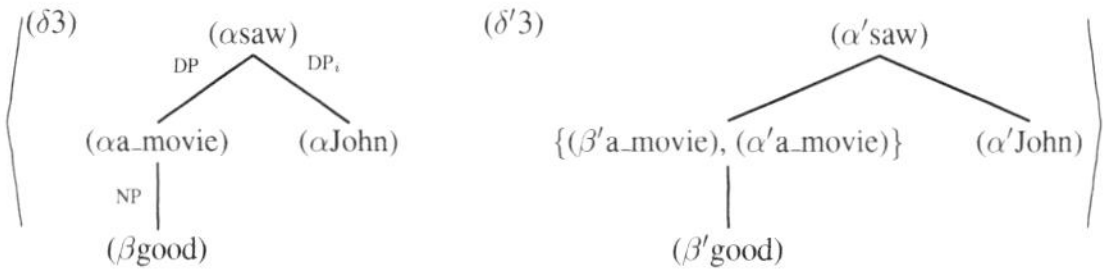

Figure 2: Derivation trees for *John saw a good movie.*

The semantic derived trees can be reduced by applying λ-conversion, as the nodes dominate typed λ-expressions and terms. When reducing semantic derived trees, in addition to λ-conversion, I propose to use Predicate Modification, as defined in Heim and Kratzer (1998) in (4).

(4) Predicate Modification
If α has the form α [β γ],

[1]In sentences with more than one quantified DPs, I assume multiple adjoining (as defined in Schabes and Shieber (1994)) of quantifier trees at the same F node, leaving the order unspecified. This provides an underspecified representation and accounts for scope ambiguity.

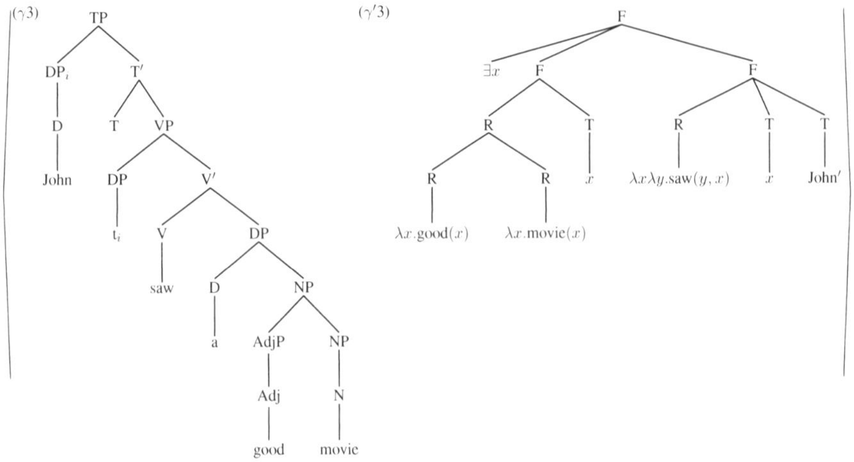

Figure 3: Derived trees for *John saw a good movie.*

and $[\![\beta]\!]^s$ and $[\![\gamma]\!]^s$ are both in $D_{<e,t>}$, then $[\![\alpha]\!]^s = \lambda x_e[\![\beta]\!]^s(x) \wedge [\![\gamma]\!]^s(x)$.

The application of Predicate Modification and λ-conversion to (γ′3) reduces it to the formula in (5).

(5) $\exists x[\text{good}(x) \wedge \text{movie}(x)]\ [\text{saw}(\text{John}', x)]$

3 An STAG analysis of pied-piping in relative clauses

I propose the elementary tree pairs in Figure 4 for the syntactic derivation and semantic composition of the relative clause in (1). In the syntax side, (αwho) substitutes into DP$_j$ in (βhit), and the pied-piping of the rest of the DP is achieved by adjoining (β's brother) onto (αwho). The tree in (β's brother) is a widely-accepted genitive structure according to the DP hypothesis, where the genitive *'s* heads the DP tree. This satisfies CETM, as a DP is an extended projection of a noun. Substituting (αmary) into DP$_i$ in (βhit) completes the derivation of the relative clause.

The derivation tree for the relative clause is in (δ1) in Figure 5 and the derived tree is in (γ1) in Figure 6.

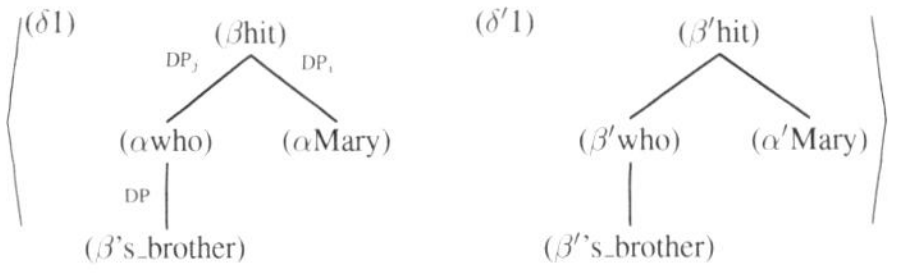

Figure 5: Derivation trees for *whose brother Mary hit*

Semantically, we must make sure that the variable coming from the *wh*-word is also the one being predicated of the head noun (*boy* in (1)), and yet the same variable does not serve as an argument of the predicate (*hit* in (1)) in the relative clause. I argue that the introduction of a generalized quantifier (GQ) node in the semantic tree in (β′who) and adjoining of (β′'s_brother) onto the GQ node guarantee this. I define the logical form of a *wh* relative pronoun as an auxiliary tree given in (β′who). In (β′who), λx binds x in the generalized quantifier, $\lambda P.P(x)$. Adjoining (β′who) onto the relative clause elementary tree in (β′hit) essentially has the effect of abstracting over the variable coming from the *wh*-word in the relative clause, turning it into a one-place predicate. This therefore ensures that the relative clause and the head noun are predicating over the same variable, deriving the interpretation of the relative clause as a modifier of the head noun. The meaning of the pied-piped material *'s brother* is added onto the meaning of *who* by adjoining the auxiliary tree defined in (β′'s_brother) onto the GQ node in (β′who). In (β′'s_brother), λy ensures that the variable coming from the DP* (*who*) is in some relation with the variable coming from the head of the pied-piped DP (*whose brother*), and λQ, by turning *whose brother* into a GQ, ensures that the variable coming from the head of the pied-piped DP is the argument of the predicate that the DP combines with. The derivation tree and the derived tree in the semantics side are given in (δ′1) in Figure 5 and (γ′1) in Figure 6. After all the λ-conversions have applied, (γ′1) can be reduced to the expression in (6).

(6) $\lambda x.\text{THE}z_1[\text{brother}(z_1) \wedge \text{Rel}(x, z_1)]\ [\text{hit}(\text{Mary}', z_1)]$

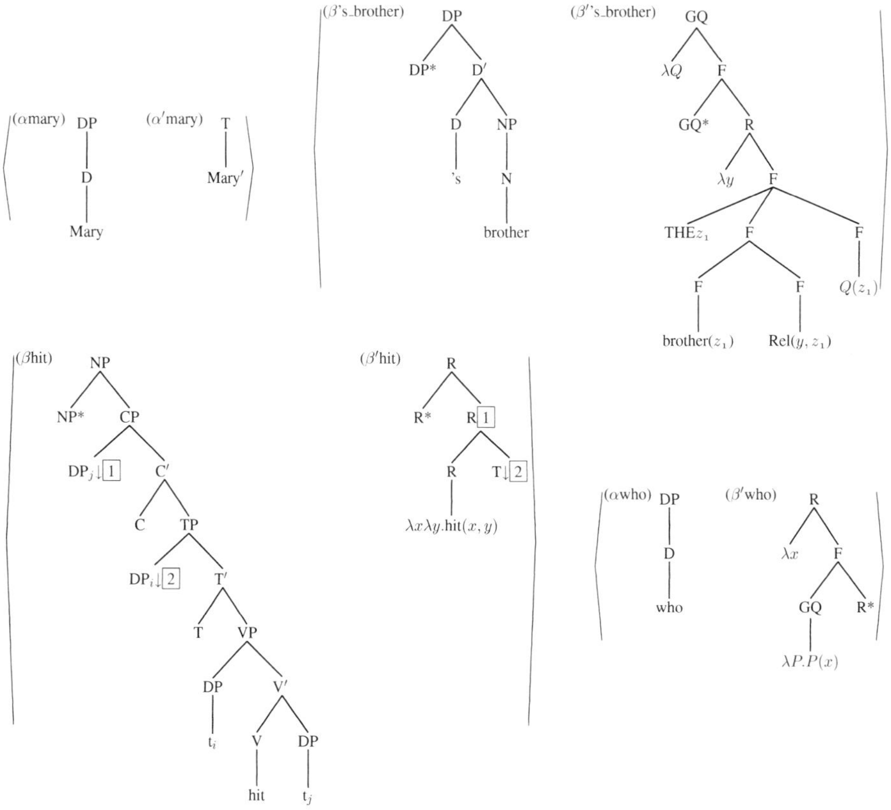

Figure 4: Elementary trees for *whose brother Mary hit*

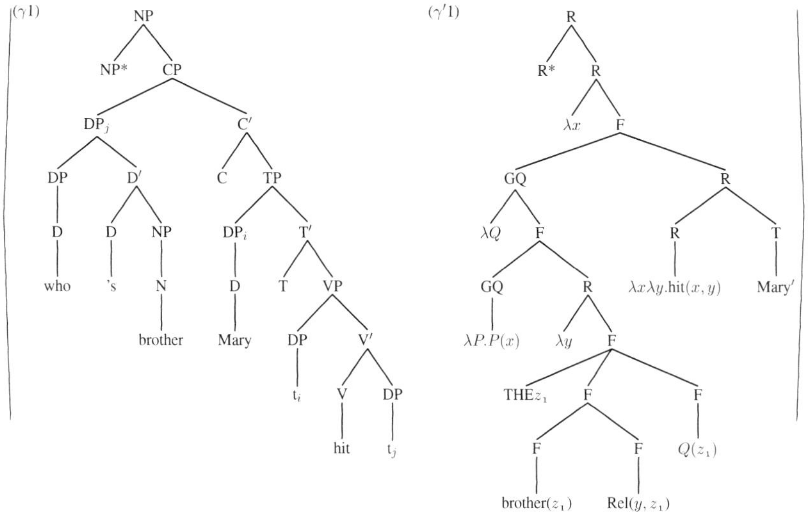

Figure 6: Derived trees for *whose brother Mary hit*

The expression in (6) is a one-place predicate which can be paraphrased as a set of all x's such that there is a unique brother z_1 and x is in some relation with z_1 and Mary hit z_1. As the semantics of relative clauses is defined to be a one-place predicate, it is analogous to attributive adjectives. This means that the semantic tree resulting from the adjoining of ($\gamma'1$) onto the logical form of the head noun *boy* can be reduced to the expression in (7) through Predication Modification.

(7) $\lambda x.\text{boy}(x) \wedge \text{THE}z_1[\text{brother}(z_1) \wedge \text{Rel}(x, z_1)]\ [\text{hit}(\text{Mary}', z_1)]$

The derivation of a sentence containing (1), *a boy whose brother Mary hit*, as the object, as in (8), proceeds in a similar fashion as in (3), yielding the semantic derived tree which is reducible to the formula in (9).

(8) John saw a boy whose brother Mary hit.

(9) $\exists x[\text{boy}(x) \wedge \text{THE}z_1[\text{brother}(z_1) \wedge \text{Rel}(x, z_1)]\ [\text{hit}(\text{Mary}', z_1)]]\ [\text{saw}(\text{John}', x)]$

For the syntactic derivation and the compositional semantics of the relative clause in (2), all we need to do is add the tree pair in Figure 7 to the set of elementary tree pairs in Figure 4. In the syntax side, (β's_friend) adjoins onto (β's_brother) and in the semantics side, (β''s_friend) adjoins onto (β''s_brother), as shown in the derivation trees in Figure 8. The derived trees are given in Figure 9. The semantic derived tree ($\gamma'2$) can be reduced to the expression in (10) through λ-conversions.

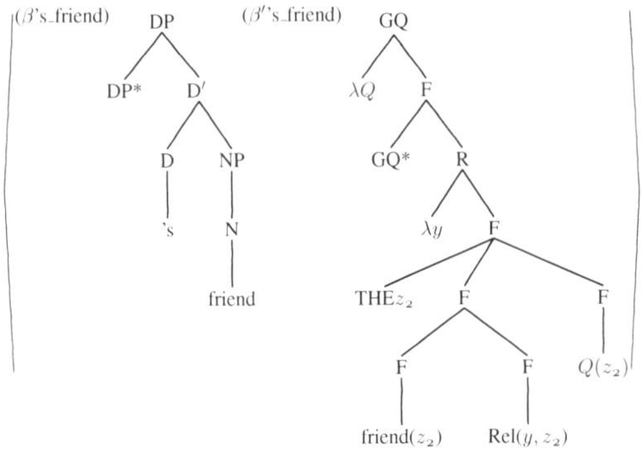

Figure 7: Elementary trees for *'s friend*

(10) $\lambda x.\text{THE}z_1[\text{brother}(z_1) \wedge \text{Rel}(x, z_1)]\ [\text{THE}z_2[\text{friend}(z_2) \wedge \text{Rel}(z_1, z_2)]\ [\text{hit}(\text{Mary}', z_2)]]$

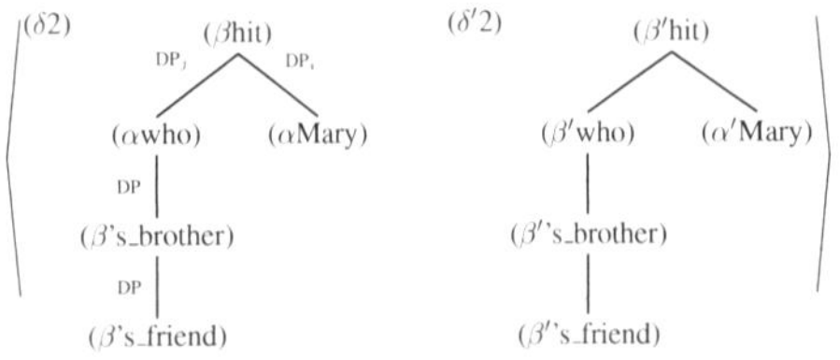

Figure 8: Derivation trees for *whose brother's friend Mary hit*

4 Extensions

The proposed syntax and the semantics of pied-piping can straightforwardly be extended to cases in which the *wh*-word is embedded in a PP, as in (11).

(11) a boy [[$_{DP}$ the brother of whom]$_i$ Mary hit t$_i$]

For the derivation of (11), we need to change two of the elementary tree pairs in Figure 4 slightly. The elementary tree pairs <(αwho), (β'who)> and <(β's_brother), β''s_brother)> need to be replaced with the pairs in Figure 10. Since the relative pronoun in (11) is *whom*, we use a DP tree anchoring *whom* in (αwhom). The corresponding semantic tree (β'whom) remains exactly the same as before. (βthe_brother_of) represents the pied-piped material in DP. It is a well-formed elementary tree according to CETM as it has a single lexical head *brother* and DP is an extended projection of this head, and PP is not subject to CETM because P is a functional head, not a lexical head. Moreover, DP* is licensed as it is an argument of the lexical head *brother*, as argued in Kroch (1989). The semantics of *the brother of whom* is equivalent to *whose brother*, and therefore, we pair up (βthe_brother_of) with the exact same semantic tree as (β''s_brother).

The derivation trees for the relative clause in (11) are given in Figure 11. They look exactly the same as the ones for the relative clause in (1), except for names of the elementary trees in a few nodes. The derived trees are given in Figure 12. While the syntactic derived tree (γ11) is different from (γ1) in Figure 6 in the structure of DP containing the pied-piped material, the semantic derived tree (γ'11) looks exactly the same as (γ'1) in Figure 6. This is as it should be given that the meaning of (1) and the meaning of (11) are equivalent.

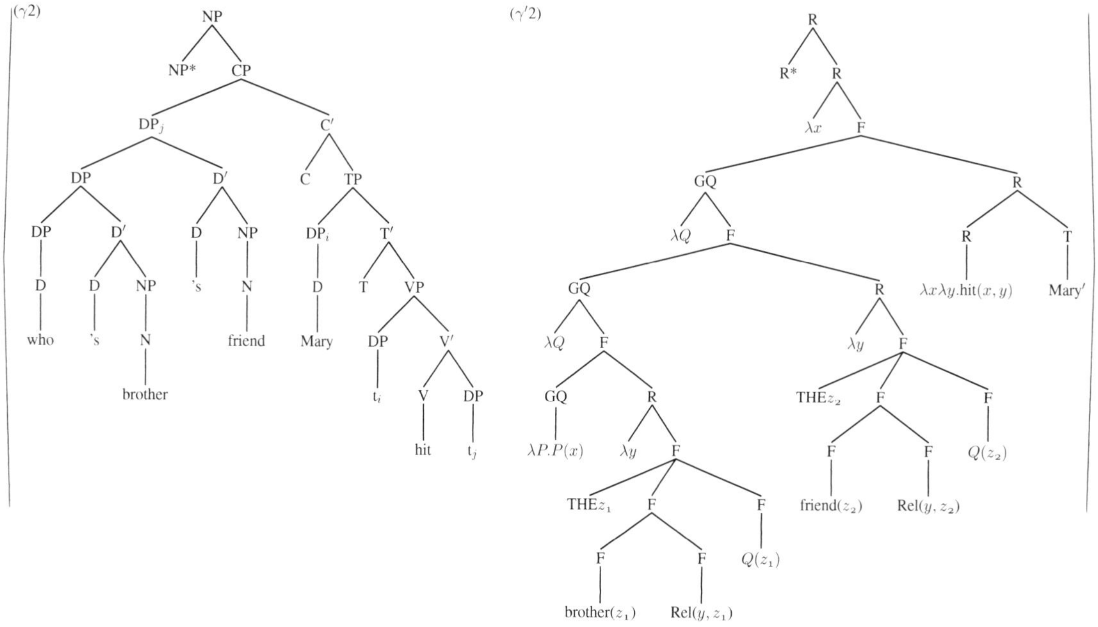

Figure 9: Derived trees for *whose brother's friend Mary hit*

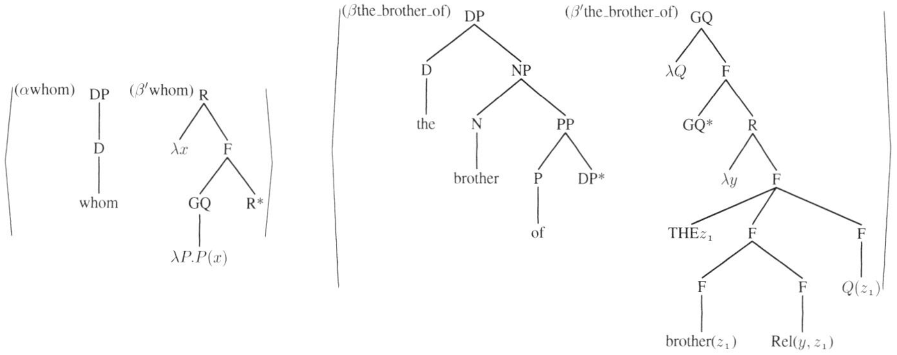

Figure 10: Elementary trees for *whom* and *the brother of*

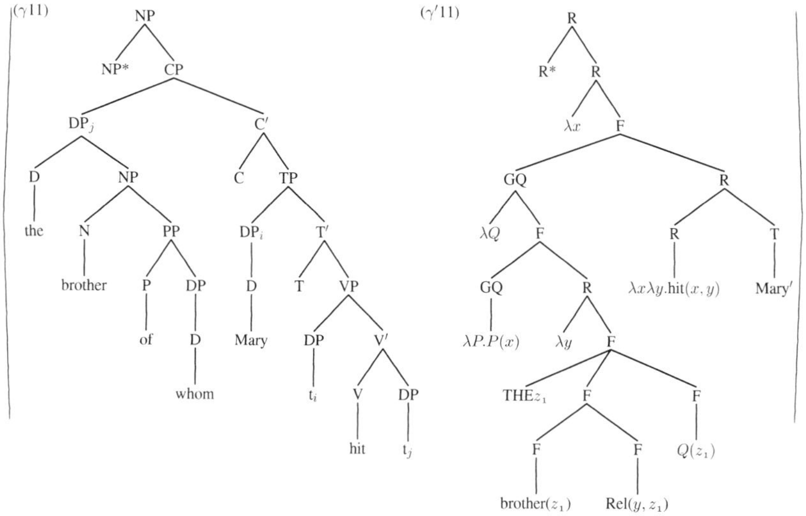

Figure 12: Derived trees for *the brother of whom Mary hit*

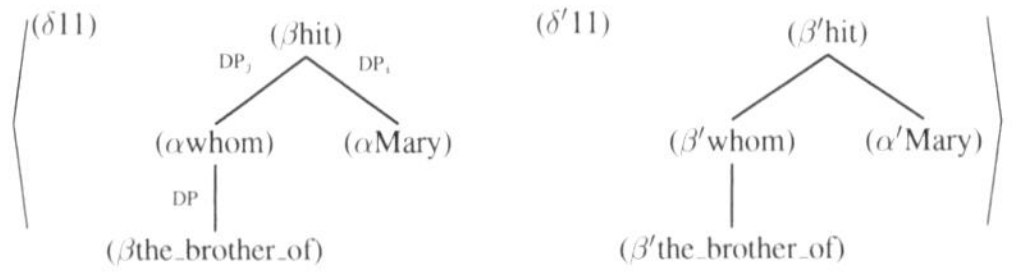

Figure 11: Derivation trees for *the brother of whom Mary hit*

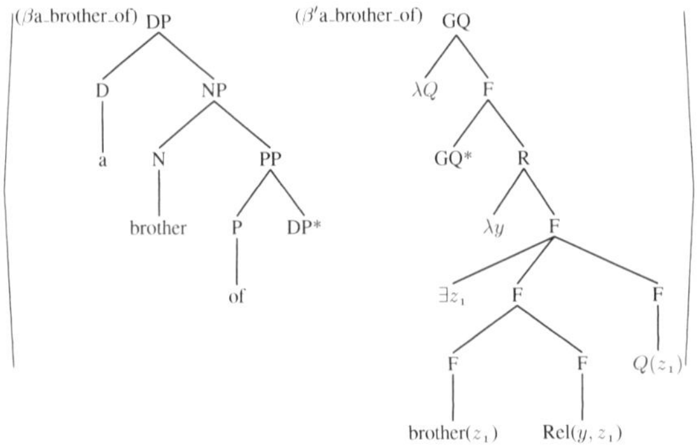

Figure 13: Elementary trees for *whom* and *a brother of*

The proposed analysis can also be extended to relative clauses in which no pied-piping has taken place. When the larger DP containing the relative pronoun is indefinite or non-specific, the DP can be stranded, as in (12). This gives us a configuration where a *wh*-word has extracted out of a DP.

(12) a boy [whom$_i$ Mary hit [$_{DP}$ a brother of t$_i$]]

Since we now have a DP with an indefinite article, a tree pair in Figure 13 is needed, for the derivation of (12). Using the semantic tree (β'a_brother_of), the semantic composition of the relative clause in (12) can proceed as before: the semantic tree (β'a_brother_of) adjoins onto the semantic tree (β'whom) in Figure 10, which then adjoins onto (β'hit) in Figure 4. In the syntax, however, we must make sure that (βa_brother_of) does not adjoin onto the relative pronoun *whom*, because if it did, we would end up with the string *a brother of whom*. Instead, what we need is for (βa_brother_of) to adjoin onto the DP dominating the trace of the extracted object in (βhit). This however is not a valid derivation in STAG, as elementary trees in a single pair are composing with two trees from two different pairs. A slight modification in the syntactic elementary tree for (αwhom) in Figure 14 can fix this problem. I propose to do this by turning (αwhom) into a multi-component set {(αwhom), (βwhom)} as in Figure 14. An auxiliary tree like (βwhom), which

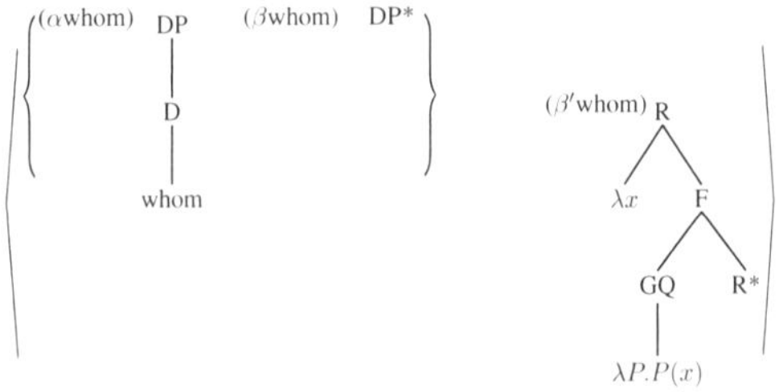

Figure 14: Elementary trees for *whom*

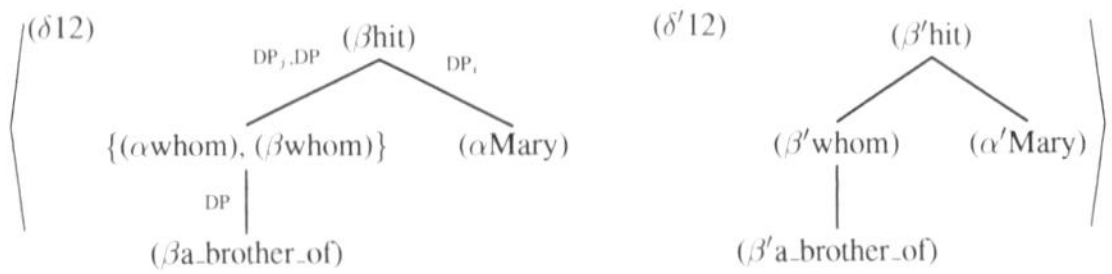

Figure 15: Derivation trees for *whom Mary hit a brother of*

does not dominate any other nodes, is a degenerate tree, and has been used in Kroch (1989) and Frank (2002) to handle extraction from a *wh*-island, as in *[Which car]$_i$ does Sally wonder how to fix t$_i$?*

In syntax, to derive the relative clause in (12), (αwhom) substitutes into DP$_j$ in (βhit) as before, and (βwhom) adjoins onto the DP dominating the trace of the extracted object in (βhit), as shown in the derivation tree (δ12) in Figure 15. And in semantics, (β'whom) adjoins onto (β'hit) as before, as shown in (δ'12) in Figure 15. Subsequently, in syntax (βa_brother_of) adjoins onto (βwhom) giving us the DP *a brother of t$_j$*, and in semantics (β'a_brother_of) adjoins onto (β'whom). Thus, by using the multi-component set {(αwhom), (βwhom)}, we now have a situation where two elementary trees in a single pair are composing with two trees belonging to another pair. The syntactic and the semantic derived trees are given in Figure 16. After λ-conversions, (γ'12) can be reduced to the expression in (13).[2]

(13) $\lambda x.\exists z_1[\text{brother}(z_1) \wedge \text{Rel}(x, z_1)]\ [\text{hit}(\text{Mary}', z_1)]$

5 Conclusion

I have shown that STAG-based compositional semantics for relative clauses with pied-piping is

[2]Partial stranding as in *a boy [a picture of whom]$_i$ Mary made a copy of t$_i$* can be handled by composing a multi-component set for *whom* containing a degenerate DP tree and another multi-component set for *a picture of* containing a degenerate DP tree. Further, the impossibility of the stranding of subject DP, as in **a boy whom$_i$ [a brother of t$_i$] hit Mary*, can be handled by placing an NA constraint on the subject DP dominating a trace in the relative clause tree.

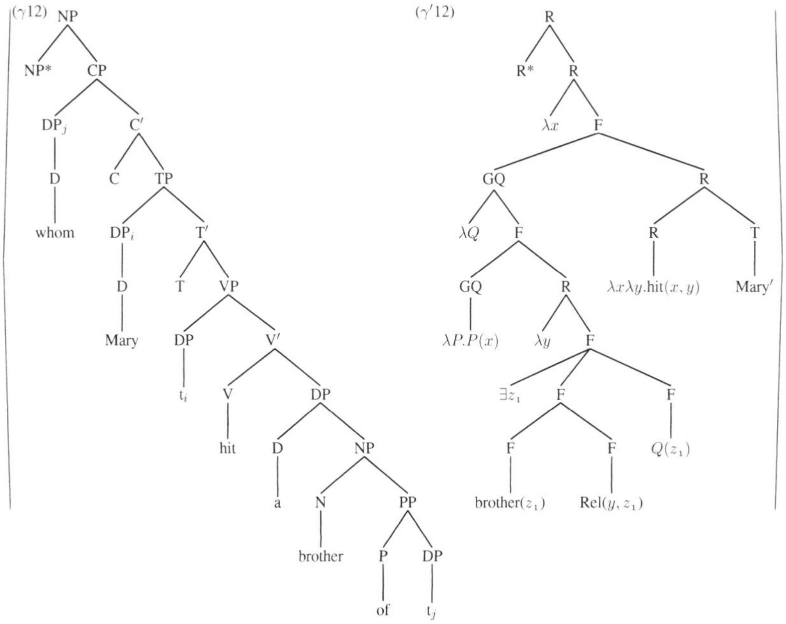

Figure 16: Derived trees for *whom Mary hit a brother of*

possible using examples in which the *wh*-word is embedded in a genitive DP, and shown that the proposed analysis can straightforwardly be extended to cases in which the *wh*-word is embedded in a PP. The main ingredients of the proposed analysis are: in syntax, the pied-piped material adjoins to the *wh*-word, and in semantics, the *wh*-word provides a GQ to which the meaning of the pied-piped material adjoins. I have also shown that similar analysis can handle cases in which the *wh*-word alone has moved to [Spec,CP], stranding the rest of the DP in situ, if we use a multi-component set containing a degenerate DP for the syntax of the relative pronoun. The proposed analysis utilizes composition operations in semantics that are already available in syntax, substitution and adjoining, thereby making syntax-semantics mapping in TAG simple and straightforward.

Acknowledgment

I thank Anoop Sarkar and the three anonymous reviewers for their insightful comments.

References

Robert Frank. 2002. *Phrase Structure Composition and Syntactic Dependencies*. MIT Press, Cambridge, MA.

Chung-hye Han. 2002. Compositional semantics for relative clauses in Lexicalized Tree Adjoining Grammar. A talk presented at TAG+6, Venice, Italy, www.sfu.ca/~chunghye/papers/tag6-rc-slides.pdf.

Irene Heim and Angelika Kratzer. 1998. *Semantics in Generative Grammar*. Blackwell, Oxford.

Laura Kallmeyer and Tatjana Scheffler. 2004. LTAG analysis for pied-piping and stranding of wh-phrases. In *Proceedings of TAG+7*, pages 32–39, Vancouver, Canada.

Laura Kallmeyer. 2003. LTAG semantics for relative clauses. In *Proceedings of the Fifth International Workshop on Computational Semantics (IWCS-5)*, Tilburg.

Anthony Kroch. 1989. Asymmetries in long-distance extraction in a Tree Adjoining Grammar. In Mark Baltin and Anthony Kroch, editors, *Alternative Conceptions of Phrase Structure*, pages 66–98. University of Chicago Press, Chicago.

Yves Schabes and Stuart M. Shieber. 1994. An alternative conception of Tree-Adjoining derivation. *Computational Linguistics*, pages 167–176.

Stuart Shieber and Yves Schabes. 1990. Synchronous Tree Adjoining Grammars. In *Proceedings of COLING'90*, Helsinki, Finland.

Stuart Shieber. 1994. Restricting the weak-generative capacity of Synchronous Tree-Adjoining Grammars. *Computational Intelligence*, 10(4).

David Weir. 1988. *Characterizing Mildly Context-Sensitive Grammar Formalisms*. Ph.D. thesis, University of Pennsylvania.

Negative Concord and Restructuring in Palestinian Arabic: A Comparison of TAG and CCG Analyses

Frederick M. Hoyt
Linguistics Department
University of Texas at Austin
1 University Station B5100
Austin, TX, USA 78712-0198
fmhoyt@mail.texas.edu

Abstract

This paper discusses interactions between negative concord and restructuring/clause union in Palestinian Arabic. Analyses formulated in Tree Adjoining Grammar and Combinatorial Categorial Grammar are compared, with the conclusion that a perspicuous analysis of the the intricacies of the data requires aspects of both formalisms; in particular, the TAG notion of the extended domain of locality and the CCG notion of flexible constituency.

1 Palestinian Arabic Negative Concord

In Palestinian Arabic (PA), negative concord occurs with the determiner **wɛla** "(not) even one," where negative concord describes the failure of an expression which expresses negation in some sentences to do so in others. Phrases formed with **wɛla** ("**wɛla**-phrases") are interpreted either as negative quantifiers ("NQ-**wɛla**)" or as polarity-sensitive indefinites ("NPI-**wɛla**"). **wɛla**-phrases have an NQ-interpretation preceding the finite verb or verb complex in a clause (1-2) or in fragment answers (3-4):

(1) **wɛla ḥada** fi:-hʊm šæ:f-ni.
not.even one.MS in-them saw.3ms-me
"Not even ONE of them saw me!"

(2) **wɛla yo:m** ʕaǧabni l-ɛkɪl.
not.even day pleased.3ms-me the-food
"There wasn't even one day the food pleased me!"

(3) Q: šu ḳal-l-ak? A: **wɛla iši**.
what said.3ms-to-you not.even thing
"What did he say to you? Nothing at all."

(4) Q: mi:n šʊfti? A: **wɛla ṣu:ṣ** ıbn yome:n.
who saw.2fs not.even chick son two-days
"Who did you see? Not even a two-day old chick!"

A preverbal **wɛla**-phrase preceding a sentential negation marker causes the sentence to have a double-negation reading (5: compare with 2):

(5) **wɛla yo:m ma**-ʕaǧabni l-ɛkɪl.
not.even day not-pleased.3ms-me the-food
"There wasn't one day the food didn't please me!"
"The food pleased me every day."

NQ-**wɛla** never occurs within the scope of negation but does occur in post-verbal positions which are not "thematically entailed" by the verb (6-7)[1]:

(6) huwwa **wɛla iši**!
he not.even thing
"He is NOTHING!"

(7) hiyya maǧru:ra ʕala **wɛla iši**.
she conceited.fs upon not.even thing
"She is conceited for absolutely NO reason!"

The NPI-interpretation is only available within the scope of antimorphic operators (Zwarts, 1993), like sentential negation or **bɪdu:n** "without" (8-9):

(8) tɪlʕti **bɪdu:n-ma** tḳu:li **wɛla iši**.
left.2fs without-that say.2fs even thing
"You left without saying even one thing!"

(9) la-s-sɛnna ma-baʕṭi:-hʊm **wɛlla lʊḳmi** ɛkl.
to-the-year not-give.1s-them even bite food
"Up to a year I don't give them even a bite of [solid] food."

More than one **wɛla**-phrase can have the NPI-interpretation at a time:

(10) ma-ḳʊlt **wɛla iši wɛla la-ḥada** fi:-hʊm.
not-said.1s even thing to-even one in-them
"I didn't give anything at all to even one of them."

It follows from the distributions of NQ- and NPI-**wɛla** that **wɛla**-phrases are blocked from post-verbal argument positions which are thematically entailed and which are not within the scope of an antimorphic operator.

[1] Following (Herburger, 2001), "thematically entailed" means that the meaning of the verb entails the existence of an entity filling the thematic role in question.

Proceedings of the 8th International Workshop on Tree Adjoining Grammar and Related Formalisms, pages 49–56,
Sydney, July 2006.

1.1 Negative Concord and Locality

PA negative concord is generally subject to strict locality constraints: a **wɛla**-phrase must be contained within the smallest inflected clause containing its licensor. It cannot be separated from its licensor by the boundary of either an indicative (11) or a subjunctive/irrealis (12) complement:

(11) * **ma**-waʕatt [ɛḥki **wɛla maʕ ḥada** fiː-hʊm].
not-promised.1s talk even with one in-them

(12) * batwakkaʕ-**ɪš** [ɪnnhæ bɪtḥɪbb **wɛla ḥada**].
believe.1s-neg that.3fs likes.3fs even one

Similar sentences with weaker polarity items such as **ḥada** or **ʔaiy ḥada** "anyone" are acceptable:

(13) ma-**waʕatt** ɛḥki maʕ (**ʔaiy**) **ḥada** fiː-hʊm.
not-promised.1s talk with any one in-them
"I didn't promise to talk with any of them."

(14) **batwakkaʕ**-ɪš ɪnnhæ bɪtḥɪbb (**ʔaiy**) **ḥada**.
believe.1s-neg that.3fs likes.3fs any one
"I don't think that she likes ANY one."

This suggests that negative concord is a strictly bounded dependency like agreement marking, argument realization, or reflexive binding.

However, there are exceptions to this generalization. "Long-distance" negative concord is possible between a matrix negation morpheme and **wɛla**-phrases inside the complements of a small class of verbs, including **bɪdd**- "want" (15), **χalla** "to allow" (16), **ḥaːwal** "to try" (17, 25 below) or **ʕɪrɪf** "to know how to, to be able to" (18 below):

(15) ma-**bɪddna** nχalli **wɛla zɛlami**.
not-want.1s leave.1p even fellow
"We don't want to leave even one man."

(16) ma-**χalluː**-niː-š æːkɔl **wɛla lʊkmi**
not-allowed.3mp-me-neg eat.1s even bite
"They wouldn't let me eat even one bite!"

The embedding can be recursive, provided that only verbs in this class are used (17).

(17) **bɪddiː**-š **aḥaːwɪl** ɛḥki wɛla maʕ ḥada.
want.1s-neg try.1s speak.1s even with one
"I don't want try to talk with anyone at all."

These verbs correspond to verbs found in many other languages which trigger a process often referred to as *restructuring* or *clause union*. I follow (Aissen and Perlmutter, 1983) in calling them *trigger verbs*. Restructuring involves the "stretching" of the domain of locality for certain kinds of bounded dependencies from the complement of a trigger verb to include the clause that it heads.

At present no other phenomena have been identified in PA which independently confirm that it has restructuring. However, long-distance negative concord is identified as a restructuring phenomenon in several languages such as West Flemish (Haegeman and Zanuttini, 1996), Polish (Dziwirek, 1998), and Serbian (Progovac, 2000). As such, I assume for now that long-distance negative concord in PA is a form of restructuring as well.

2 A TAG Analysis

Restructuring involves a seeming paradox involving a dependency which is non-local in the hierarchical structure of a sentence but local in its semantics. Tree Adjoining Grammars are well suited for analyzing restructuring because the distinction between a derived tree and the derivation tree associated with it provides two notions of locality. Restructuring phenomena which have been analyzed with TAGs include clitic-climbing in Spanish and Italian (Bleam, 2000; Kulick, 2000), long-distance scrambling in German (Rambow, 1994), and long-distance agreement in Tsez (Frank, 2006). It therefore is natural to explore a TAG analysis for long-distance negative concord in PA.

To illustrate with a simple example, the negative concord dependency in (18) is licensed within an initial tree headed by **ɛktɪb** "write," and is then "stretched" by adjunction of the auxiliary tree headed by **ʕɪrɪft** "I was able to" (19):

(18) ma-ʕɪrɪft ɛktɪb wɛla kɪlmi.
not-knew.1s write.1s even word
"I wasn't able to write even one word."

(19)

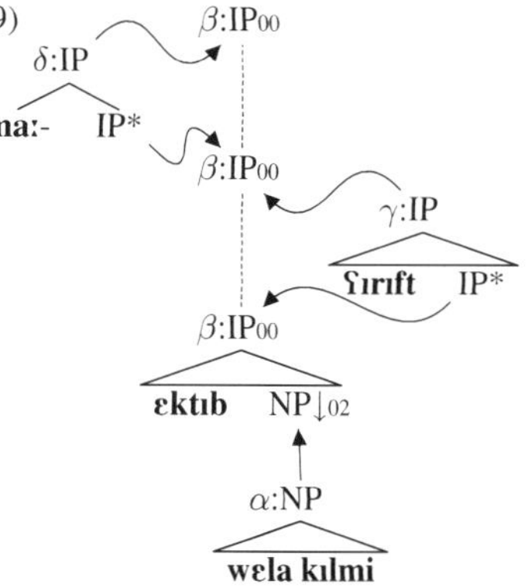

The locality constraint on negative concord can then be expressed as a generalization about the derivation tree (20): a **wɛla**-phrase and its licensor must be sisters:

(20)

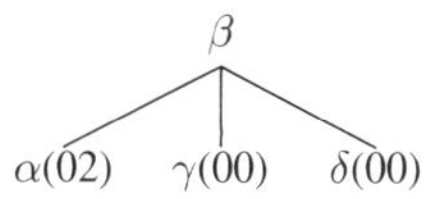

However, several properties of negative concord in PA preclude a simple analysis like this.

2.1 Clause-local Dependencies

The first property is the domain of locality of the negative concord dependency. In a simple TAG, syntactic dependencies are licensed within an elementary tree: they are *tree-local*. However, negative concord in PA is *clause-local*, because **wɛla**-phrases are not licensed within the immediate tree to which they are attached, but instead within the immediate clausal tree containing them. For example, **wɛla**-phrases can be inside prepositional phrases attached to a negative clause (21-22):

(21) ma-kaʕatt [$_{PP}$ **ǧanıb** wɛla ḥada fi:-hʊm]
not-sat.1s next.to even one in-them
"I didn't sit next to even one of them."

(22) bıtχallıfu:-š ʕan-na [$_{PP}$ **bi**-wɛla **iši**].
disagree.2mp-neg from-us with-even thing
"You don't disagree with us about even one thing."

In a simple TAG analysis, the **wɛla**-phrase first substitutes into the initial tree headed by the preposition, which is then attached to the clausal tree. The relationship between the **wɛla**-phrase and its licensor would therefore not be tree-local.

Clause-locality can be modeled with what I refer to as "Scope TAG" (Kallmeyer and Joshi, 2003), a multi-component TAG (MC-TAG) in which quantificational NPs are tree sets containing two parts: a "defective" auxiliary tree IP* which specifies the scope of the quantifier, and an NP-tree which specifies its restriction. I refer to such tree sets as "scope sets."

While Kallmeyer & Joshi's proposal is intended to capture the semantic scope of quantifiers, it can also be used to express clause locality by assigning PPs to scope sets as well, and by stipulating that scope sets can combine with each other by means of set-local adjunction. The IP*-node in the scope-set of a **wɛla**-phrase can then adjoin to the IP*-node in the PP scope set, which in turn adjoins to the IP-node of the initial tree.

For example, (21) above can be analyzed with the elementary trees in (23) (trees are in abbreviated form), producing the derivation tree in (24):

(23)
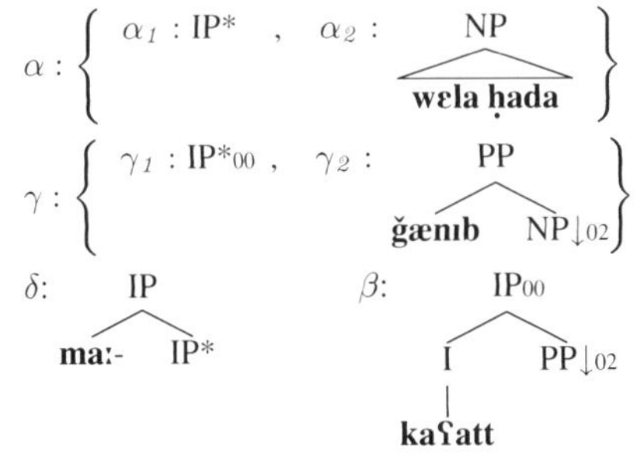

(24)
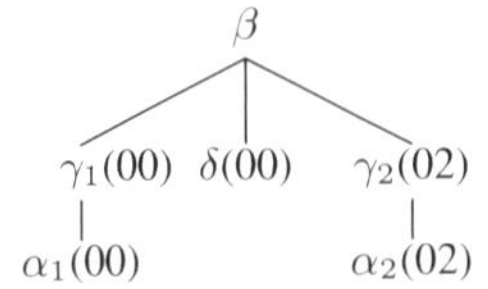

However, given (24) it is still not possible to state a generalization about negative concord locality in terms of sisterhood in the derivation tree.

This can be remedied by adopting the "node-sharing" relation proposed by (Kallmeyer, 2005). Informally, two nodes α and β are in a node-sharing relation in a derivation tree T iff they are either in a mother-daughter relation in T at a node address A, or there is a sequence S of nodes $N_1 \ldots N_n$ which is the transitive closure of a mother-daughter relation in T in which the node pairs are related in terms of the root node or foot node in an auxiliary tree.

On this basis, the negative concord locality generalization is that a **wɛla**-phrase and its licensor are "shared-node sisters" in the derivation tree, where shared-node sisters are two nodes A and B which are each in a shared-node relation with a single node C. For example, in (24) β is a shared-node parent of both α_1 and δ. Accordingly, α_1 and δ are shared-node sisters with respect to β.

2.2 Trigger Verbs and Complement Type

The second property of PA long-distance negative concord that complicates a TAG analysis has to do with the kinds of complement that they take. TAG approaches to restructuring exploit "reduced complement" analyses in which trigger verbs take "smaller" complements than other kinds of subordinating verbs do (Bleam, 2000; Kulick, 2000). However, PA trigger verbs are mixed in terms of the types of complements they take: **ḥa:wal** "try to" or **ḳıdır** "be able to" optionally allow a complementizer **ʔınn**- (25-26), while **bıdd**- "want" or **ʕırıf** "know to, be able to" exclude it (27-28):

(25) ma-ḥa:walt (**ınni**) ɛḥki wɛla maʕ ḥada.
not-tried.1s that.1s speak.1s even with one
"I didn't try to talk with even one of them."

(26) ma-ḳıdırt (**ınni**) ɛḥki wɛla maʕ ḥada.
not-could.1s that.1s speak.1s even with one
"I wasn't able to speak with even one of them."

(27) ma-bıdd-i:-ıš (***ınni**) ašu:f wɛla ḥada.
not-want.1s-neg that.1s see.1s even one
"I don't want to see even ONE of them."

(28) ma-ʕırıft (***ınni**) ɛktıb wɛla kılmi.
not-knww.1s that.1s write.1s even word
"I wan't able to write even one word."

Assuming that the presence of a complementizer indicates a CP category, and that the presence of agreement marking on the verb indicates an IP category, what these data show is that some trigger verbs allow either CP or IP complements, while others allow only IP complements. It follows that complement category cannot be exploited as a way to distinguish trigger verbs from non-trigger verbs.

This is an essential distinction because restructuring is not the only phenomenon which involves adjunction. For example, long-distance $\overline{\text{A}}$-dependencies are analyzed in TAG as involving adjunction of auxiliary trees. (29-30) show that the same verbs which block long-distance negative concord allow long-distance $\overline{\text{A}}$-dependencies, indicating that they must also be analyzed as auxiliary trees. Moreover, (30) can include the complementizer **ʔɪnn-**, indicating that it takes the same kinds of complements as do trigger verbs like **ḳɪdɪr** "be able" and **ḥa:wal** "try":

(29) mi:n **bɪtɪtwaḳḳaʕ** yaḥsal ʕala kæ:s ɪl-ʕæ:lɪm?
who believe.2ms get.3ms upon cup the-world
"Who do you think will get the World Cup?"

(30) šu **waʕatt** (ɪnnak) taʕṭi:-hæ?
what promised.2ms that.2ms give.2ms-her
"What did you promise to give her?"

A failure to distinguish between trigger verbs and non-trigger verbs will over-predict the availability of long-distance negative concord.

To make this distinction, I use Dowty's (Dowty, 1994) analysis of negative concord licensing. Dowty models negative concord with a "polarity" feature which takes "+" or "-" values. When a negative concord item combines with a clausal category it specifies (by unification) the clause as having a negative value for this feature. In addition, Dowty assumes that root clauses must have a positive value for the feature: I refer to this as the *root clause polarity constraint*. Negation morphemes (as well as **bɪdu:n** "without") take a complement specified as POL- and return a constituent with a POL+ feature. A root clause containing a negative concord item and lacking a negation morpheme will have a POL- feature for its root node and violate the root clause polarity constraint. This derives the requirement that **wɛla** phrases in root clauses be "roofed" by a negation morpheme.

Turning to long-distance negative concord, trigger verbs can be distinguished from non-trigger verbs by stipulating that non-trigger verbs take POL+ complements, while trigger verbs (and auxiliary verbs) impose no polarity specification and instead inherit the polarity feature with which their complement is specified[2]. An analysis of this kind applied to (18) would result in a derived tree (32) which satisfies the root clause polarity constraint.

(31)

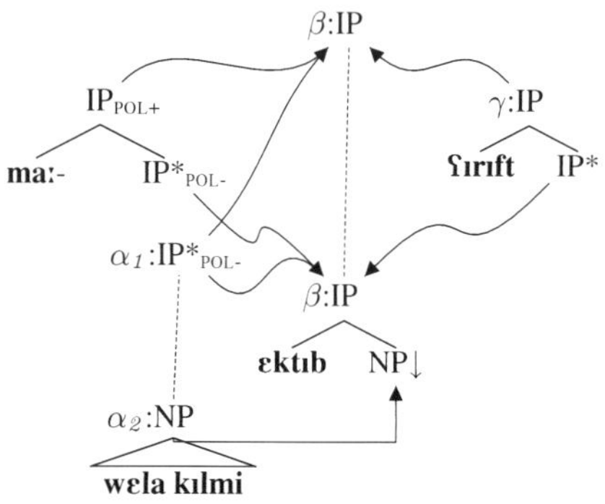

(32)

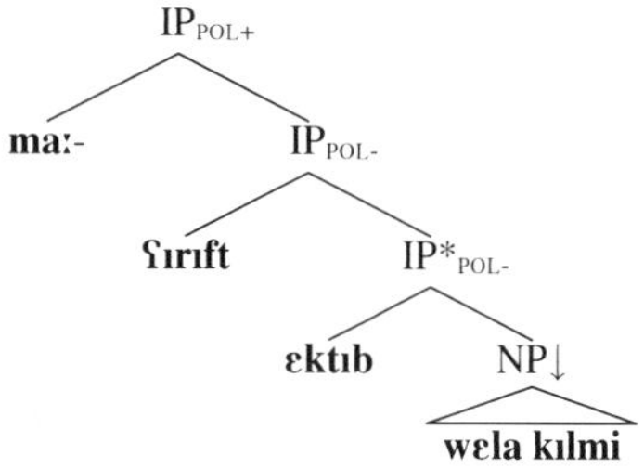

2.3 Negation Morphology

The last property of long-distance negative concord sentences to be dealt with has to do with negation morphology in PA. Negation is expressed with some combination of the proclitic **ma:**- and the enclitic -**š**. -**š** appears to be a second-position attaching to the first word-sized constituent in the string produced by an IP-constituent, provided that the word contains a morpheme expressing person features (Awwad, 1987; Eid, 1993).

The most frequent distribution has -**š** attached to the leftmost verb stem in a clause, which may be the main verb in a mono-verbal predicate (33), or to the leftmost auxiliary in a clause with compound tense-aspect-mood marking (34-35):

(33) ma-**nɪmt**-ɪš fi-l-le:l.
not-slept.1s-neg in-the-night
"I didn't sleep last night."

(34) ma-**kʊnt**-ɪš ʕa:rɪf we:n aḥʊṭṭ-u.
not-was.1s-neg know.actpart.ms where put.1s-it
"I didn't know where to put it."

(35) ma-**ʕad**-š ḳal-l-i ʔɪnnu
not-returned.3ms-neg said.3ms-to-me that.3ms
štara sayya:ra.
bought.3ms car
"He didn't tell me anymore that he bought a car."

[2]This is similar to Frank's (Frank, 2006) proposal for analyzing long-distance agreement in Tsez.

In other kinds of sentences, -š attaches to a variety of non-verbal expressions, including the indefinite pronoun **ḥada** "(any)one" (36), the existential particle **fi:** (37), inflected prepositions (38), and the adverb **ʕʊmr** "ever" (39):

(36) ma-**ḥada:**-š kæ:n yɪʕǧɪr-na.
not-one.ms-neg was.3ms rent.3ms-us
"No one would rent to us."

(37) ma-**fɪš**-š fi-d-dɪnya mɪþɪl-hɪn.
not-exist-neg in-the-word like-them.fp
"There isn't [anything] in the world like them."

(38) bæḳi:-l-ɛ faras ma-**lhæ:**-š ʊχt.
was.3ms-to-him mare not-to-her-neg sister
"He had a mare [that was] without compare."

(39) fi: næ:s ma-**ʕʊmr**-hæ:-š ḥaṭṭat mawḍu:ʕ fi-l-mʊntada.
exist people.3fs not-age-3fs-neg put.3fs subject in-the-club
"There are people who have never posted a thread on almontada.com."

What these expressions all have in common with verb stems is that they occur as the first constituent in the clause and that they all contain a morpheme expressing person features. It follows that -š is constrained to occur in the second position attached to a word that is inflected for person.

The cases in which -š attaches to a verb can be modeled by assuming that **ma:**- and -š are part of a tree set and that -š adjoins to right of an I-node:

(40) 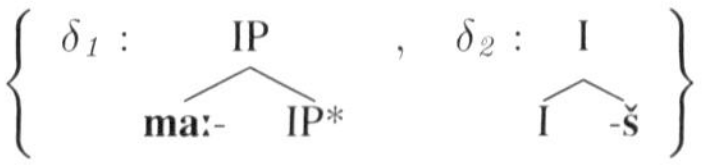

(41) 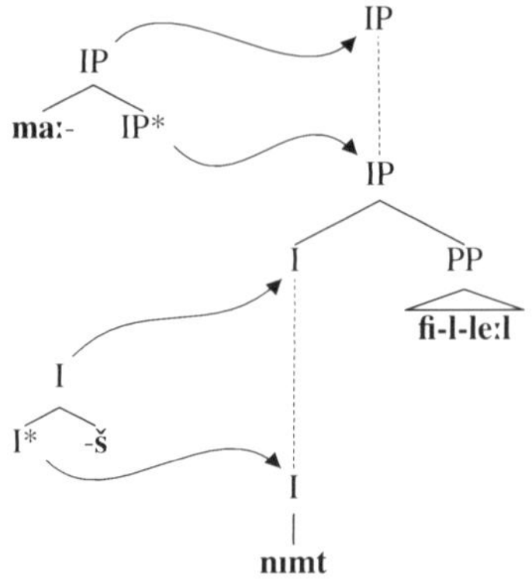

The cases with -š attached to a non-verbal expression require a second analysis. One possibility is to assume a second tree for -š like the first, except with -š preceding the foot node. This requires stipulating a morphological output filter that affixes -š to the preceding word and blocks use of δ_2 in (40):

(42) 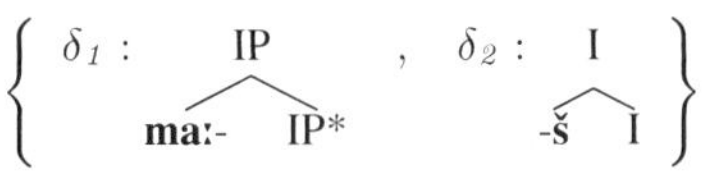

(43) 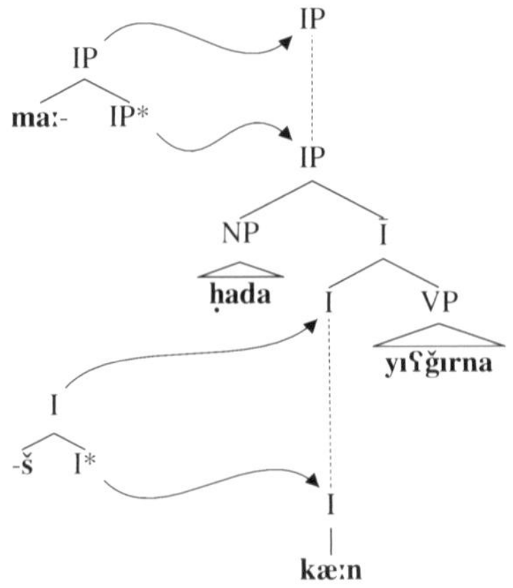

This is still not adaquate for (35), in which -š is attached to a "serial auxiliary" (Hussein, 1990), one of a small set of verb stems which function as aspectual adverbs and which "agree" with the main verb in aspectual form and agreement marking. Serial auxiliaries are plausibly analyzed as adverbial IP-auxiliary trees as in (44):

(44) 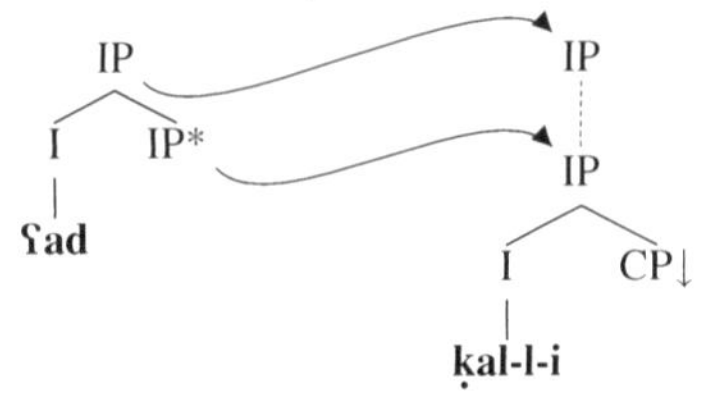

The structure resulting from (44) has two I-nodes, and another constraint would have to be stipulated forcing -š to adjoin to the leftmost of the two.

To sum up, a TAG analysis can be formulated for PA long-distance negative concord which allows the locality of negative concord licensing to be stated as a generalization about shared-node derivation trees. However, the analysis requires brute force stipulations to capture the morphological expression of negation in PA negative sentences. Moreover, the TAG analysis does not provide a way to express the simple morphological generalization that -š falls in the second position in the string generated by the clause.

3 A CCG Analysis

The TAG analysis has difficulty accommodating the distribution of -š because TAG trees are phrase structures, making it difficult to state constraints on strings of words rather than on hierarchical structure. Categorial Grammar, on the other hand, is a string calculus, and its operations result in string concatenation rather than structure expansion. For this reason, a CG can be constrained to not generate particular kinds of strings, rather than particular trees. A CG therefore provides a way to state constraints on the distribution of -**š** more directly than a phrase-structure grammar does.

I assume a *Combinatory Categorial Grammar* (Steedman, 1996; Steedman, 2000b; Baldridge, 2002). The basis of the CCG analysis is that npI-**wɛla**-phrases are treated as type-raised categories which look for an s category to their left. I continue following Dowty in assuming the *root clause polarity principle* and in assuming that **wɛla**-phrases specify a POL- feature on the s-headed category that they combine with. NQ-**wɛla** phrases, on the other hand, are treated as negative quantifiers which look for their s-headed argument to the right:

(45) NQ-**wɛla** :- $(\mathrm{S}_{pol+}\$/(\mathrm{S}_{pol+}\backslash\$/\mathrm{NP}))/\mathrm{NP}$: $\lambda P \lambda Q.\exists x[P(x)\ \&\ Q(x)]$

(46) NPI-**wɛla** :- $(\mathrm{S}_{pol-}\$\backslash(\mathrm{S}_{pol-}\$/\mathrm{NP}))/\mathrm{NP}$: $\lambda P \lambda Q.\neg\exists x[P(x)\ \&\ Q(x)]$

The negation morphemes are treated as follows (-**š** is semantically vacuous):

(47) **ma:**- :- $\mathrm{S}_{pol+}\$/\mathrm{S}_{pol-}\$: \lambda P_{st}.\neg P(e)$

(48) -**š** :- $\mathrm{S}_{pol-}\$\backslash_{\times}\mathrm{S}_{pol\pm}\$$

Verbs have the following types[3]:

(49) **šʊft** :- $\mathrm{S}\backslash\mathrm{NP}/\mathrm{NP} : \lambda y.\lambda x.[x \text{ saw } y]$

(50) **ḥa:walt** :- $\mathrm{S}\backslash\mathrm{NP}/(\mathrm{s}\backslash\mathrm{NP}) : \lambda x.\lambda P_{st}.[x \text{ tries } P(x)]$

The -**š** morpheme fixes a clause with a POL- feature, while **ma:**- takes the POL- clausal category and changes its value for the polarity feature to POL+, satisfying the root clause polarity constraint. This works much as the TAG analysis did. The slash in the type for -**š** is marked with the "crossed composition" modality. This allows -**š** to combine with a preceding s-headed category while returning a category looking for its arguments to the right (Figures 1-2)[4].

Turning to long-distance negative concord, a CCG analysis, like the TAG analysis above, has to account for the distinction between trigger verbs and non-trigger verbs. The CCG analog of auxiliary-tree adjunction is function composition. The long-distance negative concord dependency therefore involves a specific kind of composition subject to stricter constraints than is the more general kind which produces $\overline{\mathrm{A}}$-dependencies.

In order to model this, I adapt Hepple's (Hepple, 1990) approach to modeling island constraints in Categorial Type Logic. In brief, Hepple's approach is to assign unary modalities to the arguments of clausal categories (such as subordinating verbs or relative pronouns) as well as to the nominal argument of a type-raised extracted category (such as a question word or topicalized noun phrase). The former are referred to as "bounding modalities," and the latter as "penetrative modalities." *Interaction axioms* require the penetrative modality of an extraction category to be compatible with the bounding category of its argument in terms of a type hierarchy defined over modalities.

The unary modalities in CTL can be duplicated in CCG as features on category labels, so to approximate Hepple's proposal, I define a feature hierarchy as follows:

(51)
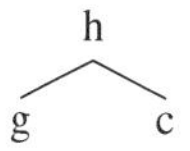

Each pair of sisters in the hierarchy consists of a "penetrative feature" and the "bounding feature" which blocks it (following Hepple's terminology). The feature *c* is an penetrative feature which is blocked by the *g* feature, and *h* is the most general or permissive bounding feature.

The idea is that categories which participate in restructuring dependencies are marked with the *c* penetrative feature, which is spread across all the arguments of a complex type:

(52) **wɛla ḥada** :- $\mathrm{S}_c\$\backslash(\mathrm{S}_c\$/\mathrm{NP}_c)$

Trigger verbs impose the *h* bounding feature on their complements, while non-trigger embedding verbs impose the *g* feature:

(53) **bɪdd**- "want," **ʕɪrɪf** "be able to," **ḥa:wal** "try to" :- $\mathrm{S}\backslash\mathrm{NP}/(\mathrm{S}_h\backslash\mathrm{NP}_h)$

(54) **waʕad-yu:ʕɪd** "promise to" :- $\mathrm{S}\backslash\mathrm{NP}/(\mathrm{S}_g\backslash\mathrm{NP}_g)$

According to (51), categories marked with feature *h* are compatible with categories marked with feature *c*, while categories marked with feature *g* clash with it. The clash between *g* and *c* expresses the restriction on restructuring dependencies.

For example, in an analysis of (18), **wɛla kɪlmi** applies to the composed constituent, **ʕɪrɪft ɛktɪb**. This is possible because the penetrative feature *c* on the **wɛla**-phrase is compatible with the *h* bounding feature which **ʕɪrɪft** passes to its complement (Figure 3).

Long-distance negative concord is blocked in two ways. A wide-scope derivation (in which the **wɛla**-phrase combines with the composition of the

[3]The type assignments ignore the representation of VS word order and pro-drop sentences.

[4]Logical forms are surpressed in the derivations.

matrix and embedded verbs) is blocked by a feature clash between the *g* and *c* features (Figure 4). A narrow scope derivation (in which the **wɛla**-phrase combines with the embedded verb only) is blocked because of a resulting clash in polarity features between the embedded clause and the matrix verb (Figure 5).

4 Comparison and Discussion

While the TAG analysis imposes certain limitations on the ordering of morphemes, it does provide a very simple and intuitive way to describe restructuring verbs as a natural class that includes auxiliary verbs, the other kinds of verb stems which are "transparent" to negative concord. In contrast, The CCG analysis has a technical flavor, and it is not clear to what extent it reflects a linguistic intuition. The CCG analysis does, however, capture the distribution of the negation morphemes in PA. It would therefore be interesting to explore further whether the Hepple-style feature/modality approach could be associated with some linguistic phenomenon.

One interesting possibility would be to use Steedman's theory of intonation (Steedman, 2000a) to explore the prosodic properties of restructuring sentences in Arabic (and in other languages) to see whether the availability of restructuring correlates with certain prosodic properties. There has been very little study of sentential intonation in Arabic, and so very little empirical basis for an investigation. However, should such an investigation bear fruit, it might suggest that Hepple's approach to extraction constraints could be recast as a theory of intonation. This would allow powerful generalizations to be stated relating the prosodic properties of sentences in PA and other languages to their syntactic properties.

References

Judith Aissen and David Perlmutter. 1983. Clause reduction in spanish. In *Studies in Relational Grammar*. University of Chicago Press.

Mohammad Amin Awwad. 1987. Free and bound pronouns as verbs in rural palestinian colloquial arabic. *Journal of Arabic Linguistics*, 16:108–118.

Jason Baldridge. 2002. *Lexically Specified Derivational Control in Combinatory Categorial Grammar*. Ph.D. thesis, University of Edinburgh.

Tonia Bleam. 2000. Clitic climbing and the power of tree adjoining grammar. In Anne Abeillé and Owen Rambow, editors, *Tree Adjoining Grammar: Formalism, Implementation, and Linguistic Analysis*. CSLI (Stanford).

David Dowty. 1994. The role of negative polarity and concord marking in natural language reasoning. In Mandy Harvey and Lynn Santelmann, editors, *Proceedings from Semantics and Linguistic Theory IV*, pages 114–144, Ithaca, New York. Cornell University.

Katarzyna Dziwirek. 1998. Reduced constructions in universal grammar: Evidence from the polish object control construction. *Natural Language and Linguistic Theory*, 16:53–99.

Mushira Eid. 1993. Negation and predicate heads in arabic. In Mushira Eid and Gregory Iverson, editors, *Principles and Predication: The Analysis of Natural Language*, pages 135–152. John Benjamins (Philadelphia).

Robert Frank. 2006. Phase theory and tree adjoining grammar. *Lingua*, 116:145–202.

Liliane Haegeman and Raffaella Zanuttini. 1996. Negative concord in west flemish. In Adriana Belleti and Luigi Rizzi, editors, *Parameters and Functional Heads*, pages 117–179. Oxford University Press.

Mark Hepple. 1990. *The Grammar and Processing of Order and Dependency: A Categorial Approach*. Phd, University of Edinburgh.

Elena Herburger. 2001. Negative concord revisited. *Natural Language Semantics*, pages 289–333.

Lutfi Hussein. 1990. Serial verbs in colloquial arabic. In B. D. Joseph and A. M. Zwicky, editors, *When Verbs Collide: Papers from the 1990 Ohio State Mini-Conference on Serial Verbs*, pages 340–354. The Ohio State University.

Laura Kallmeyer and Aravind Joshi. 2003. Factoring predicate argumenta and scope semantics: Underspecified semantics with ltag. *Research on Language and Computation*, 1:3–58.

Laura Kallmeyer. 2005. Tree-local multicomponent tree adjoining grammars with shared nodes. *Computational Linguistics*, 31(2):187–225.

Seth Kulick. 2000. *Constraining Non-Local Dependencies in Tree Adjoining Grammar: Computational and Linguistic Perspectives*. Ph.D. thesis, University of Pennsylvania.

Ljiljana Progovac. 2000. Coordination, c-command and 'logophoric' n-words. In Laurence Horn and Yasuhiko Kato, editors, *Negation and Polarity: Syntactic and Semantic Perspectives*, pages 88–114. Oxford University Press (Oxford).

Owen Rambow. 1994. *Formal and Computational Aspects of Natural Language Syntax*. Ph.D. thesis, University of Pennsylvania.

Mark Steedman. 1996. *Surface Structure and Interpretation*. MIT Press.

Mark Steedman. 2000a. Information structure and the syntax-phonology interface. *Linguistic Inquiry*, 31:649–689.

Mark Steedman. 2000b. *The Syntactic Process*. MIT Press.

Frans Zwarts. 1993. Three types of polarity items. In F. Hamm and E. Hinrichs, editors, *Semantics*.

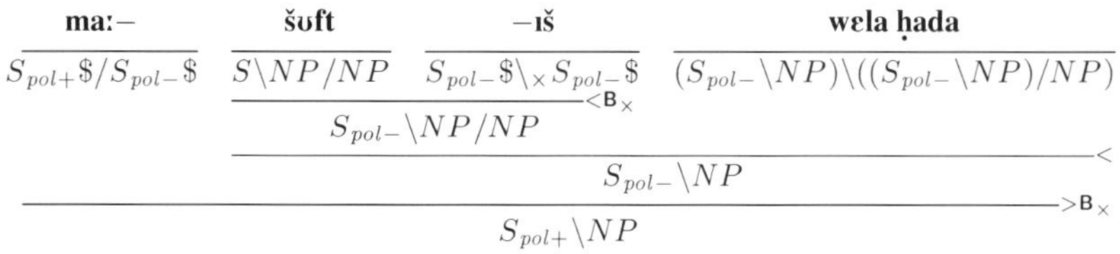

Figure 1:

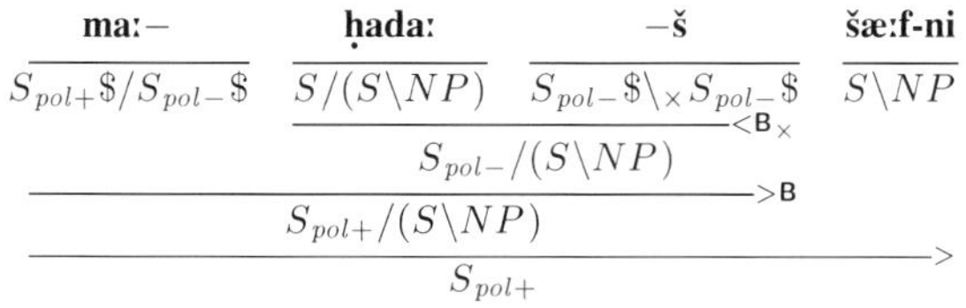

Figure 2:

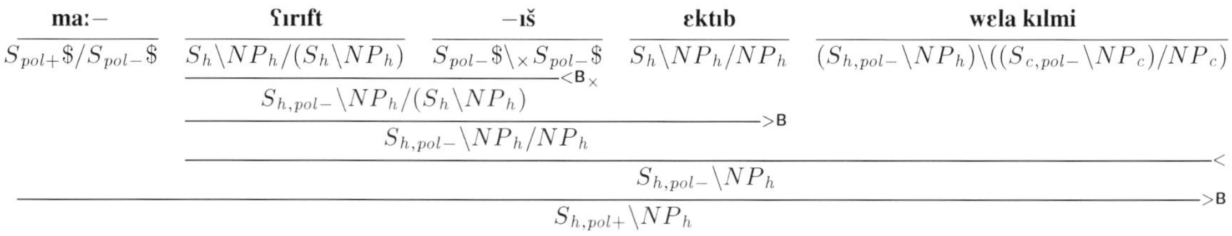

Figure 3:

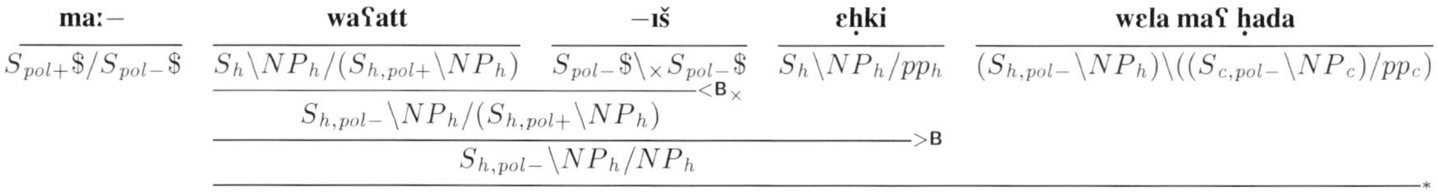

Figure 4:

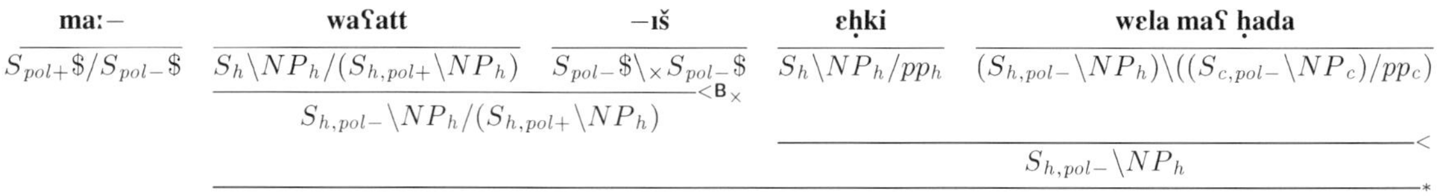

Figure 5:

Stochastic Multiple Context-Free Grammar for RNA Pseudoknot Modeling

Yuki Kato
Graduate School of Information Science,
Nara Institute of Science and Technology
8916-5 Takayama, Ikoma,
Nara 630-0192, Japan
yuuki-ka@is.naist.jp

Hiroyuki Seki
Graduate School of Information Science,
Nara Institute of Science and Technology
8916-5 Takayama, Ikoma,
Nara 630-0192, Japan
seki@is.naist.jp

Tadao Kasami
Graduate School of Information Science,
Nara Institute of Science and Technology
8916-5 Takayama, Ikoma,
Nara 630-0192, Japan
kasami@naist.jp

Abstract

Several grammars have been proposed for modeling RNA pseudoknotted structure. In this paper, we focus on multiple context-free grammars (MCFGs), which are natural extension of context-free grammars and can represent pseudoknots, and extend a specific subclass of MCFGs to a probabilistic model called SMCFG. We present a polynomial time parsing algorithm for finding the most probable derivation tree and a probability parameter estimation algorithm. Furthermore, we show some experimental results of pseudoknot prediction using SMCFG algorithm.

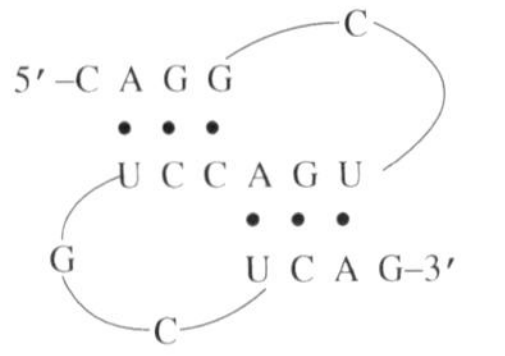

(a) Pseudoknot

(b) Arc depiction of (a)

Figure 1: Example of RNA secondary structure

1 Introduction

Non-coding RNAs fold into characteristic structures determined by interactions between mostly Watson-Crick complementary base pairs. Such a base paired structure is called the *secondary structure*. *Pseudoknot* (Figure 1 (a)) is one of the typical substructures found in the secondary structures of several RNAs, including rRNAs, tmRNAs and viral RNAs. An alternative graphic representation of a pseudoknot is arc depiction where arcs connect base pairs (Figure 1 (b)). It has been recognized that pseudoknots play an important role in RNA functions such as ribosomal frameshifting and regulation of translation.

Many attempts have so far been made at modeling RNA secondary structure by formal grammars. In a grammatical approach, secondary structure prediction can be viewed as parsing problem. However, there may be many different derivation trees for an input sequence. Thus, it is necessary to have a method of extracting biologically realistic derivation trees among them. One solution to this problem is to extend a grammar to a probabilistic model and find the most likely derivation tree, and another is to take free energy minimization into account. Eddy and Durbin (1994), and Sakakibara et al. (1994) modeled RNA secondary structure without pseudoknots by using stochastic context-free grammars (stochastic CFGs or SCFGs). For pseudoknotted structure (Figure 1 (a)), however, another approach has to be taken since a single CFG cannot represent crossing dependencies of base pairs in pseudoknots (Figure 1 (b)) for the lack of generative power. Brown and Wilson (1996) proposed a model based on intersections of SCFGs to describe RNA pseudoknots. Cai et al. (2003) introduced a model based on parallel communication grammar systems using a single CFG synchronized with a number of regular grammars. Akutsu (2000) provided dynamic programming algorithms for RNA pseudoknot prediction without using grammars. On the other hand, several grammars have been proposed where the grammar itself can fully describe pseudoknots. Rivas and Eddy (1999, 2000) provided a dynamic programming

Proceedings of the 8th International Workshop on Tree Adjoining Grammar and Related Formalisms, pages 57–64,
Sydney, July 2006.

algorithm for predicting RNA secondary structure including pseudoknots, and introduced a new class of grammars called RNA pseudoknot grammars (RPGs) for deriving sequences with gap. Uemura et al. (1999) defined specific subclasses of tree adjoining grammars (TAGs) named SL-TAGs and extended SL-TAGs (ESL-TAGs) respectively, and predicted RNA pseudoknots by using parsing algorithm of ESL-TAG. Matsui et al. (2005) proposed pair stochastic tree adjoining grammars (PSTAGs) based on ESL-TAGs and tree automata for aligning and predicting pseudoknots, which showed good prediction accuracy. These grammars have generative power stronger than CFGs and polynomial time algorithms for parsing problem.

In our previous work (Kato et al., 2005), we identified RPGs, SL-TAGs and ESL-TAGs as subclasses of *multiple context-free grammars* (MCFGs) (Kasami et al., 1988; Seki et al., 1991), which can model RNA pseudoknots, and showed a candidate subclass of the minimum grammars for representing pseudoknots. The generative power of MCFGs is stronger than that of CFGs and MCFGs have a polynomial time parsing algorithm like the CYK (Cocke-Younger-Kasami) algorithm for CFGs. In this paper, we extend the above candidate subclass of MCFGs to a probabilistic model called a stochastic MCFG (SMCFG). We present a polynomial time parsing algorithm for finding the most probable derivation tree, which is applicable to RNA pseudoknot prediction. In addition, we mention a probability parameter estimation method based on the EM (expectation maximization) algorithm. Finally, we show some experimental results on pseudoknot prediction for three RNA families using SMCFG algorithm, which show good prediction accuracy.

2 Stochastic Multiple Context-Free Grammar

A *stochastic multiple context-free grammar* (stochastic MCFG, or SMCFG) is a probabilistic extension of MCFG (Kasami et al., 1988; Seki et al., 1991) or *linear context-free rewriting system* (Vijay-Shanker et al., 1987). An SMCFG is a 5-tuple $G = (N, T, F, P, S)$ where N is a finite set of nonterminals, T is a finite set of terminals, F is a finite set of functions, P is a finite set of (production) rules and $S \in N$ is the start symbol. For each $A \in N$, a positive integer denoted by $\dim(A)$ is given and A derives $\dim(A)$-tuples of terminal sequences. For the start symbol S, $\dim(S) = 1$. For each $f \in F$, positive integers d_i $(0 \leq i \leq k)$ are given and f is a total function from $(T^*)^{d_1} \times \cdots \times (T^*)^{d_k}$ to $(T^*)^{d_0}$ where each component of f is defined as the concatenation of some components of arguments and constant sequences. Note that each component of an argument should occur in the function value at most once (linearity). For example, $f[(x_{11}, x_{12}), (x_{21}, x_{22})] = (x_{11}x_{21}, x_{12}x_{22})$. Each rule in P has the form of $A_0 \xrightarrow{p} f[A_1, \ldots, A_k]$ where $A_i \in N$ $(0 \leq i \leq k)$, $f : (T^*)^{\dim(A_1)} \times \cdots \times (T^*)^{\dim(A_k)} \to (T^*)^{\dim(A_0)} \in F$ and p is a real number with $0 \leq p \leq 1$ called the *probability* of this rule. The summation of the probabilities of the rules with the same left-hand side should be one. If we are not interested in p, we just write $A_0 \to f[A_1, \ldots, A_k]$. If $k \geq 1$, then the rule is called a *nonterminating rule*, and if $k = 0$, then it is called a *terminating rule*. A terminating rule $A_0 \to f[\,]$ with $f^{[h]}[\,] = \beta_h$ $(1 \leq h \leq \dim(A_0))$ is simply written as $A_0 \to (\beta_1, \ldots, \beta_{\dim(A_0)})$.

We recursively define the relation $\stackrel{*}{\Rightarrow}$ by the following (L1) and (L2): **(L1)** if $A \xrightarrow{p} \overline{\alpha} \in P$ $(\overline{\alpha} \in (T^*)^{\dim(A)})$, then we write $A \stackrel{*}{\Rightarrow} \overline{\alpha}$ with probability p, and **(L2)** if $A \xrightarrow{p} f[A_1, \ldots, A_k] \in P$ and $A_i \stackrel{*}{\Rightarrow} \overline{\alpha_i} \in (T^*)^{\dim(A_i)}$ $(1 \leq i \leq k)$ with probabilities $p_1, \ldots, p_k$, respectively, then we write $A \stackrel{*}{\Rightarrow} f[\overline{\alpha_1}, \ldots, \overline{\alpha_k}]$ with probability $p \cdot \prod_{i=1}^{k} p_i$. In parallel with the relation $\stackrel{*}{\Rightarrow}$, we define derivation trees as follows: **(D1)** if $A \xrightarrow{p} \overline{\alpha} \in P$ $(\overline{\alpha} \in (T^*)^{\dim(A)})$, then the ordered tree with the root labeled A which has $\overline{\alpha}$ as the only one child is a derivation tree for $\overline{\alpha}$ with probability p, and **(D2)** if $A \xrightarrow{p} f[A_1, \ldots, A_k] \in P$, $A_i \stackrel{*}{\Rightarrow} \overline{\alpha_i} \in (T^*)^{\dim(A_i)}$ $(1 \leq i \leq k)$ and $t_1, \ldots, t_k$ are derivation trees for $\overline{\alpha_1}, \ldots, \overline{\alpha_k}$ with probabilities $p_1, \ldots, p_k$, respectively, then the ordered tree with the root labeled A (or $A : f$ if necessary) which has $t_1, \ldots, t_k$ as (immediate) subtrees from left to right is a derivation tree for $f[\overline{\alpha_1}, \ldots, \overline{\alpha_k}]$ with probability $p \cdot \prod_{i=1}^{k} p_i$. Example rules are $A \xrightarrow{0.3} f[A]$ where $f[(x_1, x_2)] = (ax_1b, cx_2d)$ and $A \xrightarrow{0.7} (ab, cd)$. Then, $A \stackrel{*}{\Rightarrow} (ab, cd)$ by the second rule, which is followed by $A \stackrel{*}{\Rightarrow} f[(ab, cd)] = (aabb, ccdd)$ by the first rule. The probability of the latter derivation is $0.3 \cdot 0.7 = 0.21$. The language generated by an SMCFG G is defined as $L(G) = \{w \in T^* \mid S \stackrel{*}{\Rightarrow}$

Table 1: SMCFG G_s

Type	Rule set	Function	Transition probability	Emission probability
E	$W_v \to (\varepsilon, \varepsilon)$		1	1
S	$W_v \to J[W_y]$	$J[(x_1, x_2)] = x_1 x_2$	$t_v(y)$	1
D	$W_v \to SK[W_y]$	$SK[(x_1, x_2)] = (x_1, x_2)$	$t_v(y)$	1
B_1	$W_v \to C_1[W_y, W_z]$	$C_1[x_1, (x_{21}, x_{22})] = (x_1 x_{21}, x_{22})$	1	1
B_2	$W_v \to C_2[W_y, W_z]$	$C_2[x_1, (x_{21}, x_{22})] = (x_{21} x_1, x_{22})$	1	1
B_3	$W_v \to C_3[W_y, W_z]$	$C_3[x_1, (x_{21}, x_{22})] = (x_{21}, x_1 x_{22})$	1	1
B_4	$W_v \to C_4[W_y, W_z]$	$C_4[x_1, (x_{21}, x_{22})] = (x_{21}, x_{22} x_1)$	1	1
U_{1L}	$W_v \to UP^{a_i}_{1L}[W_y]$	$UP^{a_i}_{1L}[(x_1, x_2)] = (a_i x_1, x_2)$	$t_v(y)$	$e_v(a_i)$
U_{1R}	$W_v \to UP^{a_j}_{1R}[W_y]$	$UP^{a_j}_{1R}[(x_1, x_2)] = (x_1 a_j, x_2)$	$t_v(y)$	$e_v(a_j)$
U_{2L}	$W_v \to UP^{a_k}_{2L}[W_y]$	$UP^{a_k}_{2L}[(x_1, x_2)] = (x_1, a_k x_2)$	$t_v(y)$	$e_v(a_k)$
U_{2R}	$W_v \to UP^{a_l}_{2R}[W_y]$	$UP^{a_l}_{2R}[(x_1, x_2)] = (x_1, x_2 a_l)$	$t_v(y)$	$e_v(a_l)$
P	$W_v \to BP^{a_i a_l}[W_y]$	$BP^{a_i a_l}[(x_1, x_2)] = (a_i x_1, x_2 a_l)$	$t_v(y)$	$e_v(a_i, a_l)$

w with probability greater than $0\}$.

In this paper, we focus on an SMCFG $G_s = (N, T, F, P, S)$ that satisfies the following conditions: G_s has m different nonterminals denoted by $W_1, \ldots, W_m$, each of which uses the only one type of a rule denoted by E, S, D, B_1, B_2, B_3, B_4, U_{1L}, U_{1R}, U_{2L}, U_{2R} or P [1] (see Table 1). The type of W_v is denoted by type(v) and we predefine type$(1) =$ S, that is, W_1 is the start symbol. Consider a sample rule set $W_v \to UP^{\alpha}_{1L}[W_y] \mid UP^{\alpha}_{1L}[W_z]$ where $UP^{\alpha}_{1L}[(x_1, x_2)] = (\alpha x_1, x_2)$ and $\alpha \in T$. For each rule r, two real values called *transition probability* p_1 and *emission probability* p_2 are specified in Table 1. The probability of r is simply defined as $p_1 \cdot p_2$. In application, $p_1 = t_v(y)$ and $p_2 = e_v(a_i), \ldots$ in Table 1 are the parameters of the grammar, which are set by hand or by a training algorithm (Section 3.3) depending on the set of possible sequences to be analyzed.

3 Algorithms for SMCFG

In RNA structure analysis using stochastic grammars, we have to deal with the following three problems: **(1)** calculate the optimal alignment of a sequence to a stochastic grammar (alignment problem), **(2)** calculate the probability of a sequence given a stochastic grammar (scoring problem), and **(3)** estimate optimal probability parameters for a stochastic grammar given a set of example sequences (training problem). In this section, we give solutions to each problem for the specific SMCFG $G_s = (N, T, F, P, S)$.

3.1 Alignment Problem

The alignment problem for G_s is to find the most probable derivation tree for a given input sequence. This problem can be solved by a dynamic programming algorithm similar to the CYK algorithm for SCFGs (Durbin et al., 1998), and in this paper, we also call the parsing algorithm for G_s the CYK algorithm. We fix an input sequence $w = a_1 \cdots a_n$ ($|w| = n$). Let $\gamma_v(i, j)$ and $\gamma_y(i, j, k, l)$ be the logarithm of maximum probabilities of a derivation subtree rooted at a nonterminal W_v for a terminal subsequence $a_i \cdots a_j$ and of a derivation subtree rooted at a nonterminal W_y for a tuple of terminal subsequences $(a_i \cdots a_j, a_k \cdots a_l)$ respectively. The variables $\gamma_v(i, i-1)$ and $\gamma_y(i, i-1, j, j-1)$ are the logarithm of maximum probabilities for an empty sequence ε and a pair of ε. Let $\tau_v(i, j)$ and $\tau_y(i, j, k, l)$ be traceback variables for constructing a derivation tree, which are calculated together with $\gamma_v(i, j)$ and $\gamma_y(i, j, k, l)$. We define $\mathcal{C}_v = \{y \mid W_v \to f[W_y] \in P,\ f \in F\}$. To avoid non-emitting cycles, we assume that the nonterminals are numbered such that $v < y$ for all $y \in \mathcal{C}_v$. The CYK algorithm uses five dimensional dynamic programming matrix to calculate γ, which leads to $\log P(w, \hat{\pi} \mid \theta)$ where $\hat{\pi}$ is the most probable derivation tree and θ is an entire set of probability parameters. The detailed description of the CYK algorithm is as follows:

Algorithm 1 (CYK).
Initialization:
for $i \leftarrow 1$ **to** $n+1$, $j \leftarrow i$ **to** $n+1$, $v \leftarrow 1$ **to** m
  do if type$(v) =$ E
    then $\gamma_v(i, i-1, j, j-1) \leftarrow 0$
  else $\gamma_v(i, i-1, j, j-1) \leftarrow -\infty$
Iteration:
for $i \leftarrow n$ **downto** 1, $j \leftarrow i-1$ **to** n, $k \leftarrow n+1$ **downto** $j+1$, $l \leftarrow k-1$ **to** n, $v \leftarrow 1$ **to** m
  do if type$(v) =$ E
    then if $j = i-1$ **and** $l = k-1$
      then skip

[1] These types stand for END, START, DELETE, BIFURCATION, UNPAIR and PAIR respectively.

else $\gamma_v(i,j,k,l) \leftarrow -\infty$
if type(v) = S
then $\gamma_v(i,j)$
$\leftarrow \max_{y \in \mathcal{C}_v} \max_{h=i-1,\dots,j} [\log t_v(y) + \gamma_y(i,h,h+1,j)]$
$\tau_v(i,j)$
$\leftarrow \arg\max_{(y,h)} [\log t_v(y) + \gamma_y(i,h,h+1,j)]$
if type(v) = B_1 **and** $W_v \to C_1[W_y, W_z]$
then $\gamma_v(i,j,k,l)$
$\leftarrow \max_{h=i-1,\dots,j} [\gamma_y(i,h) + \gamma_z(h+1,j,k,l)]$
$\tau_v(i,j,k,l)$
$\leftarrow \arg\max_{(y,z,h)} [\gamma_y(i,h) + \gamma_z(h+1,j,k,l)]$
if type(v) = B_2 **and** $W_v \to C_2[W_y, W_z]$
then $\gamma_v(i,j,k,l)$
$\leftarrow \max_{h=i-1,\dots,j} [\gamma_y(h+1,j) + \gamma_z(i,h,k,l)]$
$\tau_v(i,j,k,l)$
$\leftarrow \arg\max_{(y,z,h)} [\gamma_y(h+1,j) + \gamma_z(i,h,k,l)]$
if type(v) = B_3 **and** $W_v \to C_3[W_y, W_z]$
then $\gamma_v(i,j,k,l)$
$\leftarrow \max_{h=k-1,\dots,l} [\gamma_z(i,j,h+1,l) + \gamma_y(k,h)]$
$\tau_v(i,j,k,l)$
$\leftarrow \arg\max_{(y,z,h)} [\gamma_z(i,j,h+1,l) + \gamma_y(k,h)]$
if type(v) = B_4 **and** $W_v \to C_4[W_y, W_z]$
then $\gamma_v(i,j,k,l)$
$\leftarrow \max_{h=k-1,\dots,l} [\gamma_z(i,j,k,h) + \gamma_y(h+1,l)]$
$\tau_v(i,j,k,l)$
$\leftarrow \arg\max_{(y,z,h)} [\gamma_z(i,j,k,h) + \gamma_y(h+1,l)]$
if type(v) = P
then if $j = i-1$ **or** $l = k-1$
then $\gamma_v(i,j,k,l) \leftarrow -\infty$
else $\gamma_v(i,j,k,l)$
$\leftarrow \max_{y \in \mathcal{C}_v} [\log e_v(a_i, a_l) + \log t_v(y) + \gamma_y(i+1, j, k, l-1)]$
$\tau_v(i,j,k,l)$
$\leftarrow \arg\max_{y} [\log e_v(a_i, a_l) + \log t_v(y) + \gamma_y(i+1, j, k, l-1)]$
else $\gamma_v(i,j,k,l)$
$\leftarrow \max_{y \in \mathcal{C}_v} [\log e_v(a_i, a_j, a_k, a_l) + \log t_v(y) + \gamma_y(i + \Delta_v^{1L}, j - \Delta_v^{1R}, k + \Delta_v^{2L}, l - \Delta_v^{2R})]$
$\tau_v(i,j,k,l)$
$\leftarrow \arg\max_{y} [\log e_v(a_i, a_j, a_k, a_l) + \log t_v(y) + \gamma_y(i + \Delta_v^{1L}, j - \Delta_v^{1R}, k + \Delta_v^{2L}, l - \Delta_v^{2R})]$

Note: $e_v(a_i, a_j, a_k, a_l) = e_v(a_i)$ for type(v) = $\mathrm{U_{1L}}$, $e_v(a_i, a_j, a_k, a_l) = e_v(a_j)$ for type(v) = $\mathrm{U_{1R}}$, $e_v(a_i, a_j, a_k, a_l) = e_v(a_k)$ for type(v) = $\mathrm{U_{2L}}$, $e_v(a_i, a_j, a_k, a_l) = e_v(a_l)$ for type(v) = $\mathrm{U_{2R}}$, $e_v(a_i, a_j, a_k, a_l) = 1$ for the other types except P. Also, $\Delta_v^{1L} = 1$ for type(v) = $\mathrm{U_{1L}}$, $\Delta_v^{1R} = 1$ for type(v) = $\mathrm{U_{1R}}$, $\Delta_v^{2L} = 1$ for type(v) = $\mathrm{U_{2L}}$, $\Delta_v^{2R} = 1$ for type(v) = $\mathrm{U_{2R}}$, and $\Delta_v^{1L}, \dots \Delta_v^{2R}$ are set to 0 for the other types except P. □

When the calculation terminates, we obtain $\log P(w, \hat{\pi} \mid \theta) = \gamma_1(1,n)$. If there are b BIFURCATION nonterminals and a other nonterminals, the time and space complexities of the CYK algorithm are $O(amn^4 + bn^5)$ and $O(mn^4)$, respectively. To recover the optimal derivation tree, we use the traceback variables τ. Due to limitation of the space, the full description of the traceback algorithm is omitted (see (Kato and Seki, 2006)).

3.2 Scoring Problem

As in SCFGs (Durbin et al., 1998), the scoring problem for G_s can be solved by the inside algorithm. The inside algorithm calculates the summed probabilities $\alpha_v(i,j)$ and $\alpha_y(i,j,k,l)$ of all derivation subtrees rooted at a nonterminal W_v for a subsequence $a_i \cdots a_j$ and of all derivation subtrees rooted at a nonterminal W_y for a tuple of subsequences $(a_i \cdots a_j, a_k \cdots a_l)$ respectively. The variables $\alpha_v(i, i-1)$ and $\alpha_y(i, i-1, j, j-1)$ are defined for empty sequences in a similar way to the CYK algorithm. Therefore, we can easily obtain the inside algorithm by replacing max operations with summations in the CYK algorithm. When the calculation terminates, we obtain the probability $P(w \mid \theta) = \alpha_1(1,n)$. The time and space complexities of the algorithm are identical with those of the CYK algorithm.

In order to re-estimate the probability parameters of G_s, we need the outside algorithm. The outside algorithm calculates the summed probability $\beta_v(i,j)$ of all derivation trees excluding subtrees rooted at a nonterminal W_v generating a subsequence $a_i \cdots a_j$. Also, it calculates $\beta_y(i,j,k,l)$, the summed probability of all derivation trees excluding subtrees rooted at a nonterminal W_y generating a tuple of subsequences $(a_i \cdots a_j, a_k \cdots a_l)$. In the algorithm, we will use $\mathcal{P}_v = \{y \mid W_y \to f[W_v] \in P,\ f \in F\}$. Note that calculating the outside variables β requires the inside variables α. Unlike CYK and inside algorithms, the outside algorithm recursively works its way inward. The time and space complexities of the outside algorithm are the same as those of CYK and inside algorithms. Formally, the outside algorithm is as follows:

Algorithm 2 (Outside).
Initialization:
$\beta_1(1, n) \leftarrow 1$
Iteration:
for $i \leftarrow 1$ **to** $n+1$, $j \leftarrow n$ **downto** $i-1$, $k \leftarrow j+1$ **to** $n+1$, $l \leftarrow n$ **downto** $k-1$, $v \leftarrow 1$ **to** m
do if type$(v) =$ S **and** $W_y \rightarrow C_1[W_v, W_z]$
then $\beta_v(i, j)$

$$\leftarrow \sum_{h=j}^{n} \sum_{k'=h+1}^{n+1} \sum_{l'=k'-1}^{n} \beta_y(i, h, k', l') \alpha_z(j+1, h, k', l')$$

if type$(v) =$ S **and** $W_y \rightarrow C_2[W_v, W_z]$
then $\beta_v(i, j)$

$$\leftarrow \sum_{h=1}^{i} \sum_{k'=j+1}^{n+1} \sum_{l'=k'-1}^{n} \beta_y(h, j, k', l') \alpha_z(h, i-1, k', l')$$

if type$(v) =$ S **and** $W_y \rightarrow C_3[W_v, W_z]$
then $\beta_v(i, j)$

$$\leftarrow \sum_{h=1}^{i} \sum_{k'=h-1}^{i-1} \sum_{l'=j}^{n} \beta_y(h, k', i, l') \alpha_z(h, k', j+1, l')$$

if type$(v) =$ S **and** $W_y \rightarrow C_4[W_v, W_z]$
then $\beta_v(i, j)$

$$\leftarrow \sum_{h=1}^{i} \sum_{k'=h-1}^{i-1} \sum_{l'=k'+1}^{i} \beta_y(h, k', l', j) \alpha_z(h, k', l', i-1)$$

if type$(v) \neq$ S **and** $W_y \rightarrow C_1[W_z, W_v]$
then $\beta_v(i, j, k, l)$

$$\leftarrow \sum_{h=1}^{i} \beta_y(h, j, k, l) \alpha_z(h, i-1)$$

if type$(v) \neq$ S **and** $W_y \rightarrow C_2[W_z, W_v]$
then $\beta_v(i, j, k, l)$

$$\leftarrow \sum_{h=j}^{k-1} \beta_y(i, h, k, l) \alpha_z(j+1, h)$$

if type$(v) \neq$ S **and** $W_y \rightarrow C_3[W_z, W_v]$
then $\beta_v(i, j, k, l)$

$$\leftarrow \sum_{h=j+1}^{k} \beta_y(i, j, h, l) \alpha_z(h, k-1)$$

if type$(v) \neq$ S **and** $W_y \rightarrow C_4[W_z, W_v]$
then $\beta_v(i, j, k, l)$

$$\leftarrow \sum_{h=l}^{n} \beta_y(i, j, k, h) \alpha_z(l+1, h)$$

else $\beta_v(i, j, k, l)$

$$\leftarrow \sum_{y \in \mathcal{P}_v} \beta_y(i - \Delta_y^{1L}, j + \Delta_y^{1R}, k - \Delta_y^{2L}, l + \Delta_y^{2R}) e_y(a_{i-\Delta_y^{1L}}, a_{j+\Delta_y^{1R}}, a_{k-\Delta_y^{2L}}, a_{l+\Delta_y^{2R}}) t_y(v)$$

□

3.3 Training Problem

The training problem for G_s can be solved by the EM algorithm called the inside-outside algorithm where the inside variables α and outside variables β are used to re-estimate probability parameters.

First, we consider the probability that a nonterminal W_v is used at positions i, j, k and l in a derivation of a single sequence w. If type$(v) =$ S, the probability is $\frac{1}{P(w|\theta)}\alpha_v(i, j)\beta_v(i, j)$, otherwise $\frac{1}{P(w|\theta)}\alpha_v(i, j, k, l)\beta_v(i, j, k, l)$. By summing these over all positions in the sequence, we can obtain the expected number of times that W_v is used for w as follows: for type$(v) =$ S, the expected count is

$$\frac{1}{P(w \mid \theta)} \sum_{i=1}^{n+1} \sum_{j=i-1}^{n} \alpha_v(i, j)\beta_v(i, j),$$

otherwise

$$\frac{1}{P(w \mid \theta)} \sum_{i=1}^{n+1} \sum_{j=i-1}^{n} \sum_{k=j+1}^{n+1} \sum_{l=k-1}^{n} \alpha_v(i, j, k, l) \beta_v(i, j, k, l).$$

Next, we extend these expected values from a single sequence w to multiple independent sequences $w^{(r)}$ $(1 \leq r \leq N)$. Let $\alpha^{(r)}$ and $\beta^{(r)}$ be the inside and outside variables calculated for each input sequence $w^{(r)}$. Then we can obtain the expected number of times that a nonterminal W_v is used for training sequences $w^{(r)}$ $(1 \leq r \leq N)$ by summing the above terms over all sequences: for type$(v) =$ S,

$$E(v) = \sum_{r=1}^{N} \sum_{i=1}^{n+1} \sum_{j=i-1}^{n} \frac{1}{P(w^{(r)} \mid \theta)} \alpha_v^{(r)}(i, j) \beta_v^{(r)}(i, j),$$

otherwise

$$E(v) = \sum_{r=1}^{N} \sum_{i=1}^{n+1} \sum_{j=i-1}^{n} \sum_{k=j+1}^{n+1} \sum_{l=k-1}^{n} \frac{1}{P(w^{(r)} \mid \theta)} \alpha_v^{(r)}(i, j, k, l) \beta_v^{(r)}(i, j, k, l).$$

Similarly, for a given W_y, the expected number of times that a rule $W_v \rightarrow f[W_y]$ is applied can be obtained as follows: for type(v) = S,

$$E(v \to y) = \sum_{r=1}^{N} \sum_{i=1}^{n+1} \sum_{j=i-1}^{n} \sum_{h=i-1}^{j} \frac{1}{P(w^{(r)} \mid \theta)} \beta_v^{(r)}(i,j) t_v(y) \alpha_y^{(r)}(i,h,h+1,j),$$

otherwise

$$E(v \to y) = \sum_{r=1}^{N} \sum_{i=1}^{n+1} \sum_{j=i-1}^{n} \sum_{k=j+1}^{n+1} \sum_{l=k-1}^{n} \frac{1}{P(w^{(r)} \mid \theta)} \beta_v^{(r)}(i,j,k,l) e_v(a_i,a_j,a_k,a_l) t_v(y) \alpha_y^{(r)}(i+\Delta_v^{1L}, j-\Delta_v^{1R}, k+\Delta_v^{2L}, l-\Delta_v^{2R}).$$

For a given terminal a or a pair of terminals (a,b), the expected number of times that a rule containing a (or a and b) is applied is as shown below: for type(v) = $\mathrm{U_{1L}}$,

$$E(v \to a) = \sum_{r=1}^{N} \sum_{i=1}^{n} \sum_{j=i}^{n} \sum_{k=j+1}^{n+1} \sum_{l=k-1}^{n} \frac{1}{P(w^{(r)} \mid \theta)} \delta(a_i^{(r)} = a) \beta_v^{(r)}(i,j,k,l) \alpha_v^{(r)}(i,j,k,l),$$

for type(v) = $\mathrm{U_{1R}}$,

$$E(v \to a) = \sum_{r=1}^{N} \sum_{i=1}^{n} \sum_{j=i}^{n} \sum_{k=j+1}^{n+1} \sum_{l=k-1}^{n} \frac{1}{P(w^{(r)} \mid \theta)} \delta(a_j^{(r)} = a) \beta_v^{(r)}(i,j,k,l) \alpha_v^{(r)}(i,j,k,l),$$

for type(v) = $\mathrm{U_{2L}}$,

$$E(v \to a) = \sum_{r=1}^{N} \sum_{i=1}^{n-1} \sum_{j=i-1}^{n-1} \sum_{k=j+1}^{n} \sum_{l=k}^{n} \frac{1}{P(w^{(r)} \mid \theta)} \delta(a_k^{(r)} = a) \beta_v^{(r)}(i,j,k,l) \alpha_v^{(r)}(i,j,k,l),$$

for type(v) = $\mathrm{U_{2R}}$,

$$E(v \to a) = \sum_{r=1}^{N} \sum_{i=1}^{n-1} \sum_{j=i-1}^{n-1} \sum_{k=j+1}^{n} \sum_{l=k}^{n} \frac{1}{P(w^{(r)} \mid \theta)} \delta(a_l^{(r)} = a) \beta_v^{(r)}(i,j,k,l) \alpha_v^{(r)}(i,j,k,l),$$

and for type(v) = P,

$$E(v \to ab) = \sum_{r=1}^{N} \sum_{i=1}^{n-1} \sum_{j=i}^{n-1} \sum_{k=j+1}^{n} \sum_{l=k}^{n} \frac{1}{P(w^{(r)} \mid \theta)} \delta(a_i^{(r)} = a, a_l^{(r)} = b) \beta_v^{(r)}(i,j,k,l) \alpha_v^{(r)}(i,j,k,l),$$

where $\delta(C)$ is 1 if the condition C in the parenthesis is ture, and 0 if C is false.

Now, we re-estimate probability parameters by using the above expected counts. Let $\hat{t}_v(y)$ be re-estimated transition probabilities from W_v to W_y. Also, let $\hat{e}_v(a)$ and $\hat{e}_v(a,b)$ be re-estimated emission probabilities that W_v emits a symbol a and two symbols a and b respectively. We can obtain each re-estimated probability by the following equations:

$$\hat{t}_v(y) = \frac{E(v \to y)}{E(v)}, \ \hat{e}_v(a) = \frac{E(v \to a)}{E(v)}, \quad \hat{e}_v(a,b) = \frac{E(v \to ab)}{E(v)}. \tag{3.1}$$

Note that the expected count correctly corresponding to its nonterminal type must be substituted for the above equations. In summary, the inside-outside algorithm is as follows:

Algorithm 3 (Inside-Outside)**.**

Initialization: Pick arbitrary probability parameters of the model.

Iteration: Calculate the new probability parameters using (3.1). Calculate the new log likelihood $\sum_{r=1}^{N} \log P(w^{(r)} \mid \theta)$ of the model.

Termination: Stop if the change in log likelihood is less than predefined threshold. □

4 Experimental Results

4.1 Data for Experiments

The dataset for experiments was taken from an RNA family database called "Rfam" (version 7.0) (Griffiths-Jones et al., 2003) which is a database of multiple sequence alignment and covariance models (Eddy and Durbin, 1994) representing non-coding RNA families. We selected three viral RNA families with pseudoknot annotations named Corona_pk_3 (Corona), HDV_ribozyme (HDV) and Tombus_3_IV (Tombus) (see Table 2). Corona_pk_3 has a simple pseudoknotted structure, whereas HDV_ribozyme and Tombus_3_IV have more complicated structures with pseudoknot.

Table 2: Three RNA families from Rfam ver. 7.0

Family	Range of length	# of annotated sequences	# of test sequences
Corona_pk_3	62–64	14	10
HDV_ribozyme	87–91	15	10
Tombus_3_IV	89–92	18	12

Table 3: Prediction results

Family	Precision [%]			Recall [%]			CPU time [sec]		
	Average	Min	Max	Average	Min	Max	Average	Min	Max
Corona_pk_3	99.4	94.4	100.0	99.4	94.4	100.0	27.8	26.0	30.4
HDV_ribozyme	100.0	100.0	100.0	100.0	100.0	100.0	252.1	219.0	278.4
Tombus_3_IV	100.0	100.0	100.0	100.0	100.0	100.0	244.8	215.2	257.5

4.2 Implementation

We specified a particular SMCFG G_s by utilizing secondary structure annotation of each family. Rules were determined by considering consensus secondary structure. Probability parameters were estimated in a few selected sequences by the simplest pseudocounting method known as the Laplace's rule (Durbin et al., 1998): to add one extra count to the true counts for each base configuration observed in a few selected sequences. Note that the inside-outside algorithm was not used in the experiments. The other sequences in the alignment were used as the test sequences for prediction (see Table 2). We implemented the CYK algorithm with traceback in ANSI C on a machine with Intel Pentium D CPU 2.80 GHz and 2.00 GB RAM. Straightforward implementation gives rise to a serious problem of lack of memory space due to the higher order dynamic programming matrix (remember that the space complexity of the CYK algorithm is $O(mn^4)$). The dynamic programming matrix in our specified model is sparse, and therefore, we successfully implemented the matrix as a hash table storing only nonzero probability values (equivalently, finite values of the logarithm of probabilities).

4.3 Tests

We tested prediction accuracy by calculating precision and recall (sensitivity), which are the ratio of the number of correct base pairs predicted by the algorithm to the total number of predicted base pairs, and the ratio of the number of correct base pairs predicted by the algorithm to the total number of base pairs specified by the trusted annotation, respectively. The results are shown in Table 3. A nearly correct prediction (94.4% precision and recall) for Corona_pk_3 is shown in Figure 2 where underlined base pairs agree with trusted ones. The secondary structures predicted by our algorithm agree very well with the trusted structures.

4.4 Comparison with PSTAG

We compared the prediction accuracy of our SMCFG algorithm with that of PSTAG algorithm (Matsui et al., 2005) (see Table 4). PSTAGs, as we have mentioned before, are proposed for modeling pairwise alignment of RNA sequences with pseudoknots and assign a probability to each alignment of TAG derivation trees. PSTAG algorithm, based on dynamic programming, calculates the most likely alignment for the pair of TAG derivation trees where one of them is in the form of an unfolded sequence and the other is a TAG derivation tree for known structure. SMCFG method shows better performance in accuracy than PSTAG method in the same test sets.

5 Conclusion

In this paper, we have proposed a probabilistic model named SMCFG, and designed a polynomial time parsing and a parameter estimation algorithm for SMCFG. Moreover, we have demonstrated computational experiments of RNA secondary structure prediction with pseudoknots using SMCFG parsing algorithm, which show good performance in accuracy.

Acknowledgments

This work is supported in part by Grant-in-Aid for Scientific Research from Japan Society for the Promotion of Science (JSPS). We also wish to thank JSPS Research Fellowships for Young Scientists for their generous financial assistance. The authors thank Dr. Yoshiaki Takata for his useful

Corona_pk3 (EMBL accession #: X51325.1)

[Trusted structure in Rfam]

```
CUAGUCUUAUACACAAUGGUAAGCCAGUGGUAGUAAAGGUAUAAGAAAUUUGCUACUAUGUUA
    [[[[[[[[              ((( ((((((( ]]]]]]]]  ))))))) )))
```

[Prediction by SMCFG]

```
CUAGUCUUAUACACAAUGGUAAGCCAGUGGUAGUAAAGGUAUAAGAAAUUUGCUACUAUGUUA
    [[[[[[[[              ((((((((((  ]]]]]]]]   ))))))))))
```

Figure 2: Comparison of a prediction result with a trusted structure in Rfam

Table 4: Comparison between SMCFG and PSTAG

Model	Average precision [%]			Average recall [%]		
	Corona	HDV	Tombus	Corona	HDV	Tombus
SMCFG	99.4	100.0	100.0	99.4	100.0	100.0
PSTAG	95.5	95.6	97.4	94.6	94.1	97.4

comments on implementation of high dimensional dynamic programming.

References

Tatsuya Akutsu. 2000. Dynamic programming algorithms for RNA secondary structure prediction with pseudoknots. *Discrete Applied Mathematics*, 104:45–62.

Michael Brown and Charles Wilson. 1996. RNA pseudoknot modeling using intersections of stochastic context free grammars with applications to database search. *Proc. Pacific Symposium on Biocomputing*, 109–125.

Liming Cai, Russell L. Malmberg, and Yunzhou Wu. 2003. Stochastic modeling of RNA pseudoknotted structures: a grammatical approach. *Bioinformatics*, 19(1):i66–i73.

Richard Durbin, Sean R. Eddy, Anders Krogh, and Graeme Mitchison. 1998. *Biological Sequence Analysis*, Cambridge University Press.

Sean R. Eddy and Richard Durbin. 1994. RNA sequence analysis using covariance models. *Nuc. Acids Res.*, 22(11):2079–2088.

Sam Griffiths-Jones, Alex Bateman, Mhairi Marshall, Ajay Khanna, and Sean R. Eddy. 2003. Rfam: an RNA family database. *Nuc. Acids Res.*, 31(1):439–441.

Tadao Kasami, Hiroyuki Seki, and Mamoru Fujii. 1988. Generalized context-free grammar and multiple context-free grammar. *IEICE Trans. Inf. & Syst.*, J71-D(5):758–765 (in Japanese).

Yuki Kato, Hiroyuki Seki, and Tadao Kasami. 2005. On the generative power of grammars for RNA secondary structure. *IEICE Trans. Inf. & Syst.*, E88-D(1):53–64.

Yuki Kato and Hiroyuki Seki. 2006. Stochastic multiple context-free grammar for RNA pseudoknot modeling. *NAIST Info. Sci. Tech. Rep. (NAIST-IS-TR2006002)*.

Hiroshi Matsui, Kengo Sato, and Yasubumi Sakakibara. 2005. Pair stochastic tree adjoining grammars for aligning and predicting pseudoknot RNA structures. *Bioinformatics*, 21(11):2611–2617.

Elena Rivas and Sean R. Eddy. 1999. A dynamic programming algorithm for RNA structure prediction including pseudoknots. *J. Mol. Biol.*, 285:2053–2068.

Elena Rivas and Sean R. Eddy. 2000. The language of RNA: A formal grammar that includes pseudoknots. *Bioinformatics*, 16(4):334–340.

Yasubumi Sakakibara, Michael Brown, Richard Hughey, I. Saira Mian, Kimmen Sjölander, Rebecca C. Underwood, and David Haussler. 1994. Stochastic context-free grammars for tRNA modeling. *Nuc. Acids Res.*, 22:5112–5120.

Hiroyuki Seki, Takashi Matsumura, Mamoru Fujii, and Tadao Kasami. 1991. On multiple context-free grammars. *Theor. Comput. Sci.*, 88:191–229.

Yasuo Uemura, Aki Hasegawa, Satoshi Kobayashi, and Takashi Yokomori. 1999. Tree adjoining grammars for RNA structure prediction. *Theor. Comput. Sci.*, 210:277–303.

K. Vijay-Shanker, David J. Weir, and Aravind K. Joshi. 1987. Characterizing structural descriptions produced by various grammatical formalisms. *Proc. 25th Annual Meeting of Association for Computational Linguistics (ACL87)*, 104–111.

Binding of Anaphors in LTAG

Neville Ryant
Department of Linguistics
619 Williams Hall
University of Pennsylvania
Philadelphia, PA, 19104-6305
nryant@ling.upenn.edu

Tatjana Scheffler
Department of Linguistics
619 Williams Hall
University of Pennsylvania
Philadelphia, PA, 19104-6305
tatjana@ling.upenn.edu

Abstract

This paper presents an LTAG account for binding of reflexives and reciprocals in English. For these anaphors, a multi-component lexical entry is proposed, whose first component is a degenerate NP-tree that adjoins into the anaphor's binder. This establishes the local structural relationship needed to ensure coreference and agreement. The analysis also allows a parallel treatment of reflexives and reciprocals, which is desirable because their behavior is very similar.

In order to account for non-local binding phenomena, as in raising and ECM cases, we employ flexible composition, constrained by a subject intervention constraint between the two components of the anaphor's lexical entry. Finally, the paper discusses further data such as extraction and picture-NP examples.

1 Introduction

Binding Theory (Büring, 2005; Reuland and Everaert, 2001) is an issue at the interface of syntax and semantics which has previously been avoided in the LTAG literature. While LTAGs were initially concerned only with the syntax of natural languages, recent accounts of semantic computation in the LTAG framework (Kallmeyer and Joshi, 2003; Kallmeyer and Romero, 2004) allow us now to tackle interface phenomena. An appropriate formulation of Binding Theory (BT) is needed to explain the pattern exhibited in (1–3).

(1) John$_i$ likes himself$_i$.

(2) * John$_i$ likes herself$_i$.

(3) * Himself$_i$ likes himself$_i$ / John$_i$.

Due to the incredible complexity of the data in question, we will focus here on English reflexives (*himself, herself*) and reciprocals (*each other*), typically subsumed under Condition A (Chomsky, 1981).

This paper proposes a new two-component lexical entry for reflexive pronouns that takes care of the syntactic and semantic dependencies involved in binding (agreement and coreference). In this approach, different binding options (e.g., in a ditransitive sentence) follow from different derivations.

In section 3, we show how our analysis extends straightforwardly to reciprocals. Section 4 presents the extension of our account to anaphors with nonlocal antecedents, such as the experiencers of raising verbs, and ECM subjects. Further issues, including extraction, are discussed in section 5. Section 6 concludes.

2 Basic Anaphor Binding

In traditional accounts, binding is defined representationally: an antecedent binds an anaphor iff they are are coindexed and in a certain structural relationship. In an LTAG, binding cannot be viewed in this way as the notion of coindexation is foreign to the formalism. An LTAG analysis can therefore not be a mere translation of a previous account.

Although the phenomenon is very complex, the basic properties of binding are quite well understood. Binding of an anaphor by an antecedent consists of coreference and agreement between the two items. Furthermore, it is well known that binding of English anaphors is an asymmetrical, local, structural relationship. The asymmetry of binding can be easily observed in examples (1)

Proceedings of the 8th International Workshop on Tree Adjoining Grammar and Related Formalisms, pages 65–72,
Sydney, July 2006.

versus (3). Locality is reflected by the fact that (1) is grammatical, but not (4).

(4) * John$_i$ knows that Mary likes himself$_i$.

Finally, the binding relationship is known to be structural because the positions of binder and anaphor play a crucial role. This is discussed in more detail below.

2.1 Lexical Entry

The domain of locality that LTAG provides enables us to encode a local structural relationship, such as the one between the anaphor and its antecedent, very directly. We understand binding as a lexical requirement of the anaphor: that it must be bound. Thus, we propose the lexical entry in Figure 1 for reflexives. It is a multicomponent set whose second component is the anaphor. The first component is a degenerate auxiliary tree which adjoins into the elementary tree of the antecedent.

In LTAG, elementary trees encode both syntax and semantics. Thus, the two components of binding, coreference and agreement, are simultaneously guaranteed by the coindexations between the feature structures of binder and anaphor. Furthermore, since the derivation must be tree-local, locality is also ensured. A c-command constraint between the two components accounts for the asymmetry between the antecedent and anaphor as shown in examples (1) and (3). This constraint is checked when the two components are composed into an elementary tree (by tree-locality).

2.2 Example Derivation

Consider (5), where *himself* has two possible antecedents, *John* and *Bill*. Our analysis derives both readings, given a standard tree inventory as in Figure 2.

(5) John$_i$ showed Bill$_j$ himself$_{i/j}$.

Sentence (5) is syntactically ambiguous under this analysis, since two different derivations lead to distinct readings. This seems to reflect our intuitions about this sentence well, although it contrasts with the traditional vew of BT, where the coindexation between binder and anaphor is part of the syntactic structure for the sentence, and thus no ambiguity arises.

2.3 Flexible Composition

Tree-locality requires the first component of *himself* to adjoin into a higher NP substitution node.

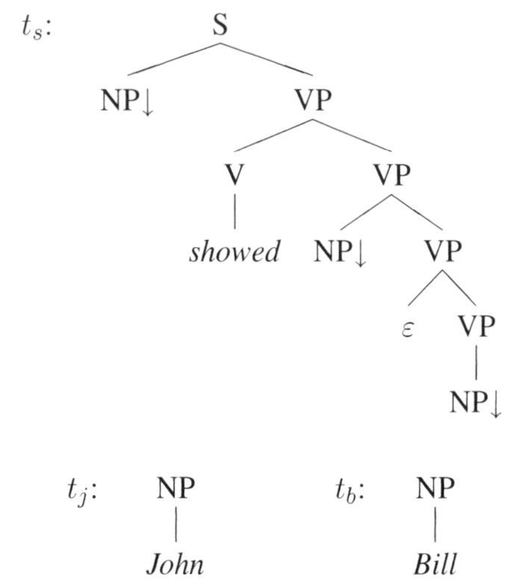

Figure 2: Tree inventory.

However, adjunction into substitution nodes is generally disallowed. Adjunction of the first component of *himself* into the root node of the *John*-tree t_j or the *Bill*-tree t_b is, however, not tree-local. Therefore, we employ flexible composition (Joshi et al., 2003) to compose t_j with the first component of t_h (t_h^1), yielding a derived multicomponent set. Composition of t_h with t_s is then tree-local. This yields the reading where *John* is the antecedent of *himself.*

Alternatively, t_b composes with t_h first, which derives the other reading. The two derivation trees representing these readings are shown in Figure 3.

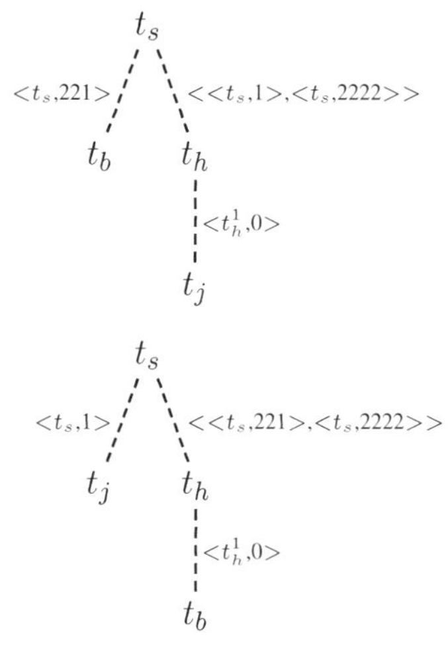

Figure 3: Derivation trees for "John showed Bill himself."

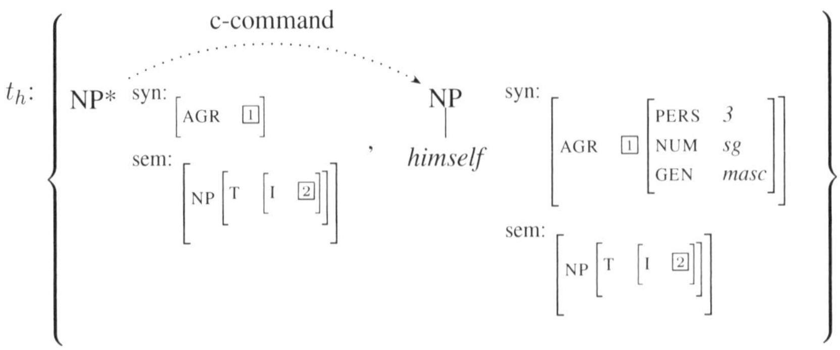

Figure 1: Lexical entry for *himself.*

2.4 Advantages

The different binding options (e.g., in double-object sentences) follow directly from the derivation and do not have to be hardcoded. Furthermore, the reflexive itself is responsible for agreement and coreference with its antecedent.

2.5 Alternative Analysis

There is at least one obvious alternative analysis for BT in LTAG. In this case, features are employed instead of a multicomponent set to derive the binding relationship. Features on each verbal elementary tree would encode whether an argument is an anaphor, and if so, what it is bound to. Just like in our analysis introduced above, a certain locality necessary for binding can be ensured under this approach. However, this approach is very stipulative. It is merely an accident that agreement and coreference go hand in hand: Two separate feature equations have to ensure agreement between the binder and anaphor, and coreference between them. Furthermore, a number of verbal trees is added; and the reflexive itself becomes syntactically and semanticially vacuous.

3 Reciprocals

Another advantage of the proposed account is that it allows an analogous treatment of reciprocals like *each other* in (6).

(6) [John and Mary]$_i$ like each other$_i$.

This is desirable given that the syntactic behavior of reciprocals resembles reflexives. Semantically, though, reciprocals are very complex (Dimitriadis, 2000). The meaning of "each other" roughly corresponds to its parts, "each", and "other". That is, "John and Mary love each other" means something like "Of John and Mary, each loves the other".[1]

These properties are neatly accounted for with our analysis of *each other* that is syntactically analogous to *himself*, but contributes additional operators in the semantics[2]. The proposed lexical entry is spelled out in Figure 4.

The fact that *each other* contributes two distinct quantifiers corresponds directly to its syntactic analysis as a two-part multicomponent set.

4 Nonlocal Antecedents

The discussion of anaphoric pronoun binding discussed in the previous section demonstrated how certain locality (7) and configurational restrictions (8) on anaphoric pronouns follow from TAG's constrained mechanisms of structural composition coupled with a multicomponent analysis of reflex-

[1] It is sometimes claimed that "long-distance" reciprocals require non-local adjunction of "each":

(i) The boxers thought they would defeat each other.
✓ each # each

The LTAG analysis proposed here does not allow this. This may constitute independent evidence for Dimitriadis' (2000) analysis of reciprocals in which "each" is not as high as it seems in these kinds of examples.

[2] The exact semantics of *each other* is a matter of ongoing discussion. We assume for simplicity that *each other* corresponds to *each+the other*, as reflected in the lexical entry.

[3] $\sqsubseteq_A$= "is an atomic part of".

In the absence of a complete analysis of plural semantics in LTAG, we assume here that plural noun phrases like "John and Mary" or "the boys" contribute at least a group (G) variable. This variable is used by certain collective predicates, for example in "The boys surrounded the castle." It corresponds to the plural individual contributed by the NP.

The semantics given here predicts strongly distributive "each other". Some adjustment is needed to account for lesser forms of distributivity.

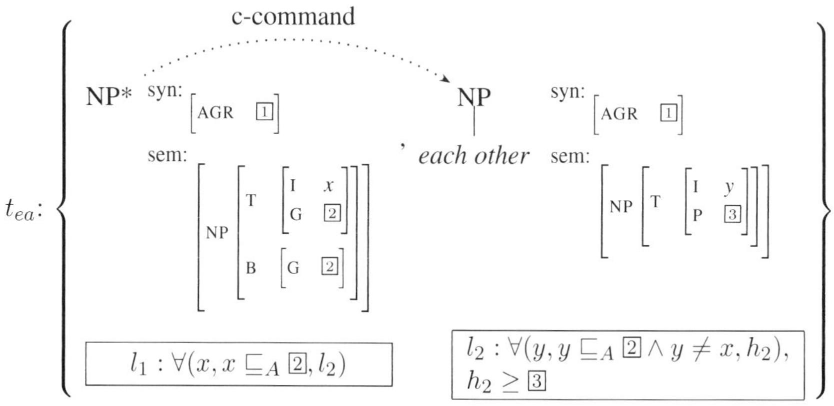

Figure 4: Lexical entry for *each other*.[3]

ives and reciprocals.

(7) a. John$_i$ likes himself$_i$.
b. *John$_i$ thinks that Mary believes that Kate likes himself$_i$.

(8) a. John believes Mary$_i$ to like herself$_i$.
b. *John believes herself$_i$ to like Mary$_i$.

A significant problem with this analysis as stands, however, is that it works too well, denying the grammaticality of certain raising (9) and ECM constructions (10) and constructions in which the anaphor is embedded within a subject (11). Under current assumptions, the antecedent-anaphor dependency must be established within an elementary tree (by adjunction of a single multicomponent set). However, for both of these constructions the anaphor and its antecedent lie in different elementary trees. In (9) the auxiliary tree of the raising verb *seems* contains no local argument for the degenerate NP* component to combine with. In (10) *himself* occurs as an argument of *like* while its antecedent occurs in another elementary tree, *believe*. In each case, generating the examples requires that we relax some of our current assumptions.

(9) John$_i$ seems to himself$_i$ to be a decent guy.

(10) John$_i$ believes himself$_i$ to be a decent guy.

(11) John$_i$ thought that the pictures of himself$_i$ were wonderful.

4.1 Raising

We see from (9) that anaphors can occur as experiencer arguments of raising verbs providing they are c-commanded by a possible antecedent. Though predicted to be ungrammatical under the current proposal, (9) can be generated if we relax the requirement that the two parts of the multicomponent set of the anaphor attach to the same elementary tree. This relaxation could take the form of simply allowing non-local adjunction for specific classes of multicomponent sets, those with a degenerate components. Alternately, we retain the restriction to tree-local MC-TAG but achieve nonlocality through more extensive use of flexible composition, already adopted for independent reasons.

Under a flexible composition analysis (Figure 6), the *John*-tree composes with the degenerate NP* member of the reflexive set as before. This yields a derived multicomponent set consisting of one derived part, *John*, and one underived part, *himself*. The *seems*-tree then composes with the *himself* component of the reflexive set, yielding a derived set (Figure 5) containing the components *John* and *seems to himself*. Finally, this derived multicomponent set combines with the *like*-tree, the *John* component substituting into the open NP slot and the *seems to himself* component adjoining at VP.

4.2 ECM

In ECM constructions such as (10) the anaphor appears as the subject of the embedded *to be a decent guy*-tree while its antecedent appears as subject of the matrix *believes*-tree. A derivation for this sentence under our account is shown in Figure 7. As before, the *John-tree* first composes with the degenerate NP* component of the reflexive tree, followed by the the substitution of the *himself*-tree

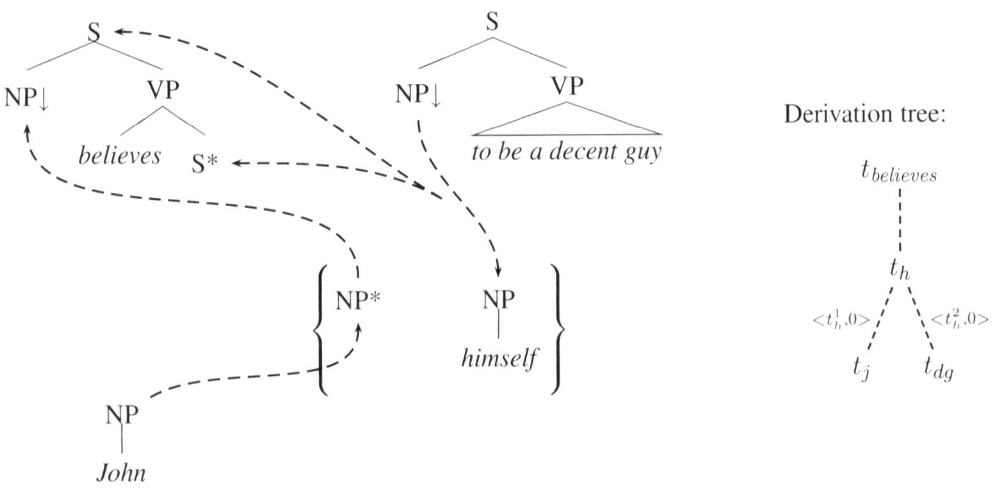

Figure 7: Derivation of "John believes himself to be a decent guy."

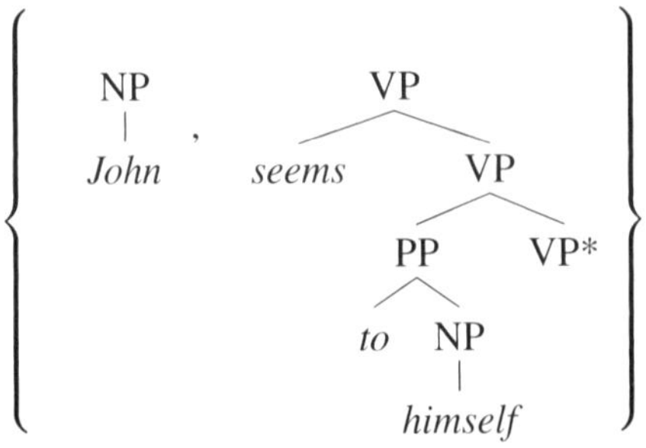

Figure 5: Derived multicomponent set for (9).

into the *to be a decent guy*-tree, yielding the derived multicomponent set containing *John* and *believes himself*, which locally composes with the *to be a decent guy*-tree.

4.3 Subject Embedding

Anaphors contained within embedded subjects[4] (12) cause the binding domain to be minimally expanded. Again, it is transparent that these cases can be derived successfully from the lexical entry in Figure 1 and repeated use of flexible composition.

(12) a. The men$_i$ knew that pictures of each other$_i$ were on sale.

b. The men$_i$ felt that the pictures of themselves$_i$ were horrid.

c. The men$_i$ knew that each other$_i$'s pictures were on sale.

[4]The absence of nonlocal binding of reflexive subjects (e.g. *John thinks that himself is grand.*) is assumed to derive from an inability of reflexives to take nominative case.

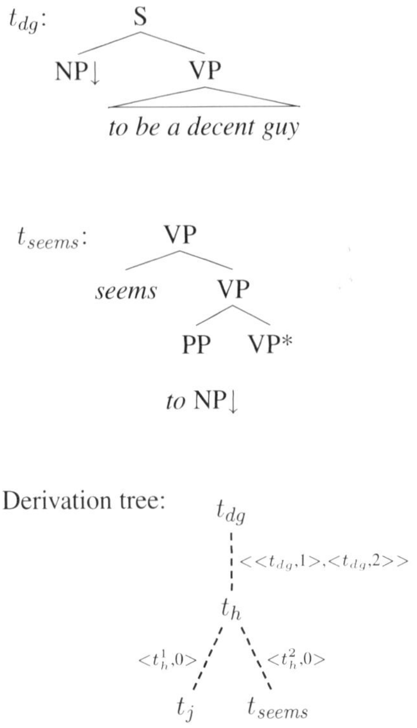

Figure 6: Derivation of "John seems to himself to be a decent guy."

4.4 Constraints on Flexible Composition

The use of flexible composition with tree-local MC-TAG is very powerful, thus able to account for the non-local binding in (9), (10), and (12). However, it is too powerful if unconstrained as it will also generate (13). It is necessary to constrain the derivation such that in the derived tree no subject node intervenes between the antecedent and anaphor (Chomsky's Subject Intervention Constraint). This is obtained by strengthening the link between NP and *himself* in the lexical entry s.t. when the two trees connected by the link are adjoined, a requirement that NP* c-command *himself* and no subject NP intervenes between the two (c-commanding *himself* and c-commanded by NP*) is checked. This constraint formalizes the descriptive account given in the linguistic literature. Note that a similar account may be active in other places in the grammar as well, due to the pervasiveness of left-edge phenomena (see section 5.4).

Computationally, this constraint can be checked as soon as the multicomponent set which contains it attaches into another elementary tree. C-command as well as subject intervention cannot be disturbed by later operations on the outer tree, if they are valid at the time of composition.

(13) * John$_i$ believes me to like himself$_i$.

5 Further Issues

5.1 Exempt Pronouns

As it currently stands, the proposal follows heavily in the footsteps of traditional configurational approaches to BT. As such, it mirrors the more traditional BT of Chomsky in it's inability to license such examples as (17b), where the antecedent does not c-command the anaphor and (14) and (15), where binding is possible despite presence of an intervening subject along the c-command path.

(14) a. I spoke to [John and Bill]$_i$ about each other$_i$.

b. Pictures of myself$_i$ frighten me$_i$.

c. John$_i$'s greatest problem is a fear of himself$_i$.

(15) [John and Mary]$_i$ are letting the honey drip on each other$_i$'s feet.

(16) Clones of each other annoy the children.

The examples in (14) can be accommodated by having the prepositions appearing before the arguments be surface case markers rather than real prepositions (as suggested in (Jackendoff, 1972)). Even so, (15) and (16) remain and seem to present an intractable problem for an LTAG account, as well as traditional accounts of English binding phenomena. This may in fact be the case and prove firm support for claims by numerous authors (Pollard and Sag, 1994; Postal, 1971; Kuroda, 1965) that at least part of the data subsumed under BT (the "exempt pronouns") is governed by pragmatic constraints such as point-of-view rather than purely structural constraints. In fact, the LTAG analysis proposed here is a relatively clean structural account of English binding data. The (un)availability of a derivation for certain examples may thus point to their classification into "exempt" and regular anaphora. These considerations are left for further work.

5.2 Extraction

A potential problem for the proposed analysis is presented by extraction phenomena, as in wh-movement or topicalization. Extraction of a phrase containing an anaphor, whether topicalization or (17) or wh-movement (18), does not induce a Condition A violation. The current proposal predicts the grammaticality of (17a) and (18a) given that in each case the reflexive is locally c-commanded by its antecedent. However, in (17b) and (18b) the reflexive fails to be c-commanded by its antecedent, hence these examples are predicted to be ungrammatical although they are clearly acceptable.

(17) a. John$_i$ saw himself$_i$.

b. Himself$_i$ John saw t$_i$.

(18) a. John$_i$ liked the color pictures of himself$_i$.

b. [Which pictures of himself$_i$] did John$_i$ like ε?

A classical solution to these facts involves reconstruction of the A$'$-moved element to its original site for the purposes of binding. Clearly, syntactic reconstruction is untenable in LTAG. However, it is possible to emulate it through an entry akin to that in Figure 8, which is capable of deriving the topicalization examples in (17). The first component is the extracted reflexive

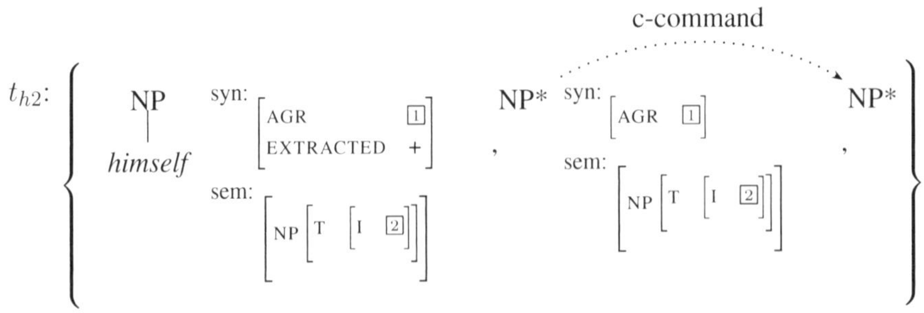

Figure 8: Lexical entry for extracted reflexive *himself*.

(A′-moved constituents are marked by extraction-features (XTAG Group, 2001)), the second component is the binder, and the third component is the position that the reflexive has been extracted from. The requirement that the antecedent locally c-command the trace of movement has the effect of emulating reconstruction.

Note, furthermore, that even if some manner of reconstruction operation were to be implemented in LTAG, we are faced with the reality of cases such as (19), which demonstrate that extraction of an element can alter its set of possible binders. GB accounts (van Riemsdijk and Williams, 1986; Clark, 1982) have explained the opposition in (19) by allowing partial reconstruction to an intermediate trace from which the matrix subject is an accessible binder of the anaphor. The LTAG analysis of wh-movement, though, neither exploits intermediate traces nor allows transformational movement over domains larger than an elementary tree, meaning that such intermediate traces are simply unavailable to us.

(19) a. *Marsha$_i$ thought that I painted a picture of herself$_i$.
b. [Which pictures of herself$_i$] did Marsha$_i$ think that I painted ε?

Instead, we suggest that Spec,IP subjects of clauses are able to bind into Spec,CP of the same clause as proposed by Reinhart (1991) and Frank and Kroch (1995). Rather than being a disadvantage, though, this seems to be a strength, predicting as it does that (20) is bad where reconstruction to a posited intermediate trace would predict acceptability.

(20) *[Which pictures of himself$_i$] did Mary think that John$_i$ believed that Sally wanted?

Future work should attempt to determine the correct form of this lexical entry as well as whether or not it is possible to collapse it with the previously proposed Figure 8.

5.3 Conditions B,C

It is often assumed that the analyses for anaphors and regular pronouns should be related, because of a certain complementarity in distribution: While anaphors must be locally bound, pronouns must be locally free. In English, however, this complementarity is not absolute (cf. 21–22). Furthermore, a negative locality constraint seems to be discouraged by the LTAG framework. This suggests that the analysis of pronouns is independent of our account of anaphors. We leave pronouns, as well as r-expressions (*Mary, the man*) for further work.

(21) John$_i$ pulled the blanket over him$_i$ / himself$_i$.

(22) a. They$_i$ saw each other$_i$'s friends.
b. They$_i$ saw their$_i$ friends.

5.4 Importance of the Left Edge

Examination of language exposes the left edge to be special with regards to certain phenomena. In Binding Theory, this is revealed in the guise of a Subject Intervention Constraint. Case assignment represents a similar case. We see that verbs can assign accusative case to objects, and subjects of the next lowest clause (ECM), but no further. Ideally, a new analysis of left-edge effects would clarify the relationship between the two components of the lexical entry proposed above.

5.5 Inherent Reflexives

English has a small number of inherently reflexive verbs, such as *behave*:

(23) John behaves himself.[5]

Note that this verb requires its object to be a reflexive pronoun which is coreferent with its subject:

[5]We would like to thank one anonymous reviewer for bringing this example to our attention.

(24) * John behaves her.

We conclude from this that *behave* has a specific lexical constraint, namely that its object should be [+ reflexive]. Since there can be no other binder for this reflexive pronoun, it must be bound by the subject of the sentence.

6 Conclusion

In conclusion, we have presented an account of the syntax and semantics of anaphoric expressions that covers basic binding as well as raising, ECM, and extraction data. Our analysis employs a multicomponent lexical entry whose first component corresponds to the anaphor's binder, thus establishing a local relationship between antecedent and anaphor. A structural constraint that links the two components accounts for the basic asymmetry that is observed in the binding of reflexives and reciprocals in English.

7 Acknowledgements

We would like to thank the members of the XTAG group, as well as the CIS 630 class of Spring 2006 at Penn for comments and discussion.

References

Büring, Daniel. 2005. *Binding Theory.* Cambridge: Cambridge University Press.

Chomsky, Noam. 1981. *Lectures on Government and Binding.* Dordrecht: Foris.

Clark, Robin. 1982. Scope assignment and modification. *Linguistic Inquiry 23*: 1-28.

Copestake, Ann, Dan Flickinger, Ivan A. Sag, and Carl Pollard. 1999. Minimal Recursion Semantics: An introduction. Manuscript, Stanford University

Dalrymple, M., M. Kanazawa, Y. Kim, S.A. Mehombo, and S. Peters. 1998. Reciprocal expressions and the concept of reciprocity. *Linguistics and Philosophy* 21:159–210

Dimitriadis, Alexis. 2000. *Syntactic locality and tree adjoining grammar: Grammatical, acquisition, and processing perspectives.* Doctoral Dissertation, University of Pennsylvania.

Frank, Robert. 1992. *Beyond Identity: Topics in Pronominal and Reciprocal Anaphora.* Doctoral Dissertation, University of Pennsylvania.

Frank, Robert and Anthony Kroch. 1995. Generalized transformations and the theory of grammar. *Studia Linguistica 49(2)*: 103-151.

Jackendoff, Ray. 1972. *Semantic Interpretation in Generative Grammar.* Cambridge, MA: MIT Press

Joshi, Aravind K., Laura Kallmeyer, and Maribel Romero. 2003. Flexible Composition in LTAG: Quantifier Scope and Inverse Linking. In *Proceedings of the International Workshop on Compositional Semantics.* Tilburg, The Netherlands

Joshi, Aravind K. and K. Vijay-Shanker. 1999. Compositional Semantics with Lexicalized Tree-Adjoining Grammar (LTAG): How Much Underspecification is Necessary? In H.C. Blunt and E.G.C. Thijsse, editors. *Proceedings of the Third International Workshop on Computational Semantics (IWCS-3)*, pp. 131-145. Tilburg, The Netherlands

Kallmeyer, Laura and Aravind K. Joshi. 2003. Factoring predicate argument and scope semantics: Underspecified semantics with LTAG. *Research on Language and Computation* 1:3–58

Kallmeyer, Laura and Maribel Romero. 2004. LTAG semantics with semantic unification. In *Proceedings of TAG+7.* Vancouver, Canada

Kuroda, S.Y.. 1965. *Generative Gramamtical Studies in the Japanese Language.* MIT: PhD. dissertation.

Pollard, Carl and Ivan Sag. 1994. *Head-driven Phrase Structure Grammar.* Chicago, Il: University of Chicago Press.

Postal, Paul. 1971. *Crossover Phenomena.* New York: Holt.

Reinhart, Tanya. 1991. Definite NP anaphora and c-command domains. *Linguistic Inquiry 12(4)*: 605-635.

Reuland, Eric and Martin Everaert. 2001. Deconstructing Binding. In M. Baltin and C. Collins, editors. *The Handbook of Contemporary Syntactic Theory.* Oxford

van Riemsdijk, Henk and Edwin Williams. 1986. *Introduction to the Theory of Grammar.* Cambridge, MA: MIT Press

XTAG Group. 2001. A Lexicalized Tree Adjoining Grammar for English. IRCS Technical Report, University of Pennsylvania

Quantifier Scope in German: An MCTAG Analysis

Laura Kallmeyer
University of Tübingen
Collaborative Research Center 441
lk@sfs.uni-tuebingen.de

Maribel Romero
University of Pennsylvania
Department of Linguistics
romero@ling.upenn.edu

Abstract

Relative quantifier scope in German depends, in contrast to English, very much on word order. The scope possibilities of a quantifier are determined by its surface position, its base position and the type of the quantifier. In this paper we propose a multicomponent analysis for German quantifiers computing the scope of the quantifier, in particular its minimal nuclear scope, depending on the syntactic configuration it occurs in.

1 Introduction: The data

(1) A man loves every woman.
$\exists > \forall, \forall > \exists$

In English, in sentences with several quantificational NPs, in principle all scope orders are possible independent from word order. (1) for example has two readings, the $\exists > \forall$ reading and the inverse scope $\forall > \exists$ reading. This is different in German where word order is crucial for scope possibilities.

(2) a. Viele Männer haben mindestens eine
many men_{nom} have at least one
Frau hofiert.
woman_{acc} flattered.
'Many men have flattered at least one woman.'
$viele > eine$, $^{*}eine > viele$

b. Mindestens eine Frau haben viele
at least one woman_{acc} have many
Männer hofiert.
men_{nom} flattered.
'Many men have flattered at least one woman.'
$viele > eine$, $eine > viele$

In German, for quantifiers in base order, the surface order determines scope.[1] (2a) has only the scope order $viele > eine$ corresponding to surface order, that is, the inverse order $eine > viele$ is not available. In contrast to this, if the word order differs from the base order, ambiguities are possible. (2b) for example displays both scope orders, $viele > eine$ and $eine > viele$.

In the literature, the following generalizations have been noticed for German: For two quantifiers Q_1, Q_2 with Q_1 preceding Q_2 in the surface order of a sentence, the scope order $Q_1 > Q_2$ is always possible. Furthermore, the inverse reading $Q_2 > Q_1$ is possible if

(Q1) Q_1 has been moved so that Q_2 c-commands the trace of Q_1 ((Frey, 1993)), and

(Q2) Q_1 is a weak quantifier (e.g., *irgendein* 'some', *viele* 'many', cardinals) ((Lechner, 1998)).

Evidence for (Q2) –and further evidence for (Q1)– are the examples in (3)–(4). In (3), the (a)-example is in base order and thus has only surface scope, but moving the weak quantifier over the dative quantifier in the (b)-version results in scope ambiguity. This contrasts with (4). In (4), the (a)-version with base order has only surface scope, as before. But now we move the strong quantifier over the dative quantifier, and this does not yield ambiguity. That is, even though the dative quantifier c-commands the trace of the moved quantifier both in (3b) and in (4b), only when the moved

[1]Throughout the paper we assume an unmarked intonation. With a different intonation, other scope orders become available because of the change in information structure. But this lies outside the scope of this paper.
The base order depends on the verb; in most cases it is Subject - (Indirect Object) - Direct Object.

Proceedings of the 8th International Workshop on Tree Adjoining Grammar and Related Formalisms, pages 73–80,
Sydney, July 2006.

element is a weak quantifier do we obtain scope ambiguity.

(3) a. ... dass er [fast jedem Verlag]
... that he almost every publisher
[mindestens ein Gedicht] anbot.
at least one poem proposed_to.
'... that he proposed some poem to almost every publisher.'
$jedem > ein$, $^{*}ein > jedem$

b. ... dass er [mindestens ein Gedicht]$_1$
... that he some poem
[fast jedem Verlag] t_1 anbot.
almost every publisher proposed_to.
$jedem > ein$, $ein > jedem$

(4) a. ... dass er [mindestens einem Verleger]
... that he at least one publisher
[fast jedes Gedicht] anbot.
almost every poem proposed_to
'... that he proposed almost every poem to at least one publisher.'
$jedes > einem$, $^{*}einem > jedes$

b. ... dass er [fast jedes Gedicht]$_1$
... that he almost every poem
[mindestens einem Verleger] t_1
at least one publisher
anbot.
proposed_to.
$jedes > einem$, $^{*}einem > jedes$

(Kiss, 2000) claims that if two quantifiers have been moved such that among themselves they remain in base order, inverse scope is not possible between them. Because of this, he argues for a non-movement-based theory of German quantifier scope. However, Kiss' claim is not true as can be seen with the example (5) from (Frey, 1993):

(5) a. weil der freundliche Museumsdirektor
because the friendly curator$_{nom}$
[mindestens einer Frau]$_1$
at least one woman$_{dat}$
[fast jedes Gemälde]$_2$ gezeigt hat
almost every painting$_{acc}$ has shown
'because the friendly curator has shown almost every painting to at least one woman'
$Q_1 > Q_2$, $^{*}Q_2 > Q_1$

b. weil [mindestens einer Frau]$_1$ [fast jedes Gemälde]$_2$ der freundliche Museumsdirektor t_1 t_2 gezeigt hat
$Q_1 > Q_2$, $Q_2 > Q_1$

In both cases, (5a) and (5b), the two quantifiers are in base order. According to Kiss there should be, contrary to fact, no ambiguity in (5b). The difference between the two is that in (5a) the quantifiers are in base position while in (5b) both of them have been scrambled with the result that Q_2 c-commands the trace of Q_1. We assume with (Frey, 1993) that this is why the inverse scope order becomes available.

We therefore stick to the above-mentioned generalizations (Q1) and (Q2) and try to capture them in our LTAG analysis. This means that, in order to capture (Q1), we need a syntactic analysis of German NPs that takes into account movement and base positions.

2 English quantifier scope in LTAG

We use the LTAG semantics framework from (Kallmeyer and Romero, 2004; Kallmeyer and Romero, 2005). Semantic computation is done on the derivation tree. Each elementary tree is linked to a semantic representation (a set of Ty2 formulas and scope constraints). Ty2 formulas (Gallin, 1975) are typed λ-terms with individuals and situations as basic types. The scope constraints of the form $x \geq y$ specify subordination relations between Ty2 expressions. In other words, $x \geq y$ indicates that y is a component of x.

A semantic representation is equipped with a semantic feature structure description. Semantic computation consists of certain feature value identifications between mother and daughter nodes in the derivation tree. The feature structure descriptions do not encode the semantic expressions one is interested in. They only encode their contributions to functional applications by restricting the argument slots of certain predicates in the semantic representations: They state which elements are contributed as possible arguments for other semantic expressions and which arguments need to be filled. They thereby simulate lambda abstraction and functional application. A sample feature for this simulation of functional application is the feature I that serves to pass the individual contributed by an NP to the predicate taking it as an argument. Besides this functional application aspects, the feature structure descriptions also contain features that determine the scope semantics, i.e., features specifying boundaries for the scope of different operators. Sample features for scope are MINS and MAXS encoding the minimal and maximal scope of attaching quantifiers.

Features can be global (feature GLOBAL, here abbreviated with GL) or they can be linked to specific node positions (features S, VP, ...). The latter are divided into top (T) and bottom (B) features. The equations of top and bottom features linked to specific node positions in the elementary trees are parallel to the syntactic unifications in FTAG (Vijay-Shanker and Joshi, 1988). The global features that are not linked to specific nodes can be passed from mothers to daughters and vice versa in the derivation tree.

(6) Everybody laughs.

As a sample derivation let us sketch the analysis of quantificational NPs in English from (Kallmeyer, 2005). Fig. 1 shows the LTAG analysis of (6). More precisely, it shows the derivation tree with the semantic representations and feature structure descriptions of *laughs* and *everybody* as node labels. The feature identifications are depicted by dotted lines. The semantic representation of the NP *everybody* contains the generalized quantifier every that binds the variable x and that has a restrictive scope $\boxed{4}$ and a nuclear scope $\boxed{5}$. Furthermore, it contains the proposition person(x) that must be part of the restrictive scope (constraint $\boxed{4} \geq l_3$). Concerning functional application, the NP provides the individual variable x in the global feature I as a possible argument for the verb predicate laugh.

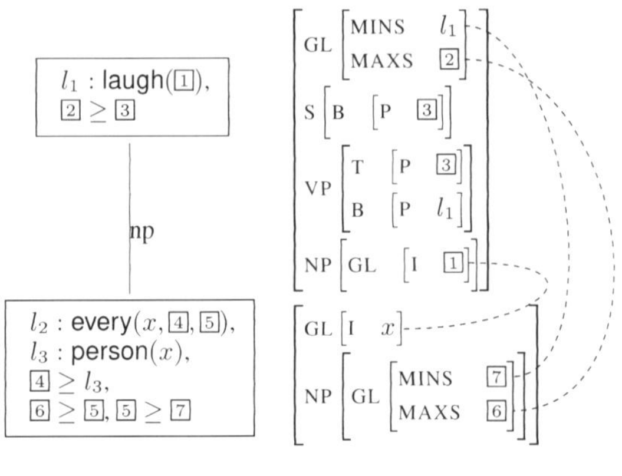

Figure 1: LTAG analysis of (6) *everybody laughs*

Quantificational NPs in English can in principle scope freely; an analysis of quantifier scope must guarantee only two things: 1. the proposition corresponding to the predicate to which a quantifier attaches must be in its nuclear scope, and 2. a quantifier cannot scope higher than the first finite clause. (Kallmeyer and Romero, 2005) model this by defining a scope window delimited by some maximal scope (global feature MAXS and some minimal scope (global feature MINS) for a quantifier. In Fig. 1, the nuclear scope $\boxed{5}$ of the quantifier is delimited by the maximal and minimal scope boundaries provided by the verb the quantifier attaches to (constraints $\boxed{6} \geq \boxed{5}, \boxed{5} \geq \boxed{7}$). The feature identifications in Fig. 1 lead then to the constraints $\boxed{2} \geq \boxed{5}, \boxed{5} \geq l_1$.

Applying the assignments following from the feature identifications and building the union of the semantic representations leads to the underspecified representation (7):

(7)
l_1 : laugh(x),
l_2 : every$(x, \boxed{4}, \boxed{5})$, l_3 : person(x)
$\boxed{2} \geq l_1$,
$\boxed{4} \geq l_3, \boxed{2} \geq \boxed{5}, \boxed{5} \geq l_1$

As the only possible disambiguation, we obtain $\boxed{2} \rightarrow l_2, \boxed{4} \rightarrow l_3, \boxed{5} \rightarrow l_1$ which yields the semantics every$(x$, person(x), laugh$(x))$.

3 Syntax of German quantificational NPs

Recall that, according to criterion (Q1), not only the position of an NP but also -if the NP was moved- the position of its trace are crucial for the scope properties. In order to capture this, our analysis needs to take into account movements (scrambling, topicalization, etc.) of NPs including traces at base positions. We therefore cannot adopt the analyses proposed by (Rambow, 1994) in V-TAG where the slot for the NP is generated at the surface position and there is only one initial tree for NPs, whether moved or not.[2]

(8) a. ... dass jeder/irgendeiner
... that everybody/someone
irgendein Buch/jedes Buch liest
some book/every book reads
'... that everybody/someone reads some book/every book'
SUBJ > DOBJ

b. ... dass [jedes Buch]$_1$ irgendeiner t_1 liest
... that every book someone reads
DOBJ > SUBJ

[2]To avoid misunderstandings, let us emphasize that in LTAG, there is no movement outside the lexicon. Therefore, either the NP or the slot of the NP must be localized together with the corresponding trace inside one elementary structure. This elementary structure can be a tree or, in MCTAG, a set of trees.

c. ... dass [irgendein Buch]$_1$ jeder t_1 liest
... that some book everybody reads
SUBJ > DOBJ, DOBJ > SUBJ

To illustrate our analysis, in this and the following section, we restrict ourselves to the sentences in (8). For the syntax, we adopt a multicomponent analysis for NPs that have been moved consisting of an auxiliary tree for the moved material and an initial tree for the trace. Our analysis can be adopted using V-TAG (Rambow, 1994) or something in the style of SN-MCTAG (Kallmeyer, 2005). Note that, in order to account for scrambling, we need some type of MCTAG anyway, independent from quantifier scope.

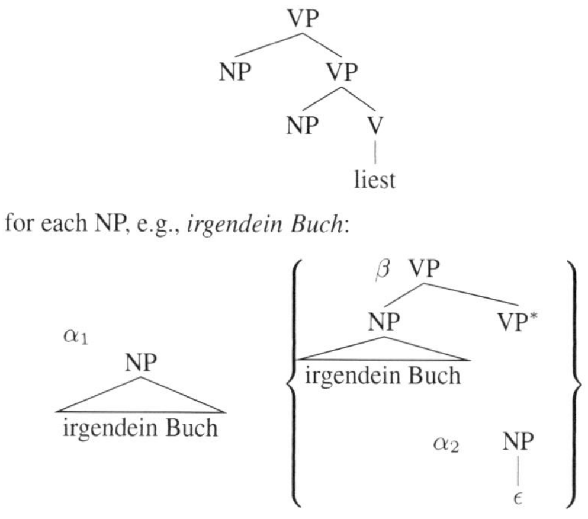

Figure 2: Elementary trees for (8)

The elementary trees for (8) are in Fig. 2. α_1 is used for NPs in base position, while the set $\{\alpha_2, \beta\}$ is used for moved NPs. We assume that, if possible, α_1 is used. I.e., starting from the verb, trees of type α_1 are substituted to its left as long as possible. $\{\alpha_2, \beta\}$ sets are used when α_1 could not possibly yield the desired surface word order. Fig. 3 shows a derivation of a sentence of type (8a) (with no movement). Fig. 4 shows the derivation of (8b). ((8c) is similar to (8b).)

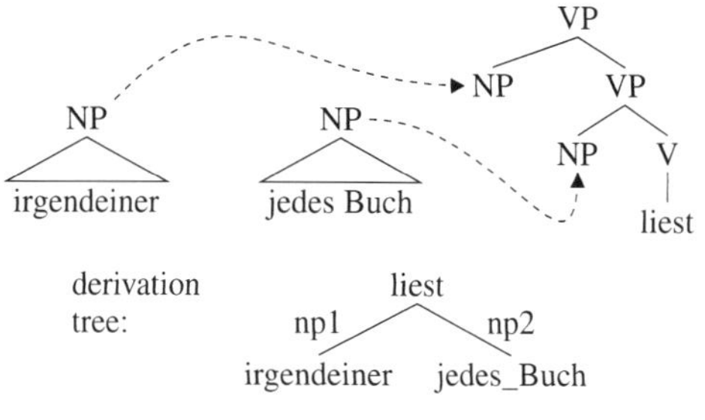

Figure 3: Derivation for (8a)

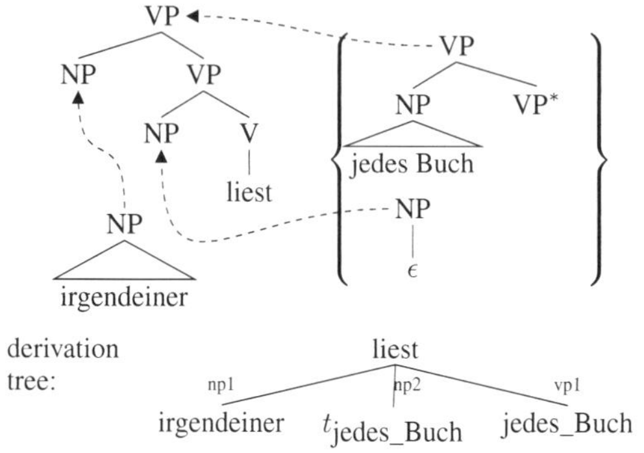

Figure 4: Derivation for (8b)

Note that, in the derivation trees, each node represents a single elementary tree, not a set of elementary trees from the grammar. An MCTAG derivation tree as defined in (Weir, 1988) with each node representing a set is available only for tree-local or set-local MCTAG, not for the MCTAG variants we need (SN-MCTAG or V-TAG). Therefore we take the undelying TAG derivation tree as the derivation structure semantics will be computed on.

4 Semantics of German quantificational NPs

Because of the generalizations above, the following must be guaranteed: i) Strong quantifiers scope over the next element in surface order (take scope where they attach).[3] ii) The minimal nuclear scope of a weak quantifier is the closest "unmoved" element following its base position. Consequently, we need different lexical entries for weak and strong quantifiers.

We characterize the scope possibilities of a quantifier in terms of its minimal scope. Consider first the verb tree for *liest* 'read' in Fig. 5. In contrast to English, MINS is not a global feature since, depending on the position where the quantifier attaches, its minimal scope is different. In the *liest*-tree, MINS appears in the feature structure of different nodes, with each MINS value determined in the following way: the value of MINS at the NP_2 address is the label l_1 of the verb; the value of MINS at the NP_1 address depends on what is attached at NP_2 (see variables $\boxed{4}$ and $\boxed{0}$, which in this case will be identified with each other); and the value of MINS at the top VP address depends on what is attached at NP_1 ($\boxed{5}$).

[3]But see section 5, where more complex examples show that this generalization needs to be refined.

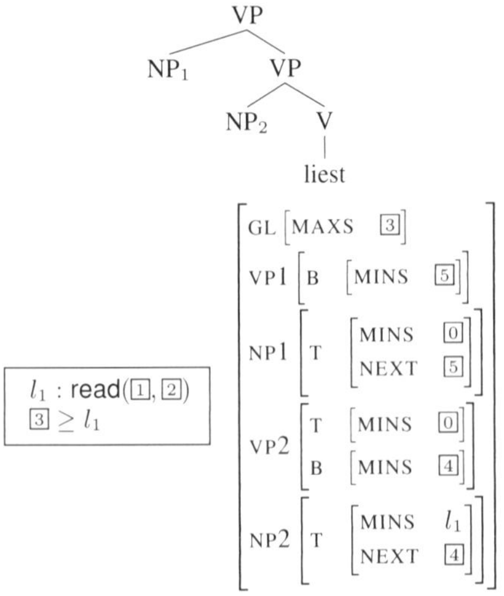

Figure 5: Semantics for *liest*

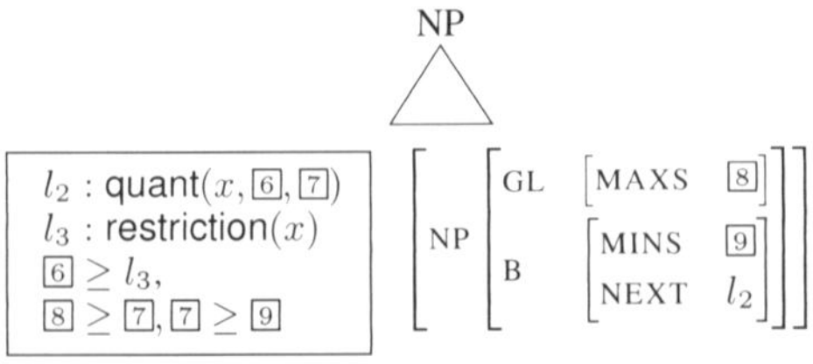

Figure 6: Quantifiers in base position

The idea is that, when an NP (part) is attached at a given address, the label of that NP is the new MINS to be passed up the verb tree; when a trace (part) is attached instead, the MINS of the verb address is passed up unmodified. This feature passing is technically achieved by articulating the VP spine with the feature MINS (much like the use of the P feature in English for adverbial scope in Kallmeyer and Romero, 2005), and by adding the feature NEXT for passing between NP substitution nodes (since substitution nodes do not have T and B features that allow feature percolations between mothers and daughters).

The lexical entries for the three types of quantifiers we must distinguish (non-moved quantifiers, weak moved quantifiers and strong moved quantifiers) are shown in Fig. 6–8. Quantificational NPs that have not been moved (Fig. 6) receive their MINS boundary (variable $\boxed{9}$) simply from their attachment position. Weak and strong quantifiers that have been moved differ in how their own MINS is determined: Strong quantifiers (see Fig. 7) get their MINS from the VP node they attach to, i.e., from their surface position (see variable $\boxed{13}$). In contrast to this, weak quantifiers (see Fig. 8) get their MINS from the base order position, i.e., from their trace position (see variable $\boxed{18}$).

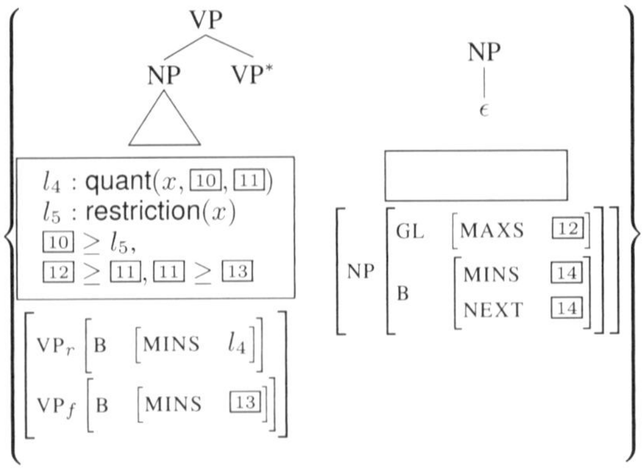

Figure 7: Strong quantifiers that have been moved

As sample analyses consider Fig. 9 and Fig. 10 showing the analyses of (8b) and (8c) where the accusative object quantifier has been moved. (The features of the internal VP node are omitted since they are not relevant here.) In the first case, it is a strong quantifier, in the second case a weak quantifier. For Fig. 9, we obtain the identifications $\boxed{12} = l_1 = \boxed{4} = \boxed{8}, \boxed{5} = l_2 = \boxed{11}$ (depicted with dotted lines). Consequently, the only scope order is wide scope of *jedes Buch*: $l_4 > \boxed{10} \geq l_2 > \boxed{7} \geq l_1$. In Fig. 10, we obtain $\boxed{11} = l_1 = \boxed{4} = \boxed{8}, \boxed{5} = l_2$ which leads to the scope constraints $l_2 > \boxed{7} \geq l_1$ and $l_4 > \boxed{10} \geq l_1$. Consequently, we have an underspecified representation allowing for both scope orders.

The analysis proposed in this section has demonstrated that some features –in this case MINS– are global in some languages (e.g. English) while being local in other languages (e.g. German). We take this as further evidence that the distinction between the two kinds of features, advocated in (Kallmeyer and Romero, 2005) is em-

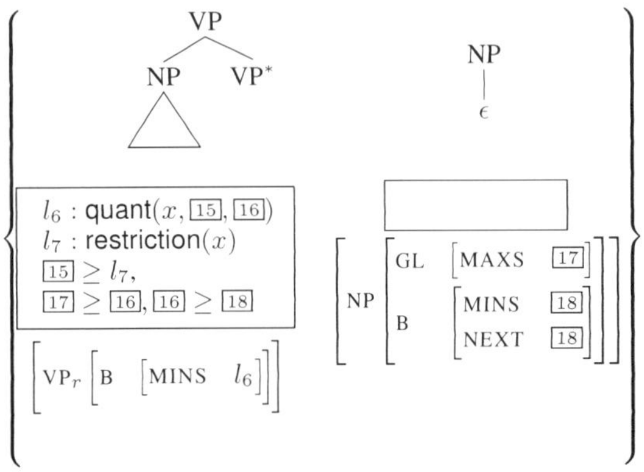

Figure 8: Weak quantifiers that have been moved

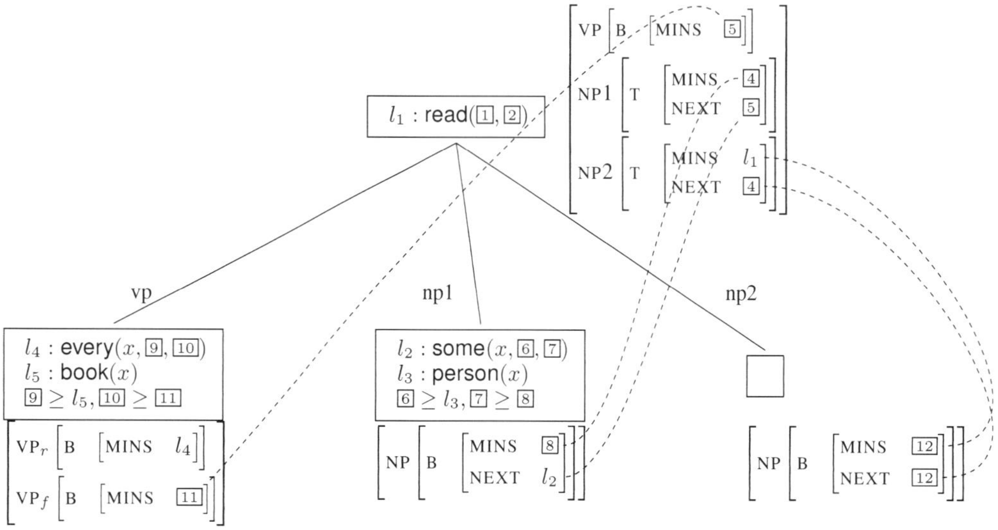

Figure 9: Analysis of *dass [jedes Buch]$_1$ irgendeiner t_1 liest*

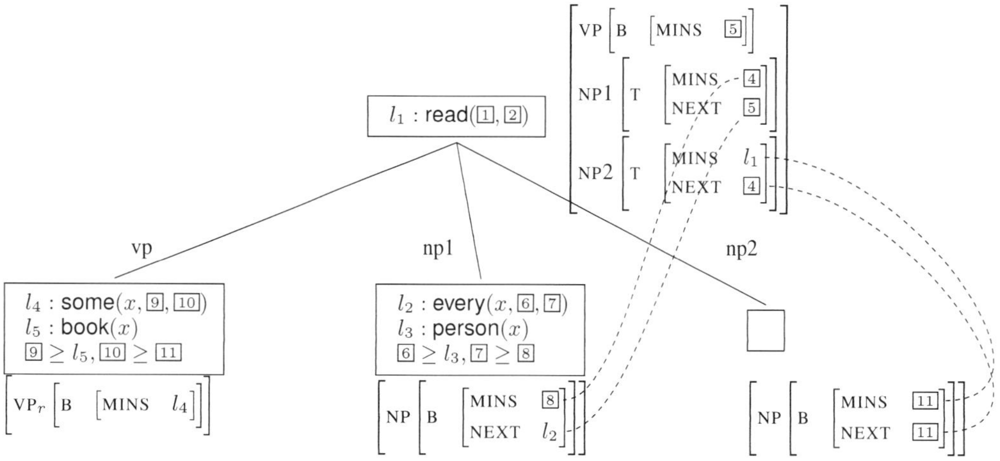

Figure 10: Semantic analysis of *dass [irgendein Buch]$_1$ jeder t_1 liest*

pirically justified.

5 Long-distance scrambling and quantifier scope

So far we have examined cases where local scrambling affects quantifier scope order. In this section, we will demonstrate how our analysis carries over to long-distance scrambling.

(9) ... dass [irgendein Lied]$_1$ Maria
... that some song$_{acc}$ Maria$_{nom}$
[fast jedem]$_2$ [t_1 zu singen]
almost everybody$_{dat}$ to sing
versprochen hat
promised has
'that Maria has promised almost everybody to sing some song'
$Q_1 > Q_2$, $Q_2 > Q_1$

In (9) both scope orders are possible.

Fig. 11 shows the syntactic analysis for (9). According to the treatment of weak quantifiers proposed above, the minimal nuclear scope of *irgendein Lied* is determined by the position of the trace; it is therefore the proposition of *singen*. As for *fast jedem*, its minimal nuclear scope is required to include the proposition of *versprochen hat*. Nothing else is required, and consequently *irgendein* can scope over or under *fast jedem*.

A problematic configuration that can occur with scrambling concerns cases where two weak quantifiers Q_2 and Q_3 have been moved with a third quantifier Q_1 preceding them where Q_1 is either a strong quantifier or a weak quantifier in base position. Then Q_1 has scope over Q_2 and Q_3 but the scope order between Q_2 and Q_3 is unspecified. An example is (10):

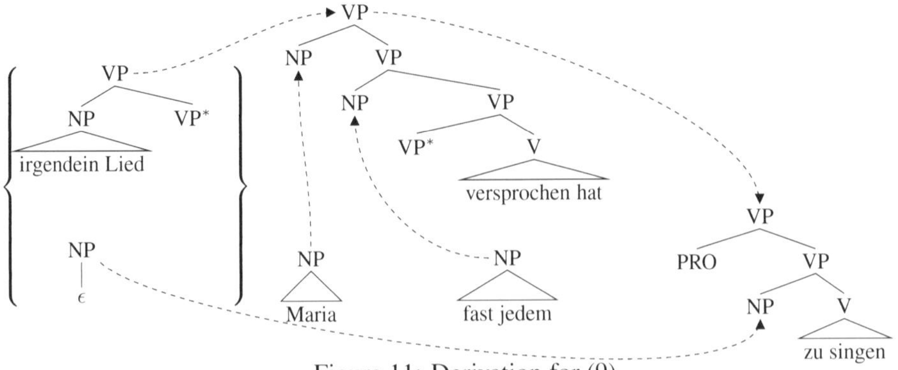

Figure 11: Derivation for (9)

(10) ... dass [jeder Mitarbeiter]$_1$
... that [every colleague]
[vielen Besuchern]$_2$ [mindestens ein Bild]$_3$
[many visitors]$_{dat}$ [at least one picture]$_{acc}$
gerne [t_2 t_3 zu zeigen] bereit war
with pleasure to show willing was
'... that every colleague is happy to show at least one picture to many visitors.'
$Q_1 > Q_2 > Q_3$, $Q_1 > Q_3 > Q_2$

The syntactic derivation is shown in Fig. 12. Such examples are problematic for our analysis: our approach predicts that Q_2 and Q_3 have the same minimal scope, namely the *zeigen* proposition, and that the minimal scope of Q_1 is the quantifier it precedes, namely Q_2. But nothing in the analysis prevents Q_3 from having scope over Q_1, contrary to fact.

This example indicates that the generalization (i) in section 4 -that the minimal scope of a strong quantifier is the proposition of the next quantifier in surface order- needs to be refined. More accurately, the minimal scope of a strong quantifier is the highest proposition following in surface order. We propose to model this using the feature NEXT also in VP nodes. Here NEXT stands for the maximal scope of all quantifiers following in surface order. An attaching weak quantifier has to do two things: 1. equate the current NEXT feature with the new MINS that provides the minimal scope for higher strong quantifiers, and 2. state that NEXT is its own maximal scope. The corresponding revised lexical entry for moved weak quantifiers is shown in Fig. 13.

Fig. 14 shows the way the minimal scope for the unmoved quantifier in (10) is computed from combining the auxiliary trees of the moved weak quantifiers with *bereit*. (The adverb is left aside.) In the tree of a verb and also in the auxiliary trees of moved strong quantifiers, an additional feature

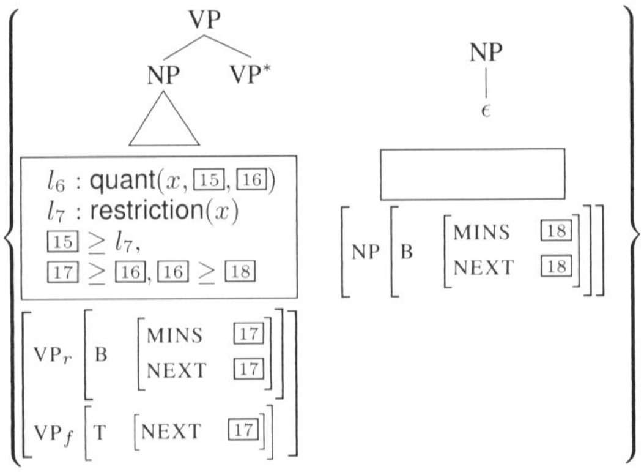

Figure 13: Moved weak quantifiers (revised)

NEXT is added, linked to the bottom of VP nodes. The value of this feature is required to be higher than the value of the bottom MINS at that position. Whenever a moved strong quantifier adjoins, nothing happens with this NEXT feature. Moved weak quantifiers take the NEXT feature as their maximal scope and pass it as the new MINS. This is how in Fig. 14, the final MINS at the top of the root of the leftmost moved weak quantifier contains all moved quantifiers and is passed to the NP node as new MINS limit. A (weak or strong) quantifier substituting into the NP slot takes this new MINS as its minimal scope. Consequently, it scopes over both moved weak quantifiers.

6 Conclusion

It has been shown that, although quantifier scope is usually read off surface word order in German, ambiguities can arise from movement of weak quantifiers. We have developed an MCTAG analysis using traces. In our approach, the scope possibilities of a quantifier are characterized in terms of its minimal scope. In contrast to English, MINS in German is not global but depends on the po-

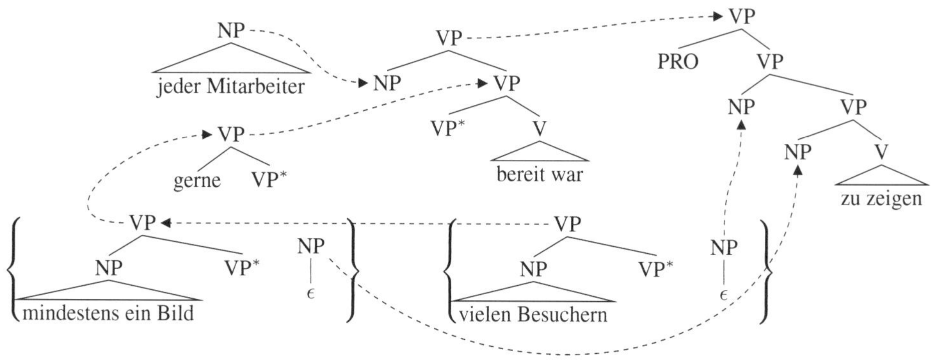

Figure 12: Derivation for (10)

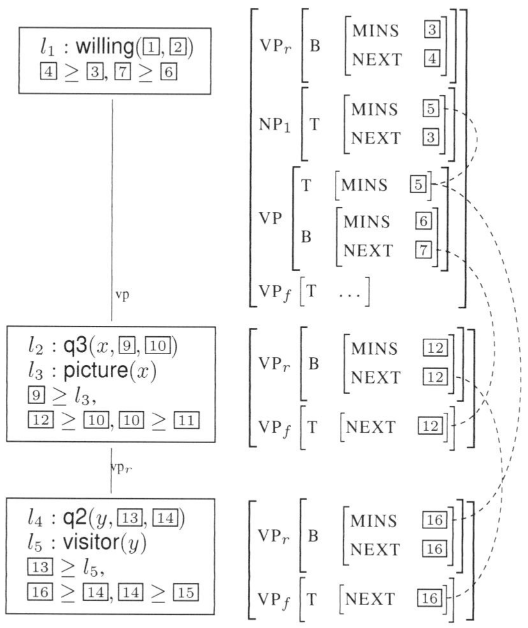

q2 = many, q3 = at_least_one

Figure 14: Attaching the moved weak quantifiers in (10)

sition of the quantifier. The minimal scope of weak and strong quantifiers is determined differently: The minimal scope of a moved weak quantifier depends on its trace; the minimal scope of a moved strong quantifier depends on the position of the moved material.

Acknowledgments

For fruitful discussions of the work presented in this paper, we want to thank Timm Lichte and Wolfgang Maier. Furthermore, we are grateful to three anonymous reviewers for helpful comments.

References

Tilman Becker, Aravind K. Joshi, and Owen Rambow. 1991. Long-distance scrambling and tree adjoining grammars. In *Proceedings of ACL-Europe*.

Werner Frey. 1993. *Syntaktische Bedingungen für die semantische Interpretation: Über Bindung, implizite Argumente und Skopus*. studia grammatica. Akademie Verlag, Berlin.

Daniel Gallin. 1975. *Intensional and Higher-Order Modal Logic with Applications to Montague Semantics*. North Holland mathematics studies 19. North-Holland Publ. Co., Amsterdam.

Laura Kallmeyer and Maribel Romero. 2004. LTAG Semantics with Semantic Unification. In *Proceedings of TAG+7*, pages 155–162, Vancouver.

Laura Kallmeyer and Maribel Romero. 2005. Scope and Situation Binding in LTAG using Semantic Unification. Submitted to *Research on Language and Computation*. 57 pages., December.

Laura Kallmeyer. 2005. Tree-local multicomponent tree adjoining grammars with shared nodes. *Computational Linguistics*, 31(2):187–225.

Tibor Kiss. 2000. Configurational and Relational Scope Determination in German. In Tibor Kiss and Detmar Meurers, editors, *Constraint-Based Approaches to Germanic Syntax*, pages 141–176. CSLI.

Winfried Lechner. 1998. Two Kinds of Reconstruction. *Studia Linguistica*, 52(3):276–310.

Owen Rambow. 1994. *Formal and Computational Aspects of Natural Language Syntax*. Ph.D. thesis, University of Pennsylvania.

K. Vijay-Shanker and Aravind K. Joshi. 1988. Feature structures based tree adjoining grammar. In *Proceedings of COLING*, pages 714–719, Budapest.

David J. Weir. 1988. *Characterizing mildly context-sensitive grammar formalisms*. Ph.D. thesis, University of Pennsylvania.

Licensing German Negative Polarity Items in LTAG

Timm Lichte
University of Tübingen
Collaborative Research Center 441
timm.lichte@uni-tuebingen.de

Laura Kallmeyer
University of Tübingen
Collaborative Research Center 441
lk@sfs.uni-tuebingen.de

Abstract

Our paper aims at capturing the distribution of negative polarity items (NPIs) within lexicalized Tree Adjoining Grammar (LTAG). The condition under which an NPI can occur in a sentence is for it to be in the scope of a negation with no quantifiers scopally intervening. We model this restriction within a recent framework for LTAG semantics based on semantic unification. The proposed analysis provides features that signal the presence of a negation in the semantics and that specify its scope. We extend our analysis to modelling the interaction of NPI licensing and neg raising constructions.

1 Introduction

1.1 Negative Polarity Items

NPIs are distributionally restricted to linguistic environments that exhibit a trigger for negativity (see e.g., Ladusaw, 1980; Linebarger, 1987; Zwarts, 1997). More precisely, NPIs seek to be placed within the scope of a negative operator at the level of semantics. We say that the NPI has to be *licensed* by an exponent of negativity, the *licenser*. Examples in German can be found in (1)–(5) (the NPI is underlined while the licenser is in bold face).

(1) a. Hans war **nicht** <u>sonderlich</u> zufrieden mit seiner Arbeit
Hans was not very happy with his work
b. *Hans war <u>sonderlich</u> zufrieden mit seiner Arbeit

(2) a. Er hat es **nicht** <u>wahrhaben</u> wollen
he has it not accept_to_be_true want
('He did not want to accept it to be true')
b. *Er hat es <u>wahrhaben</u> wollen.

(3) a. Es <u>schert</u> ihn **nicht**
it bothers him not
('He does not give a damn about it')
b. *Es <u>schert</u> ihn.

(4) a. Du <u>brauchst</u> diese Bücher **nicht** zu lesen
you need these books not to read
('You need not read these books')
b. *Du <u>brauchst</u> diese Bücher zu lesen.

(5) a. **Niemand** hat <u>auch nur einen Cent</u> gespendet.
nobody has even one cent donated
('Nobody has donated any cent at all.')
b. *<u>Auch nur einen Cent</u> hat **niemand** gespendet.

We will mainly be concerned with verbal NPIs such as *wahrhaben wollen* ('accept to be true') and *scheren* ('to give a damn about'). Another group of NPIs we will pay closer attention to are *minimizers*, here exemplified by *auch nur ein Cent* ('any Cent at all'). They are quantifiers denoting the bottom line of a scale and therefore show affinity with negation due to pragmatic reasons. Furthermore, minimizers as quantifiers are subject to particular position restrictions with respect to negation (see next section). A group of NPIs we will leave aside in this paper, however, is that of adjectival NPIs such as *sonderlich* ('very').

1.2 NPI Licensers

Various items and constructions can license NPIs. Besides the more obvious ones such as *not*, *nobody* and *never*, also (among others) *few*, re-

Proceedings of the 8th International Workshop on Tree Adjoining Grammar and Related Formalisms, pages 81–90,
Sydney, July 2006.

strictors of universal quantifiers, conditional antecendents and questions can license at least some of the NPIs. There has been much controversy about what the characterizing logical property of licensers is. One proposal is based on the notion of *downward entailment* (DE, Ladusaw, 1980), which holds for operators whose truth value is persistent over specification. While the DE property can be found in most of the licensers, there are some, such as questions, where it is hard to detect (see van der Wouden, 1997 for an overview).[1]

In our proposal we don't make use of DE as an NPI licensing criterion. Instead we only require the negation operator ($\neg$) in the semantic representation as licensing feature. We thereby restrict ourselves to triggers of 'classic' negation; we go even further and only implement *non-contrastive* negation. We use this term after Jacobs (1982) where *non-contrastive negation* (NCN) and *contrastive negation* (CN) are examined for German. They differ in that sentences with CN can be extended by a but-phrase (*Sondern*-Phrase) while adding a but-phrase to sentences with NCN gives odd results. Put differently, CN focuses on parts of a sentence while NCN does not.[2] Whether CN or NCN is available, is indicated by intonation and position of the negative element. However, ambiguous indications are possible. In our analysis, we leave aside intonation and stick to unambiguous NCN as far as possible.

1.3 Semantic Scope and Range of Licensing

It is not sufficient for an NPI to just co-occur with a licenser in the same sentence; it has to be in the licenser's scope. Furthermore, additional constraints have been proposed in the literature. One of the most extensively discussed requires the NPI to be c-commanded by the licenser on surface structure (*c-command constraint*, Ladusaw, 1980). As Hoeksema (2000) points out, the c-command constraint is too restrictive when applied to languages with a considerably freer word order than English, e.g. Dutch and German (see (4) for an example that does not respect the c-command constraint). He also points out that the need for the c-command constraint only arises from capturing the distribution of minimizers. All other NPIs obey a simple scope constraint in terms of Linebarger's immediate scope constraint (ISC, Linebarger, 1980; Linebarger, 1987), namely that no other propositional operators (i.e. "logical elements" that are capable of entering into scope ambiguities) may intervene between the licenser and the NPI on LF.

While the ISC seems to hold for quantifiers, quantificational adverbs and operators that conjoin propositions such as *because*, there are in fact some operators that may scopally intervene. Among them are non-quantificational adverbs, minimizers and modals, as in (6):

(6) Peter hat **keinen** Finger rühren müssen.
Peter has no finger move must
('Peter didn't need to lift a finger.')

In (6), the negation always has wide scope with respect to the modal *müssen* (must), hence *müssen* intervenes between negation and NPI, but still the sentence is grammatical.

Thus, our criterion for an NPI to be licensed is 1. to be in the scope of a negation that is semantically interpreted in the same finite clause, and 2. not to allow regular quantifiers to scopally intervene between negation and NPI. In this paper, we will also refer to these criterions as *immediate scope*.[3] Minimizers seem to add a third criterion, namely that the licenser has to syntactically c-command the minimizer.

Independently from the ISC, one has to keep in mind that negative elements in German are able to cancel each other out, that is to constitute double negation. We will come back to this briefly in section 3.

1.4 Neg Raising Constructions

We extend our analysis to so-called *neg raising* (NR, cf. Horn, 1978) constructions because there are interesting interactions between NPI licensing and neg raising.

[1] Giannakidou (1997) therefore proposes the idea of *non-veridicality* as being the basic logical property of NPI-licensers - eventually facing the problem of being less restrictive than required.

[2] If CN is available NPIs can only be licensed in the part focused by CN.

[3] Note that with this approach, one negation can even license several NPIs as in (i):

(i) **Kein** Schüler hat jemals in den Ferien
no pupil has ever in the holidays
sonderlich viel gelernt.
particularly much learned
('No pupil has ever learned very much during the holidays.')

An example of a NR-verb is *glauben* ('believe') in (7).

(7) Hans glaubt **nicht**, dass Peter kommt.
Hans believes not that Peter comes
('Hans does not believe that Peter is coming.')

The negation can either take scope at its surface position, i.e., scope over *glauben*, or it can scope within the embedded sentence. Hence, two interpretations are generally available: (a) $\neg\mathsf{believe}(p)$ and (b) $\mathsf{believe}(\neg p)$. The second reading is possible only with NR-verbs.

In LTAG, lexical material is generated at its surface structure position, there is no movement outside the lexicon. Therefore it is natural to assume with respect to sentences as (7), that the negation is syntactically generated in the matrix clause and that neg raising attitude verbs such as *glauben* allow for semantic lowering of an attached negation. This negation then receives wide scope within the sentential complement. In this, we follow the HPSG analysis proposed in Sailer (to appear).

The presence of an NPI in the embedded sentence as in (8) forces the negation to scope under the bridge verb, that is the (b)-interpretation is chosen.

(8) Hans glaubt **nicht**, dass Peter
Hans believes not that Peter
sonderlich glücklich sein wird.
very happy be will
('Hans does not believe that Peter will be very happy.')

2 The LTAG Semantics Framework

We use the Kallmeyer and Romero (2005) framework for semantics. Each elementary tree is linked to a semantic representation containing Ty2 terms and scope constraints. Ty2 terms are typed λ-terms providing individuals and situations as basic types. The terms can be labeled, and they can contain meta-variables. The scope constraints are subordination constraints of the form $x \geq y$ ('y is a component of x') with x and y being either propositional labels or propositional meta-variables.

The semantic representations are equipped with feature structure descriptions. Semantic computation is done on the derivation tree and consists of certain feature value equations between mother and daughter nodes of edges in the derivation tree.

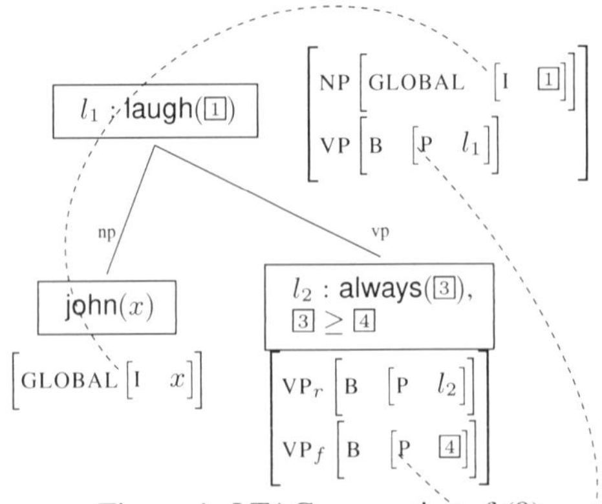

Figure 1: LTAG semantics of (9)

The meta-variables from the semantic representations can occur in the feature structure descriptions. In this case they can receive values following from the feature value equations performed on the derivation tree.

As an example see Fig. 1 showing the derivation tree for (9) with semantic representations and semantic feature structure descriptions as node labels.

(9) John always laughs

The additional feature equations in this example are depicted with dotted links. They arise from top-bottom feature identifications parallel to the unifications performed in FTAG (Vijay-Shanker and Joshi, 1988) and from identifications of global features. They yield $\boxed{1} = x$ and $\boxed{4} = l_1$. Applying these identities to the semantic representations after having built their union leads to (10). The constraint $\boxed{3} \geq l_1$ states that $l_1 : \mathsf{laugh}(x)$ is a component of $\boxed{3}$.

(10)

$\mathsf{john}(x), l_2 : \mathsf{always}(\boxed{3}),$ $l_1 : \mathsf{laugh}(x),$ $\boxed{3} \geq l_1$

We assume a scope window for quantifiers specifying an upper boundary MAXS ('maximal scope') and a lower boundary MINS ('minimal scope') for the nuclear scope. In this we follow Kallmeyer and Romero (2005). In addition, however, we make use of the feature MINP ('minimal proposition'). In their analysis, which was developed for English, MINS and MINP are the same, in other words, there is no separate MINP feature. In German, the minimal scope of a quantifier seems to depend not only on the verb the quantifier attaches to but also on other factors (see Kallmeyer and Romero, 2006 in this volume for the influence of word order on quantifier scope in German). This justifies the assumption that German MINS if different from English MINS. The scope order is of course such that MAXS is higher than MINS which is in turn higher than MINP.

In order to deal with NPI-licensing we introduce three new features: a global and a local NEG-feature and the global feature N-SCOPE. Not surprisingly, the latter represents the scope of a negative operator, while the former is needed to check the presence of a negative operator. The next section offers detailed examples.

3 The Analysis of Licensers

In this section we give the elementary trees for non-contrastive *nicht* (not) and *niemand* (nobody).

A strong trigger for NCN is *nicht* attached to the verb. Based on the topological field theory for German the attachment takes place at the right satzklammer, a position that together with the left satzklammer contains the verbal expression.[4] As an example see the derivation for (11) in Fig. 2.

(11) Peter ruft Hans nicht an
Peter calls Hans not PART
('Peter does not call Hans')

Similar to Gerdes (2002), the VP nodes carry features VF ('Vorfeld'), LK ('Linke Satzklammer'), MF ('Mittelfeld'), and RK ('Rechte Satzklammer') for the topological fields. In German, the vorfeld, the position preceding the left satzklammer, must be filled by exactly one constituent. We guarantee this with the feature VF: The different VF features at the highest VP node in the tree for *ruft an* make sure that adjunction to the vorfeld is obligatory. At the same time, elements adjoining to any of the topological fields (see the tree for *Peter*) have a foot node feature VF $= -$ and have equal top and bottom features VF at their root. When

[4]Exceptions to this generalization are found with verbs that express movement:

(i) a. Peter geht nicht ins Kino.
Peter goes not to_the movies
('Peter does not go to the movies')
b. *... dass Peter ins Kino nicht geht.
... that Peter to_the movies not goes
('... that Peter does not go to the movies')

Here the NC-*nicht* is always attached to the adverb that expresses the direction or target of the movement, thus not to the second satzklammer directly. For this paper, we leave these cases aside.

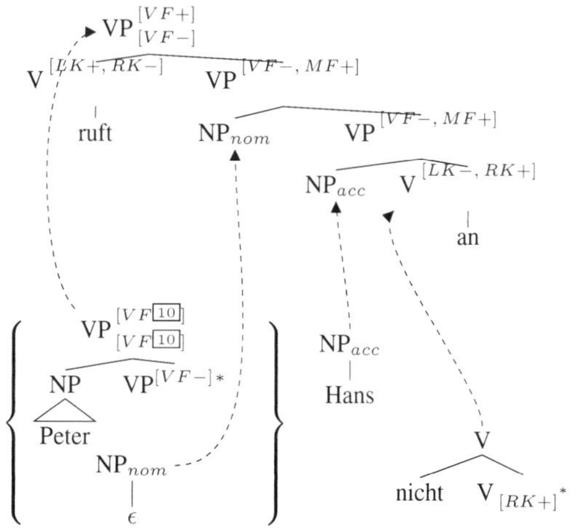

Figure 2: Syntactic analysis for (11)

adjoining to the vorfeld, these receive values $+$. Consequently, further adjunctions of similar elements at the new root node are not possible. An adjunction at the foot node of the auxiliary tree of the vorfeld element can be excluded by some other feature. This guarantees that exactly one element gets adjoined into the vorfeld.

Note that we consider the base position of the subject NP being in the mittelfeld and consider the subject as being moved into the vorfeld. Alternatively, any other element could be moved in to the vorfeld instead.

The semantic combination of *nicht* and *ruft_an* is shown in Fig. 3.

The MINP feature from *ruft* indicates the proposition contributed by the verb which is the minimal proposition of the whole elementary tree. It is included in the scope of all operators (quantifiers, negation, modals, ...) attaching to this verb (An exception is of course neg raising where the scope of the negation does not include the MINP value of the NR-verb.).

The unifications between the two feature structures in Fig. 3 are depicted with dotted lines. They yield in particular $\boxed{9} = \boxed{7}$, therefore, with constraint $\boxed{7} \geq l_1$, l_1 is in the scope of the negation.

The presence of a negation is indicated by a global NEG $= yes$. In case there is no negation, we have to make sure we obtain NEG = no and not just an unspecified NEG value. Therefore, the VP spine is articulated with non-global NEG features that switch from no to yes once a negation occurs. Here this is the case at node position V, consequently $\boxed{6} = \boxed{5} = \boxed{4} = \boxed{3} = yes$. The topmost

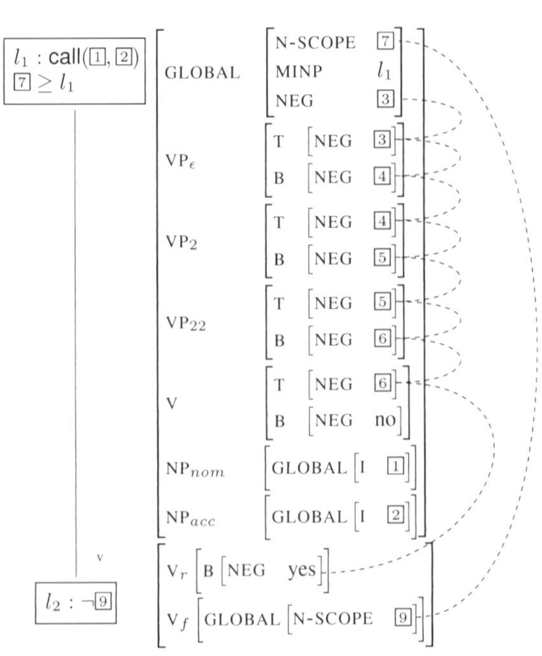

Figure 3: Semantic computation for ... *ruft* ... *nicht an*

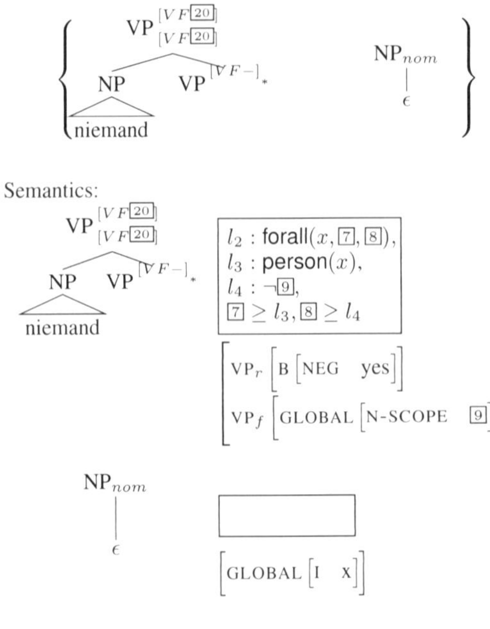

Figure 4: Lexical entry for *niemand*

NEG then becomes the global NEG.

Cases of double negation, though not considered here, could be captured by assuming that each negation on the verbal spine makes the value of the local NEG feature switch (from *no* to *yes* or, if there was already negation, from *yes* to *no*). This way, double negation would lead to a global NEG feature with value *no*.

The negative quantifier *niemand* has the distribution of an NP. The elementary trees in Fig. 4 for *niemand* reflect the $\forall\neg$ reading which is preferred by an analysis assuming that the NPI must be in the scope of a negation with no quantifiers intervening. The features NEG, MINP and N-SCOPE work in the same way as in the case of *nicht*. The global I feature linked to the initial tree with the trace passes the argument variable to the verb.

Note that this is an analysis for the case where *niemand* is 'moved'. If *niemand* is in base position, the lexical item comes with an initial tree that is substituted at the corresponding NP slot. However, since the NEG-feature can only be switched to yes by adjoining an auxiliary tree carrying negation to a VP node, even in these cases we need an additional VP auxiliary tree contributing the sentential negation.[5]

[5]Another option would be to let the initial tree of *niemand* directly access the semantic features of a VP node.

4 The Analysis of NPIs

For this paper we restrict ourselves to verbal NPIs and minimizers.

As an example for a verbal NPI consider *scheren* ('to give a damn about sth.') in (3). Its lexical entry is shown in Fig. 5. As in the case of *ruft*, the verbal spine is articulated with the NEG feature. Furthermore, GLOBAL contains the requirement of a negation (NEG $= yes$). In particular, the topmost NEG feature on the verbal spine is yes while the value of the lowest NEG feature is no. This means that at some point on the verbal spine a negation must be added that switches the value from no to yes.

Concerning the scope relation between NPI and negation, the following should hold: 1. the NPI must be in the scope of the negation, and 2. quantifiers must not intervene between negation and NPI.

The first condition is guaranteed with constraint $\boxed{9} \geq l_1$.

In order to capture the second restriction, the distinction between MINS and MINP allows us to draw a border line between the domain where quantifiers can take scope and the domain where the negation and the NPI are positioned. Other scope taking operators (modals, adverbs, ...) are not concerned by this limit. This border line is the MINS value, and the crucial NPI-specific constraint is $\boxed{8} \geq \boxed{9}$ stating that the negation must

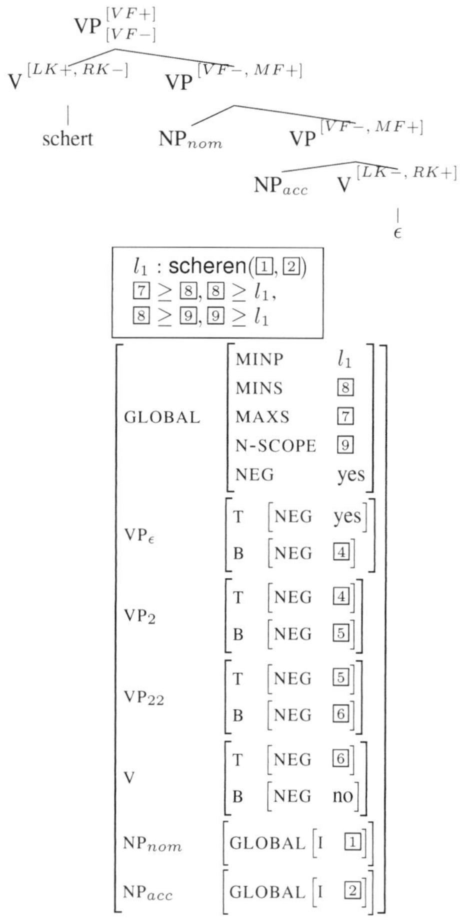

Figure 5: Lexical entry for *schert*

scope under the minimal scope of all quantifiers. The scope relations then can be summarised as in Fig. 6.

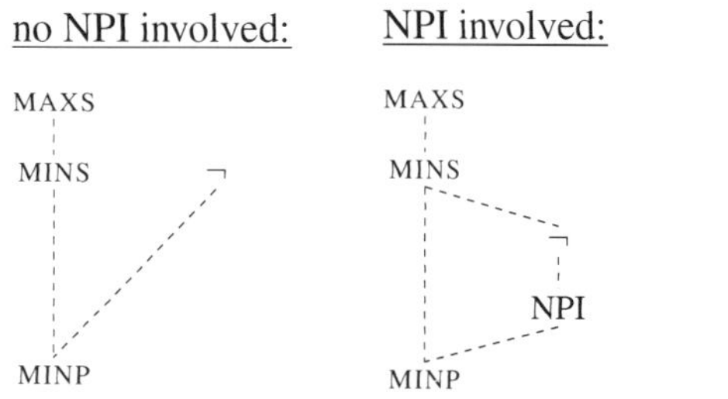

Figure 6: Scope relations of MAXS, MINS and ¬ with and without the involvement of an NPI.

As mentioned in 1.3 minimizers show a more restrictive distribution than verbal NPIs. In addition to the two licensing conditions of verbal NPIs stated above minimizers also obey a third licensing condition in German: the negation must precede the minimizer in the same clause or the negation must have wide scope with respect to the sentence containing the minimizer, such as in NR constructions. Consider the minimizer *auch nur einen Cent* ('any cent at all') in example (5) and its proposed lexical entry in Fig. 7.

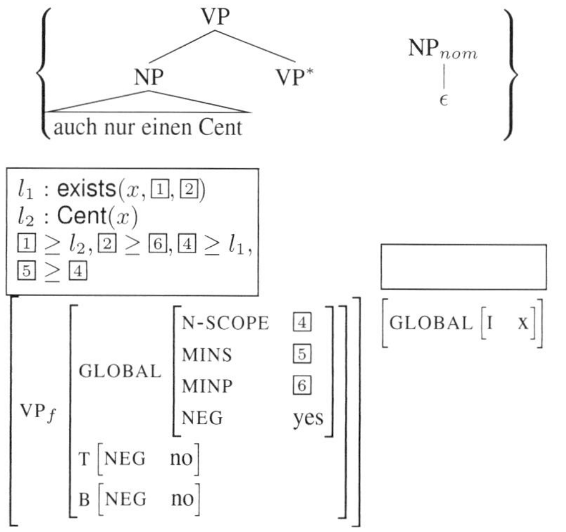

Figure 7: Lexical entry for *auch nur einen Cent*

We propose a multicomponent lexical entry for minimizers here, since they have to access the semantic feature structure of the VP spine, and therefore have to be adjoined. This is different from verbal NPIs (that are part of the VP spine by definition), but similar to the negative quantifier *niemand*. As for verbal NPIs the presence of a negation is ensured by the global NEG feature, that is required to be *yes*. The scope condition is satisfied by the constraints 4 ≥ l_1 and 5 ≥ 4: the former one ensures that the semantic contribution of *auch nur einen Cent* is part of N-SCOPE, while the latter one prohibits any intervening regular quantifier (by requiring N-SCOPE to be a subexpression of MINS).[6]

In order to meet the third condition we have to make sure that the negation appears somewhere to the left of the minimizer. In other words, the negation is not attached between the right satzklammer and the minimizer, but somewhere else (as ensured by the global NEG feature). Remember that the position of a negation is signaled by the local NEG feature on the VP spine and its switch from *no* to *yes*. One way to exploit this is to let the minimizer semantically specify the VP node to which

[6] Note that, though being quantifiers, minimizers are not concerned by the MAXS-MINS scope window. Instead, their scope window is specified by N-SCOPE as upper limit and MINP as lower limit (the latter results from constraint 2 ≥ 6.

it can be attached. This is accomplished by the VP_f feature in the lexical entry for *auch nur einen Cent*, where the local NEG is required to be *no*, while the global NEG is *yes*. Thereby it is guaranteed that somewhere between the position where the adjunction of the minimizer takes place and the maximal projection of the VP the NEG feature has to switch to *yes* with the aid of a negative item.

5 The Analysis of Neg Raising

Now let us turn to the neg raising examples from section 1.4. Attitude verbs that optionally offer neg raising are mapped onto two lexical entries representing a non-NR- and a NR-reading. In the latter, the negation takes wide scope within the embedded clause. In other words, quantifiers cannot scopally intervene between the embedding verb and the negation. This is exemplified in (12).

(12) Peter glaubt nicht, dass jeder seiner
Peter believes not that each of_his
Freunde kommen wird.
friends come will.
('Peter does not believe that each of his friends will come')

The NR-reading ($\text{believes}(p, \cdots \neg \cdots)$ does not exclude that Peter believes that some of his friends will come. A reading where Peter believes that none of his friends will come is not available. In other words, the quantifier has to scope under the negation.

The lexical entry for *glaubt* with the NR-reading is shown in Fig. 8. In the syntax we assume a substitution node for the sentential complement. Long-distance dependencies are then analysed with multicomponents. This choice was motivated because in German, taking into account scrambling, more movement-based word order variations are possible than in English. For these we need multicomponents anyway (see the elementary tree set for *niemand*), and then sentential complements might be treated in parallel. The S substitution node carries a syntactic feature NR indicating that this is a neg raising construction.

The lowering of the negation is expressed as follows: the N-SCOPE of *glaubt* (variable [7]), i.e., the scope of the attaching negation, does not contain the MINP of *glaubt* as in non-NR readings. Instead, it contains the MAXS (variable [9]) of the embedded sentence (constraint [7] $\geq$ [9]). This MAXS is usually contained in the propositional argument

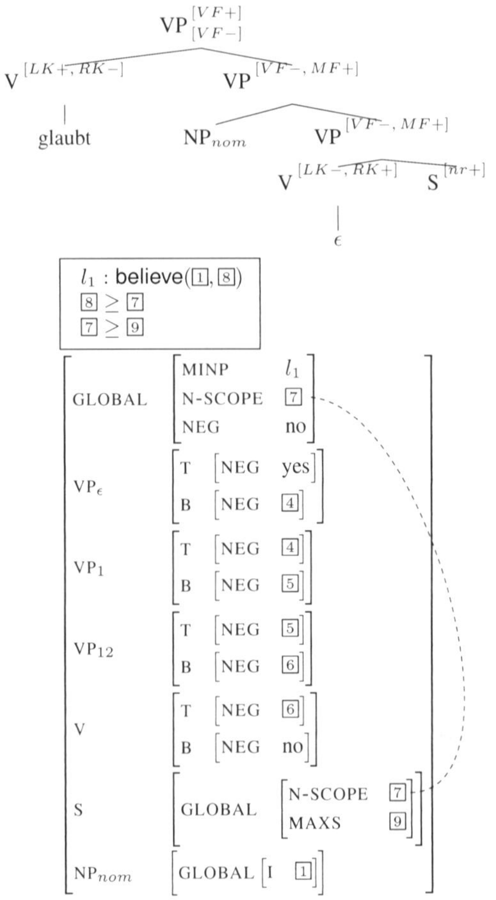

Figure 8: Lexical entry for *glaubt*

of believe (see Kallmeyer and Romero, 2005); in this special neg raising entry we even require the N-SCOPE to be contained in this argument (constraint [8] $\geq$ [7]). The MAXS feature [9] marks the upper limit for the scope of all quantifiers occurring inside the embedded clause. Consequently, wide scope of the lowered negation with respect to the embedded sentence is ensured.

The lexical entry for *glaubt* with NR-reading also has to make sure that a negative element is attached to its verbal spine. In this respect its semantic feature structure resembles the one of a verbal NPI, that is the NEG value has to be switched to *yes* by adjunction. However, semantically the negation is interpreted in the embedded sentence and NPIs cannot be licensed in the matrix clause. Therefore, the value of the global NEG feature is *no*.

The complementizer of the embedded clause takes care of setting the value of the embedded global NEG to *yes* by identifying the NEG feature of its S node with the topmost NEG feature on the verbal spine of the embedded clause. In a non-NR-reading, the complementizer only passes the NEG value upwards, i.e., the global NEG of the embedded clause specifies whether a negation is present in the embedded clause.

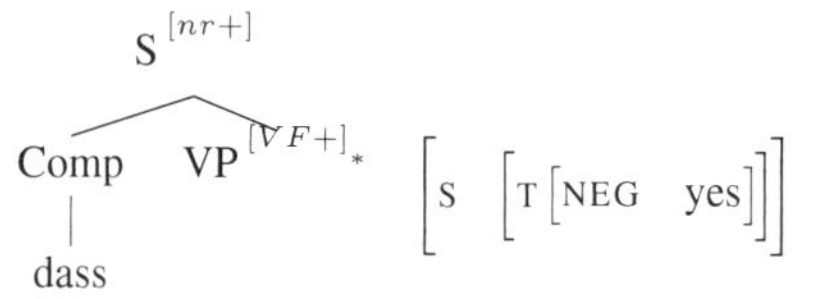

Figure 9: Complementizer *dass* in neg raising construction

With this analysis, if a NR-verb embeds an NPI as in (8), the NPI requires the NR-reading; otherwise the global NEG feature of the embedded clause is *no*.

Next, we want to give an example derivation of a sentence that contains an *un*licensed NPI and which amounts to contradicting scope constraints. It concerns the following sentence:

(13) *Hans glaubt **nicht**, dass es jeden
Hans believes not, that it everybody
schert.
bothers
('Hans doesn't believe that everybody gives a damn about it.')

The NPI *schert* is not licensed due to the intervening quantifier *jeden* (every). The defective dervation of (13) is shown in Fig. 10. Syntactically, the S leaf of the $Hans\_glaubt\_nicht$ tree is substituted by the $dass\_es\_schert$ tree and the $jeder$ tree is substituted into the $dass\_es\_schert$ tree. This works fine. In the semantic representation, however, we observe a clash of the scope constraints. Remember that we analyse the verbal NPI *schert* as requiring immediate scope, that is MINS $\geq$ N-SCOPE. On the other side, the NR-verb *glauben* demands the negation to have wide scope with respect to the embedded sentence, hence N-SCOPE $\geq$ MAXS (constraint $l_2 \geq \boxed{3}$) . If we put these two constraints together we obtain the constraint MINS = MAXS, which means that the area where quantifiers take scope (the MAXS-MINS window) is empty and hence there cannot be any quantifiers. A quantifer such as *jeden* is then ruled out due to two semantic constraints it contributes: its semantic content is a subexpression of MAXS (constraint $\boxed{3} \geq l_3$) and MINS is a subexpression of its nuclear scope (constraint $\boxed{6} \geq l_2$). However, this can only hold if MINS $\neq$ MAXS which is not true for (13) as has been shown.

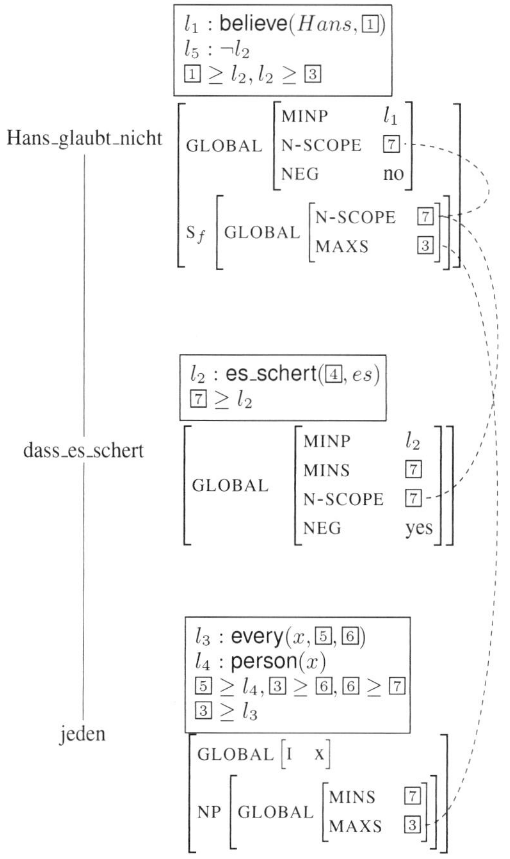

Figure 10: Defective derivation tree for *Hans glaubt nicht, dass es jeden schert*

6 Conclusion and further research

We propose an LTAG analysis of the distribution of German NPIs. The crucial criterion for an NPI is the requirement to be in the scope of a negation that is semantically in the same finite clause such that no quantifier can scopally intervene between negation and NPI. Technically we achieved this using the features NEG and N-SCOPE, that signal the presence of a negation and make its immediate scope available for the NPI. [7] The specific constraints for quantifiers when occurring with

[7]Note however, that, even though we have called the feature signalling the presence of a potential NPI licenser NEG, we might as well call it differently and give it a different meaning (for example, encoding downward entailment instead of negation). The licensing mechanism and the way this feature is used could stay the same. In this sense our analysis is independent from the concrete logical characterization of NPI licensers.

NPI licensing negations are obtained by a distinction between the feature MINS characterizing the lower boundary of quantifier scope and the minimal proposition contributed by a verb that characterizes the lower boundary for the scope of negations.

We think LTAG is particularly well suited to describe this phenomenon since the relation between licenser and licensee can be localized within single elementary trees.[8] The only exception are neg raising constructions where the licensing property needs to be passed down to the embedded clause. This is not non-local either and can be easily modelled in LTAG. This shows that LTAG's extended domain of locality has advantages not only for syntax (see Kroch, 1987) but also for semantics.

The analyses discussed in this paper have demonstrated the usefulness of semantic feature structure descriptions that specify the combination possibilities of semantic representations and that are separated from the semantic representations themselves. On the one hand the semantic features encode the contributions of the semantic representations to functional applications. I.e., they state which elments are contributed as possible arguments for other semantic expressions and which arguments need to be filled. They thereby simulate lambda abstraction and functional application. On the other hand they also serve to model the scopal behaviour of different operators and to capture the different boundaries for scope. The combination of LTAG's extended domain of locality with a semantics using feature structure unification enables us to capture these constraints within a mildly context-sensitive framework: The structures underlying the computation of syntax and semantics are the context-free derivation trees.

One line of further research we want to pursue is an extension of the proposed analysis to adjectival and adverbial NPIs. We already started working on this. But for reasons of space we left this out in this paper.

Acknowledgements

For many inspiring discussions of the topics treated in this paper, we are grateful to our colleagues Wolfgang Maier, Frank Richter, Manfred Sailer and Jan-Philipp Söhn. Furthermore, the paper benefitted a lot from the useful comments of three anonymous reviewers.

[8] In the HPSG analysis from Soehn (2006) for example, where we do not have an extended domain of locality, one has to specify explicitely that the licenser of an NPI must be found within the next complete clause containing the NPI.

References

Kim Gerdes. 2002. DTAG? In *Proceedings of TAG+6 Workshop*, pages 242–251. Venice.

Anastasia Giannakidou. 1997. *The Landscape of Polarity Items*. Ph.D. thesis, Rijksuniversiteit Groningen.

Jack Hoeksema. 2000. Negative Polarity Items: Triggering, Scope and C-Command. In Laurence Horn and Yasuhiko Kato, editors, *Negation and Polarity*, pages 115–146. Oxford University Press, Oxford.

Laurence R. Horn. 1978. Remarks on Neg-Raising. In Peter Cole, editor, *Pragmatics*, pages 129–220. Academic Press, New York, San Francisco, London.

Joachim Jacobs. 1982. *Syntax und Semantik der Negation im Deutschen*. Wilhelm Fink Verlag, München.

Laura Kallmeyer and Maribel Romero. 2005. Scope and Situation Binding in LTAG using Semantic Unification. *Research on Language and Computation*. 57 pages, submitted.

Laura Kallmeyer and Maribel Romero. 2006. Quantifier Scope in German: An MCTAG Analysis. In *Proceedings of The Eighth International Workshop on Tree Adjoining Grammar and Related Formalisms (TAG+8)*, Sydney, Australia, July.

Anthony S. Kroch. 1987. Unbounded Dependencies and Subjacency in a Tree Adjoining Grammar. In A. Manaster-Ramer, editor, *Mathematics of Language*, pages 143–172. John Benjamins, Amsterdam.

William Ladusaw. 1980. *Polarity Sensitivity as Inherent Scope relations*. Garland Press, New York.

Marcia Linebarger. 1980. *The Grammar of Negative Polarity*. Ph.D. thesis, MIT. cited after the reproduction by the Indiana University Linguistics Club, Indiana, 1981.

Marcia Linebarger. 1987. Negative Polarity and Grammatical Representation. *Linguistics and Philosophy*, 10:325–387.

Manfred Sailer. to appear. "Don't Believe" in Underspecified Semantics. an LRS Analysis of Neg Raising. *Empirical Issues in Formal Syntax and Semantics 6*.

Jan-Philipp Soehn. 2006. *Über Bärendienste und erstaunte Bauklötze - Idiome ohne freie Lesart in der HPSG*. Ph.D. thesis, Fiedrich-Schiller Universität Jena.

Ton van der Wouden. 1997. *Negative Contexts. Collocation, Polarity and Multiple Negation*. Routledge, London.

K. Vijay-Shanker and Aravind K. Joshi. 1988. Feature Structures Based Tree Adjoining Grammar. In *Proceedings of COLING*, pages 714–719, Budapest.

Frans Zwarts. 1997. Three Types of Polarity. In Fritz Hamm and Erhard W. Hinrichs, editors, *Plurality and Quantification*, pages 177–237. Kluwer Academic Publishers, Dordrecht.

Semantic Interpretation of Unrealized Syntactic Material in LTAG

Olga Babko-Malaya
University of Pennsylvania
malayao@ldc.upenn.edu

Abstract

This paper presents a LTAG-based analysis of gapping and VP ellipsis, which proposes that resolution of the elided material is part of a general disambiguation procedure, which is also responsible for resolution of underspecified representations of scope.

1 Introduction

The problem of ellipsis resolution is to recover the interpretation of the elided material. For example, in (1), the elided VP is interpreted as being identical to the verb in the preceding sentence. Likewise, in the gapping structures, as shown in (2), the interpretation of a gap is being identified with the interpretation of the preceding verb.

(1) Mary likes Bill. Jane does too.
(2) Mary ate beans and others -- rice.

Whereas some approaches assume syntactic identity between the antecedent and the elided material (e.g. Fiengo and May 1994), others suggest that VP ellipsises are proforms, semantically identified with their antecedents (see Dalrymple et al 1991, Shieber et al 1996, Hardt 1993, 1999).

This paper follows semantic approaches to ellipsis resolution. It adopts the LTAG semantics of Kallmeyer and Romero 2004 and proposes that resolution of ellipsises and gaps is part of a general disambiguation procedure, which is also responsible for resolution of underspecified representations of scope.

2 LTAG Semantics with Semantic Unification

In LTAG framework (Joshi and Schabes 1997), the basic units are (elementary) trees, which can be combined into bigger trees by substitution or adjunction. LTAG derivations are represented by derivation trees that record the history of how the elementary trees are put together. Given that derivation steps in LTAG correspond to predicate-argument applications, it is usually assumed that LTAG semantics is based on the derivation tree, rather than the derived tree (Kallmeyer and Joshi 2003).

Semantic composition which we adopt is based on LTAG semantics with semantic unification (Kallmeyer and Romero 2004). In the derivation tree, elementary trees are replaced by their semantic representations and corresponding feature structures. Semantic representations are as defined in Kallmeyer and Joshi 2003, except that they do not have argument variables. These representations consist of a set of formulas (typed λ-expressions with labels) and a set of scope constraints.

Each semantic representation is linked to a feature structure. Feature structures, as illustrated by different examples below, include a feature i whose values are individual variables and features p and MaxS, whose values are propositional labels. Semantic composition consists of feature unification. After having performed all unifications, the union of all semantic representations is built.

Consider, for example, the semantic representations and feature structures associated with the elementary trees of the sentence shown in (3).

(3) *Mary dates Bill*

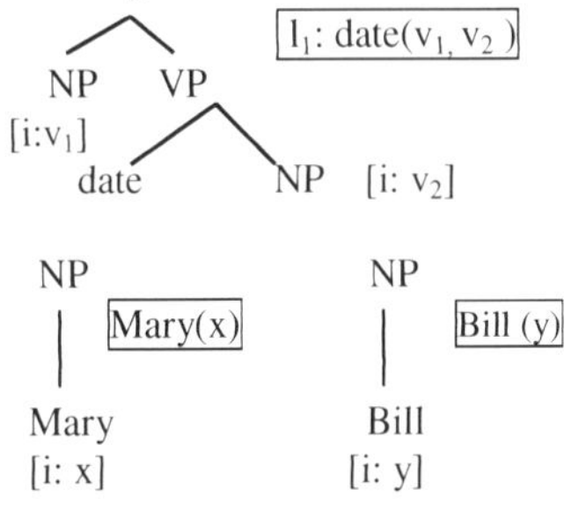

Proceedings of the 8th International Workshop on Tree Adjoining Grammar and Related Formalisms, pages 91–96,
Sydney, July 2006.

Derivation tree:

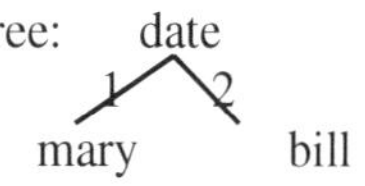

Semantic composition proceeds on the derivation tree and consists of feature unification:

(4)

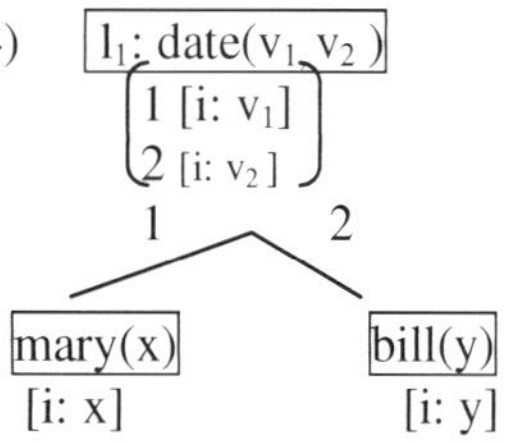

Performing two unifications, v_1=x, v_2=y, we arrive at the final interpretation of this sentence: l_1: date(x, y), bill(y), mary(x). This representation is interpreted conjunctively, with free variables being existentially bound.

Quantificational NPs are analyzed as multicomponent TAGs, where the scope part of the quantifier introduces the proposition containing the quantifier, and the predicate-argument part introduces the restrictive clause (see Kallmeyer and Joshi 2003).

(5) Every student likes some course

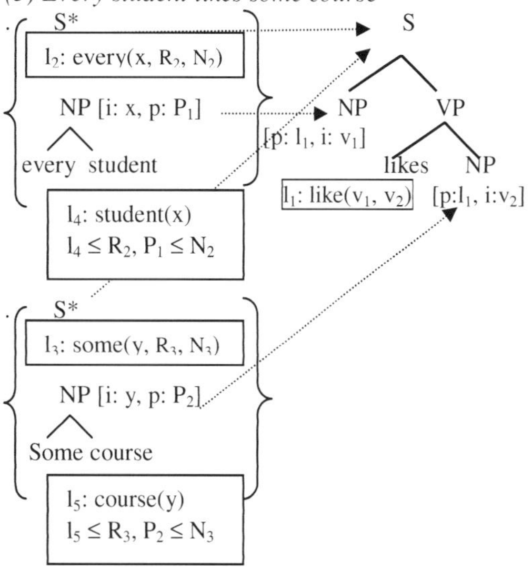

Final representation

l_2: every(x, R_2, N_2)
l_4: student(x) $l_4 \leq R_2$
l_3: some(y, R_3, N_3)
l_5: course(y) $l_5 \leq R_3$
l_1: like(x, y) $l_1 \leq N_2$ $l_1 \leq N_3$

The final representation of this sentence is underspecified for scope, given that there are no constraints which restrict the relative scope of every and some. In order to obtain one of the readings, a disambiguation mapping is needed:

Disambiguations:

1. $R_2 \rightarrow l_4$, $R_3 \rightarrow l_5$, $N_2 \rightarrow l_1$, $N_3 \rightarrow l_2$:
some(y,course(y), every(x,student(x), like(x, y)))
2. $R_2 \rightarrow l_4$, $R_3 \rightarrow l_5$, $N_3 \rightarrow l_1$, $N_2 \rightarrow l_3$:
every(x, student(x), some(y, course(y), like(x, y))

Disambiguations are functions from propositional variables to propositional labels that respect the scope constraints, such that after having applied this mapping, the transitive closure of the resulting scope is a partial order.

3 The Problem of Ellipsis Resolution in LTAG semantics

Given LTAG semantics, there are two possible approaches to resolution of the elided material: reconstruction can be done as part of the unification process or as part of the disambiguation procedure. If reconstruction was done as unification, the semantic representation of the elided material would be disambiguated in the final representation. On the other hand, it is well known that resolution of ellipsises and gaps can be ambiguous. For example, the sentence in (6), discussed in Siegel 1987 and Johnson 2003 among others, has 2 interpretations:[1]

(6) *Ward can't eat caviar and his guests -- dried beans*

Can't (eat (ward, caviar)) & **eat** (his guests, dried beans))

Can't (eat(ward, caviar)) & **can't (eat**(his guests, dried beans))

As this example shows, the gap in (6) can be reconstructed by selecting either the verb or the negated modal as its antecedent. The two interpretations represent different scope readings between the conjunction and negation, which should be analyzed as underspecified in LTAG semantics. Resolution of gaps, therefore, cannot be done as part of unification, since it depends on the disambiguated interpretation. The question is whether it is possible to define an underspecified representation of these two readings, and what kind of resolution mechanism can be used to disambiguate these interpretations?

[1] Other cases of ambiguous interpretations of the elided material are discussed in section 7.

4 LTAG Semantics of Gapping

In LTAG semantics, semantic representations are introduced by lexicalized trees. In order to account for the analysis of gapping and VP ellipsis, this paper proposes that semantics should be defined on both lexicalized and non-lexicalized trees. Specifically, we propose that

Interpretation of a gap (or elided VP) is the semantic interpretation of a non-lexicalized S tree.

The semantic representations of lexicalized S trees under this new approach are derived compositionally, given the meaning of a nonlexicalized S tree and the meaning of a verb.

(7)

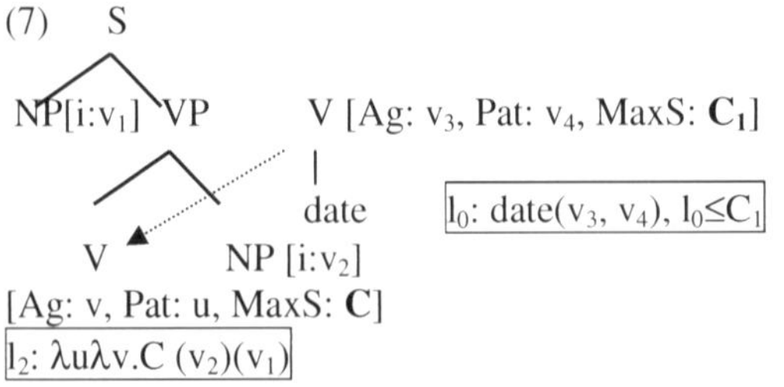

Non-lexicalized trees introduce a propositional label and a propositional variable, illustrated by l_2 and C above. If a tree is a transitive S-tree, there are two lambda bound variables, which correspond to the Agent and Patient features of the verb. Performing feature unifications (v_3=v, v_4=u,C_1=C) and scope constraint disambiguations (C->l_0), the proposition l_2 will be reduced to: $\lambda u.\lambda v.date(v, u)(v_2)(v_1)= date(v_1, v_2)$.

Given this proposal, we suggest that the semantics of gaps, VPE and other types of elided material is introduced by non-lexicalized trees. For example, the analysis of the sentence in (2) is shown in (7). Performing feature unifications ($l_2=P_1$, $l_3=P_2$, $v=v_1=v_2$, $u=u_1=u_2$, $C=C_1=C_2$) yields the final representation, where l_2 and l_3 are underspecified. There is only one disambiguation of the variable C in this sentence: C -> l_0, which gives us the desired interpretation of the sentence:

l_2: $\lambda u\lambda v.eat(v, u)\ (y)(x) = eat(x, y)$
l_3: $\lambda u\lambda v.eat(v, u)\ (w)(z) = eat(z, w)$

Resolution of the gap in this sentence is enforced by the feature structure of 'and', which unifies MaxS as well as Agent and Patient features. This analysis therefore accounts for the fact that gapping "is intimately entangled with the syntax of coordination (as opposed to VP ellipsis)" (Johnson 2003). On the other hand, as the next example illustrates, it is crucial that propositional variables introduced by non-lexicalized trees are not unified during semantic composition, but rather are identified with their antecedents as part of the disambiguation procedure.

(7) *Mary ate beans and others -- rice.*

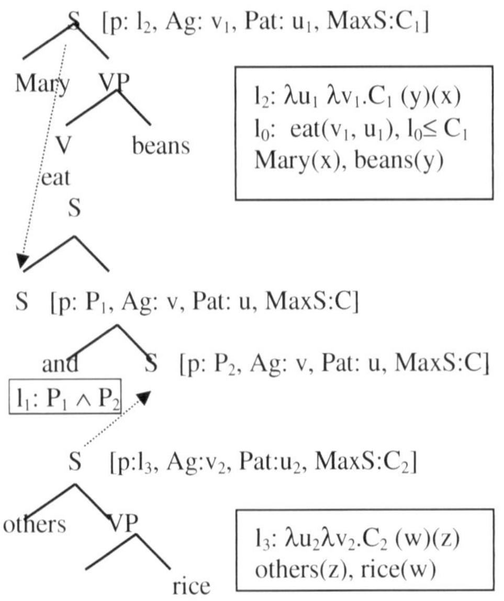

Final Representation:

l_1: $l_2 \wedge l_3$
l_2: $\lambda u\lambda v.C\ (y)(x)$ l_3: $\lambda u\lambda v.C\ (w)(z)$
l_0: eat(v, u) $l_0 \leq C$
mary(x), beans(y), others(z), rice(w)

The sentence in (8), shown below, differs from the previous one in the presence of a negated modal. The interpretation of this modal introduces a proposition l_9: can't(N_9) and a constraint $P_3 \leq N_9$. After P_3 is unified with the proposition l_0, the final representation has two constraints on the variable l_0: $l_0 \leq C$ and $l_0 \leq N_9$, and therefore two possible disambiguations. In the disambiguation 1, C is mapped to l_0, introduced by the verb 'eat', and propositions l_2 and l_3 are reduced to eat(x, y) and eat(z, w). In the disambiguation 2, the variable C is mapped to l_9, introduced by the modal, and l_2 and l_3 are reduced to can't(eat(x, y)) and can't(eat(z, w)). These disambiguations yield the desired interpretations of this sentence.

(8) *Ward can't eat caviar and his guests -- dried beans*

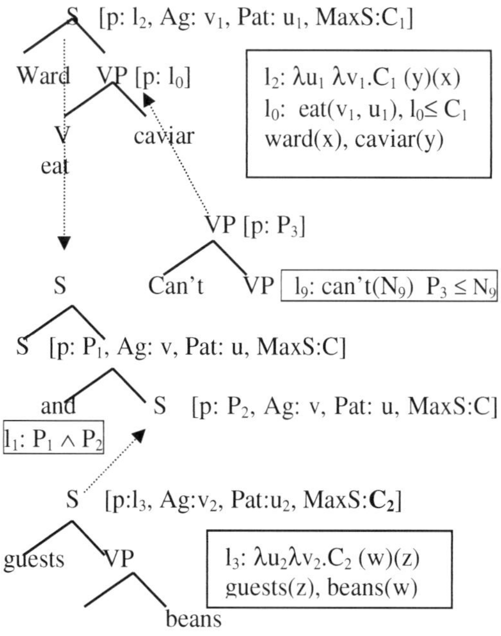

Final Representation

l_1: $l_2 \wedge l_3$	l_0: eat(v, u)
l_9: can't(N_9)	$l_0 \leq N_9$ $l_0 \leq C$
l_2: $\lambda u \lambda v$ C (y)(x)	l_3: $\lambda u \lambda v$ C (w)(z)
guests(z), beans(w), caviar(y), ward(x)	

Disambiguation 1: C->l_0, N_9 ->l_1:
can't (eat(x, y) $\wedge$ eat(z, w))
l_2 l_3

Disambiguation 2: C->l_9, N_9->l_0:
can't(eat(x, y)) $\wedge$ can't (eat(z, w))
l_2 l_3

Resolution of gaps under this analysis is done as part of the scope resolution procedure on underspecified representations. A crucial feature of this analysis is that the propositions l_2 and l_3 are 'underspecified' in the final representation and the variable C is computed during the disambiguation, i.e. when all scope ambiguities are being resolved. In this respect this analysis differs from previous approaches, where the final representation did not include any variables, except for the arguments of quantifiers or other scopal elements.[2]

[2] However, see Babko-Malaya 2004, where a similar analysis is proposed to account for the semantics of coordinated structures with quantified NPs.

5 LTAG Analysis of VP Ellipsis

The analysis of gapping presented above can be easily extended to the analysis of VP ellipsis. VPE differs from gapping in that it is not restricted to coordinated structures. Whereas in the examples above resolution of gaps was enforced by the feature structure of 'and', in the case of VPE, a similar unification, forced by pragmatic constraints, results in recovering the elided material.

As the example in (9) illustrates, our analysis of VPE assumes the following modification of the semantics of non-lexicalized trees: propositions introduced by non-lexicalized trees have one lambda-bound variable, so that each argument is introduced by a separate proposition. For example, the interpretation of a transitive tree below has two propositions l_1 and l_2, and two propositional variables C_1 and C_2. The proposition l_2 corresponds to the meaning of a VP, which is missing in the standard TAG-based analyses. This decomposition of the meaning of a nonlexicalized tree, therefore, can be independently motivated by the existence of modifiers which predicate of VPs. We further assume that the MaxS feature of the S tree corresponds to the variable introduced by the agent (or the highest-ranked argument).

(9) *Mary likes Bill. Jane does too.*

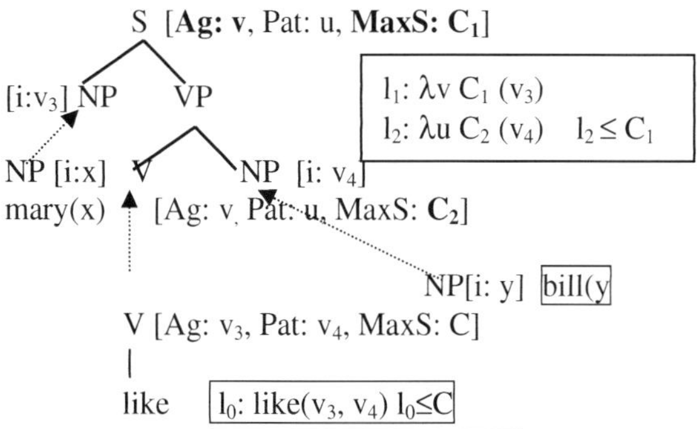

Final Representation:

l_1: λv C_1 (x)
l_2: λu C_2 (y) $l_2 \leq C_1$
l_0: like(v, u), $l_0 \leq C_2$
Mary(x), Bill(y)

Applying disambiguations C_2 -> l_0, C_1 -> l_2, we derive the following propositions:

l_2: λu.like(v, u) (y)=like(v, y)
l_1: λv.like(v, y) (x)=like(x, y)

Now consider the second sentence: *Jane does too:*

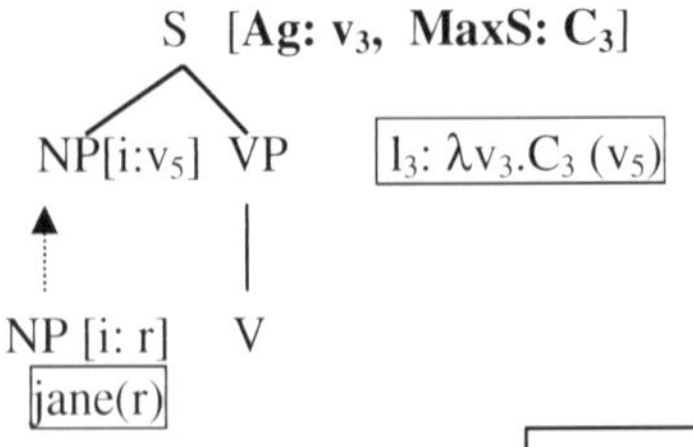

Final Representation:

l_3: λv_3 C_3 (r)
Jane(r)

This sentence introduces an intransitive tree and one propositional variable C_3. This variable is not constrained within the sentence, and parallel to other pro-forms, it gets its interpretation from the previous discourse. Specifically, the interpretation of the second sentence is derived by unification of the S features of the second and the first S-trees in (9): $C_3=C_1$, $v_3=v$. Given that C_1 is mapped to l_2 above, it corresponds to the proposition being reconstructed: $C_3(=C_1)$ -> l_2

l_3: λv.like(v, u) (r) = like(r, u)

6 Scope Parallelism

Many previous approaches impose parallelism constraints on the interpretation of the elided material (e.g. Fox 2000, Asher et al 2001 among others). Under the present analysis, scope parallelism comes for free. Consider, for example, the following sentence discussed in Dalrymple et al 1991, among others, where ambiguity is resolved in the same way in both the antecedent and at the ellipsis site: *John gave every student a test, and Bill did too.* The final interpretation of the first sentence is given in (10) and has 2 possible disambiguations.

(10) John gave every student a test.

l_0: give(v, u, w)
l_1: λv.C_1 (x) l_2: λu.C_2 (y) $l_2 \leq C_1$
l_3: λw.C_3 (z) $l_3 \leq C_2$
l_7: every(y, R_7, N_7) l_5: some(z, R_5, N_5)
l_8: student(y) l_9: test(z) john(x)
$l_0 \leq C_3$ $l_0 \leq N_5$ $l_0 \leq N_7$ $l_8 \leq R_7$ $l_9 \leq R_5$

The surface reading (every >> some) is derived by the following mapping: C_3->l_0, C_2->l_3, R_7->l_8, N_5 -> l_2, **C_1-> l_7**, R_5->l_9, N_7 -> l_5
l_2: give(v, y, z)
l_5: some(x, test(x), give(v, y, z))
l_7:every(y,student(y),some(x,test(x),give(v,y, z)))
l_1:every(y,student(y),some(x,test(x),give(x, y, z)))

The interpretation of the second sentence is derived by unifying the S-features of the S-trees (as shown in the previous section). As the result, the variables C_3 and v_3 are unified with the variables C_1 and v. Given that C_1 is being mapped to the proposition l_7 above, C_3 is being reconstructed as the proposition every(y, student(y), some(x, test(x), give(v, y, z)) and l_3 corresponds to the desired reading of this sentence:

(11) Bill did too.

l_4: Bill(r)
l_3: λv_3.C_3 (r)

C_3 (=C_1) -> l_7
v_3=v

l_3: λv. every(y, student(y),some(x, test(x), give(v, y, z))) (r) = every(y, student(y), some(x, test(x), give(r, y, z)))

The inverse reading (where *some>>every)* can be obtained by the following mapping C_3->l_0, C_2->l_3, R_7->l_8, N_7 -> l_2, **C_1-> l_5**, R_5->l_9, N_5 -> l_7
l_2: give(v, y, z)
l_7: every(y, student(y), give(v, y, z))
l_5:some(x,test(x),every(y,student(y),give(v,y, z)))
l_1: some(x,test(x),every(y,student(y),give(x, y, z)))

Now, when the second sentence is interpreted, C_3 is unified with C_1, which is being mapped to l_5: $C_3(=C_1)$ -> l_5. The proposition l_3, then, is reduced to: λv.some(x, test(x), every(y, student(y), give(v, y, z))) (r) = some(x, test(x), every(y, student(y), give(r, y, z)))

As this example illustrates, scope parallelism follows from the present analysis, given that C_3 is unified with a disambiguated interpretation of a VP. It can also be shown that the wide scope puzzle (Sag 1980), shown in (12) is not unexpected under this approach, however, the analysis of this phenomenon is beyond the scope of this paper. [3]

(12) A nurse saw every patient. Dr.Smith did too.
some(x, nurse(x), every(y, patient(y), see(x, y)))
*every(y, patient(y), some(x, nurse(x), see(x, y)))

[3] As Hirschbuhler 1982, Fox 2000 among others noted, there are constructions where subjects of VPE can have narrow scope relative to nonsubjects. For example, the sentence *A Canadian flag was hanging in front of every building. An American flag was too* has a reading in which each building has both an American and a Canadian flag standing in front of it. The existence of such readings does not present a problem for the present analysis, if we adopt an analysis of quantificational NPs proposed in Babko-Malaya 2004.

7 Antecedent Contained Deletion(ACD)

Further evidence for the proposed analysis comes from sentences with ACD, discussed in Sag 1980, Egg and Erk 2001, Asher et al 2001, Jacobson (to appear), and illustrated in (13):

(13) *John wants Mary to read every book Bill does.*

The elided material in this sentence is understood as either "Bill reads" or "Bill wants Mary to read". Given that 'want' and 'every' can take different scope, four possible readings are expected. However, puzzling in this case is the unavailability of one of these readings: *John wants that for every book that Bill wants Mary to read, she reads it. Let us consider the final interpretation of this sentence:

l_4: want(v_0, N_4) l_0: $\lambda v_0.C_{2\,(want)}$ (r)
l_1: read(v, u) l_2: $\lambda v.C_{1\,(read)}$ (x)
l_6: $\lambda u.C_{4\,(read)}$ (y) $l_6 \leq C_1$ l_8: book(y) $\wedge$ l_3
l_5: every(y, R_5, N_5) l_3: λv_3.C (z)
mary(x), john(r), bill(z)
$l_1 \leq C_1$, $l_4 \leq C_2$, $l_1 \leq N_5$, $l_8 \leq R_5$, $l_1 \leq N_4$

The non-lexicalized S tree introduces a proposition l_3 and variables C and v_3. These variables can be unified with either S features of the 'read'-tree (i.e. C_1 and v), or S features of the 'want'-tree (i.e. C_2 and v_0). In the first case, the small ellipsis interpretation is derived, and both scope readings are available: C = C_1, v_3 = v
C/C_1 -> l_6, C_4-> l_1
l_2: read(x, y), l_3: read(z, y)
every >> want:
N_5 -> l_o, C_2 -> l_4, N_4 -> l_2, R_5 ->l_8

$$l_5\text{:every(y, book(y)\&}\underbrace{\text{read}(\mathbf{z}, y)}_{l_3}\text{,want(r, }\underbrace{\text{read}(\mathbf{x}, y)}_{l_2}))$$

want >> every:
C_2 -> l_4, N_4 -> l_5, N_5 -> l_2, R_5 ->l_8

$$l_0\text{:want(r,every(y,book(y)\&}\underbrace{\text{read}(\mathbf{z},y)}_{l_3}\text{, }\underbrace{\text{read}(\mathbf{x}, y)}_{l_2}))$$

If C and v_3 are unified with S features of the 'want'-tree, then the large ellipsis interpretation is derived: C = C_2, v_3 = v_0, **C/C_2 -> l_4**, N_4 -> l_2, C_4 -> l_1, C_1 -> l_6
l_0: want(r, read(x, y)), l_3: want(z, read(x, y))

The reading where *every* >> *want* is derived by the following constraints: N_5-> l_0, C_1-> l_1, R_5 ->l_8

$$l_5\text{: every(y, book(y) \& }\underbrace{\text{want}(\mathbf{z}, \text{read}(x,y))}_{l_3}\text{), }\underbrace{\text{want}(\mathbf{r}, \text{read}(x, y))}_{l_0}$$

The fourth possible reading, where *want* >> *every*, however, is predicted to be unavailable under the present assumptions. This reading, *want(r, every(y, book(y) & <u>want(z, read(x, y))</u>, read(x, y)),* cannot be derived, since it requires the proposition l_3 to be 'inserted' within the proposition l_0.

References

Asher N., D. Hardt and J.Busquets. 2001. Discourse Parallelism, Scope, and Ellipsis", Journal of Semantics, 18(1), pp. 1-25.

Babko-Malaya O. 2004 "LTAG Semantics of NP-Coordination" in Proc. of TAG+7, Vancouver

Dalrymple M., S.Shieber and F.Pereira 1991. Ellipsis and Higher-Order Unification. In Linguistics and Philosophy 14.

Egg, M. and K.Erk 2001. A compositional approach to VP ellipsis 8th International Conference on HPSG,Trondheim, Norway

Fiengo R. and R. May 1994. Indices and Identity. MIT Press, Cambridge

Fox, D. 2000 Economy and Semantic Intepretation, MIT Press

Hardt, D. 1993. VP Ellipsis: Form, Meaning and Processing. PhD Diss. Univ. of PA

Hardt, D. 1999. Dynamic Interpretation of VP Ellipsis. Linguistics and Philosophy. 22.2. Heim, I. 2001

Jacobson, P. (to appear) Direct Compositionality and Variable-Free Semantics: The Case of Antecedent Contained Deletion", in K. Johnson (ed.), Topics in Ellipsis, Oxford University Press.

Johnson, K. 2003. In search of the Middle Field. Ms. Univ. of Mass.

Joshi A. and Y. Schabes 1997. Tree-Adjoining Grammars, in G. Rozenberg and A. Salomaa (eds.) Handbook of Formal Languages, Springer, Berlin

Kallmeyer, L. and A.K Joshi 2003. Factoring Predicate Argument and Scope Semantics: Underspecified Semantics with LTAG. Research on Language and Computation 1(1-2), 358.

Kallmeyer, L. and M. Romero. 2004. LTAG Semantics with Semantic Unification. In Proceedings of TAG+7, Vancouver, Canada

Sag, Ivan 1980 Deletion and Logical Form. Garland Press: New York

Shieber, S., F.Pereira, and M.Dalrymple 1996. Interactions of Scope and Ellipsis. In *Linguistics and Philosophy 19,* pp.527-552.

Three reasons to adopt TAG-based surface realisation

Claire Gardent
CNRS / LORIA
615, rue du Jardin Botanique
F-54 600 Villers-Lès-Nancy
gardent@loria.fr

Eric Kow
INRIA / LORIA
Université Henri Poincaré
615, rue du Jardin Botanique
F-54 600 Villers-Lès-Nancy
kow@loria.fr

Abstract

Surface realisation from flat semantic formulae is known to be exponential in the length of the input. In this paper, we argue that TAG naturally supports the integration of three main ways of reducing complexity: polarity filtering, delayed adjunction and empty semantic items elimination. We support these claims by presenting some preliminary results of the TAG-based surface realiser GenI.

1 Introduction

Surface realisation consists in producing all the sentences associated by a grammar with a given semantic formula. For lexicalist grammars such as LTAG (Lexicalised Tree Adjoining Grammar), surface realisation usually proceeds bottom-up from a set of flat semantic literals[1]. However, surface realisation from flat semantic formulae is known to be exponential in the length of the input (Kay96; Bre92; KS02). In this paper, we abstract from the TAG based surface realiser for French GenI, (GK05) and argue that TAG naturally supports the integration of various proposals made to help reduce either surface realisation or parsing complexity into a TAG based, lexically driven surface realiser. Specifically, we show:

1. that TAG elementary trees naturally support the implementation of a technique called *polarity filtering* used to reduce the exponential factor introduced by *lexical ambiguity* (Per03),
2. that TAG two operations of substitution and adjunction provides a natural framework for implementing a delayed adjunction mechanism capable of reducing the complexity due to the *lack of ordering information* and
3. that TAG extended domain of locality helps reduce the potential complexity increment introduced by *semantically empty items* such as infinitival *"to"* or complementiser *"that"*.

2 Surface realisation, flat semantics and computational complexity

Why is surface realisation exponential in the length of the input? As shown in (Kay96), one reason for this is the *lack of ordering information*. Contrary to parsing where the input is a string i.e., an ordered list of words, the input to surface realisation is a set of literals. Supposing each literal selects exactly one constituent in the lexicon, then the number of possible combinations between these constituents will be 2^n (the number of subsets obtainable from a set of size n).

In practice of course, there are possible restrictions on constituent combination. In particular, most existing realisers impose the constraint that only constituents with non overlapping semantics and compatible indices can be combined. Because of this restriction, the core of the complexity stems in practice from *intersective modifiers* (Bre92; Kay96). Given a set of n modifiers all modifying the same structure, all possible intermediate structures will be constructed i.e. 2^{n+1}.

A second reason for the exponential complexity of surface realisation is *lexical ambiguity*. As for bottom-up parsing, in surface realisation from flat semantics, the input is used to select a set of lexical entries namely all lexical entries whose seman-

[1] See e.g., (CCFP99) for a discussion summarising the reasons for this choice.

Proceedings of the 8th International Workshop on Tree Adjoining Grammar and Related Formalisms, pages 97–102,
Sydney, July 2006.

tics subsumes one or more of the input literals. In a realistic grammar, one literal will be associated with more than one lexical entries. So if Lex_i is the number of lexical entries associated with literal l_i, then for an input semantics comprising n literals, the number of sets of lexical constituents covering the input semantics is: $\prod_{i=1}^{i=n} Lex_i$

The two sources of complexity interact by multiplying out so that the potential number of combinations of constituents is:

$$2^n \times \prod_{i=1}^{i=n} Lex_i$$

In what follows, we show that TAG naturally supports various optimisations that have been proposed to reduce the search space.

3 Polarity filtering

To restrict the impact of lexical ambiguity on parsing efficiency, (Per03) introduces a method called *Polarity filtering*. This method is based on the observation that many of the combinations of lexical entries which cover the input semantics are in fact syntactically invalid either because a syntactic requirement is not fulfilled or because a syntactic resource is not used. Accordingly, polarity based filtering eliminates such combinations by:

- assigning each lexical entry with a set of polarities reflecting its syntactic requirements and resources,
- computing for each possible combination of lexical entries the sum of its polarities and
- only allowing surface realisation on combinations which have a net sum of zero (all requirements are satisfied and all resources are used).

By filtering the initial search space before the tree combination phase, polarity filtering in effect reduces the impact of lexical ambiguity i.e. decreases $\prod_{i=1}^{i=n} Lex_i$.

The definitory properties of TAG elementary trees provide a natural way to assign polarities to a TAG lexical entries: each elementary tree can be associated with a polarity $+C$, where C is the category of its root node and each substitution or foot node in that tree, a polarity $-C$ is added, where C is the category of that node.

We implemented polarity filtering in `GenI` based on this way of associating lexical entries with polarities[2]. We then measured the impact of this filtering on the initial search space (the number of sets of lexical items actually explored by the realiser), on space (measured by the number of chart items created) and on time.

Table 1 summarises the impact of polarity filtering on the initial search space[3]. **possible** indicates the number of combinations of lexical entries which cover the input semantics and thus can potentially lead to a valid syntactic tree realising the input semantics and **explored** gives the number of combinations actually explored by the surface realiser after polarity filtering has ruled out combinations which cannot possibly lead to a valid syntactic tree).

As is to be expected, the impact increases with the number of input literals so that while polarity filtering divides the initial search space by 35.6 for an input ranging between 1 and 6 literals, it divides it by 441.6 for an input size ranging between 14 and 16 literals

literals	possible	explored	(×)
1-6	199.10	5.60	35.6
7-9	6460.88	40.06	161.3
10-13	43028.25	137.06	313.9
14-16	292747.64	662.91	441.6

Figure 1: Polarity filtering and initial space (Sets of initial trees covering the input semantics)

Table 2 gives the impact of polarity filtering on space as measured by the number of created chart items (or constituents). The first column (**w/o pol.**) gives the number of created charted items when polarity filtering is switched off and the second, (**with pol.**) when polarity filtering is on. As can be seen, the effect is particularly pronounced when the input exceeds 10 literals.

Finally, Figure 3 shows that the overhead introduced by the construction of the polarity automaton means that formulae under 10 literals are realised in roughly the same time with or without polarity filtering. However, for larger sentences, polarity filtering is increasingly important in keeping realisation times reasonable. For instance, given an input ranging between 14 and 16 literals, polar-

[2]See (GK05) for more details.

[3]For each group of input (1-6 literals, 7-9, etc.), measures are based on an average of 15 cases.

literals	w/o pol.	with pol.	(×)
1-6	146.40	83.60	1.8
7-9	3273.50	1281.25	2.6
10-13	7468.06	702.50	10.6
14-16	17502.36	1613.91	10.8

Figure 2: With and without Polarity filtering (Chart items)

ity filtering divides realisation time by 5, that is, yields a realisation time of 2.21 seconds instead of 11.61.

literals	w/o pol.	with pol.	(×)
1-6	0.81	0.79	1.0
7-9	1.68	1.35	1.2
10-13	3.56	1.88	1.9
14-16	11.61	2.21	5.3

Figure 3: With and without Polarity filtering (CPU times)

4 Substitution/adjunction distinction

One important specificity of TAG is that it includes two combination operations namely, adjunction and substitution. We now show that this feature of TAG is particularly useful in improving surface realisation performance.

4.1 Reducing the impact of intersective modifiers

To restrict the combinatorics induced by modifiers, (CCFP99; CO05) proposes either to handle modifiers after a complete syntactic tree is built (i.e., after all syntactic requirements are fulfilled) or before the modifiee is combined with other items (e.g., before the head noun has combined with a determiner). Although the number of intermediate structures generated is still 2^n for n modifiers, both strategies have the effect of blocking these 2^n structures from multiplying out with other structures in the chart. More precisely, given an input semantics of size n where k of its literals are to be realised as modifiers, the number of intermediate structures possible in the two phase approach is $2^k + 2^{n-k}$, which can be considerably smaller than 2^n, depending on the size of k.

In TAG, we can make use of the fact that substitution and adjunction apply independently of each other to implement a two-phase generation strategy where modifiers are handled only after a complete syntactic tree is built. In the first phase, only substitutions are performed and in the second, only adjunctions. Additionally, before adjunction starts, all unsaturated trees (trees with unfilled substitution sites) are discarded from the chart thereby ensuring that modifiers do not combine with structures that cannot possibly lead to a valid result (since no constituent could be found to fill the unsaturated substitution sites).

Since in TAG, modifiers always involve the use of adjunction, modifiers will always be handled by the second phase of the algorithm and thereby adjoined into "saturated trees" i.e., trees devoid of unfilled substitutions sites. In this way, the proliferation of structures induced by the modifiers can be restricted.

The substitution-before-adjunction strategy was integrated in `GenI` yielding the improvements indicated in Figures 4 and 5.

literals	1 phase	2 phase	(×)
≤ 3	0.73	0.73	1.0
4	0.74	0.75	1.0
5	0.97	0.93	1.0
6	2.91	0.89	3.3
7	4.24	1.30	3.3
≥ 8	Time out		

Figure 4: With and without SBA (CPU times)

literals	1 phase	2 phase	(×)
≤ 3	47.00	44.33	1.1
4	107.00	108.00	1.0
5	310.00	263.00	1.2
6	1387.33	883.00	1.6
7	2293.50	761.33	3.0

Figure 5: With and without SBA (Chart items)

As table 4 shows, when there is more than 7 literals in the input, the one-phase algorithm times out. More in general, for the data shown, the two phase strategy leads to an average decrease in time ranging between 1 and 3.3% and a decrease in space varying between 1.1% and 3% respectively.

Although the poor performance of the 1 phase algorithm is in part due to a very large and strongly overgenerating grammar[4] , the data clearly shows that SBA is essential in supporting large scale TAG based surface realisation.

[4]The grammar used is a grammar for French which contains roughly 3 400 initial trees (CD04).

4.2 Substitution-before-adjunction combined with Polarity Filtering

The substitution-before-adjunction strategy limits the impact of intersective modifiers by restricting the number of constituents the modifiers can combine with *within one set of lexical items*. Because polarity filtering reduces the number of sets of lexical items to be considered, it trivially also reduces the number of sets of lexical items involving adjunctions.

The space improvement provided by combining the substitution-before-adjunction (SBA) strategy with polarity filtering is illustrated in Figures 6 and 7 which show the space reduction associated with cases ordered either according to their number of literals or according to their number of foot nodes (i.e., adjunction cases). As should be expected, the number of foot nodes is more highly correlated with a space reduction. Specifically, a combined SBA/polarity strategy divides by 3.4 the space used for cases involving between 1 and 12 auxiliary trees; and by 18.8 the space used for cases involving between 14 and 16 auxiliary trees.

literals	**w/o pol.**	**with pol.**	(×)
1-6	367.90	109.50	3.4
7-9	6192.69	1550.19	4.0
10-13	11211.06	711.06	15.8
14-16	30660.27	1631.64	18.8

Figure 6: SBA + Polarity (Chart items)

# aux trees	**w/o pol.**	**with pol.**	(×)
1-12	2124.27	620.82	3.4
13-120	8751.53	1786.47	4.9
121-190	11528.43	611.50	18.9
191-350	25279.75	1085.75	23.3

Figure 7: SBA + Polarity (Chart items)

4.3 Filtering out unusable trees

Another interesting aspect of TAG's use of two combination operations and more specifically of the substitution-before-adjunction strategy is that it naturally supports the inclusion of a third phase to filter out unusable trees that is, trees which can be determined not to be integrable in any valid derivation. Specifically, this third phase occurs between substitution and adjunction and filters out:

- all trees with an unfilled substitution site
- all saturated trees whose root node is not labelled with an S category

The first filter (elimination of unsaturated trees) is required, as indicated above, to restrict the impact of intersective modifiers: by discarding them, we restrict adjunction to saturated trees. The second, makes use of the property of auxiliary trees which insists that root and foot node be labelled with the same category. Because of this property, adjunction cannot affect the category of the tree it adjoins to. In particular, a tree which after all possible substitutions have been performed, has root label C with $C \neq S$ can never lead to the creation by adjunction of a tree with root label S. Hence it can be discarded (provided of course, the generator is seeking to build sentences).

Figures 8 and 9 illustrate the impact of this second filter (called the *Root Node Filter*, RNF) on the chart size when polarity filtering is switched off. As for SAB, the figures show a higher correlation between the RNF and the number of adjunction nodes than with the number of literals. Intriguingly, the impact of the filter is proportionally higher on sentences with fewer foot nodes. Although this needs to be checked more thoroughly, the explanation for this could be the following. The trees removed by the Root Node Filter are saturated tree not rooted in S hence essentially saturated NP trees. Examination of the data reveals that the number of these trees removed by the RNF remains almost constant (though this might be an ad hoc property of the specific testsuite used). Hence in proportion, the effect of the RNF diminishes.

Note however that in absolute terms, the number of trees whose derivation is avoided by the RNF remains quite high thus contributing to an overall better performance.

literals	**w/o RNF**	**with RNF**	(×)
1-6	367.90	146.40	2.5
7-9	6192.69	3273.50	1.9
10-13	11211.06	7468.06	1.5
14-16	30660.27	17502.36	1.8

Figure 8: Root node filter w/o Pol (Chart Items).

As Figures 10 and 11 show, combining the Root Node Filter with polarity filtering simply reinforces the biases noted above: Root Node Filtering is proportionally more effective for short input but can remain useful in absolute terms. A more thor-

# aux trees	w/o RNF	with RNF	(×)
1-12	2124.27	527.36	4.0
13-120	8751.53	5570.33	1.6
121-190	11528.43	6490.14	1.8
191-350	25279.75	15469.17	1.6

Figure 9: Root node filter w/o Pol (Chart Items).

ough investigation of the data and further experiments are needed however to determine whether such behaviour is not tied to some ad hoc property of our (still too limited) testsuite.

literals	w/o RNF	with RNF	(×)
1-6	109.50	83.60	1.3
7-9	1550.19	1281.25	1.2
10-13	711.06	702.50	1.0
14-16	1631.64	1613.91	1.0

Figure 10: Root node filter + Pol (Chart Items).

# aux trees	w/o RNF	with RNF	(×)
1-12	422	621	1.5
13-120	1627	1786	1.1
121-190	600	612	1.0
191-350	1073	1086	1.0

Figure 11: Root Node Filter + Pol (Chart Items).

5 TAG extended domain of locality

Arguably there are words such as complementiser *that* or infinitival *to* whose semantics is empty. These words are to surface realisation what gaps (or empty categories) are to parsing. In a naive approach, they require that all trees with an empty semantics be considered as potential constituent candidate at each combining step. In terms of efficiency, this roughly means increasing the size of the input n (just like postulating gaps at all position in an input string increases the size of that string).

To avoid this shortcoming, a common practice (CCFP99) consists in specifying a set of rules which selects empty semantic items on the basis of the input literals. However these rules fail to reflect the fact that empty semantic items are usually functional words and hence governed by syntactic rather than semantic constraints.

By contrast, in a TAG based surface realiser, TAG elementary trees provide a natural way to specify the syntactic environment in which empty semantic items can occur. For instance, complementiser *that* occurs with verbs taking a sentential argument which is generally captured by including the complementiser as a co-anchor in the trees of these verbs.

More in general, the extended domain of locality provided by TAG elementary trees, together with the possibility of specifying co-anchors means that empty semantic items can be avoided altogether. Hence they do not require specific treatment and have no impact on efficiency.

6 Discussion

We have argued that TAG presents several features that makes it particularly amenable to the development of an optimised surface realiser. We now summarise these features and briefly compare TAG with CCG (Combinatory Categorial Grammar) and HPSG (Head Driven Phrase Structure Grammar) based surface realisation.

6.1 Using tree node types

The *different types of tree nodes* identified by TAG can be used to support polarity filtering whereby substitution nodes can be associated with negative polarities (requirements) and root nodes with positive polarities (resources). As our preliminary experiments show, polarity filtering has a significant impact on the initial search space, on the space used and on CPU times.

So far, this particular type of global filtering on the initial search space has been used neither in the HPSG (CCFP99; CO05) nor in the CCG (Whi04) approach. Although it could presumably be adapted to fit these grammars, such an adaptation is in essence less straightforward than in TAG.

In CCG, the several combination rules mean that a subcategory can function either as a resource or as a requirement depending on the rule that applies. For instance, in the verbal category $(S\backslash NP)/NP$, the subcategory $S\backslash NP$ functions as a resource when NPs are type raised (it satisfies the requirement of a type raised NP with category $S/(S\backslash NP)$). However it will need to be further decomposed into a resource and a requirement if they are not. More in general, polarity specification in CCG would need to take into account the several combination rules in addition to the category structure. In HPSG, it is the interaction of lexical categories with lexical and phrasal rules that will need to be taken into consideration.

6.2 Using rule types

The *two types of tree combining operations* permitted by TAG can be used to structure the surface realisation algorithm. As we've shown, performing all substitutions before allowing for adjunction greatly reduces the exponential impact of intersective modifiers. Moreover, combining such a substitution-before-adjunction strategy with polarity filtering further improves performance.

In comparison, the HPSG and the CCG approach do not support such a natural structuring of the algorithm and intersective modifiers induce either a pre- or a post-processing.

In HPSG, intersective modifiers are discarded during the chart generation phase and adjoined into the generated structures at a later stage. This is inelegant in that (i) intersective modifiers are artificially treated separately and (ii) structures subject to adjunction have to be non monotonically recomputed to reflect the impact of the adjunction in that part of the tree dominating the adjunction.

In CCG, the input logical form is chunked into subtrees each corresponding to a separate generation subproblem to be solved independently. Again the approach is ad hoc in that it does not rely on a given grammatical or linguistic property. As a result, e.g., negation needs special treatment to avoid incompleteness (if the heuristic applies, negated sentences cannot be generated). Similarly, it is unclear how long distance dependencies involving modifiers (e.g., *Which office did you say that Peter work in ?*) are handled.

6.3 Using TAG extended domain of locality

TAG extended domain of locality means that empty semantic items need no special treatment. In contrast, both the HPSG and the CCG approach resort to ad hoc filtering rules which, based on a scan of the input semantics, add semantically empty items to the chart.

7 Further research

Although the results presented give strong evidence for the claim that TAG naturally supports the development of an optimised surface based realiser, they are based on a limited testsuite and on a core grammar for French that heavily overgenerates. Hence they do not truly reflect the potential of the proposed optimisations on the performance of a large scale surface realiser. Current work concentrates on remedying these shortcomings. In particular, we are working on developing a *structured* test suite which permits a precise measure of the impact of different factors both on complexity and on the optimisations used. In this testsuite for instance, each item is associated with a series of indicators concerning its potential complexity: number of literals in the corresponding input semantics, number of trees, number of nodes, number of substitutions nodes and number of foot nodes in the corresponding selection of initial trees.

Further work also includes restricting overgeneration and exploring in how far, polarity filtering can be used to select one among the many paraphrases

References

C. Brew. Letting the cat out of the bag: Generation for shake-and-bake MT. In *Proceedings of COLING '92*, Nantes, France, 1992.

J. Carroll, A. Copestake, D. Flickinger, and V. Paznański. An efficient chart generator for (semi-)lexicalist grammars. In *Proceedings of EWNLG '99*, 1999.

B. Crabbé and D. Duchier. Metagrammar redux. In *International Workshop on Constraint Solving and Language Processing - CSLP 2004, Copenhagen*, 2004.

J. Carroll and S. Oepen. High efficiency realization for a wide-coverage unification grammar. In R. Dale and K-F. Wong, editors, *Proceedings of the Second International Joint Conference on Natural Language Processing*, volume 3651 of *Springer Lecture Notes in Artificial Intelligence*, pages 165–176, 2005.

C. Gardent and E. Kow. Generating and selecting grammatical paraphrases. In *Proceedings of the 10th European Workshop on Natural Language Generation*, Aberdeen, Scotland, 2005.

M. Kay. Chart Generation. In *34th ACL*, pages 200–204, Santa Cruz, California, 1996.

A. Koller and K. Striegnitz. Generation as dependency parsing. In *Proceedings of the 40th ACL*, Philadelphia, 2002.

G. Perrier. Les grammaires d'interaction, 2003. Habilitation à diriger les recherches en informatique, université Nancy 2.

M. White. Reining in CCG chart realization. In *INLG*, pages 182–191, 2004.

Generating XTAG Parsers from Algebraic Specifications*

Carlos Gómez-Rodríguez and **Miguel A. Alonso**
Departamento de Computación
Universidade da Coruña
Campus de Elviña, s/n
15071 A Coruña, Spain
{cgomezr, alonso}@udc.es

Manuel Vilares
E. S. de Ingeniería Informática
Universidad de Vigo
Campus As Lagoas, s/n
32004 Ourense, Spain
vilares@uvigo.es

Abstract

In this paper, a generic system that generates parsers from parsing schemata is applied to the particular case of the XTAG English grammar. In order to be able to generate XTAG parsers, some transformations are made to the grammar, and TAG parsing schemata are extended with feature structure unification support and a simple tree filtering mechanism. The generated implementations allow us to study the performance of different TAG parsers when working with a large-scale, wide-coverage grammar.

1 Introduction

Since Tree Adjoining Grammars (TAG) were introduced, several different parsing algorithms for these grammars have been developed, each with its peculiar characteristics. Identifying the advantages and disadvantages of each of them is not trivial, and there are no comparative studies between them in the literature that work with real-life, wide coverage grammars. In this paper, we use a generic tool based on parsing schemata to generate implementations of several TAG parsers and compare them by parsing with the XTAG English Grammar (XTAG, 2001).

The parsing schemata formalism (Sikkel, 1997) is a framework that allows us to describe parsers in a simple and declarative way. A parsing schema is a representation of a parsing algorithm as a set of inference rules which are used to perform deductions on intermediate results called items. These items represent sets of incomplete parse trees which the algorithm can generate. An input sentence to be analyzed produces an initial set of items. Additionally, a parsing schema must define a criterion to determine which items are final, i.e. which items correspond to complete parses of the input sentence. If it is possible to obtain a final item from the set of initial items by using the schema's inference rules (called deductive steps), then the input sentence belongs to the language defined by the grammar. The parse forest can then be retrieved from the intermediate items used to infer the final items, as in (Billot and Lang, 1989).

As an example, we introduce a CYK-based algorithm (Vijay-Shanker and Joshi, 1985) for TAG. Given a tree adjoining grammar $G = (V_T, V_N, S, I, A)$[1] and a sentence of length n which we denote by $a_1\ a_2\ \ldots\ a_n$[2], we denote by $P(G)$ the set of productions $\{N^\gamma \rightarrow N_1^\gamma N_2^\gamma \ldots N_r^\gamma\}$ such that N^γ is an inner node of a tree $\gamma \in (I \cup A)$, and $N_1^\gamma N_2^\gamma \ldots N_r^\gamma$ is the ordered sequence of direct children of N^γ.

The parsing schema for the TAG CYK-based algorithm (Alonso et al., 1999) is a function that maps such a grammar G to a deduction system whose domain is the set of items

$$\{[N^\gamma, i, j, p, q, adj]\}$$

verifying that N^γ is a tree node in an elementary

* Partially supported by Ministerio de Educación y Ciencia and FEDER (TIN2004-07246-C03-01, TIN2004-07246-C03-02), Xunta de Galicia (PGIDIT05PXIC30501PN, PGIDIT05PXIC10501PN, PGIDIT05SIN044E and PGIDIT05SIN059E), and Programa de becas FPU (Ministerio de Educación y Ciencia). We are grateful to Eric Villemonte de la Clergerie and François Barthelemy for their help in converting the XTAG grammar to XML.

[1] Where V_T denotes the set of terminal symbols, V_N the set of nonterminal symbols, S the axiom, I the set of initial trees and A the set of auxiliary trees.

[2] From now on, we will follow the usual conventions by which nonterminal symbols are represented by uppercase letters ($A, B\ldots$), and terminals by lowercase letters ($a, b\ldots$). Greek letters (α, β...) will be used to represent trees, N^γ a node in the tree γ, and R^γ the root node of the tree γ.

Proceedings of the 8th International Workshop on Tree Adjoining Grammar and Related Formalisms, pages 103–108,
Sydney, July 2006.

tree $\gamma \in (I \cup A)$, i and j $(0 \leq i \leq j)$ are string positions, p and q may be undefined or instantiated to positions $i \leq p \leq q \leq j$ (the latter only when $\gamma \in A$), and $adj \in \{true, false\}$ indicates whether an adjunction has been performed on node N^γ.

The positions i and j indicate that a substring $a_{i+1} \ldots a_j$ of the string is being recognized, and positions p and q denote the substring dominated by γ's foot node. The final item set would be

$$\{[R^\alpha, 0, n, -, -, adj] \mid \alpha \in I\}$$

for the presence of such an item would indicate that there exists a valid parse tree with yield $a_1\ a_2 \ldots a_n$ and rooted at R^α, the root of an initial tree; and therefore there exists a complete parse tree for the sentence.

A *deductive step* $\frac{\eta_1 \ldots \eta_m}{\xi}\ \Phi$ allows us to infer the item specified by its consequent ξ from those in its antecedents $\eta_1 \ldots \eta_m$. *Side conditions* (Φ) specify the valid values for the variables appearing in the antecedents and consequent, and may refer to grammar rules or specify other constraints that must be verified in order to infer the consequent. The deductive steps for our CYK-based parser are shown in figure 1. The steps $\mathcal{D}^{\text{Scan}}_{\text{CYK}}$ and $\mathcal{D}^{\epsilon}_{\text{CYK}}$ are used to start the bottom-up parsing process by recognizing a terminal symbol for the input string, or none if we are using a tree with an epsilon node. The $\mathcal{D}^{\text{Binary}}_{\text{CYK}}$ step (where the operation $p \cup p'$ returns p if p is defined, and p' otherwise) represents the bottom-up parsing operation which joins two subtrees into one, and is analogous to one of the deductive steps of the CYK parser for CFG. The $\mathcal{D}^{\text{Unary}}_{\text{CYK}}$ step is used to handle unary branching productions. $\mathcal{D}^{\text{Foot}}_{\text{CYK}}$ and $\mathcal{D}^{\text{Adj}}_{\text{CYK}}$ implement the adjunction operation, where a tree β is adjoined into a node N^γ; their side condition $\beta \in \text{adj}(N^\gamma)$ means that β must be adjoinable into the node N^γ (which involves checking that N^γ is an adjunction node, comparing its label to $\mathbf{R}^\beta$'s and verifying that no adjunction constraint disallows the operation). Finally, the $\mathcal{D}^{\text{Subs}}_{\text{CYK}}$ step implements the substitution operation in grammars supporting it.

As can be seen from the example, parsing schemata are simple, high-level descriptions that convey the fundamental semantics of parsing algorithms while abstracting implementation details: they define a set of possible intermediate results and allowed operations on them, but they don't specify data structures for storing the results or an order for the operations to be executed. This high abstraction level makes schemata useful for defining, comparing and analyzing parsers in pencil and paper without worrying about implementation details. However, if we want to actually execute the parsers and analyze their results and performance in a computer, they must be implemented in a programming language, making it necessary to lose the high level of abstraction in order to obtain functional and efficient implementations.

In order to bridge this gap between theory and practice, we have designed and implemented a system able to automatically transform parsing schemata into efficient Java implementations of their corresponding algorithms. The input to this system is a simple and declarative representation of a parsing schema, which is practically equal to the formal notation that we used previously. For example, this is the $\mathcal{D}^{\text{Binary}}_{\text{CYK}}$ deductive step shown in figure 1 in a format readable by our compiler:

```
@step CYKBinary
[ Node1 , i , k , p , q , adj1 ]
[ Node2 , k , j , p' , q' , adj2 ]
-------------------------------- Node3 -> Node1 Node2
[ Node3 , i , j , Union(p;p') , Union(q;q') , false ]
```

The parsing schemata compilation technique used by our system is based on the following fundamental ideas (Gómez-Rodríguez et al., 2006a):

- Each deductive step is compiled to a Java class containing code to match and search for antecedent items and generate the corresponding conclusions from the consequent.
- The step classes are coordinated by a deductive parsing engine, as the one described in (Shieber et al., 1995). This algorithm ensures a sound and complete deduction process, guaranteeing that all items that can be generated from the initial items will be obtained.
- To attain efficiency, an automatic analysis of the schema is performed in order to create indexes allowing fast access to items. As each different parsing schema needs to perform different searches for antecedent items, the index structures we generate are schema-specific. In this way, we guarantee constant-time access to items so that the computational complexity of our generated implementations is never above the theoretical complexity of the parsers.
- Since parsing schemata have an open notation, for any mathematical object can potentially appear inside items, the system includes an extensibility mechanism which can be used to define new kinds of objects to use in schemata.

$$\mathcal{D}^{\text{Scan}}_{\text{CYK}} = \frac{[a,i,i+1]}{[N^\gamma,i,i+1 \mid -,- \mid \text{false}]} \quad a = \text{label}(N^\gamma) \qquad \mathcal{D}^{\epsilon}_{\text{CYK}} = \frac{}{[N^\gamma,i,i \mid -,- \mid \text{false}]} \quad \epsilon = \text{label}(N^\gamma)$$

$$\mathcal{D}^{\text{Unary}}_{\text{CYK}} = \frac{[M^\gamma,i,j \mid p,q \mid adj]}{[N^\gamma,i,j \mid p,q] \mid \text{false}]} \quad N^\gamma \to M^\gamma \in \mathcal{P}(\gamma) \qquad \mathcal{D}^{\text{Binary}}_{\text{CYK}} = \frac{\begin{array}{c}[M^\gamma,i,k \mid p,q \mid adj1],\\ [P^\gamma,k,j \mid p',q' \mid adj2]\end{array}}{[N^\gamma,i,j \mid p\cup p',q\cup q' \mid \text{false}]} \quad N^\gamma \to M^\gamma P^\gamma \in \mathcal{P}(\gamma)$$

$$\mathcal{D}^{\text{Foot}}_{\text{CYK}} = \frac{[N^\gamma,i,j \mid p,q \mid \text{false}]}{[\mathbf{F}^\beta,i,j \mid i,j \mid \text{false}]} \quad \beta \in \text{adj}(N^\gamma) \qquad \mathcal{D}^{\text{Adj}}_{\text{CYK}} = \frac{\begin{array}{c}[\mathbf{R}^\beta,i',j' \mid i,j \mid adj],\\ [N^\gamma,i,j \mid p,q \mid \text{false}]\end{array}}{[N^\gamma,i',j' \mid p,q \mid \text{true}]} \quad \beta \in \text{adj}(N^\gamma)$$

$$\mathcal{D}^{\text{Subs}}_{\text{CYK}} = \frac{[\mathbf{R}^\alpha,i,j \mid -,- \mid adj]}{[N^\gamma,i,j \mid -,- \mid \text{false}]} \quad \alpha \in \text{subs}(N^\gamma)$$

Figure 1: A CYK-based parser for TAG.

2 Generating parsers for the XTAG grammar

By using parsing schemata as the ones in (Alonso et al., 1999; Nederhof, 1999) as input to our system, we can easily obtain efficient implementations of several TAG parsing algorithms. In this section, we describe how we have dealt with the particular characteristics of the XTAG grammar in order to make it compatible with our generic compilation technique; and we also provide empirical results which allow us to compare the performance of several different TAG parsing algorithms in the practical case of the XTAG grammar. It shall be noted that similar comparisons have been made with smaller grammars, such as simplified subsets of the XTAG grammar, but not with the whole XTAG grammar with all its trees and feature structures. Therefore, our comparison provides valuable information about the behavior of various parsers on a complete, large-scale natural language grammar. This behavior is very different from the one that can be observed on small grammars, since grammar size becomes a dominant factor in computational complexity when large grammars like the XTAG are used to parse relatively small natural language sentences (Gómez-Rodríguez et al., 2006b).

2.1 Grammar conversion

The first step we undertook in order to generate parsers for the XTAG grammar was a full conversion of the grammar to an XML-based format, a variant of the TAG markup language (TAGML). In this way we had the grammar in a well-defined format, easy to parse and modify. During this conversion, the trees' anchor nodes were duplicated in order to make our generic TAG parsers allow adjunctions on anchor nodes, which is allowed in the XTAG grammar.

2.2 Feature structure unification

Two strategies may be used in order to take unification into account in parsing: feature structures can be unified after parsing or during parsing. We have compared the two approaches for the XTAG grammar (see table 1), and the general conclusion is that unification during parsing performs better for most of the sentences, although its runtimes have a larger variance and it performs much worse for some particular cases.

In order to implement unification during parsing in our parsing schemata based system, we must extend our schemata in order to perform unification. This can be done in the following way:

- Items are extended so that they will hold a feature structure in addition to the rest of the information they include.
- We need to define two operations on feature structures: the unification operation and the "keep variables" operation. The "keep variables" operation is a transformation on feature structures that takes a feature structure as an argument, which may contain features, values, symbolic variables and associations between them, and returns a feature structure containing only the variable-value associations related to a given elementary tree, ignoring the variables and values not associated through these relations, and completely ignoring features.
- During the process of parsing, feature structures that refer to the same node, or to nodes that are taking part in a substitution or adjunction and

Strategy	Mean	T. Mean 10%	T. Mean 20%	1st Quart.	Median	3rd Quart.	Std. Dev.	Wilcoxon
During	108,270	12,164	7,812	1,585	4,424	9,671	388,010	0.4545
After	412,793	10,710	10,019	2,123	9,043	19,073	14,235	

Table 1: Runtimes in ms of an Earley-based parser using two different unification strategies: unification during and after parsing. The following data are shown: mean, trimmed means (10 and 20%), quartiles, standard deviation, and p-value for the Wilcoxon paired signed rank test (the p-value of 0.4545 indicates that no statistically significant difference was found between the medians).

are going to collapse to a single node in the final parse tree, must be unified. For this to be done, the test that these nodes must unify is added as a side condition to the steps that must handle them, and the unification results are included in the item generated by the consequent. Of course, considerations about the different role of the top and bottom feature structures in adjunction and substitution must be taken into account when determining which feature structures must be unified.

- Feature structures in items must only hold variable-value associations for the symbolic variables appearing in the tree to which the structures refer, for these relationships hold the information that we need in order to propagate values according to the rules specified in the unification equations. Variable-value associations referring to different elementary trees are irrelevant when parsing a given tree, and feature-value and feature-variable associations are local to a node and can't be extrapolated to other nodes, so we won't propagate any of this information in items. However, it must be used locally for unification. Therefore, steps perform unification by using the information in their antecedent items and recovering complete feature structures associated to nodes directly from the grammar, and then use the "keep-variables" operation to remove the information that we don't need in the consequent item.
- In some algorithms, such as CYK, a single deductive step deals with several different elementary tree nodes that don't collapse into one in the final parse tree. In this case, several "keep variables" operations must be performed on each step execution, one for each of these nodes. If we just unified the information on all the nodes and called "keep variables" at the end, we could propagate information incorrectly.
- In Earley-type algorithms, we must take a decision about how predictor steps handle feature structures. Two options are possible: one is propagating the feature structure in the antecedent item to the consequent, and the other is discarding the feature structure and generating a consequent whose associated feature structure is empty. The first option has the advantage that violations of unification constraints are detected earlier, thus avoiding the generation of some items. However, in scenarios where a predictor is applied to several items differing only in their associated feature structures, this approach generates several different items while the discarding approach collapses them into a single consequent item. Moreover, the propagating approach favors the appearance of items with more complex feature structures, thus making unification operations slower. In practice, for XTAG we have found that these drawbacks of propagating the structures overcome the advantages, especially in complex sentences, where the discarding approach performs much better.

2.3 Tree filtering

The full XTAG English grammar contains thousands of elementary trees, so performance is not good if we use the whole grammar to parse each sentence. Tree selection filters (Schabes and Joshi, 1991) are used to select a subset of the grammar, discarding the trees which are known not to be useful given the words in the input sentence.

To emulate this functionality in our parsing schema-based system, we have used its extensibility mechanism to define a function *Selects-tree(a,T)* that returns *true* if the terminal symbol *a* selects the tree *T*. The implementation of this function is a Java method that looks for this information in XTAG's syntactic database. Then the function is inserted in a filtering step on our schemata:

$$\frac{[a,i,j]}{[Selected,\alpha]}\ alpha \in Trees/\text{SELECTS-TREE}(\text{A};\alpha)$$

The presence of an item of the form $[Selected, \alpha]$ indicates that the tree α has been selected by the filter and can be used for parsing. In order for the filter to take effect, we add $[Selected, \alpha]$ as an antecedent to every step in our schemata introducing a new tree α into the parse (such as initters, substitution and adjoining steps). In this way we guarantee that no trees that don't pass the filter will be used for parsing.

3 Comparing several parsers for the XTAG grammar

In this section, we make a comparison of several different TAG parsing algorithms — the CYK-based algorithm described at (Vijay-Shanker and Joshi, 1985), Earley-based algorithms with (Alonso et al., 1999) and without (Schabes, 1994) the valid prefix property (VPP), and Nederhof's algorithm (Nederhof, 1999) — on the XTAG English grammar (release 2.24.2001), by using our system and the ideas we have explained. The schemata for these algorithms without unification support can be found at (Alonso et al., 1999). These schemata were extended as described in the previous sections, and used as input to our system which generated their corresponding parsers. These parsers were then run on the test sentences shown in table 2, obtaining the performance measures (in terms of runtime and amount of items generated) that can be seen in table 3. Note that the sentences are ordered by minimal runtime.

As we can see, the execution times are not as good as the ones we would obtain if we used Sarkar's XTAG distribution parser written in C (Sarkar, 2000). This is not surprising, since our parsers have been generated by a generic tool without knowledge of the grammar, while the XTAG parser has been designed specifically for optimal performance in this grammar and uses additional information (such as tree usage frequency data from several corpora, see (XTAG, 2001)).

However, our comparison allows us to draw conclusions about which parsing algorithms are better suited for the XTAG grammar. In terms of memory usage, CYK is the clear winner, since it clearly generates less items than the other algorithms, and a CYK item doesn't take up more memory than an Earley item.

On the other hand, if we compare execution times, there is not a single best algorithm, since the performance results depend on the size and complexity of the sentences. The Earley-based algorithm with the VPP is the fastest for the first, "easier" sentences, but CYK gives the best results for the more complex sentences. In the middle of the two, there are some sentences where the best performance is achieved by the variant of Earley that doesn't verify the valid prefix property. Therefore, in practical cases, we should take into account the most likely kind of sentences that will be passed to the parser in order to select the best algorithm.

Nederhof's algorithm is always the one with the slowest execution time, in spite of being an improvement of the VPP Earley parser that reduces worst-case time complexity. This is probably because, when extending the Nederhof schema in order to support feature structure unification, we get a schema that needs more unification operations than Earley's and has to use items that store several feature structures. Nederhof's algorithm would probably perform better in relation to the others if we had used the strategy of parsing without feature structures and then performing unification on the output parse forest.

4 Conclusions

A generic system that generates parsers from algebraic specifications (parsing schemata) has been applied to the particular case of the XTAG grammar. In order to be able to generate XTAG parsers, some transformations were made to the grammar, and TAG parsing schemata were extended with feature structure unification support and a simple tree filtering mechanism.

The generated implementations allow us to compare the performance of different TAG parsers when working with a large-scale grammar, the XTAG English grammar. In this paper, we have shown the results for four algorithms: a CYK-based algorithm, Earley-based algorithms with and without the VPP, and Nederhof's algorithm. The result shows that the CYK-based parser is the least memory-consuming algorithm. By measuring execution time, we find that CYK is the fastest algorithm for the most complex sentences, but the Earley-based algorithm with the VPP is the fastest for simpler cases. Therefore, when choosing a parser for a practical application, we should take

1. He was a cow	9. He wanted to go to the city
2. He loved himself	10. That woman in the city contributed to this article
3. Go to your room	11. That people are not really amateurs at intelectual duelling
4. He is a real man	12. The index is intended to measure future economic performance
5. He was a real man	13. They expect him to cut costs throughout the organization
6. Who was at the door	14. He will continue to place a huge burden on the city workers
7. He loved all cows	15. He could have been simply being a jerk
8. He called up her	16. A few fast food outlets are giving it a try

Table 2: Test sentences.

Sentence	Runtimes in milliseconds				Items generated			
	Parser				Parser			
	CYK	Ear. no VPP	Ear. VPP	Neder.	CYK	Ear. no VPP	Ear. VPP	Neder.
1	2985	**750**	**750**	2719	1341	1463	**1162**	1249
2	3109	1562	**1219**	6421	**1834**	2917	2183	2183
3	4078	1547	**1406**	6828	**2149**	2893	2298	2304
4	4266	1563	**1407**	4703	1864	1979	**1534**	2085
5	4234	1921	**1421**	4766	1855	1979	**1534**	2085
6	4485	1813	**1562**	7782	**2581**	3587	2734	2742
7	5469	2359	**2344**	11469	**2658**	3937	3311	3409
8	7828	4906	**3563**	15532	**4128**	8058	4711	4716
9	10047	4422	**4016**	18969	**4931**	6968	5259	5279
10	13641	**6515**	7172	31828	**6087**	8828	7734	8344
11	16500	**7781**	15235	56265	**7246**	12068	13221	13376
12	16875	17109	**9985**	39132	**7123**	10428	9810	10019
13	25859	**12000**	20828	63641	**10408**	12852	15417	15094
14	54578	**35829**	57422	178875	**20760**	31278	40248	47570
15	**62157**	113532	109062	133515	**22115**	37377	38824	59603
16	**269187**	3122860	3315359		**68778**	152430	173128	

Table 3: Runtimes and amount of items generated by different XTAG parsers on several sentences. The machine used for all the tests was an Intel Pentium 4 / 3.40 GHz, with 1 GB RAM and Sun Java Hotspot virtual machine (version 1.4.2_01-b06) running on Windows XP. Best results for each sentence are shown in boldface.

into account the kinds of sentences most likely to be used as input in order to select the most suitable algorithm.

References

M. A. Alonso, D. Cabrero, E. de la Clergerie, and M. Vilares. 1999. Tabular algorithms for TAG parsing. *Proc. of EACL'99*, pp. 150–157, Bergen, Norway.

S. Billot and B. Lang. 1989. The structure of shared forest in ambiguous parsing. *Proc. of ACL'89*, pp. 143–151, Vancouver, Canada.

C. Gómez-Rodríguez, J. Vilares and M. A. Alonso. 2006. Automatic Generation of Natural Language Parsers from Declarative Specifications. *Proc. of STAIRS 2006*, Riva del Garda, Italy. Long version available at http://www.grupocole.org/GomVilAlo2006a_long.pdf

C. Gómez-Rodríguez, M. A. Alonso and M. Vilares. 2006. On Theoretical and Practical Complexity of TAG Parsers. *Proc. of Formal Grammars 2006*, Malaga, Spain.

M.-J. Nederhof. 1999. The computational complexity of the correct-prefix property for TAGs. *Computational Linguistics*, 25(3):345–360.

A. Sarkar. 2000. Practical experiments in parsing using tree adjoining grammars. *Proc. of TAG+5*, Paris.

Y. Schabes and A. K. Joshi. 1991. Parsing with lexicalized tree adjoining grammar. In Masaru Tomita, editor, *Current Issues in Parsing Technologies*, pp. 25–47. Kluwer Academic Publishers, Norwell.

Y. Schabes. 1994. Left to right parsing of lexicalized tree-adjoining grammars. *Computational Intelligence*, 10(4):506–515.

S. M. Shieber, Y. Schabes, and F. C. N. Pereira. 1995. Principles and implementation of deductive parsing. *Journal of Logic Programming*, 24(1–2):3–36.

K. Sikkel. 1997. *Parsing Schemata — A Framework for Specification and Analysis of Parsing Algorithms*. Springer-Verlag, Berlin.

K. Vijay-Shanker and A. K. Joshi. 1985. Some computational properties of tree adjoining grammars. *Proc. of ACL'85*, pp. 82–93, Chicago, USA.

XTAG Research Group. 2001. A lexicalized tree adjoining grammar for english. Technical Report IRCS-01-03, IRCS, University of Pennsylvania.

Constraint-based Computational Semantics: A Comparison between LTAG and LRS

Laura Kallmeyer
University of Tübingen
Collaborative Research Center 441
lk@sfs.uni-tuebingen.de

Frank Richter
University of Tübingen
Collaborative Research Center 441
fr@sfs.uni-tuebingen.de

Abstract

This paper compares two approaches to computational semantics, namely semantic unification in Lexicalized Tree Adjoining Grammars (LTAG) and Lexical Resource Semantics (LRS) in HPSG. There are striking similarities between the frameworks that make them comparable in many respects. We will exemplify the differences and similarities by looking at several phenomena. We will show, first of all, that many intuitions about the mechanisms of semantic computations can be implemented in similar ways in both frameworks. Secondly, we will identify some aspects in which the frameworks intrinsically differ due to more general differences between the approaches to formal grammar adopted by LTAG and HPSG.

1 Introduction

This paper contrasts two frameworks for computational semantics, the proposal for semantics in LTAG described in (Kallmeyer and Romero, 2005) and LRS (Richter and Sailer, 2004), a computational semantics framework formulated in Head-Driven Phrase Structure Grammar (HPSG).

There are significant differences between LTAG and HPSG. LTAG is a mildly context-sensitive lexicalized formalism characterized by an extended domain of locality. HPSG is based on the idea of a separation of the lexicon and syntactic structure and on the strict locality of general grammar principles that are formulated in an expressive and very flexible logical description language. These fundamental differences are reflected in the respective architectures for semantics: LTAG assumes a separate level of underspecified semantic representations; LRS uses the description logic of syntax for semantic specifications.

However, despite the different mathematical structures, we find striking similarities between LTAG semantics with unification and LRS. They both show similar intuitions underlying specific analyses, use the same higher order type-theoretic language (Ty2, (Gallin, 1975)) as a means for specifying the truth conditions of sentences, and employ a feature logic in the combinatorial semantics instead of the lambda calculus. Because of these similarities, analyses using both approaches are closely related and can benefit from each other.

The paper is structured as follows: Sections 2 and 3 will introduce the two frameworks. The next three sections (4–6) will sketch analyses of some phenomena in both frameworks that will reveal relevant relations between them. Section 7 presents a summary and conclusion.

2 LTAG semantics

In (Kallmeyer and Romero, 2005), each elementary tree is linked to a semantic representation (a set of Ty2 formulas and scope constraints). Ty2 formulas (Gallin, 1975) are typed λ-terms with individuals and situations as basic types. The scope constraints of the form $x \geq y$ specify subordination relations between Ty2 terms. In other words, $x \geq y$ indicates that y is a component of x.

A semantic representation is equipped with a semantic feature structure description. Semantic computation is done on the derivation tree and consists of certain feature value equations between mother and daughter nodes in the derivation tree.

(1) John always laughs.

As an example, see Fig. 1 showing the derivation tree for (1) with semantic representations and

Proceedings of the 8th International Workshop on Tree Adjoining Grammar and Related Formalisms, pages 109–114, Sydney, July 2006.

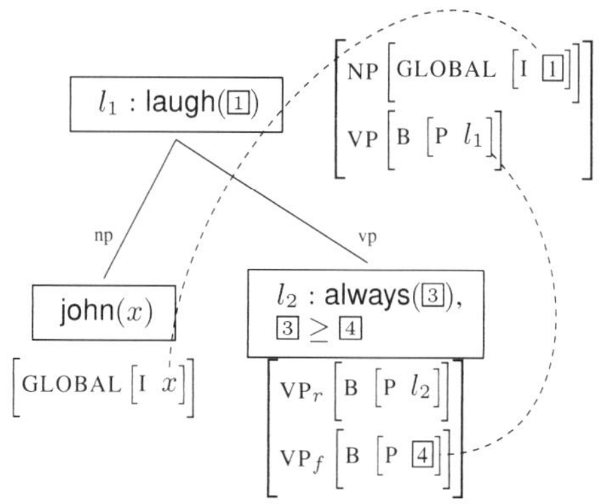

Figure 1: LTAG semantics of (1)

semantic feature structure descriptions as node labels. The additional feature equations in this example are depicted using dotted lines. They arise from top-bottom feature identifications parallel to the unifications performed in FTAG (Vijay-Shanker and Joshi, 1988) and from identifications of global features. They yield $\boxed{1} = x$ and $\boxed{4} = l_1$. Applying these identities to the semantic representations after having built their union leads to (2). The constraint $\boxed{3} \geq l_1$ states that l_1 : laugh(x) is a component of $\boxed{3}$.

(2) john(x), l_2 : always($\boxed{3}$), l_1 : laugh(x), $\boxed{3} \geq l_1$

Note that the feature structure descriptions do not encode the semantic expressions one is interested in. They only encode their contributions to functional applications by restricting the argument slots of certain predicates in the semantic representations: They state which elements are contributed as possible arguments for other semantic expressions and which arguments need to be filled. They thereby simulate lambda abstraction and functional application while assembling the semantic representations. To achieve this, a restricted first order logic is sufficient.

Semantic computation is local on the derivation tree: The new feature equations that are added depend only on single edges in the derivation tree. Because of this, even with the extension to semantics, the formalism is still mildly context-sensitive.

3 LRS

In LRS the feature logic specifies the entire grammar, including well-formed Ty2 terms as semantic representations, and their mode of composition. Instead of the lambda calculus of traditional Montague Grammar, LRS crucially uses a novel distinction between three aspects of the logical representations of signs (external content, internal content, and parts). LRS constraints establish sub-term relationships between pieces of semantic representations within and across signs, thereby specifying the combinatorial properties of the semantics. The subterm or component-of conditions (symbolized as $\triangleleft$) are imposed by grammar principles. Since these principles are descriptions of object-language expressions, they permit the application of various underspecification techniques of computational semantics, although an LRS grammar does not employ underspecified semantic representations, in contrast to LTAG semantics.

Fig. 2 shows an HPSG description of the syntactic tree and the LRS specifications of (1). The syntactic trees in HPSG correspond to the derived trees of LTAG. Since HPSG does not have derivation trees, the LRS principles refer to derived trees.

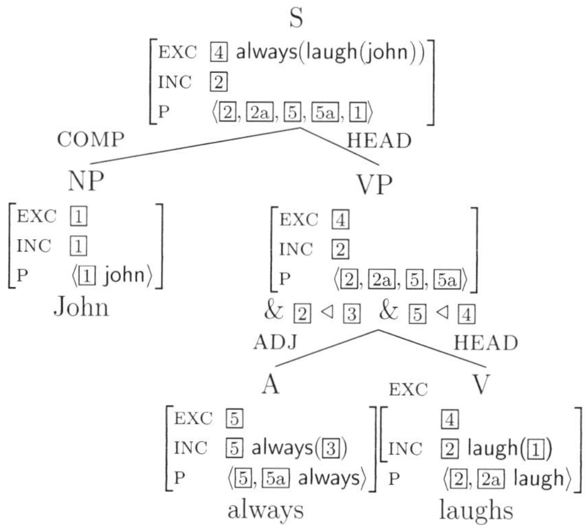

Figure 2: LRS analysis of (1)

Each word lexically specifies its contribution to the overall meaning of the sentence (P(ARTS)), the part of its semantics which is outscoped by all signs the word combines with (INC(ONT)), and the overall semantic contribution of its maximal projection (EXC(ONT)). Feature percolation principles identify INC and EXC, respectively, along head projections and collect the elements of the PARTS lists of the daughters at each phrase. The combination of the adjunct with a verbal projection introduces two component-of constraints: The EXC of *always* must be within the EXC of *laughs*, and the INC of *laughs* must be in the scope of *always*. The semantic argument of *laughs* (john) is identified by subcategorization (not shown in Fig. 2). A closure condition requires that the semantic representation of an utterance use up all and only the PARTS contributions of all signs, which yields $\boxed{4}$ = always(laugh(john)).

4 Quantifier scope

4.1 Specifying a scope window

(3) Exactly one student admires every professor: $\exists > \forall, \forall > \exists$

(4) John seems to have visited everybody: $seem > \forall, \forall > seem$

Quantificational NPs in English can in principle scope freely (see (3) and (4)). An analysis of quantifier scope must guarantee only two things: 1. the proposition to which a quantifier attaches must be in its nuclear scope, and 2. a quantifier cannot scope higher than the next finite clause. One way to model this is to define a scope window delimited by a maximal scope and a minimal scope for a quantifier. Both LTAG and LRS, specify such scope windows for quantifiers. We will now outline the two analyses.

(5) Everybody laughs.

(Kallmeyer and Romero, 2005) use global features MAXS and MINS for the limits of the scope window. Fig. 3 shows the LTAG analysis of (5). The feature identifications (indicated by dotted lines) lead to the constraints $\boxed{2} \geq \boxed{5}, \boxed{5} \geq l_1$. These constraints specify an upper and a lower boundary for the nuclear scope $\boxed{5}$. With the assignments following from the feature identifications we obtain the semantic representation (6):

$$(6)\quad \begin{array}{l} l_1 : \mathsf{laugh}(x), \\ l_2 : \mathsf{every}(x, \boxed{4}, \boxed{5}),\ l_3 : \mathsf{person}(x) \\ \boxed{2} \geq l_1, \\ \boxed{4} \geq l_3, \boxed{2} \geq \boxed{5}, \boxed{5} \geq l_1 \end{array}$$

There is one possible disambiguation consistent with the scope constraints, namely $\boxed{2} \rightarrow l_2$, $\boxed{4} \rightarrow l_3, \boxed{5} \rightarrow l_1$. This leads to the semantics every(x, person(x), laugh(x)).

In LRS, the EXCONT value of the utterance is the upper boundary while the INCONT value of the syntactic head a quantifier depends on is the lower boundary for scope, as illustrated in Fig. 4. The upper boundary is obtained through the interaction of 1) a PROJECTION PRINCIPLE stating that the

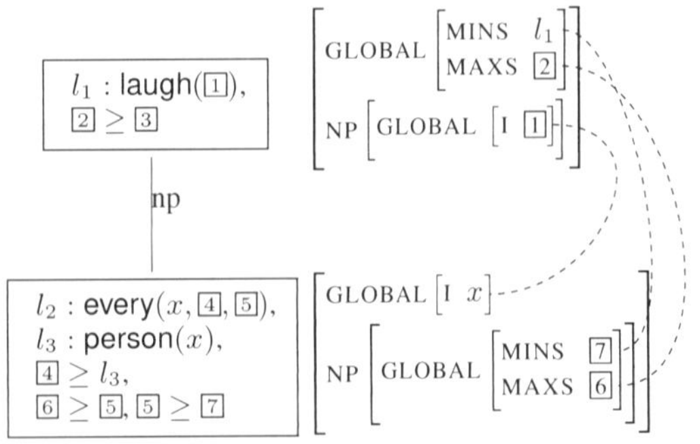

Figure 3: LTAG analysis of (5) *Everybody laughs*

PARTS list of a phrase contains all elements on the PARTS lists of its daughters, and 2) the EXCONT PRINCIPLE which states that a) the PARTS list of each non-head contains its own EXCONT, and b) in an utterance, everything on the PARTS list is a component of the EXCONT. This leads to the constraint $\boxed{4} \triangleleft \boxed{6}$ in Fig. 4, among others. The lower boundary is obtained from the SEMANTICS PRINCIPLE which states that if the non-head of a headed phrase is a quantifier, then the INCONT of the head is a component of its nuclear scope. This yields $\boxed{1} \triangleleft \beta$ in Fig. 4.

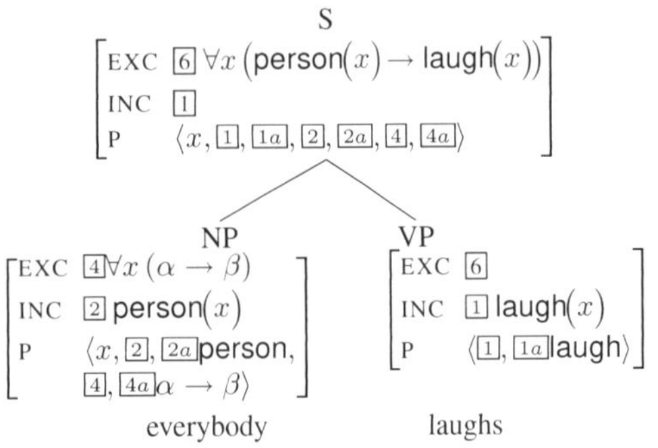

Relevant subterm constraints: $\boxed{2} \triangleleft \alpha$ (from the lexical entry of *everybody*), $\boxed{1} \triangleleft \beta$, $\boxed{4} \triangleleft \boxed{6}$

Figure 4: LRS analysis of (5) *Everybody laughs*

The striking similarity between the two analyses shows that, despite the fundamental differences between the frameworks, central insights can be modelled in parallel.

4.2 Nested quantifiers

The use of the upper limit of the scope windows is, however, slightly different: EXCONT contains the quantifier itself as a component while MAXS limits only the nuclear scope, not the quantifier. Consequently, in LTAG the quantifier can scope higher than the MAXS limiting its nuclear scope but in this case it takes immediate scope over the MAXS.

(7) Two policemen spy on someone from every city: $\forall > \exists > 2$ (among others)

The LTAG analysis is motivated by nested quantifiers. In sentences such as (7), the embedded quantifier can take scope over the embedding one but if so, this must be immediate scope. In other words, other quantifiers cannot intervene. In (7), the scope order $\forall > 2 > \exists$ is therefore not possible.[1] The LTAG analysis is such that the maximal nuclear scope of the embedded quantifier is the propositional label of the embedding quantifier.[2]

In LRS, the way the scope window is specified, a corresponding constraint using the EXCONT of the embedded quantifier cannot be obtained. The LRS principle governing the distribution of embedded quantifiers in complex NPs states directly that in this syntactic environment, the embedded quantifier may only take direct scope over the quantifier of the matrix NP. This principle does not refer to the notion of external content at all. At this point it is an open question whether LRS could learn from LTAG here and adapt the scope window so that an analogous treatment of nested quantifiers would be possible.

5 LTAG's extended domain of locality

Whereas the treatment of quantification sketched in the preceding section highlights the similarities between LTAG semantics and LRS, this and the following section will illustrate some fundamental differences between the frameworks.

In spite of the parallels mentioned above, even INCONT and MINS differ sometimes, namely in sentences containing bridge verbs. This is related to the fact that LTAG has an extended domain of locality whereas HPSG does not. Let us illustrate the difference with the example (8).

(8) Mary thinks John will come.

[1](Joshi et al., 2003) propose an extra mechanism that groups quantifi ers into sets in order to derive these constraints. (Kallmeyer and Romero, 2005) however show that these constraints can be derived even if the upper limit MAXS for nuclear scope is used as sketched above.

[2]Note that this approach requires constraints of the form $l \geq \boxed{n}$ with l being a label, $\boxed{n}$ a variable. This goes beyond the polynomially solvable *normal dominance constraints* (Althaus et al., 2003). This extension, though, is probably still polynomially solvable (Alexander Koller, personal communication).

In LTAG, the two elementary verb trees (for *thinks* and *will come*) have different global MINS features. The one for *thinks* is the label of the think proposition while the one for *will come* is the label of the embedded proposition. As a consequence, a quantifier which attaches to the matrix verb cannot scope into the embedded clause. This distinction of different MINS values for different verb trees is natural in LTAG because of the extended domain of locality.

In LRS, all verbal nodes in the constituent structure of (8) carry the same INCONT value, namely the proposition of the embedded verb. Consequently, the minimal scope of quantifiers attaching either to the embedding or to the embedded verb is always the proposition of the embedded verb. However, due to the requirement that variables be bound, a quantifier binding an argument of the embedding verb cannot have narrow scope over the embedded proposition.

How to implement the LTAG idea of different INCONT values for the embedding and the embedded verb in LRS is not obvious. One might introduce a new principle changing the INCONT value at a bridge verb, whereby the new INCONT would get passed up, and the embedded INCONT would no longer be available. This would be problematic: Take a raising verb as in (9) (adjoining to the VP node in LTAG) instead of a bridge verb:

(9) Most people seem to everybody to like the film.

Here the minimal scope of *most people* should be the *like* proposition while the minimal scope of *everybody* is the *seem* proposition. In LTAG this does not pose a problem since, due to the extended domain of locality, *most people* attaches to the elementary tree of *like* even though the *seem* tree is adjoined in between. If the INCONT treatment of LRS were modified as outlined above and *seem* had an INCONT value that differed from the INCONT value of the embedded *like* proposition, then the new INCONT value would be passed up and incorrectly provide the minimal scope of *most people*. LRS must identify the two INCONTs.

The difference between the two analyses illustrates the relevance of LTAG's extended domain of locality not only for syntax but also for semantics.

6 Negative Concord

The analysis of negative concord in Polish described in this section highlights the differences in the respective implementation of underspecification techniques in LTAG and LRS. Recall that both LTAG and LRS use component-of constraints. But in LTAG, these constraints link actual Ty2-terms (i.e., objects) to each other, while in LRS, these constraints are part of a description of Ty2-terms.

(10) Janek nie pomaga ojcu.
Janek NM helps father
'Janek doesn't help his father.'

(11) a. Janek nie pomaga nikomu.
Janek NM helps nobody
'Janek doesn't help anybody.'

b. *Janek pomaga nikomu.

(12) Nikt nie przyszedł.
nobody NM came
'Nobody came.'

The basic facts of sentential negation and negative concord in Polish are illustrated in (10)–(12): The verbal prefix *nie* is obligatory for sentential negation, and it can co-occur with any number of n-words (such as *nikt*, 'anybody') without ever leading to a double negation reading. As a consequence, (12) expresses only one logical sentential negation, although the negation prefix *nie* on the verb and the n-word *nikt* can carry logical negation alone in other contexts. LRS takes advantage of the fact that its specifications of semantic representations are descriptions of logical expressions which can, in principle, mention the same parts of the expressions several times. Fig. 5 shows that both *nikt* and the verb *nie przyszedł* introduce descriptions of negations (4 and 2, respectively). The constraints of negative concord in Polish will then conspire to force the negations contributed by the two words to be the same in the overall logical representation 6 of the sentence.

Such an analysis is not possible in LTAG. Each negation in the interpretation corresponds to exactly one negated term introduced in the semantic representations. Therefore, the negative particle *nie* necessarily introduces the negation while the n-word *nikt* requires a negation in the proposition it attaches to. An analysis along these lines is sketched in Fig. 6 ("GL" stands for "GLOBAL"). The requirement of a negation is checked with a feature NEG indicating the presence of a negation. The scope of the negation (feature N-SCOPE) marks the maximal scope of the existential quantifier of the n-word *nikt* (constraint $\boxed{7} \geq \boxed{6}$).[3]

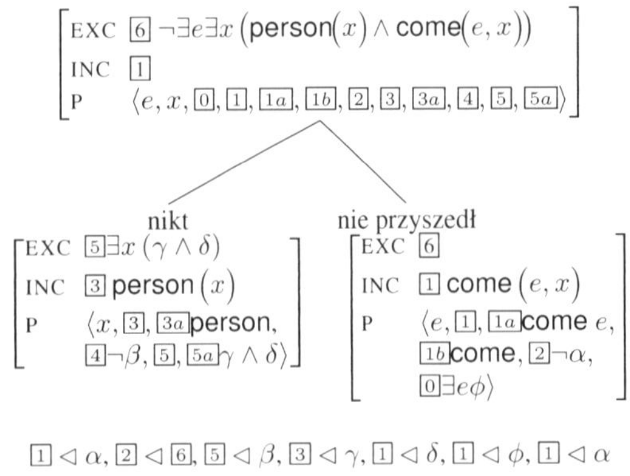

Figure 5: LRS analysis of (12) *Nikt nie przyszedł*

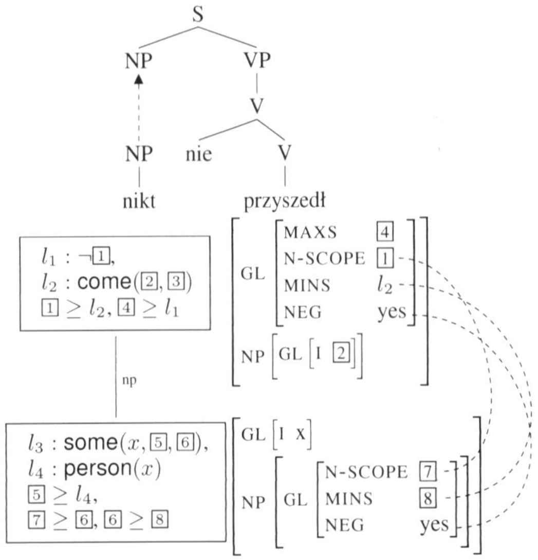

Figure 6: LTAG analysis of (12) *Nikt nie przyszedł*

This example illustrates that the two frameworks differ substantially in their treatment of underspecification: 1. LRS employs partial descriptions of fully specified models, whereas LTAG generates underspecified representations in the style of (Bos, 1995) that require the definition of a disambiguation (a "plugging" in the terminology of Bos). 2. LRS constraints contain not Ty2 terms but descriptions of Ty2 terms. Therefore, in contrast to LTAG, two descriptions can denote the same formula. Here, LTAG is more limited compared to LRS. On the other hand, the way semantic representations are defined in LTAG guarantees

[3]See (Lichte and Kallmeyer, 2006) for a discussion of NEG and N-SCOPE in the context of NPI-licensing.

that they almost correspond to *normal dominance constraints*, which are known to be polynomially parsable. The difference in the use of underspecification techniques reflects the more general difference between a generative rewriting system such as LTAG, in which the elements of the grammar are objects, and a purely description-based formalism such as HPSG, in which token identities between different components of linguistic structures are natural and frequently employed.

7 Summary and Conclusion

LTAG and LRS have several common characteristics: They both 1. use a Ty2 language for semantics; 2. allow underspecification (LTAG scope constraints $\geq$ versus LRS component-of constraints $\triangleleft$); 3. use logical descriptions for semantic computation; 4. are designed for computational applications. Due to these similarities, some analyses can be modelled in almost identical ways (e.g., the quantifier scope analyses, and the identification of arguments using attribute values rather than functional application in the lambda calculus). We take the existence of this clear correspondence as indicative of deeper underlying insight into the functioning of semantic composition in natural languages.

Additionally, the differences between the frameworks that can be observed on the level of syntax carry over to semantics: 1. LTAG's extended domain of locality allows the localization within elementary trees of syntactic and semantic relations between elements far apart from each other on the level of constituent structure. 2. LTAG (both syntax and semantics) is a formalism with restricted expressive power that guarantees good formal properties. The restrictions, however, can be problematic. Some phenomena can be more easily described in a system such as HPSG and LRS while their description is less straightforward, perhaps more difficult or even impossible within LTAG. The concord phenomena described in section 7 are an example of this.

A further noticable difference is that within the (Kallmeyer and Romero, 2005) framework, the derivation tree uniquely determines both syntactic and semantic composition in a context-free way. Therefore LTAG semantics is mildly context-sensitive and can be said to be compositional. As far as LRS is concerned, it is not yet known whether it is compositional or not; compositionality (if it holds at all) is at least less straightforward to show than in LTAG.

In conclusion, we would like to say that the similarities between these two frameworks permit a detailed and direct comparison. Our comparative study has shed some light on the impact of the different characteristic properties of our frameworks on concrete semantic analyses.

Acknowledgments

For many long and fruitful discussions of various aspects of LTAG semantics and LRS, we would like to thank Timm Lichte, Wolfgang Maier, Maribel Romero, Manfred Sailer and Jan-Philipp Söhn. Furthermore, we are grateful to three anonymous reviewers for helpful comments.

References

Ernst Althaus, Denys Duchier, Alexander Koller, Kurt Mehlhorn, Joachim Niehren, and Sven Thiel. 2003. An effi cient graph algorithm for dominance constraints. *Journal of Algorithms*, 48(1):194–219.

Johan Bos. 1995. Predicate logic unplugged. In Paul Dekker and Martin Stokhof, editors, *Proceedings of the 10th Amsterdam Colloquium*, pages 133–142.

Daniel Gallin. 1975. *Intensional and Higher-Order Modal Logic with Applications to Montague Semantics*. North Holland mathematics studies 19. North-Holland Publ. Co., Amsterdam.

Aravind K. Joshi, Laura Kallmeyer, and Maribel Romero. 2003. Flexible Composition in LTAG: Quantifi er Scope and Inverse Linking. In Harry Bunt, Ielka van der Sluis, and Roser Morante, editors, *Proceedings of the Fifth International Workshop on Computational Semantics IWCS-5*, pages 179–194, Tilburg.

Laura Kallmeyer and Maribel Romero. 2005. Scope and Situation Binding in LTAG using Semantic Unifi cation. Submitted to *Research on Language and Computation*. 57 pages., December.

Timm Lichte and Laura Kallmeyer. 2006. Licensing German Negative Polarity Items in LTAG. In *Proceedings of The Eighth International Workshop on Tree Adjoining Grammar and Related Formalisms (TAG+8)*, Sydney, Australia, July.

Frank Richter and Manfred Sailer. 2004. Basic concepts of lexical resource semantics. In Arnold Beckmann and Norbert Preining, editors, *ESSLLI 2003 – Course Material I, (=* Collegium Logicum, *5)*, pages 87–143. Kurt Gödel Society, Wien.

K. Vijay-Shanker and Aravind K. Joshi. 1988. Feature structures based tree adjoining grammar. In *Proceedings of COLING*, pages 714–719, Budapest.

SemTAG, the LORIA toolbox for TAG-based Parsing and Generation

Eric Kow
INRIA / LORIA
Université Henri Poincaré
615, rue du Jardin Botanique
F-54 600 Villers-Lès-Nancy
kow@loria.fr

Yannick Parmentier
INRIA / LORIA
Université Henri Poincaré
615, rue du Jardin Botanique
F-54 600 Villers-Lès-Nancy
parmenti@loria.fr

Claire Gardent
CNRS / LORIA
615, rue du Jardin Botanique
F-54 600 Villers-Lès-Nancy
gardent@loria.fr

Abstract

In this paper, we introduce SEMTAG, a toolbox for TAG-based parsing and generation. This environment supports the development of wide-coverage grammars and differs from existing environments for TAG such as XTAG, (XTAG-Research-Group, 2001) in that it includes a semantic dimension. SEMTAG is open-source and freely available.

1 Introduction

In this paper we introduce a toolbox that allows for both parsing and generation with TAG. This toolbox combines existing software and aims at facilitating grammar development, More precisely, this toolbox includes[1]:

- XMG: a grammar compiler which supports the generation of a TAG from a factorised TAG (Crabbé and Duchier, 2004),
- LLP2 and DyALog: two chart parsers, one with a friendly user interface (Lopez, 2000) and the other optimised for efficient parsing (Villemonte de la Clergerie, 2005)[2]
- GenI: a chart generator which has been tested on a middle size grammar for French (Gardent and Kow, 2005)

[1]All these tools are freely available, more information and links at http://trac.loria.fr/~semtag.

[2]Note that DyALog refers in fact to a logic programming language, and a tabular compiler for this language. The DyALog system is well-adapted to the compilation of efficient tabular parsers.

2 XMG, a grammar writing environment for Tree Based Grammars

XMG provides a grammar writing environment for tree based grammars[3] with three distinctive features. First, XMG supports a highly factorised and fully declarative description of tree based grammars. Second, XMG permits the integration in a TAG of a semantic dimension. Third, XMG is based on well understood and efficient logic programming techniques. Moreover, it offers a graphical interface for exploring the resulting grammar (see Figure 1).

Factorising information. In the XMG framework, a TAG is defined by a set of classes organised in an inheritance hierarchy where classes define tree fragments (using a tree logic) and tree fragment combinations (by conjunction or disjunction). XMG furthermore integrates a sophisticated treatment of names whereby variables scope can be local, global or user defined (i.e., local to part of the hierarchy).

In practice, the resulting framework supports a very high degree of factorisation. For instance, a first core grammar (FRAG) for French comprising 4 200 trees was produced from roughly 300 XMG classes.

Integrating semantic information. In XMG, classes can be multi-dimensional. That is, they can be used to describe several levels of linguistic knowledge such as for instance, syntax, semantics or prosody. At present, XMG supports classes including both a syntactic and a semantic dimension. As mentioned above, the syntactic dimen-

[3]Although in this paper we only mention TAG, the XMG framework is also used to develop so called Interaction Grammars i.e., grammars whose basic units are tree descriptions rather than trees (Parmentier and Le Roux, 2005).

Proceedings of the 8th International Workshop on Tree Adjoining Grammar and Related Formalisms, pages 115–120,
Sydney, July 2006.

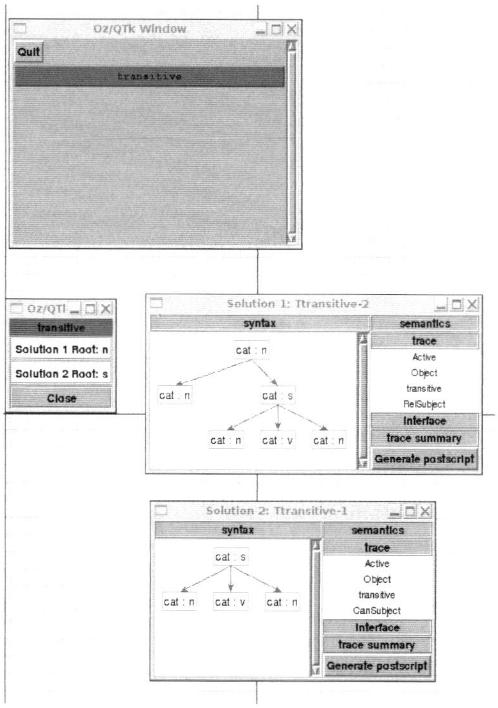

Figure 1: XMG's graphical interface

sion is based on a tree logic and can be used to describe (partial) tree fragments. The semantic dimension on the other hand, can be used to associate with each tree a flat semantic formula. Such a formula can furthermore include identifiers which corefer with identifiers occurring in the associated syntactic tree. In other words, XMG also provides support for the interface between semantic formulae and tree decorations. Note that the inclusion of semantic information remains optional. That is, it is possible to use XMG to define a purely syntactic TAG.

XMG was used to develop a core grammar for French (FRAG) which was evaluated to have 75% coverage[4] on the Test Suite for Natural Language Processing (TSNLP, (Lehmann et al., 1996)). The FRAG grammar was furthermore enriched with semantic information using another 50 classes describing the semantic dimension (Gardent, 2006). The resulting grammar (SEMFRAG) describes both the syntax and the semantics of the French core constructions.

Compiling an XMG specification. By building on efficient techniques from logic programming and in particular, on the Warren's Abstract

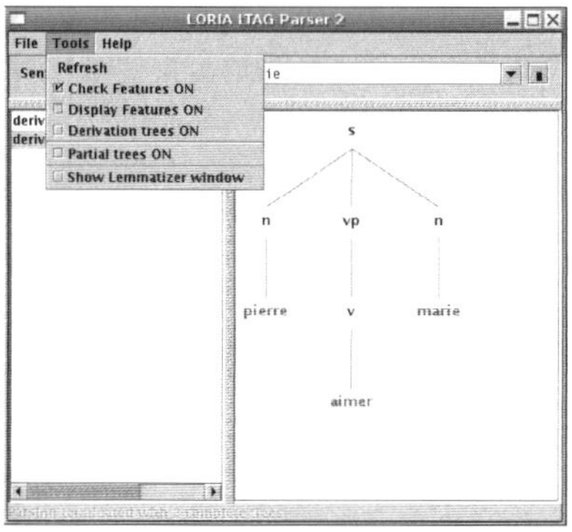

Figure 2: The LLP2 parser.

Machine idea (Ait-Kaci, 1991), the XMG compiler allows for very reasonable compilation times (Duchier et al., 2004). For instance, the compilation of a TAG containing 6 000 trees takes about 15 minutes with a Pentium 4 processor 2.6 GHz and 1 GB of RAM.

3 Two TAG parsers

The toolbox includes two parsing systems: the LLP2 parser and the DyALog system. Both of them can be used in conjunction with XMG. First we will briefly introduce both of them, and then show that they can be used with a semantic grammar (e.g., SEMFRAG) to perform not only syntactic parsing but also semantic construction.

LLP2 The LLP2 parser is based on a bottom-up algorithm described in (Lopez, 1999). It has relatively high parsing times but provides a user friendly graphical parsing environment with much statistical information (see Figure 2). It is well suited for teaching or for small scale projects.

DyALog The DyALog system on the other hand, is a highly optimised parsing system based on tabulation and automata techniques (Villemonte de la Clergerie, 2005). It is implemented using the DyALog programming language (*i.e.*, it is bootstrapped) and is also used to compile parsers for other types of grammars such as *Tree Insertion Grammars*.

The DyALog system is coupled with a semantic construction module whose aim is to associate with each parsed string a semantic representation[5]. This module assumes a TAG of the type described in (Gardent and Kallmeyer, 2003; Gardent, 2006)

[4]This means that for 75 % of the sentences, a TAG parser can build at least one derivation.

[5]The corresponding system is called SemConst (*cf* section 6).

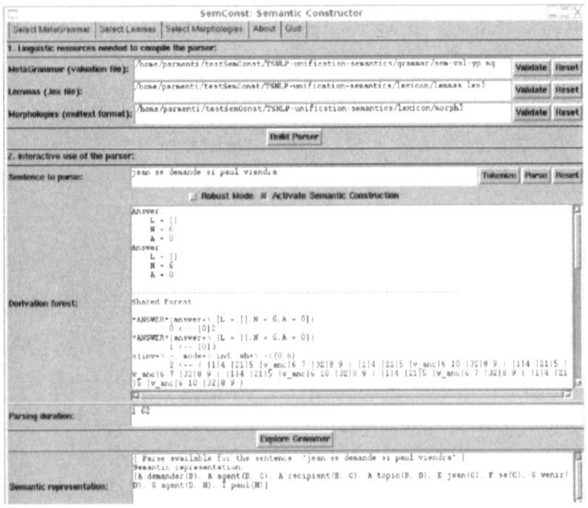

Figure 3: The SemConst system

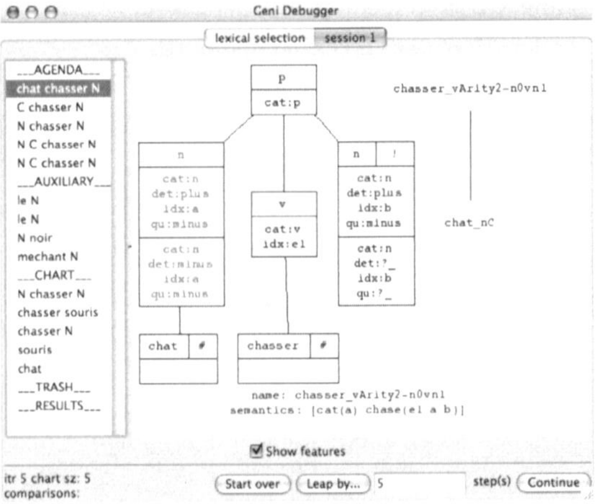

Figure 4: The GenI debugger

where initial trees are associated with semantic information and unification is used to combine semantic representations. In such a grammar, the semantic representation of a derived tree is the union of the semantic representations of the trees entering in the derivation of that derived tree modulo the unifications entailed by analysis. As detailed in (Gardent and Parmentier, 2005), such grammars support two strategies for semantic construction.

The first possible strategy is to use the full grammar and to perform semantic construction during derivation. In this case the parser must manipulate both syntactic trees and semantic representations. The advantage is that the approach is simple (the semantic representations can simply be an added feature on the anchor node of each tree). The drawback is that the presence of semantic information might reduce chart sharing.

The second possibility involves extracting the semantic information contained in the grammar and storing it into a semantic lexicon. Parsing then proceeds with a purely syntactic grammar and semantic construction is done after parsing on the basis of the parser output and of the extracted semantic lexicon. This latter technique is more suitable for large scale semantic construction as it supports better sharing in the derivation forests. It is implemented in the LORIA toolbox where a module permits both extracting a semantic lexicon from a semantic TAG and constructing a semantic representation based on this lexicon and on the derivation forests output by `DyALog` (see Figure 3).

The integration of the `DyALog` system into the toolbox is relatively new so that parsing evaluation is still under progress. So far, evaluation has been restricted to parsing the TSNLP with `DyALog` with the following preliminary results. On sentences ranging from 1 to 18 words, with an average of 7 words per sentence, and with a grammar containing 5 069 trees, `DyALog` average parsing time is of 0.38 sec with a P4 processor 2.6 GHz and 1 GB of RAM[6].

4 A TAG-based surface realiser

The surface realiser `GenI` takes a TAG and a flat semantic logical form as input, and produces all the sentences that are associated with that logical form by the grammar. It implements two bottom up algorithms, one which manipulates derived trees as items and one which is based on Earley for TAG. Both of these algorithms integrate a number of optimisations such as delayed adjunction and polarity filtering (Kow, 2005; Gardent and Kow, 2005).

`GenI` is written in Haskell and includes a graphical debugger to inspect the state of the generator at any point in the surface realisation process (see Figure 4). It also integrates a test harness for automated regression testing and benchmarking of the surface realiser and the grammar. The harness `gtester` is written in Python. It runs the surface realiser on a test suite, outputting a single document with a table of passes and failures and various performance charts (see Figures 5 and 6).

Test suite and performance The test suite is built with an emphasis on testing the surface re-

[6]These features only concern classic syntactic parsing as the semantic construction module has not been tested on real grammars yet.

test	expected	simple	earley
t1	il le accepter	pass	pass
t32	il nous accepter	pass	pass
t83	le ingnieur le lui apprendre	pass	DIED
t114	le ingnieur nous le prsenter	pass	pass
t145	le ingnieur vous le apprendre	pass	pass
t180	vous venir	pass	pass

Figure 5: Fragment of test harness output - The Earley algorithm timed out.

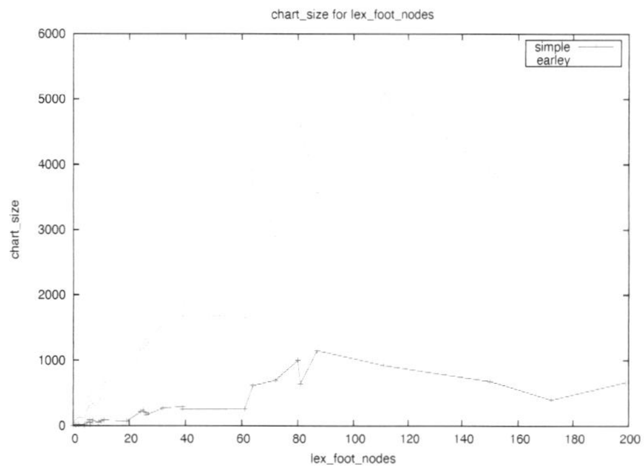

Figure 6: Automatically generated graph of performance data by the test harness.

aliser's performance in the face of increasing paraphrastic power i.e., ambiguity. The suite consists of semantic inputs that select for and combines verbs with different valencies. For example, given a hypothetical English grammar, a valency (2,1) semantics might be realised in as *Martin thinks Faye drinks* (*thinks* takes 2 arguments and *drinks* takes 1), whereas a valency (2,3,2) one would be *Dora says that Martin tells Bob that Faye likes music*. The suite also adds a varying number of intersective modifiers into the mix, giving us for instance, *The girl likes music*, *The pretty scary girl likes indie music*.

The sentences in the suite range from 2 to 15 words (8 average). Realisation times for the core suite range from 0.7 to 2.84 seconds CPU time (average 1.6 seconds).

We estimate the ambiguity for each test case in two ways. The first is to count the number of paraphrases. Given our current grammar, the test cases in our suite have up to 669 paraphrases (average 41). The second estimate for ambiguity is the number of combinations of lexical items covering the input semantics.

This second measure is based on optimisation known as polarity filtering (Gardent and Kow, 2005). This optimisation detects and eliminates combinations of lexical items that cannot be used to build a result. It associates the syntactic resources (root nodes) and requirements (substitution nodes) of the lexical items to polarities, which are then used to build "polarity automata". The automata are minimised to eliminate lexical combinations where the polarities do not cancel out, that is those for which the number of root and substitution nodes for any given category do not equal each other.

Once built, the polarity automata can also serve to estimate ambiguity. The number of paths in the automaton represent the number of possible combinations of lexical items. To determine how effective polarity filtering with respect to ambiguity, we compare the combinations before and after polarity filtering. Before filtering, we start with an initial polarity automaton in which all items are associated with a zero polarity. This gives us the lexical ambiguity before filtering. The polarity filter then builds upon this to form a final automaton where all polarities are taken into account. Counting the paths on this automaton gives us the ambiguity after filtering, and comparing this number with the lexical initial ambiguity provides an estimate on the usefulness of the polarity filter. In our suite, the initial automata for each case have 1 to 800 000 paths (76 000 average). The final automata have 1 to 6000 paths (192 average). This can represent quite a large reduction in search space, 4000 times in the case of the largest automaton. The effect of this search space reduction is most pronounced on the larger sentences or those with the most modifiers. Indeed, realisation times with and without filtering are comparable for most of the test suite, but for the most complicated sentence in the core suite, polarity filtering makes surface realisation 94% faster, producing a result in 2.35 seconds instead of 37.38.

5 Benefits of an integrated toolset

As described above, the LORIA toolbox for TAG based semantic processing includes a lexicon, a grammar, a parser, a semantic construction module and a surface realiser. Integrating these into a single platform provides some accrued benefits which we now discuss in more details.

Simplified resource management The first advantage of an integrated toolkit is that it facilitates the management of the linguistic resources used namely the grammar and the lexicon. Indeed it is common that each NLP tool (parser or generator) has its own representation format. Thus, managing the resources gets tiresome as one has to deal with several versions of a single resource. When one version is updated, the others have to be recomputed. Using an integrated toolset avoid such a drawback as the intermediate formats are hidden and the user can focus on linguistic description.

Better support for grammar development When developing parsers or surface realisers, it is useful to test them out by running them on large, realistic grammars. Such grammars can explore nooks and crannies in our implementations that would otherwise have been overlooked by a toy grammar. For example, it was only when we ran `GenI` on our French grammar that we realised our implementation did not account for auxiliary trees with substitution nodes (this has been rectified). In this respect, one could argue that `XMG` could almost be seen as a parser/realiser debugging utility because it helps us to build and extend the large grammars that are crucial for testing.

This perspective can also be inverted; parsers and surface realiser make for excellent grammar-debugging devices. For example, one possible regression test is to run the parser on a suite of known sentences to make sure that the modified grammar still parses them correctly. The exact reverse is useful as well; we could also run the surface realiser over a suite of known semantic inputs and make sure that sentences are generated for each one. This is useful for two reasons. First, reading surface realiser output (sentences) is arguably easier for human beings than reading parser output (semantic formulas). Second, the surface realiser can tell us if the grammar overgenerates because it would output nonsense sentences. Parsers, on the other hand, are much better adapted for testing for undergeneration because it is easier to write sentences than semantic formulas, which makes it easier to test phenomena which might not already be in the suite.

Towards a reversible grammar Another advantage of using such a toolset relies on the fact that we can manage a common resource for both parsing and generation, and thus avoid inconsistency, redundancy and offer a better flexibility as advocated in (Neumann, 1994).

On top of these practical questions, having a unique reversible resource can lead us further. For instance, (Neumann, 1994) proposes an interleaved parsing/realisation architecture where the parser is used to choose among a set of paraphrases proposed by the generator; paraphrases which are ambiguous (that have multiple parses) are discarded in favour of those whose meaning is most explicit. Concretely, we could do this with a simple pipeline using `GenI` to produce the paraphrases, `DyALog` to parse them, and a small shell script to pick the best result. This would only be a simulation, of course. (Neumann, 1994) goes as far as to interleave the processes, keeping the shared chart and using the parser to iteratively prune the search space as it is being explored by the generator. The version we propose would not have such niceties as a shared chart, but the point is that having all the tools at our disposable makes such experimentation possible in the first place.

Moreover, there are several other interesting applications of the combined toolbox. We could use the surface realiser to build artificial corpora. These can in turn be parsed to semi-automatically create rich treebanks containing syntactico-semantic analyses à la Redwoods (Oepen et al., 2002).

Eventually, another use for the toolbox might be in components of standard NLP applications such as machine translation, questioning answering, or interactive dialogue systems.

6 Availability

The toolbox presented here is open-source and freely available under the terms of the GPL[7]. More information about the requirements and installation procedure is available at `http://trac.loria.fr/~semtag`. Note that this toolbox is made of two main components: the GenI[8] system and the SemConst[9] system, which respectively performs generation and parsing from common linguistic resources. The first is written in Haskell (except the `XMG` part written in Oz) and is multi-platform (Linux, Windows, Mac OS). The latter is written in Oz (except the `DyALog` part which is bootstrapped and contains some Intel assembler code) and is available on Unix-like plat-

[7] Note that `XMG` is released under the terms of the CeCILL license (`http://www.cecill.info/index.en.html`), which is compatible with the GPL.

[8] `http://trac.loria.fr/~geni`

[9] `http://trac.loria.fr/~semconst`

forms only.

7 Conclusion

The LORIA toolbox provides an integrated environment for TAG based semantic processing: either to construct the semantic representation of a given sentence (parsing) or to generate a sentence verbalising a given semantic content (generation).

Importantly, both the generator and the parsers use the same grammar (SemFraG) so that both tools can be used jointly to improve grammar precision. All the sentences outputted by the surface realiser should be parsed to have at least the semantic representation given by the test suite, and all parses of a sentence should be realised into at least the same sentence.

Current and future work concentrates on developing an automated error mining environment for both parsing and generation; on extending the grammar coverage; on integrating further optimisations both in the parser (through parsing with factorised trees) and in the generator (through packing and accessibility filtering cf. (Carroll and Oepen, 2005); and on experimenting with different semantic construction strategies (Gardent and Parmentier, 2005).

References

H. Ait-Kaci. 1991. Warren's Abstract Machine: A Tutorial Reconstruction. In K. Furukawa, editor, *Proc. of the Eighth International Conference of Logic Programming*. MIT Press, Cambridge, MA.

J. Carroll and S. Oepen. 2005. High efficiency realization for a wide-coverage unification grammar. In R. Dale and K-F. Wong, editors, *Proceedings of the Second International Joint Conference on Natural Language Processing*, volume 3651 of *Springer Lecture Notes in Artificial Intelligence*, pages 165–176.

B. Crabbé and D. Duchier. 2004. Metagrammar Redux. In *Proceedings of CSLP 2004, Copenhagen.*

D. Duchier, J. Le Roux, and Y. Parmentier. 2004. The Metagrammar Compiler: An NLP Application with a Multi-paradigm Architecture. In *2nd International Mozart/Oz Conference (MOZ'2004)*, Charleroi.

C. Gardent and L. Kallmeyer. 2003. Semantic construction in FTAG. In *Proceedings of EACL'03, Budapest.*

C. Gardent and E. Kow. 2005. Generating and selecting grammatical paraphrases. *ENLG, Aberdeen.*

C. Gardent and Y. Parmentier. 2005. Large scale semantic construction for tree adjoining grammars. In *Proceedings of The Fifth International Conference on Logical Aspects of Computational Linguistics (LACL05).*

C. Gardent. 2006. Intégration d'une dimension sémantique dans les grammaires d'arbres adjoints. In *Actes de la conférence TALN'2006 Leuven.*

E. Kow. 2005. Adapting polarised disambiguation to surface realisation. In *17th European Summer School in Logic, Language and Information - ESSLLI'05, Edinburgh, UK*, Aug.

S. Lehmann, S. Oepen, S. Regnier-Prost, K. Netter, V. Lux, J. Klein, K. Falkedal, F. Fouvry, D. Estival, E. Dauphin, H. Compagnion, J. Baur, L. Balkan, and D. Arnold. 1996. TSNLP — Test Suites for Natural Language Processing. In *Proceedings of COLING 1996*, Kopenhagen.

P. Lopez. 1999. *Analyse d'énoncés oraux pour le dialogue homme-machine à l'aide de grammaires lexicalisées d'arbres.* Ph.D. thesis, Université Henri Poincaré – Nancy 1.

P. Lopez. 2000. Extended Partial Parsing for Lexicalized Tree Grammars. In *Proceedings of the International Workshop on Parsing Technology (IWPT2000), Trento, Italy.*

G. Neumann. 1994. *A Uniform Computational Model for Natural Language Parsing and Generation.* Ph.D. thesis, University of the Saarland, Saarbrücken.

S. Oepen, E. Callahan, C. Manning, and K. Toutanova. 2002. Lingo redwoods—a rich and dynamic treebank for hpsg.

Y. Parmentier and J. Le Roux. 2005. XMG: an Extensible Metagrammatical Framework. In *Proceedings of the Student Session of the 17th European Summer School in Logic, Language and Information, Edinburg, Great Britain*, Aug.

E. Villemonte de la Clergerie. 2005. DyALog: a tabular logic programming based environment for NLP. In *Proceedings of CSLP'05*, Barcelona.

XTAG-Research-Group. 2001. A lexicalized tree adjoining grammar for english. Technical Report IRCS-01-03, IRCS, University of Pennsylvania. Available at http://www.cis.upenn.edu/~xtag/gramrelease.html.

Extended cross-serial dependencies in Tree Adjoining Grammars

Marco Kuhlmann and **Mathias Möhl**
Programming Systems Lab
Saarland University
Saarbrücken, Germany
{kuhlmann|mmohl}@ps.uni-sb.de

Abstract

The ability to represent cross-serial dependencies is one of the central features of Tree Adjoining Grammar (TAG). The class of dependency structures representable by lexicalized TAG derivations can be captured by two graph-theoretic properties: a bound on the *gap degree* of the structures, and a constraint called *well-nestedness*. In this paper, we compare formalisms from two strands of extensions to TAG in the context of the question, how they behave with respect to these constraints. In particular, we show that multi-component TAG does not necessarily retain the well-nestedness constraint, while this constraint is inherent to Coupled Context-Free Grammar (Hotz and Pitsch, 1996).

1 Introduction

The ability to assign 'limited cross-serial dependencies' to the words in a sentence is a hallmark of mildly context-sensitive grammar formalisms (Joshi, 1985). In the case of TAG, an exact definition of this ability can be given in terms of two graph-theoretic properties of the dependency structures induced by TAG derivations: the *gap degree restriction* and the *well-nestedness* constraint (Bodirsky et al., 2005).

Gap degree and well-nestedness can be seen as the formal correspondents of what Joshi (1985) refers to as 'a limited amount of cross-serial dependencies' and 'the nesting properties as in the case of context-free grammars.' More specifically, the gap degree of a dependency structure counts the number of discontinuities in a dependency subtree, while well-nestedness constrains the positions of disjoint subtrees relative to one another. The dependency structures that correspond to the derivations in a lexicalized TAG are well-nested, and their gap degree is at most 1.

In the present paper, we compare formalisms from two strands of extensions to TAG in the context of the question, what classes of dependency structures they are able to induce.

We are particularly interested in formalisms that induce only well-nested dependency structures. This interest is motivated by two observations: First, well-nestedness is interesting as a generalization of projectivity (Marcus, 1967)—while more than 23% of the 73 088 dependency structures in the Prague Dependency Treebank of Czech (Hajič et al., 2001) are non-projective, only 0.11% are not well-nested (Kuhlmann and Nivre, 2006). Second, well-nestedness is interesting for processing. Specifically, parsers for well-nested grammar formalisms are not confronted with the 'crossing configurations' that make the universal recognition problem of Linear Context-Free Rewriting Systems NP-complete (Satta, 1992). In summary, it appears that well-nestedness can strike a successful balance between empirical coverage and computational tractability. If this is true, then a formalism that has the well-nestedness constraint hardwired is preferable over one that has not.

The results of this paper can be summarized as follows: Derivations in lexicalized multi-component TAGs (Weir, 1988; Kallmeyer, 2005), in which a single adjunction adds a set of elementary trees, either induce exactly the same dependency structures as TAG, or induce all structures of bounded gap degree, even non-well-nested ones. This depends on the decision whether one takes 'lexicalized' to mean 'one lexical anchor per tree', or 'one lexical anchor per tree set'. In contrast, multi-foot extensions of TAG (Abe, 1988; Hotz and Pitsch, 1996), where a single elementary tree may have more than one foot node, only induce well-nested dependency structures of bounded gap degree. Thus, from the dependency point of view, they constitute the structurally more conservative extension of TAG.

Proceedings of the 8th International Workshop on Tree Adjoining Grammar and Related Formalisms, pages 121–126,
Sydney, July 2006.

2 Dependency structures for TAG

We start with a presentation of the dependency view on TAG that constitutes the basis for our work, and introduce the relevant terminology. The main objective of this section is to provide intuitions; for the formal details, see Bodirsky et al. (2005).

2.1 The dependency view on TAG

Let $s = w_1 \cdots w_n$ be a sentence (a sequence of tokens). By a *dependency structure* for s, we mean a tuple $(W, \to, \prec)$, where $W = \{w_1, \ldots, w_n\}$, and

$$\to \;=\; \{\, (w_i, w_j) \in W \times W \mid w_j \text{ depends on } w_i \,\}$$
$$\prec \;=\; \{\, (w_i, w_j) \in W \times W \mid i < j \,\}$$

To interpret a grammar formalism as a specification for a set of dependency structures, we need to assign meaning to the relation 'depends' in terms of this formalism. For TAG, this can be done based on the Fundamental Hypothesis that 'every syntactic dependency is expressed locally within a single elementary tree' (Frank, 2002). More specifically, a derivation in a (strongly) lexicalized TAG can be viewed as a dependency structure as follows: The set W contains the (occurences of) lexical anchors involved in the derivation. For two anchors $w_i, w_j \in W$, $w_i \to w_j$ if the elementary tree anchored at w_j was substituted or adjoined into the tree anchored at w_i. We then have $w_i \prec w_j$ if w_i precedes w_j in the yield of the derived tree corresponding to the derivation. Notice that the relation $\to$ in such a dependency structure is almost exactly the derivation tree of the underlying TAG derivation; the only difference is that elementary trees have been replaced by their lexical anchors.

Figure 1 shows a TAG grammar together with a dependency structure induced by a derivation of this grammar. Tokens in the derived string are represented by labelled nodes; the solid arcs between the nodes represent the dependencies.

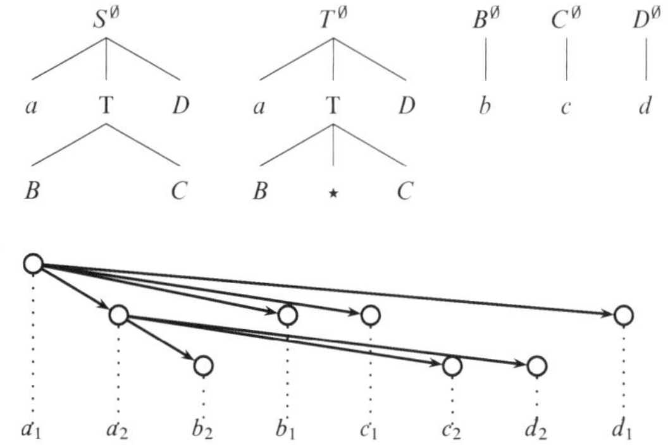

Figure 1: TAG grammar for $a^n b^n c^n d^n$, and a dependency structure induced by this grammar

2.2 Gap degree and well-nestedness

An interesting feature of the dependency structure shown in Figure 1 is that it violates a standard constraint on dependency structures known as *projectivity* (Marcus, 1967). We introduce some terminology for non-projective dependency structures:

A set $T \subseteq W$ is *convex*, if for no two tokens $w_1, w_2 \in T$, there exists a token w from $W - T$ such that $w_1 \prec w \prec w_2$. The *cover* of T, $\mathcal{C}(T)$, is the smallest convex set that contains T. For $w \in W$, we write $\downarrow w$ for the set of tokens in the subtree rooted at w (including w itself). A *gap* in $\downarrow w$ is a largest convex set in $\mathcal{C}(\downarrow w) - \downarrow w$. The *gap degree* of w, $gd(w)$, is the number of gaps in $\downarrow w$. The gaps in $\downarrow w$ partition $\downarrow w$ into $gd(w) - 1$ largest convex blocks; we write $\downarrow_i w$ to refer to the i-th of these blocks, counted from left to right (with respect to $\prec$). The gap degree of a dependency structure is the maximum over the gap degrees of its subtrees; we write $\mathcal{D}_g$ for the set of all dependency structures with a gap degree of at most g.

The gap degree provides a quantitative measure for the non-projectivity of dependency structures. *Well-nestedness* is a qualitative property: it constrains the relative positions of disjoint subtrees. Let $w_1, w_2 \in W$ such that $\downarrow w_1$ and $\downarrow w_2$ are disjoint. Four tokens $w_1^1, w_1^2 \in \downarrow w_1$, $w_2^1, w_2^2 \in \downarrow w_2$ *interleave*, if $w_1^1 \prec w_2^1 \prec w_1^2 \prec w_2^2$. A dependency structure is *well-nested*, if it does not contain interleaving tokens. We write $\mathcal{D}_{wn}$ for the set of all well-nested dependency structures.

For illustration, consider again the dependency structure shown in Figure 1. It has gap degree 1: a_2 is the only token w for which $\downarrow w$ is not convex; the set $\{b_1, c_1\}$ forms a gap in $\downarrow a_2$. The structure is also well-nested. In contrast, the structure shown in the right half of Figure 2 is not well-nested; the tokens b, c, d, e interleave. Bodirsky et al. (2005) show that TAG induces precisely the set $\mathcal{D}_{wn} \cap \mathcal{D}_1$.

3 Multi-component extensions

Multi-component TAG (MCTAG) extends TAG with the ability to adjoin a whole set of elementary trees (*components*) simultaneously. To answer the question, whether this extension also leads to an extended class of dependency structures, we first need to decide how we want to transfer the Fundamental Hypothesis (Frank, 2002) to MCTAGs.

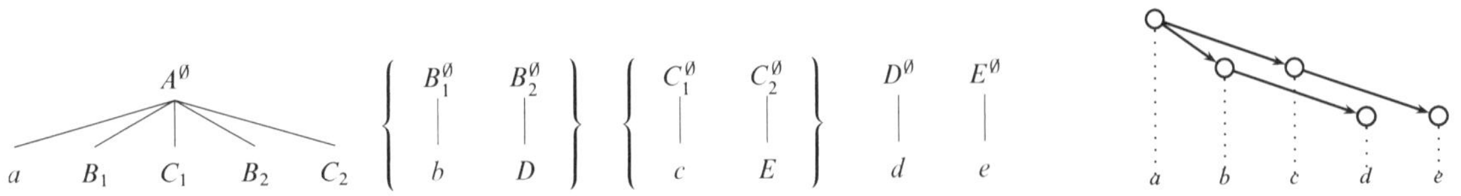

Figure 2: An MCTAG and a not well-nested dependency structure derived by it.

3.1 One anchor per component

If we commit to the view that each component of a tree set introduces a separate lexical anchor and its syntactic dependencies, the dependency structures induced by MCTAG are exactly the structures induced by TAG. In particular, each node in the derivation tree, and therefore each token in the dependency tree, corresponds to a single elementary tree. As Kallmeyer (2005) puts it, one can then consider an MCTAG as a TAG G 'where certain derivation trees in G are disallowed since they do not satisfy certain constraints.' The ability of MCTAG to perform multiple adjunctions simultaneously allows one to induce more complex *sets* of dependency structures—each individual structure is limited as in the case of standard TAG.

3.2 One anchor per tree set

If, on the other hand, we take a complete tree set as the level on which syntactic dependencies are specified, MCTAGs can induce a larger class of dependency structures. Under this perspective, tokens in the dependency structure correspond not to individual components, but to tree sets (Weir, 1988). For each token w, $\downarrow w$ then contains the lexical anchors of all the subderivations starting in the tree set corresponding to w. As there can be a gap between each two of these subderivations, the gap degree of the induced dependency structures is bounded only by the maximal number of components per tree set. At the same time, even non-well-nested structures can be induced; an example is shown in Figure 2. Here, $\downarrow b$ is distributed over the components rooted at B_1 and B_2, and $\downarrow c$ is distributed over C_1 and C_2. The elementary tree rooted at A arranges the substitution sites such that b, c, d, e interleave. Note that the MCTAG used in this example is heavily restricted: it is tree-local and does not even use adjunction. This restricted form suffices to induce non-well-nested dependency structures.

4 Multi-foot extensions

A second way to extend TAG, orthogonal to the multi-component approach, is to allow a single elementary tree to have more than one foot node. For this kind of extension, the Fundamental Hypothesis does not need to be re-interpreted. Probably the most prominent multi-foot extension of TAG is Ranked Node Rewriting Grammar (RNRG) (Abe, 1988); however, the properties that we are interested in here can be easier investigated in a notational variant of RNRG, Coupled Context-Free Grammar (Hotz and Pitsch, 1996).

Terminology Multi-foot formalisms require a means to specify which foot node gets what material in an adjunction. To do so, they use ranked symbols. A *ranked alphabet* is a pair $\Pi = (\Sigma, \rho)$, where Σ is an alphabet, and $\rho \in \Sigma \to \mathbb{N}$ is a total function that assigns every symbol $\sigma \in \Sigma$ a (positive) *rank*. Define $\Pi[r] := \{\, \sigma \in \Sigma \mid \rho(\sigma) = r \,\}$. The *components* of σ, *comp*(σ), are the elements of the set $\{\, (\sigma, i) \mid 1 \leq i \leq \rho(\sigma) \,\}$. We write σ_i instead of (σ, i). Let $comp(\Pi) := \bigcup_{\sigma \in \Pi} comp(\sigma)$.

4.1 Coupled Context-Free Grammar

Coupled Context-Free Grammar (CCFG) is a generalization of context-free grammar in which non-terminals come from a ranked alphabet, and components of a non-terminal can only be substituted simultaneously. The 'TAG-ness' of CCFG is reflected in the requirement, that the RHS of productions must be words from a bracket-like language, and thus have the same hierarchical structure as elementary trees in a TAG. As an example, the second elementary tree from Figure 1 can be linearized as

$$\langle T_1 a T_1 B_1, C_1 T_2 D_1 T_2 \rangle ,$$

where each pair (T_1, T_2) of matching components corresponds to an inner node in the tree, and the boundary between the first and the second part of the tuple marks the position of the foot node. The required structure of the RHS can be formalized as follows:

Definition 1 Let Π be a ranked alphabet, and let Σ be an unranked alphabet. The *extended semi-Dyck set* over Π and Σ, ESD(Π, Σ), is the smallest set that satisfies the following properties:

(a) $\Sigma^* \subseteq \text{ESD}(\Pi, \Sigma)$; (b) $\Pi[1] \subseteq \text{ESD}(\Pi, \Sigma)$; (c) if $s_1, \dots, s_k \in \text{ESD}(\Pi, \Sigma)$ and $\pi \in \Pi[k+1]$, then $\pi_1 s_1 \pi_2 \cdots \pi_k s_k \pi_{k+1} \in \text{ESD}(\Pi, \Sigma)$; (d) if $s_1, s_2 \in \text{ESD}(\Pi, \Sigma)$, then $s_1 s_2 \in \text{ESD}(\Pi, \Sigma)$.

Definition 2 Let N be a ranked alphabet of non-terminals, and let T be an (unranked) alphabet of terminals. A *ranked rewriting system* over $\text{ESD}(N, T)$ is a finite, non-empty set of productions of the form $X \to \langle \alpha_1, \dots, \alpha_r \rangle$, where $X \in N[r]$, and $\alpha := \alpha_1 \cdots \alpha_r \in \text{ESD}(N, T)$.

We write $\rho(p)$ to refer to the rank of the non-terminal on the LHS of a production p.

RNRG and CCFG are notational variants because each RNRG elementary tree with $r - 1$ foot nodes can be linearized into the RHS of a production $X \to \langle \alpha_1, \dots, \alpha_r \rangle$ in a ranked rewriting system, as indicated by the example above.

Definition 3 A *coupled context-free grammar* is a tuple $G = (N, T, P, S)$ where: N is a ranked alphabet of *non-terminal symbols*; T is an unranked alphabet of *terminal symbols*; P is a ranked rewriting system over $\text{ESD}(N, T)$; $S \in N[1]$ is a *start symbol*.

We say that a CCFG G is an r-CCFG, if the maximal rank among all non-terminals in G is r.

Definition 4 Put $V := comp(N) \cup T$, and let

$$\begin{aligned} \phi \in V^* &= u_1 X_1 u_2 \cdots u_r X_r u_{r+1} \\ \psi \in V^* &= u_1 \alpha_1 u_2 \cdots u_r \alpha_r u_{r+1} \end{aligned}$$

such that $u_2, \dots, u_r \in \text{ESD}(N, T)$, and $X \in N[r]$. We say that ψ can be derived from ϕ in one step, and write $\phi \Rightarrow_G \psi$, if G contains a production $X \to \langle \alpha_1, \dots, \alpha_r \rangle$. The *string language* of G is the set $L(G) := \{ s \in T^* \mid S \Rightarrow_G^* s \}$.

Based on this definition, the notions of *derivation tree* and *derived tree* are defined in the usual way. In particular, the nodes of the derivation tree are labelled with productions, while the nodes of the corresponding derived tree are labelled with components from $comp(\Pi)$ (inner nodes) and terminal symbols (leaves). We write $(T^\sharp, T^\flat)$ to refer to a derivation in CCFG: $T^\sharp$ stands for the derivation tree, $T^\flat$ for the corresponding derived tree.

4.2 The dependency view on CCFG

A CCFG G is *strongly lexicalized*, if each production p contains exactly one terminal symbol, written as *anchor*(p). Just as in the case of TAG, a strongly lexicalized CCFG G can be interpreted as a dependency grammar: Let $(T^\sharp, T^\flat)$ be a derivation in G. Since G is strongly lexicalized, there is a one-to-one mapping between the nodes of the derivation tree $T^\sharp$ (labelled with productions) and the leaves of the derived tree $T^\flat$ (labelled with terminals); we refer to this mapping by the name f_L.

Definition 5 A dependency structure D is *induced* by a derivation $(T^\sharp, T^\flat)$, written $(T^\sharp, T^\flat) \vdash D$, if (a) $anchor(p_1) \to anchor(p_2)$ in D if and only if $p_1 \to p_2$ in $T^\sharp$; (b) $anchor(p_1) \prec anchor(p_2)$ in D if and only if $f_L(p_1) \prec f_L(p_2)$ in $T^\flat$.

We write $\mathcal{D}(G)$ for the set of all dependency structures induced by derivations in G. Figure 3 shows a sample CCFG G, a derivation in G, and the dependency structure induced by this derivation.

4.3 Projections

To reason about the structural properties of the dependency languages induced by CCFGs, we need some additional definitions. In the following, we use the notation $(u : \sigma)$ to refer to a node u with label σ in some given labelled tree.

Let $D \in \mathcal{D}(G)$ be a dependency structure such that $(T^\sharp, T^\flat) \vdash D$, and let $(u : p) \in T^\sharp$ be a node. Somewhere in the course of the derivation represented by $T^\sharp$, the $\rho(p)$ components of the non-terminal on the LHS of the production p are simultaneously rewritten. Let $f_I(u)$ be the $\rho(p)$-tuple of nodes in $T^\flat$ that correspond to these components. Note that, while f_L maps nodes in the derivation tree $T^\sharp$ to leaves in the derived tree $T^\flat$, f_I takes nodes in $T^\sharp$ to *tuples* of inner nodes in $T^\flat$. Define

$$\begin{aligned} down(u) &= \{ v \mid u \to^* v \text{ in } T^\sharp \}, \\ proj(u, i) &= \{ v \mid f_I(u)_i \to^* f_L(v) \text{ in } T^\flat \}. \end{aligned}$$

The set $down(u)$ contains the lexical anchors in the sub-derivation starting at u. The set $proj(u, i)$ identifies that part of this sub-derivation that is derived from the i-th component of the non-terminal at the LHS of the production corresponding to u. For the derivation shown in Figure 3, we have

$$f_I(p_2) = \langle B_1, B_2, B_3 \rangle, \quad proj(p_2, 1) = \{p_2\}.$$

Lemma 6 For all nodes $u \in T^\sharp$,

$$down(u) = \biguplus_{1 \le i \le \rho(p)} proj(u, i).$$

4.4 Results

In this section, we prove the main technical results of this paper: that all dependency structures

Grammar G^*: $p_1\colon A \to \langle a \rangle$, $p_2\colon B \to \langle b, D_1, D_1 \rangle$, $p_3\colon C \to \langle A_1 B_1 c A_1 B_2 A_1 B_3 \rangle$, $p_4\colon D \to \langle d \rangle$

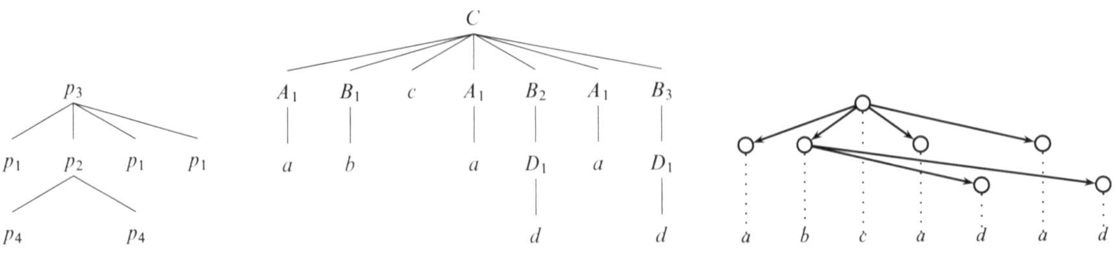

(a) Derivation tree (b) Derived tree (c) Induced dependency structure

Figure 3: A CCFG derivation and the dependency structure induced by it

induced by an r-CCFG have a gap degree that is bounded by r; that they are all well-nested; and that each well-nested structure with a gap degree bounded by r can be induced by an r-CCFG. In the following, let G be an r-CCFG, and write $\mathcal{G}_r$ for the set of all r-CCFGs.

Lemma 7 $\mathcal{D}(G) \subseteq \mathcal{D}_{r-1}$

Proof Let $(T^\sharp, T^\flat) \vdash D$, and let $(u : p) \in T^\sharp$. By definition of *proj*, for each $1 \leq i \leq \rho(p)$, the set $proj(u, i)$ forms a contiguous region of the sentence derived by $T^\sharp$. Using Lemma 6, we then see that $down(u)$ is distributed over at most $\rho(u)$ contiguous regions of that sentence. This means that the dependency subtree rooted at $anchor(p)$ has at most $\rho(p) - 1$ gaps.

Lemma 8 $\mathcal{D}(G) \subseteq \mathcal{D}_{wn}$

Proof Choose a $D \in \mathcal{D}(G)$, and assume that D is not well-nested. Then there is a governor $u \in D$ with two distinct dependents v, w such that $\downarrow v$ contains tokens v_1, v_2, and $\downarrow w$ contains tokens w_1, w_2 such that $v_1 \prec w_1 \prec v_2 \prec w_2$. For the derivation $(T^\sharp, T^\flat)$ that induces D, this means that there is a node $(u : p)$ with children $(v : p_v)$ and $(w : p_w)$ in $T^\sharp$ such that

$$\exists(v_1, v_2 \in down(v))\colon \exists(w_1, w_2 \in down(w))\colon$$
$$f_L(v_1) \prec f_L(w_1) \prec f_L(v_2) \prec f_L(w_2) \text{ in } T^\flat .$$

Since $down(v)$ and $down(w)$ are disjoint; v_1 and v_2 must come from distinct convex blocks in $down(v)$, and w_1 and w_2 must come from distinct convex blocks in $down(w)$. Therefore,

$$v_1 \in proj(v, i_1),\ v_2 \in proj(v, i_2),\ i_1 < i_2 \quad \text{and}$$
$$w_1 \in proj(w, j_1),\ w_2 \in proj(w, j_2),\ j_1 < j_2 .$$

By definition, $proj(x, k)$ ($x \in \{v, w\}$) is the projection of a node $f_I(x)_k$ in $T^\flat$; the label of this node is $\text{LHS}(p_x)_k$. Assume now that the non-terminal on the LHS of p_v is V, and that the non-terminal on the LHS of p_w is W. Given that p_v and p_w are used to rewrite p, $\text{RHS}(p)$ contains the substring $V_{i_1} \cdots W_{j_1} \cdots V_{i_2} \cdots W_{j_2}$. This contradicts the fact that $\text{RHS}(p) \in \text{ESD}(N, T)$.

Lemma 9 $\mathcal{D}_{wn} \cap \mathcal{D}_{r-1} \subseteq \bigcup_{G \in \mathcal{G}_r} \mathcal{D}(G)$

Proof Let $D = (W, \to, \prec)$ be a dependency structure from $\mathcal{D}_{wn} \cap \mathcal{D}_{r-1}$. We construct an r-CCFG $G = (N, T, P, S)$ that induces D. For the ranked alphabet N of non-terminals, put

$$N = \{\, N^w \mid w \in W \,\},\ \rho(N^w) = gd(w) + 1 .$$

The set S of start symbols is $\{N^\top\}$, where $\top$ is the root of D. For the terminal alphabet, put $T = W$. The set P consists of $|W|$ productions of the form $N^w \to \vec{\alpha}$, where $w \in W$, and $\vec{\alpha}$ is a tuple with arity $gd(w) + 1$ that contains the terminal w and non-terminal components for all children of w as follows. Consider the following family of sets:

$$\mathcal{C}_w = \{\{w\}\} \cup \{\, \downarrow_i v \mid w \to v, 1 \leq i \leq gd(v) + 1 \,\} .$$

All sets in $\mathcal{C}_w$ are disjoint, and their union equals the set $\downarrow w$. We define a function $[\cdot]$ that interprets the elements of $\mathcal{C}_w$ as elements from $N \cup T$ as follows: $[\{w\}] := w$, and $[\downarrow_i v] := N_i^v$. Now the RHS of a rule $N^w \to \vec{\alpha}$ is fully specified by the following equivalences, where $C \in \mathcal{C}_w$:

$$[C] \text{ occurs in } \alpha_i \text{ iff } C \subseteq \downarrow_i w$$
$$[C_1] \text{ precedes } [C_2] \text{ in } \vec{\alpha} \text{ iff } C_1 \times C_2 \subseteq \prec$$

Applied to the dependency structure of Figure 3c, this constructs the given grammar G^*. Note that, due to the well-nestedness of D, the RHS of each rule forms a valid extended semi-Dyck word.

5 Summary

Starting from the fact that TAG is able to derive well-nested dependency structures with a gap degree of at most 1, we have investigated how multi-component and multi-foot extensions of TAG alter this expressivity. Our results are as follows:

- For multi-component TAG, the notion of 'induced dependency structures' depends on the assumed notion of lexicalization. Therefore, either the same structures as in TAG, or arbitrary gap-bounded dependency structures are derivable. In the former case, MCTAG has the same structural limits as standard TAG; in the latter case, even non-well-nested dependency structures are induced.

- The multi-foot extension CCFG (and its equivalent RNRG) is restricted to well-nested dependency structures, but in contrast to TAG, it can induce structures with any bounded gap degree. The rank of a grammar is an upper bound on the gap degree of the dependency structures it induces.

Since the extensions inherent to MCTAG and CCFG are orthogonal, it is possible to combine them: Multi-Component Multi-Foot TAG (MMTAG) as described by Chiang (2001) allows to simultaneously adjoin sets of trees, where each tree may have multiple foot nodes. The structural limitations of the dependency structures inducible by MCTAG and CCFG generalize to MMTAG as one would expect. As in the case of MCTAG, there are two different understandings of how a dependency structure is induced by an MMTAG. Under the 'one anchor per component' perspective, MMTAG, just like CCFG, derives well-nested structures of bounded gap-degree. Under the 'one anchor per tree set' perspective, just like MCTAG, it also derives non-well-nested gap-bounded structures.

Acknowledgements We thank Jan Schwinghammer, Guido Tack, and Stefan Thater for fruitful discussions during the preparation of this paper, and three anonymous reviewers for their detailed comments on an earlier version. The work of Marco Kuhlmann is funded by the Collaborative Research Centre 'Resource-Adaptive Cognitive Processes' of the Deutsche Forschungsgemeinschaft.

References

Naoki Abe. 1988. Feasible learnability of formal grammars and the theory of natural language acquisition. In *12th International Conference on Computational Linguistics*, pages 1–6, Budapest, Hungary.

Manuel Bodirsky, Marco Kuhlmann, and Mathias Möhl. 2005. Well-nested drawings as models of syntactic structure. In *Tenth Conference on Formal Grammar and Ninth Meeting on Mathematics of Language (FG-MoL)*, Edinburgh, UK.

David Chiang. 2001. Constraints on strong generative power. In *39th Annual Meeting and Tenth Conference of the European Chapter of the Association for Computational Linguistics*, pages 124–131, Toulouse, France.

Robert Frank. 2002. *Phrase Structure Composition and Syntactic Dependencies*. MIT Press.

Jan Hajič, Barbora Vidova Hladka, Jarmila Panevová, Eva Hajičová, Petr Sgall, and Petr Pajas. 2001. Prague Dependency Treebank 1.0. LDC, 2001T10.

Günther Hotz and Gisela Pitsch. 1996. On parsing coupled-context-free languages. *Theoretical Computer Science*, 161:205–233.

Aravind K. Joshi. 1985. Tree adjoining grammars: How much context-sensitivity is required to provide reasonable structural descriptions? In David R. Dowty, Lauri Karttunen, and Arnold M. Zwicky, editors, *Natural Language Parsing*, pages 206–250. Cambridge University Press, Cambridge, UK.

Laura Kallmeyer. 2005. A descriptive characterization of multicomponent tree adjoining grammars. In *Traitement Automatique des Langues Naturelles (TALN)*, volume 1, pages 457–462, Dourdan, France.

Marco Kuhlmann and Joakim Nivre. 2006. Mildly non-projective dependency structures. In *22nd International Conference on Computational Linguistics and 43rd Annual Meeting of the Association for Computational Linguistics (COLING-ACL), Companion Volume*, Sydney, Australia.

Solomon Marcus. 1967. *Algebraic Linguistics: Analytical Models*, volume 29 of *Mathematics in Science and Engineering*. Academic Press, New York.

Giorgio Satta. 1992. Recognition of linear context-free rewriting systems. In *30th Meeting of the Association for Computational Linguistics (ACL)*, pages 89–95, Newark, Delaware, USA.

David J. Weir. 1988. *Characterizing Mildly Context-Sensitive Grammar Formalisms*. Ph.D. thesis, University of Pennsylvania, Philadelphia, USA.

Using LTAG-Based Features for Semantic Role Labeling

Yudong Liu and **Anoop Sarkar**
Computing Science Department
Simon Fraser University
British Columbia, Canada, V5A 1S6
yudongl,anoop@cs.sfu.ca

Abstract

Semantic role labeling (SRL) methods typically use features from syntactic parse trees. We propose a novel method that uses Lexicalized Tree-Adjoining Grammar (LTAG) based features for this task. We convert parse trees into LTAG derivation trees where the semantic roles are treated as hidden information learned by supervised learning on annotated data derived from PropBank. We extracted various features from the LTAG derivation trees and trained a discriminative decision list model to predict semantic roles. We present our results on the full CoNLL 2005 SRL task.

1 Introduction

Semantic role labeling (SRL) is a natural extension of the syntactic parsing task. In SRL, particular syntactic constituents in a parse tree for a sentence are identified with semantic roles. The labels assigned to various types of arguments and adjuncts differ in different annotation schemes. In this paper, we use the PropBank corpus of predicate-argument structures (Palmer, Gildea and Kingsbury, 2005). We assume we are given a syntactic parse tree and a particular predicate in the sentence for which we then identify the arguments and adjuncts and their labels. In this paper we compare two models for the identification of semantic role labels in a parse tree: A model that uses a path in the parse tree (or the derived tree in TAG terminology) and various associated features related to this, and we compare this model with a model that converts the syntactic parse tree into a Lexicalized Tree-Adjoining Grammar (LTAG) derivation tree and uses features extracted from the elementary trees and the LTAG derivation tree.

In each model the features of that model are used in a discriminative model for semantic role labeling. The model is a simple decision list learner that uses tree patterns extracted from the LTAG derivation trees in order to classify constituents into their semantic roles. We present results on the full CoNLL 2005 SRL task (Carreras and Màrquez, 2005) a dataset built by combining the Treebank and parser data with the PropBank annotations.

2 Background about SRL

A semantic role is defined to be the relationship that a syntactic constituent has with the predicate. For example, the following sentence, taken from the PropBank corpus, shows the annotation of semantic roles:

> [A0 *Late buying*] [V *gave*] [A2 *the Paris Bourse*] [A1 *a parachute*] [AM-TMP *after its free fall early in the day*].

Here, the arguments for the predicate *gave* are defined in the PropBank Frame Scheme (Palmer, Gildea and Kingsbury, 2005) as:

V: verb	A2: beneficiary
A0: giver	AM-TMP: temporal
A1: thing given	

Recognizing and labeling semantic arguments is a key task for answering "*Who*", "*When*","*What*", "*Where*", "*Why*", etc. questions in Information Extraction, Question Answering, Summarization (Melli et al, 2005), and, in general, in all NLP tasks in which some kind of semantic interpretation is needed.

Most previous research treats the semantic role labeling task as a classification problem, and divides it into two phases: *argument identification* and *argument classification*. Argument identification involves classifying each syntactic element in a sentence into either an argument or a non-argument. Argument classification involves classifying each argument identified into a specific semantic role. A variety of machine learning methods have been applied to this task. One of the most important steps in building an accurate classifier is feature selection. Different from the widely used

Proceedings of the 8th International Workshop on Tree Adjoining Grammar and Related Formalisms, pages 127–132,
Sydney, July 2006. ©2006 Association for Computational Linguistics

feature functions that are based on the syntactic parse tree (Gildea and Jurafsky, 2002), we explore the use of LTAG-based features in a simple discriminative decision-list learner.

3 LTAG Based Feature Extraction

In this section, we introduce the main components of our system. First, we do a pruning on the given parse trees with certain constraints. Then we decompose the pruned parse trees into a set of LTAG elementary trees. For each constituent in question, we extract features from its corresponding derivation tree. We train using these features in a decision list model.

3.1 Pruning the Parse Trees

Given a parse tree, the pruning component identifies the predicate in the tree and then only admits those nodes that are sisters to the path from the predicate to the root. It is commonly used in the SRL community (cf. (Xue and Palmer, 2004)) and our experiments show that 91% of the SRL targets can be recovered despite this aggressive pruning. There are two advantages to this pruning: the machine learning method used for prediction of SRLs is not overwhelmed with a large number of non-SRL nodes; and the process is far more efficient as 80% of the target nodes in a full parse tree are pruned away in this step. We make two enhancements to the pruned Propbank tree: we enrich the sister nodes with their head information, which is a part-of-speech tag and word pair: $\langle t, w \rangle$ and PP nodes are expanded to include the NP complement of the PP (including the head information). Note that the target SRL node is still the PP. Figure 1 shows the pruned parse tree for a sentence from PropBank section 24.

3.2 LTAG-based Decomposition

As next step, we decompose the pruned tree around the predicate using standard head-percolation based heuristic rules[1] to convert a Treebank tree into a LTAG derivation tree. We do not use any sophistical adjunct/argument or other extraction heuristics using empty elements (as we don't have access to them in the CoNLL 2005 data). Also, we do not use any substitution nodes in our elementary trees: instead we exclusively use adjunction or sister adjunction for the attachment of sub-derivations. As a result the root node in an LTAG derivation tree is a *spinal* elementary tree and the derivation tree provides the path from the predicate to the constituent in question. Figure 2 shows the resulting elementary tree after decomposition of the pruned tree. For each of the elementary trees we consider their labeling in the derivation tree to be their semantic role labels from the training data. Figure 3 is the derivation tree for the entire pruned tree.

Note that the LTAG-based decomposition of the parse tree allows us to use features that are distinct from the usual parse tree path features used for SRL. For example, the typical parse tree feature from Figure 2 used to identify constituent *(NP (NN terminal))* as A0 would be the parse tree fragment: $NP \uparrow NP \downarrow SBAR \downarrow S \downarrow VP \downarrow S \downarrow VP \downarrow VBG$ *cover* (the arrows signify the path through the parse tree). Using the LTAG-based decomposition means that our SRL model can use any features from the derivation tree such as in Figure 2, including the elementary tree shapes.

3.3 Decision List Model for SRL

Before we train or test our model, we convert the training, development and test data into LTAG derivation trees as described in the previous section. In our model we make an independence assumption that each semantic role is assigned to each constituent independently, conditional only on the path from the predicate elementary tree to the constituent elementary tree in the derivation tree. Different elementary tree siblings in the LTAG derivation tree do not influence each other in our current models. Figure 4 shows the different derivation trees for the target constituent *(NP (NN terminal))*: each providing a distinct semantic role labeling for a particular constituent. We use a decision list learner for identifying SRLs based on LTAG-based features. In this model, LTAG elementary trees are combined with some distance information as features to do the semantic role labeling. The rationale for using a simple DL learner is given in (Gildea and Jurafsky, 2002) where essentially it based on their experience with the setting of backoff weights for smoothing, it is stated that the most specific single feature matching the training data is enough to predict the SRL on test data. For simplicity, we only consider one intermediate elementary tree (if any) at one time instead of multiple intermediate trees along the path from the predicate to the argument.

[1] using http://www.isi.edu/~chiang/software/treep/treep.html

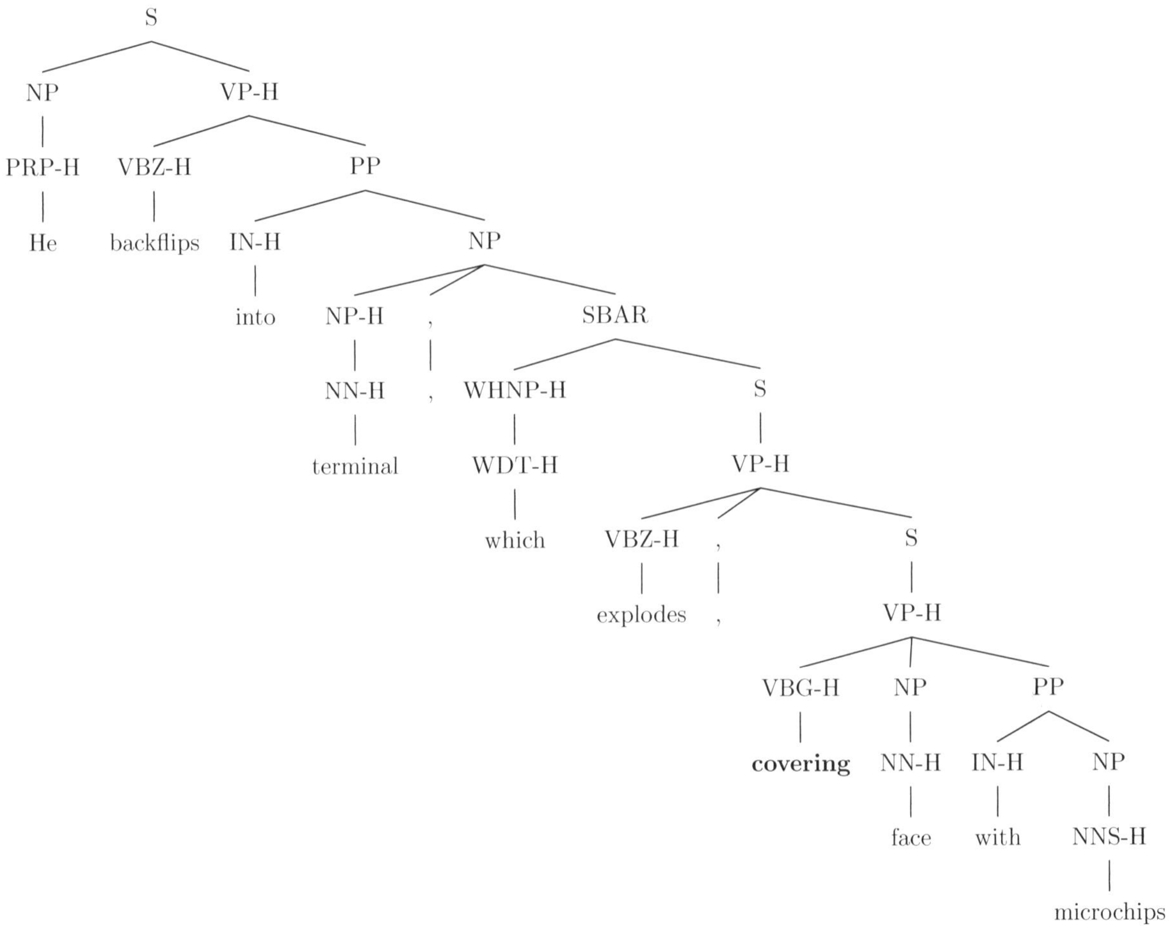

Figure 1: The pruned tree for the sentence "*He backflips into a desktop computer terminal, which explodes, covering Huntz Hall 's face with microchips.*"

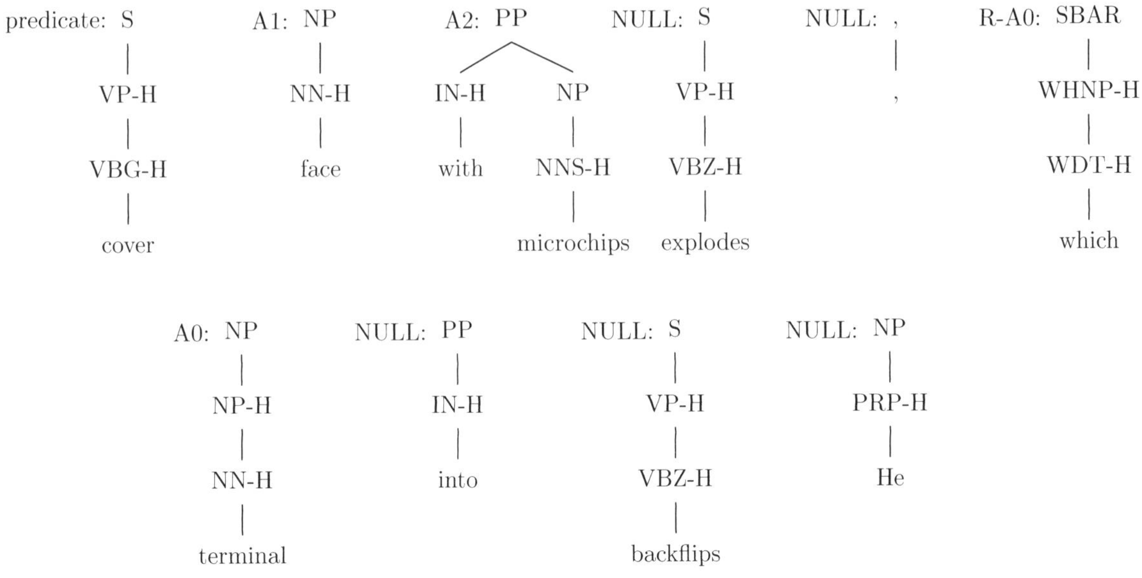

Figure 2: The resulting elementary trees after decomposition of the pruned tree.

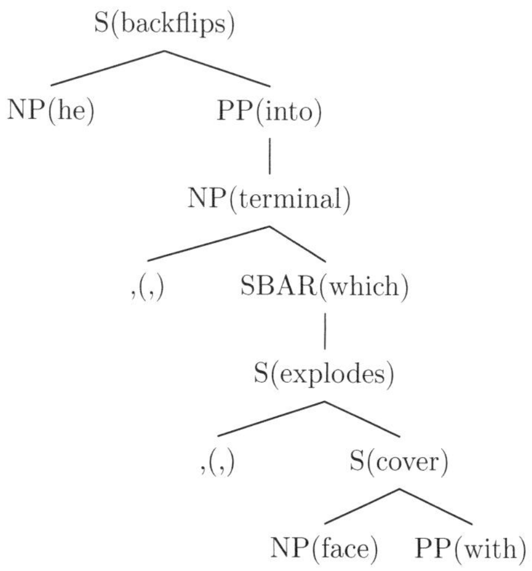

Figure 3: The LTAG derivation tree (with no semantic role labels) corresponding to the pruned tree.

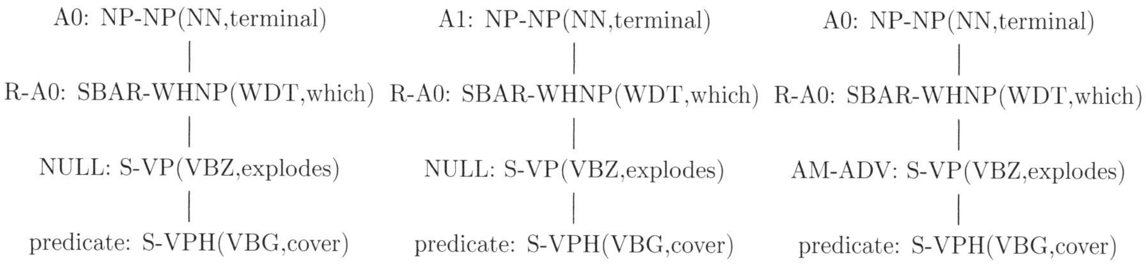

Figure 4: Different LTAG derivation trees corresponding to different assignments of semantic roles to constituents. The constituent in question is *(NP (NN terminal))*.

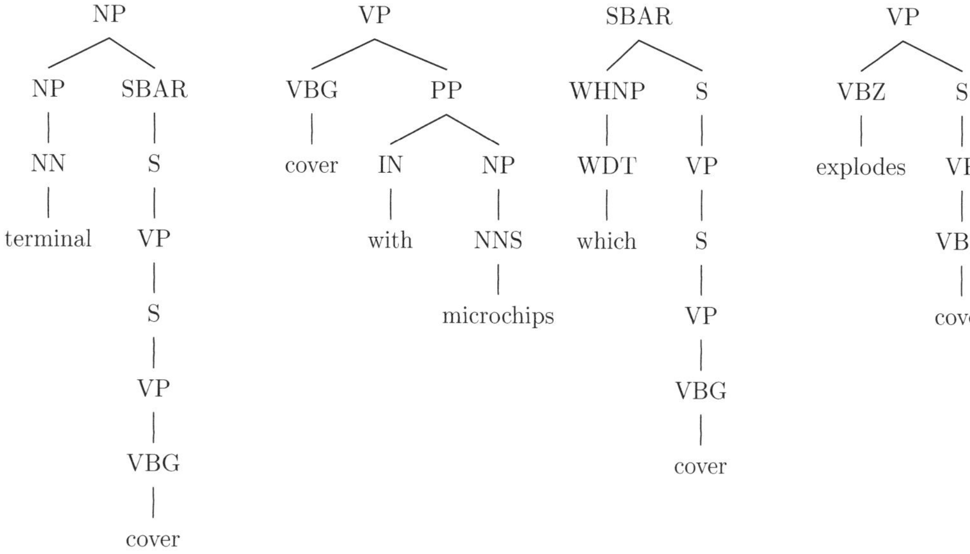

Figure 5: Tree patterns in tree pattern matching

The input to the learning algorithm is labeled examples of the form $(\mathbf{x_i}, y_i)$. y_i is the label (either NULL for no SRL, or the SRL) of the ith example. $\mathbf{x_i}$ is a feature vector $\langle P, A, Dist, Position, R\text{-}type, t_i \in t_I, Dist_{t_i}\rangle$, where P is the predicate elementary tree, A is the tree for the constituent being labeled with a SRL, t_I is a set of intermediate elementary trees between the predicate tree and the argument tree. Each P, A, I tree consists of the elementary tree template plus the tag, word pair: $\langle t, w\rangle$.

All possible combinations of fully-lexicalized/postag/un-lexicalized elementary trees are used for each example. $Dist$ and $Dist_{t_i}$ denote the distance to the predicate from the argument tree and the intermediate elementary tree respectively. $Position$ is interpreted as the position that the target is relative to the predicate. $R\text{-}type$ denotes the relation type of the predicate and the target constituent. 3 types are defined: if the predicate dominates (directly or undirectly) the argument in the derivation tree, we have the relation of type-1; if the other way around, the argument dominates (directly or undirectly) the predicate then we have the relation of type-2; and finally type-3 means that neither the predicate or the argument dominate each other in the derivation tree and instead are dominated (again, directly or indirectly) by another elementary tree.

The output of the learning algorithm is a function $h(\mathbf{x}, y)$ which is an estimate of the conditional probability $p(y \mid \mathbf{x})$ of seeing SRL y given pattern $\mathbf{x}$. h is interpreted as a decision list of rules $x \Rightarrow y$ ranked by the score $h(\mathbf{x}, y)$. In testing, we simply pick the first rule that matches the particular test example $\mathbf{x}$. We trained different models using the same learning algorithm. In addition to the LTAG-based method, we also implemented a pattern matching based method on the derived (parse) tree using the same model. In this method, instead of considering each intermediate elementary tree between the predicate and the argument, we extract the whole path from the predicate to the argument. So the input is more like a tree than a discrete feature vector. Figure 5 shows the patterns that are extracted from the same pruned tree.

4 Experiments and Results

We use the PropBank corpus of predicate-argument structures (Palmer, Gildea and Kingsbury, 2005) as our source of annotated data for the SRL task. However, there are many different ways to evaluate performance on the PropBank, leading to incomparable results. To avoid such a situation, in this paper we use the CoNLL 2005 shared SRL task data (Carreras and Màrquez, 2005) which provides a standard train/test split, a standard method for training and testing on various problematic cases involving coordination. However, in some cases, the CoNLL 2005 data is not ideal for the use of LTAG-based features as some "deep" information cannot be recovered due to the fact that trace information and other empty categories like PRO are removed entirely from the training data. As a result some of the features that undo long-distance movement via trace information in the TreeBank as used in (Chen and Rambow, 2003) cannot be exploited in our model. Our results are shown in Table 1. Note that we test on the gold standard parse trees because we want to compare a model using features from the derived parse trees to the model using the LTAG derivation trees.

dev = Sec24 test = Sec23	p(%)	r(%)	f(%)
M1: dev	78.42	77.03	77.72
M1: test	80.52	79.40	79.96
M2: dev	81.11	79.39	80.24
M2: test	83.47	81.82	82.64
M3: dev	80.98	79.56	80.26
M3: test	81.86	83.34	82.60

Table 1: Results on the CoNLL 2005 shared task using gold standard parse trees. M1 is the LTAG-based model, M2 is the derived tree pattern matching Model, M3 is a hybrid model

5 Related Work

In the community of SRL researchers (cf. (Gildea and Jurafsky, 2002; Punyakanok, Roth and Yih, 2005; Pradhan et al, 2005; Toutanova et al., 2005)), the focus has been on two different aspects of the SRL task: (a) finding appropriate features, and (b) resolving the parsing accuracy problem by combining multiple parsers/predictions. Systems that use parse trees as a source of feature functions for their models have typically outperformed shallow parsing models on the SRL task. Typical features extracted from a parse tree is the path from the predicate to the constituent and various generalizations based on this path (such as phrase type, position, etc.). Notably the voice (passive or active) of the verb is often used and recovered using a heuristic rule. We also use the passive/active voice by labeling this information into the parse tree. However, in contrast with other work, in this paper we do not focus on the problem of parse accuracy: where the parser output may not contain the constituent that is required for recovering all SRLs.

There has been some previous work in SRL that uses LTAG-based decomposition of the parse tree and we compare our work to this more closely. (Chen and Rambow, 2003) discuss a model for SRL that uses LTAG-based decomposition of parse trees (as is typically done for statistical LTAG parsing). Instead of using the typical parse tree features used in typical SRL models, (Chen and Rambow, 2003) uses the path within the elementary tree from the predicate to the constituent argument. They only recover semantic roles for those constituents that are localized within a single elementary tree for the predicate, ignoring cases that occur outside the elementary tree. In contrast, we recover all SRLs regardless of locality within the elementary tree. As a result, if we do not compare the machine learning methods involved in the two approaches, but rather the features used in learning, our features are a natural generalization of (Chen and Rambow, 2003).

Our approach is also very akin to the approach in (Shen and Joshi, 2005) which uses PropBank information to recover an LTAG treebank as if it were hidden data underlying the Penn Treebank. This is similar to our approach of having several possible LTAG derivations representing recovery of SRLs. However, (Shen and Joshi, 2005) do not focus on the SRL task, and in both of these instances of previous work using LTAG for SRL, we cannot directly compare our performance with theirs due to differing assumptions about the task.

6 Conclusion and Future Work

In this paper, we proposed a novel model for SRL using features extracted from LTAG derivation trees. A simple decision list learner is applied to train on the tree patterns containing new features. This simple learning method enables us to quickly explore new features for this task. However, this work is still preliminary: a lot of additional work is required to be competitive with the state-of-the-art SRL systems. In particular, we do not deal with automatically parsed data yet, which leads to a drop in our performance. We also do not incorporate various other features commonly used for SRL, as our goal in this paper was to make a direct comparison between simple pattern matching features on the derived tree and compare them to features from LTAG derivation trees.

References

X. Carreras and L. Màrquez 2005. Introduction to the CoNLL-2005 Shared Task. In Proc. of CoNLL 2005.

J. Chen and O. Rambow. 2003. Use of Deep Linguistic Features for the Recognition and Labeling of Semantic Arguments. In Proceedings of the 2003 Conference on Empirical Methods in Natural Language Processing, Sapporo, Japan, 2003.

D. Gildea and D. Jurafsky. 2002. Automatic Labeling of Semantic Roles. Computational Linguistics, 58(3):245–288

M. Palmer, D. Gildea, and P. Kingsbury. 2005. The Proposition Bank: An Annotated Corpus of Semantic Roles. Computational Linguistics, 31(1).

G. Melli and Y. Wang and Y. Liu and M. Kashani and Z. Shi and B. Gu and A. Sarkar and F. Popowich 2005. Description of SQUASH, the SFU Question Answering Summary Handler for the DUC-2005 Summarization Task. In Proceeding of Document Understanding Conference (DUC-2005)

S. Pradhan, K. Hacioglu, W. Ward, J. H. Martin, and D. Jurafsky. 2005. Semantic Role Chunking Combining Complementary Syntactic Views, In Proceedings of the 9th Conference on Natural Language Learning (CoNLL 2005), Ann Arbor, MI, 2005.

V. Punyakanok, D. Roth, and W Yih. 2005. Generalized Inference with Multiple Semantic Role Labeling Systems (shared task paper). Proc. of the Annual Conference on Computational Natural Language Learning (CoNLL) pp. 181-184

Ruppenhofer, Josef, Collin F. Baker and Charles J. Fillmore. 2002. The FrameNet Database and Software Tools. In Braasch, Anna and Claus Povlsen (eds.), Proceedings of the Tenth Euralex International Congress. Copenhagen, Denmark. Vol. I: 371-375.

L. Shen and A. Joshi. 2005. Building an LTAG Treebank. Technical Report MS-CIS-05-15, CIS Department, University of Pennsylvania.

K. Toutanova, A. Haghighi, and C. D. Manning. 2005. Joint learning improves semantic role labeling. ACL 2005

N. Xue and M. Palmer. 2004. Calibrating Features for Semantic Role Labeling, In Proceedings of EMNLP-2004. Barcelona, Spain.

Extracting Syntactic Features from a Korean Treebank

Jungyeul Park
UFR Linguistique
Laboratoire de linguistique formelle
Université Paris VII - Denis Diderot
jungyeul.park@linguist.jussieu.fr

Abstract

In this paper, we present a system which can extract syntactic feature structures from a Korean Treebank (*Sejong* Treebank) to develop a Feature-based Lexicalized Tree Adjoining Grammars.

1 Introduction

In a Tree Adjoining Grammar, a feature structure is associated with each node in an elementary tree (Vijay-Shanker and Joshi, 1991). This feature structure contains information about how the node interacts with other nodes in the tree. It consists of a top part, which generally contains information relating to the super-node, and a bottom part, which generally contains information relating to the sub-node.

In this paper, we present a system which can extract syntactic feature structures from a Treebank to develop a Feature-based Lexicalized Tree Adjoining Grammars. Several works have been on extracting grammars, especially using TAG formalism proposed. Chen (2001) has extracted lexicalized grammars from English Penn Treebank and there are other works based on Chen's procedure such as Nasr (2004) for French and Habash and Rambow (2004) for Arabic. Xia *et al.* (2000) developed the uniform method of a grammar extraction for English, Chinese and Korean. Neumann (2003) extracted Lexicalized Tree Grammars from English Penn Treebank for English and from NEGRA Treebank for German. However, none of these works have tried to extract syntactic features for FB-LTAG.

We use with *Sejong* Treebank (SJTree) which contains 32 054 *eojeol*s (the unity of segmentation in the Korean sentence), that is, 2 526 sentences. SJTree uses 43 part-of-speech tags and 55 syntactic tags (Sejong Project 2003).

2 Extracting a Feature structure for FB-LTAG

FB-LTAG grammars eventually use reduced tagset because FB-LTAG grammars contain their syntactic information in features structures. For example, NP_SBJ syntactic tag in LTAG is changed into NP and a syntactic feature <case=nominative> is added. Therefore, we use actually a 13 reduced tagset for FB-LTAG grammars compared with a 55 syntactic tagset for an LTAG without features. From full-scale syntactic tags which end with _SBJ (subject), _OBJ (object) and _CMP (attribute), we extract <case> features which describe argument structures in the sentence.

Alongside <case> features, we also extract <mode> and <tense> from morphological analyses in SJTree. Since however morphological analyses for verbal and adjectival endings in SJTree are simply divided into EP, EF and EC which mean non-final endings, final endings and conjunctive endings, respectively, <mode> and <tense> features are not extracted directly from SJTree. In this paper, we analyze 7 non-final endings (EP) and 77 final endings (EF) used in SJTree to extract automatically <mode> and <tense> features. In general, EF carries <mode> inflections, and EP carries <tense> inflections. Conjunctive endings (EC) are not concerned with <mode> and <tense> features and we only extract <ec> features with its string value. <ef> and <ep> features are also extracted with their string values. Some of non-final endings like *si* are extracted as <hor> features which have honorary meaning. In extracted FB-LTAG grammars, we present their lexical heads in a bare infinitive with morphological features such as <ep>, <ef> and <ec> which make correspond with its inflected forms.

Proceedings of the 8th International Workshop on Tree Adjoining Grammar and Related Formalisms, pages 133–136,
Sydney, July 2006. ©2006 Association for Computational Linguistics

<det> is another automatically extractable feature in SJTree and it is extracted from both syntactic tag and morphological analysis unlike other extracted features. For example, while <det=-> is extracted from dependant nouns which always need modifiers (extracted by morphological analyses), <det=+> is extracted from _MOD phrases (extracted by syntactic tags). From syntactic tag DP which contains MMs (determinative or demonstrative), <det=+> is also extracted. See Table 1 for all the extractable features from SJTree.

Feature	Description	Values
<case>	a case feature assigned by predicate	nom(inative), acc(usative), attr(ibut)
<det>	determiner, modifier	+/-
<mode>	mode	ind(icative), imp(erative), int(errogative), exc(lamatory)
<temps>	tense	pre(sent), past, fut(ure)
<ep>, <ef>, <ec>	a feature marked for different ways of instantiating mode and tense	string values like *eoss*, *da*, *go*, etc.
<hor>	honorific	+/-

Table 1. Extractable Features from SJTree

Korean does not need features <person> or <number> as in English. Han *et al.* (2000) proposed several features for Korean FBLTAG which we do not use in this paper, such as <adv-pp>, <top> and <aux-pp> for nouns and <clause-type> for predicates. While postpositions are separated from *eojeol* during our grammar extraction procedure, Han *et al.* considered them as "one" inflectional morphology of noun phrase *eojeol*. <aux-pp> adds semantic meaning of auxiliary postpositions such as only, also etc. which we can not extract automatically from SJTree or other Korean Treebank corpora because syntactically annotated Treebank corpora generally do not contain such semantic information. <top> marks the presence or absence of a topic marker in Korean like *neun*, however topic markers are annotated like a subject in SJTree which means that only <case=nominative> is extracted for topic markers. <clause-type> indicates the type of the clause which has its values such as main, coord(inative), subordi(native), adnom(inal), nominal, aux-connect. Since the distinction of the type of the clause is very vague except main clause in Korea, we do not adopt this feature. Instead, <ef> is extracted if a clause type is a main clause and for <ec> is extracted for other types.

3 Experimentations

The actual procedure of feature extraction is implemented by two phases. In the first phase, we convert syntactic tags and morphological analysis into feature structure as explained above (see Table 2 for our conversion scheme for syntactic tags and see Table 3 for morphological analyses). In the second phase, we complete feature structure onto nodes of the "spine (path between root and anchor, node in an initial tree and path between root and foot node in an auxiliary tree)". For example, we put the same feature of VV bottom in Figure 1a onto VV top, VP top/bottom and S bottom because nodes in dorsal spine share certain number of feature of VV bottom. The initial tree for a verb *balpyoha.eoss.da* ('announced') in (1) is completed like Figure 1b for a FB-LTAG.

(1) 일본 외무성은 즉각 해명 성명을 발표했다.
ilbon oimuseong.eun
Japan ministy_of_foreign_affairs.Nom
jeukgak haemyeng seongmyeng.eul
immediately elucidation declaration.Acc
balpyo.ha.eoss.da
announce.Pass.Ter
'The ministry of foreign affairs in Japan immediately announced their elucidation'

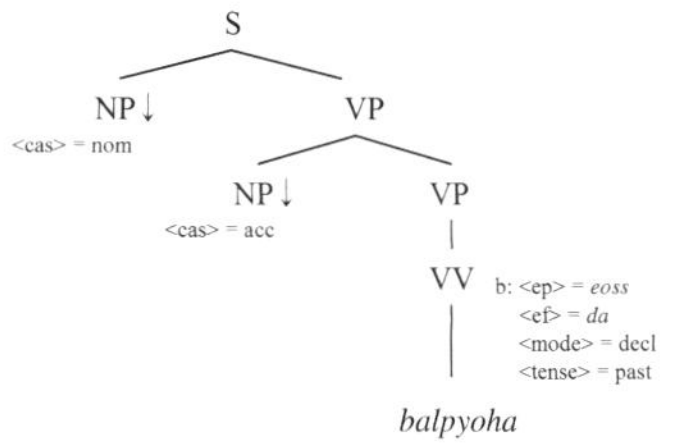

a. First phase

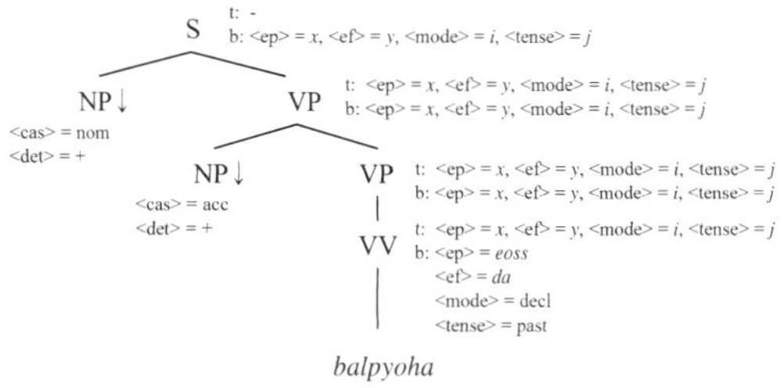

b. Second phase

Figure 1. Extracted FB-LTAG grammar for *balpyoha.eoss.da* ('announced')

Table 4 shows the results of experiments in extracting feature-based lexicalized grammars. See Park (2006) for the detail extraction scheme.

4 Evaluations

Finally, extracted grammars are evaluated by its size (see Figure 2) and its coverage (see Table 5). The number of tree schemata is not stabilized at the end of the extraction process, which seems to indicate that the size of Treebank is not enough to reach the convergence of extracted grammars. However, the number of tree schemata appearing at least twice and three times (threshold = 2 and 3) in Treebank is much stabilized at the end of the extraction process than that of tree schemata appearing only once (threshold = 1).

The coverage of extracted grammars is calculated not only by the frequency of tree schemata but also by the number of tree schemata.

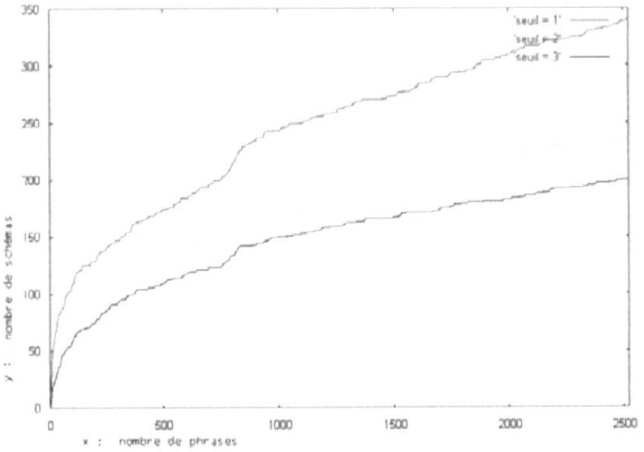

Figure 2. Size of tree schemata

We manually overlap our 163 tree schemata for predicates, which contain 14 subcategorization frames with 11 subcategorization frames of a FB-LTAG grammar proposed in Han *et al.* (2000) to evaluate the coverage of hand-crafted grammars[1]. Our extracted template grammars cover 72.7 % of their hand-crafted subcategorization frames[2].

[1] Our extracted tree schemata contain not only subcategorization frames but also some phenomena of syntactic variations, the number of lexicalized trees and the frequency information while Han *et al.* (2000) only presents subcategorization frames and some phenomena.

[2] Three subcategorization frames in Han *et al.* (2000) which contain prepositional phrases are not covered by our extracted tree schemata. Generally, prepositional phrases in SJTree are labeled with _AJT which is marked for adjunction operation. Since there is no difference between noun adverbial phrase and prepositional phrases in SJTree like [S *na.neun* [NP_AJT *ojeon.e* 'morning'] [NP_AJT *hakgyo.e* 'to school'] *ga.ss.da*] ('I went to school this morning'), we do not consider _AJT phrases as arguments.

5 Conclusion

In this paper, we have presented a system for automatic grammar extraction that produces feature-based lexicalized grammars from a Treebank. Also, we evaluated by its size and its coverage, and overlap our automatically extracted tree schemata from a Treebank with a manually written subcategorization frames to evaluate the coverage of hand-crafted grammars.

References

Alexis Nasr. 2004. *Analyse syntaxique probabiliste pour grammaires de dépendances extraites automatiquement.* Habilitation à diriger des recherches, Université Paris 7.

Chunghye Han, Juntae Yoon, Nari Kim, and Martha Palmer. 2000. *A Feature-Based Lexicalized Tree Adjoining Grammar for Korean.* IRCS Technical Report 00-04. University of Pennsylvania.

Fei Xia, Martha Palmer, and Aravind K. Joshi. 2000. A Uniform Method of Grammar Extraction and Its Application. In *The Joint SIGDAT Conference on Empirical Methods in Natural Language Processing and Very Large Corpora (EMNLP/VLC-2000)*, Hong Kong, Oct 7-8, 2000.

Günter Neumann. 2003. A Uniform Method for Automatically Extracting Stochastic Lexicalized Tree Grammar from Treebank and HPSG, In A. Abeillé (ed) *Treebanks: Building and Using Parsed Corpora*, Kluwer, Dordrecht.

John Chen. 2001. *Towards Efficient Statistical Parsing Using Lexicalized Grammatical Information.* Ph.D. thesis, University of Delaware.

Jungyeul Park. 2006. *Extraction automatique d'une grammaire d'arbres adjoints à partir d'un corpus arboré pour le coréen.* Ph.D. thesis, Université Paris 7.

K. Vijay-Shanker and Aravind K. Joshi. 1991. Unification Based Tree Adjoining Grammar, in J. Wedekind ed., *Unification-based Grammars*, MIT Press, Cambridge, Massachusetts.

Nizar Habash and Owen Rambow. 2004. Extracting a Tree Adjoining Grammar from the Penn Arabic Treebank. In *Proceedings of Traitement Automatique du Langage Naturel (TALN-04).* Fez, Morocco, 2004.

Sejong Project. 2003. *Final Report of Sejong Korean Treebank.* Ministry of Education & Human Resources Development in Korea.

<table>
<tr><th>Anchor</th><th>Tree type</th><th>Syntactic tag</th><th>Node type</th><th>Conversion example</th></tr>
<tr><td>verb</td><td>α</td><td>NP_SBJ</td><td>subst</td><td>NP
[<cas> = nom
<det> = +]</td></tr>
<tr><td>verb</td><td>α|β</td><td>VP, VP_MOD</td><td>–</td><td>VP
[<ep> <ef>
<mode> <tense>]</td></tr>
<tr><td>anchored by _MOD phrase</td><td>β</td><td>NP | NP_CMP | NP_MOD | NP_OBJ | | NP_SBJ</td><td>root</td><td>NP
[<det> = +]</td></tr>
<tr><td>postposition</td><td>α</td><td>NP_SBJ</td><td>root</td><td>NP
[<cas> = nom]</td></tr>
<tr><td>postposition</td><td>α</td><td>NP_SBJ</td><td>subst</td><td>NP
[<cas> = NONE]</td></tr>
</table>

Table 2. Conversion example for syntactic tags

Verbal ending	Ending type	Conversion example
eoss	EP	<ep> = *eoss*, <tense> = past
si	EP	<ep> = *si*, <hor> = +
da	EF	<ef> = *da*, <mode> = ind

Table 3. Conversion example for morphological analyses

	# of lexicalized tree (α + β)	Average frequencies per lexicalized tree	# of tree schemata (α + β)	Average frequencies per tree schemata
G	12 239 (7 315 + 4 766)	3.26	338 (109 + 229)	118.1

Table 4. Results of experiments in extracting feature-based lexicalized grammars

	Coverage of grammars by the frequency of tree schemata			Coverage of grammars by the number of tree schemata		
Threshold	1	2	3	1	2	3
60 % of training set	60.75 %	60.7 %	60.66 %	81.66 %	83.83 %	83.5 %
90 % of training set	91.14 %	91.14 %	91.11 %	95.86 %	98.3 %	96.5 %

Table 5. Coverage of grammars: 60% of training set (1511 sentences) and 90% of training set (2265 sentences)

Handling Unlike Coordinated Phrases in TAG by Mixing Syntactic Category and Grammatical Function

Carlos A. Prolo
Faculdade de Informática - PUCRS
Porto Alegre, RS, 90619-900, Brazil
prolo@inf.pucrs.br

Abstract

Coordination of phrases of different syntactic categories has posed a problem for generative systems based only on syntactic categories. Although some prefer to treat them as exceptional cases that should require some extra mechanism (as for elliptical constructions), or to allow for unrestricted cross-category coordination, they can be naturally derived in a grammatic functional generative approach. In this paper we explore the ideia on how mixing syntactic categories and grammatical functions in the label set of a Tree Adjoining Grammar allows us to develop grammars that elegantly handle both the cases of same- and cross-category coordination in an uniform way.

1 Introduction

Generative grammars that we commonly hear about in computational linguistics are usually based on syntactic categories. This is also the case when the formalism used is the Tree Adjoining Grammars (TAGs). Large scale handcrafted grammars for many languages have been built based on this paradigm (Joshi, 2001; XTAG Research Group, 2001; Kroch and Joshi, 1985; Abeillé and Candito, 2000; Candito, 1998; Becker, 1993; Frank, 2002; Joshi and Schabes, 1997; Abeillé and Rambow, 2000) as well as grammars extracted from corpora (Chen and Vijay-Shanker, 2000; Chiang, 2000; Hwa, 1999; Xia et al., 2001; Xia, 2001). The latter is partly due to the fact that large scale annotated corpora such as the Penn Treebank (Marcus et al., 1994; Bies et al., 1995) give primacy to syntactic categories. After all this is the most strongly sedimented generative approach at least since (Chomsky, 1957).

Computational approaches of grammar based on grammatical function such as that of Susumu Kuno (Kuno, 1987) have been given less importance. Although we can think of simply inserting functional labels in elementary trees or use them in a meta-level to generate the grammar, such as in (Candito, 1998; Kinyon, 2000; Clément and Kinyon, 2003), such tags are generally not seen as an essential part of the derivational process.

Nevertheless coordination is such an inherently functional phenomenon as we show next. Consider the sentences in (1) and (2). These are examples of regular coordination between phrases of the same category. They can easily be handled in the traditional grammar approaches of syntactic category.

(1) She flew [$_{PP}$ on May 1st and on July 4th].

(2) They sell [$_{ADJP}$ electric and electronic] products.

Now look at the cases in (3) and (4). They are different in the sense that the coordination is across categories. This poses a strong problem to the traditional grammar of syntactic categories. This has been noticed for TAGs in (Prolo, 2002). Recently this has also been tackled in the HPSG framework by (Sag, 2003) and (Abeillé, 2004). The Penn Treebank calls this constituents *UCP* for *"Unlike Coordinated Phrases"* (Bies et al., 1995). The problem is that we would need rules of the kind below (using context-free rules for short – see (Prolo, 2002) for TAGs). Basically all pairs of constituents can be coordinated but we can not assign to the resulting constituents either of the subconstituent tags.

Proceedings of the 8th International Workshop on Tree Adjoining Grammar and Related Formalisms, pages 137–140,
Sydney, July 2006.

UCP → ADVP CC PP

UCP → PP CC ADVP

UCP → ADJP CC NP

UCP → NP CC ADJP

(3) She flew [$_{??}$ yesterday and on July 4th].

(4) They sell [$_{??}$ electronic and computer] devices.

However, UCP coordination is not random. Two constituents can be coordinated only when they are fulfilling the same grammatical function (with respect to a third head). In (3) they are playing the role of adverbial adjuncts of *went*. Either one can engage in that relation individually and hence they can be coordinated while playing that role. Likewise in (4) the adjective *electronic* and the noun *computer* are both fine as left NP modifiers. Therefore they can be conjoined as such. As a final example, consider the sentences in (5). Because the direct object of the verb *know* can be realized as either an NP or a sentential complement, they can be coordinated in that role as shown in (6).

(5) I know the answer.
I know that you don't know it.

(6) I know [the answer and that you don't know it].

Clearly the recursive process of conjoining the constituents is at the grammatic functional level. We show next how we can solve this problem elegantly by mixing grammatical function and syntactic category in the set of symbols for the tree nodes of a TAG.

2 A Grammar of Grammatical Functions and Syntactic Categories

The elementary trees in our grammar are the projection of a lexical item as usual in Lexicalized TAGs. However, root nodes do not correspond to syntactic categories, but to grammatical functions. The node for the function then dominates syntactic category nodes, according to the way the function is realized syntactically. Figure 1 shows trees for an intransitive main clause and an NP subject.[1]

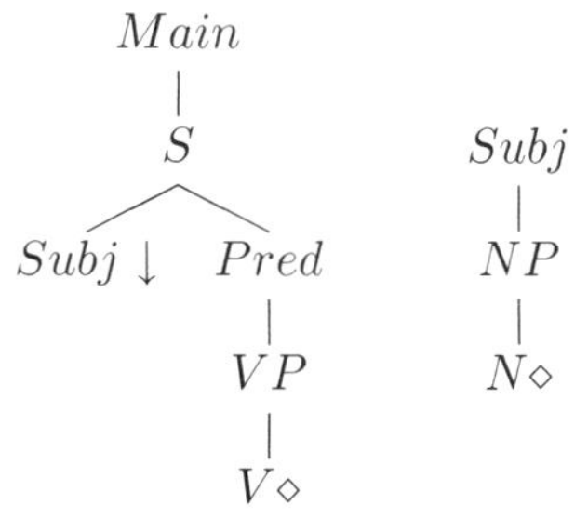

Figure 1: Elementary trees for Intransitive Main Clause and NP Subject.

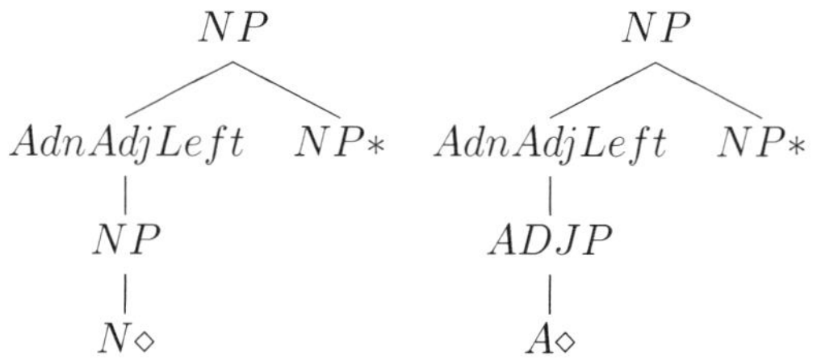

Figure 2: Elementary trees for Left Adnominal Adjuncts.

Figure 2 has trees for NP left modifiers (adnominal adjunct) realized either as an NP or an ADJP.

Finally, in Figure 3 we can see the trees for coordination of left adnominal adjuncts. Notice that they adjoin at the function node (*AdnAdjLeft*) therefore allowing for the coordination of anything that can fulfill that role, be them equal categories as in (2) or the UCP case in (4). In Figure 4 we show an additional example with a PP right NP modifier. It should be straightforward to see how to build trees for *AdnAdjRight* coordination of constituents realized by a PP or a relative clause.

In Figure 5 we finally get to subcategorization. In any approach to grammar development we have to make decisions between explicitly modeling certain restrictions in the tree structure or through features (of a *feature based* TAG). That can be seen ubiquitously in the XTAG grammar (XTAG Research Group, 2001). We can use the tree of the figure with verbs such like *eat* and *know*, having trees to realize the direct object as either an NP or a sentence. Features in the lexical items would prevent the derivation of *eat* with a sentential complement. Another approach would be to further detail the tree into one with a built in NP object

[1] Figures generally show templates where a diamond indicates where the lexical item would be substituted in, though occasionally we insert the lexical item itself.

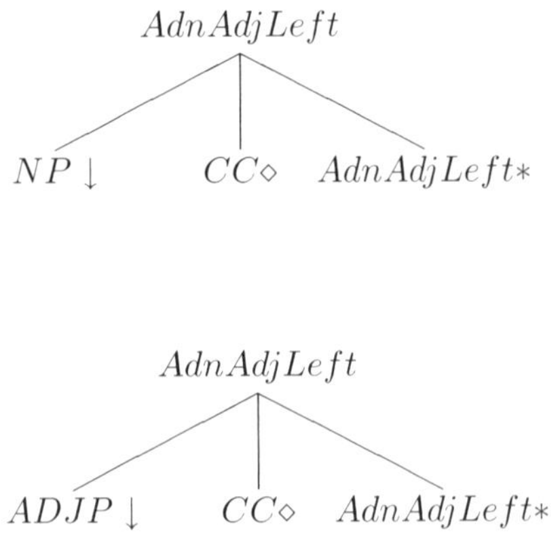

Figure 3: Elementary trees for Coordination of Left Adnominal Adjuncts.

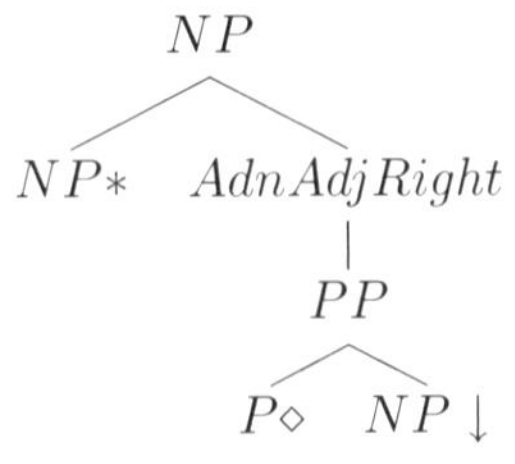

Figure 4: Elementary trees for a PP as Right Adnominal Adjunct.

and another with a sentential complement. However, realization constraints would still have to be present to allow for the coordination of only the constituents that are allowed for the specific verb. For the reader unfamiliar with grammar modeling we notice this is not a drawback of the approach. Constraints beyond those represented in the structure are constantly made as a way to avoid irrational growth of a grammar.

In Figure 6 we show still another interesting case: the predicative clauses.[2] We include it for

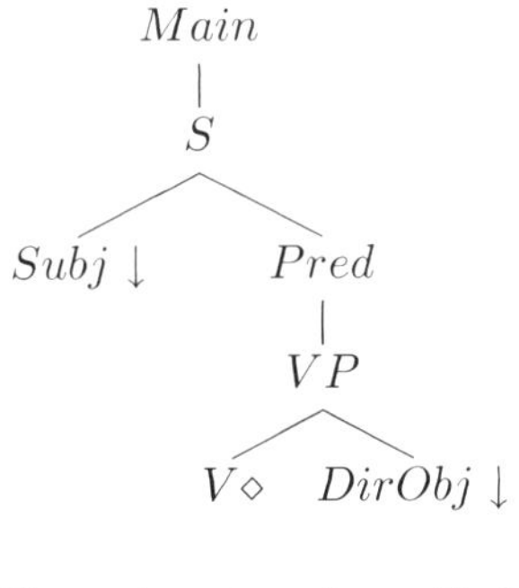

Figure 5: Elementary tree for a Verb that has a Direct Object

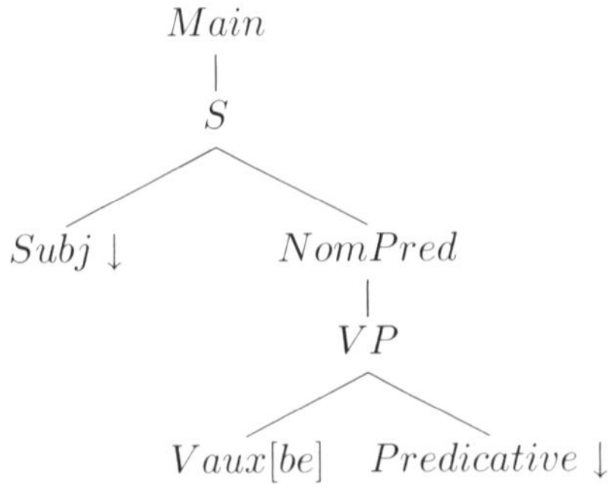

Figure 6: Elementary tree for Predicative Clauses

this is a rich context for unlike coordination. One can easily see how to generate trees for coordinating NPs, PPs and ADJPs, as predicative constituents so as to allow for (7).

(7) John was [a gentlemen, always happy, and never in bad mood].

3 Conclusions

We showed in this paper how to build a Tree Adjoining Grammar of grammatical functions and syntactic categories, mixed together in a principled way of function and possible realizations. It brings the benefits of allowing handling language phenomena which are generative at each of the two sides.

In particular, we showed how it solves the problem of coordination of constituents of distinct syntactic categories.

Elementary trees are not clumsy. On the contrary they bring additional information to the structure with minimal addition of nodes. This information could otherwise be hidden in *node features*, which are generally used to represent information that would be costly to maintain explicit in the tree structure.

Finally we can see that this structure can be easily incorporated in a supervised grammar inference algorithm such as that of (Xia, 2001), provided the annotated corpus has grammatical function information. In fact this is the case in the Penn Treebank, and Xia's algorithm allows it to be used [3]. Inferring the different kinds of verbs, with respect to the functions they subcategorize for and

[2]Again this is one approach to modeling predicatives, with the auxiliary verb *be* anchoring the tree and the predicative as a substitution node. The alternative used in the XTAG grammar of having the predicative head as anchor would be possible as well.

[3]The same is true of other algorithms such as (Chen and Vijay-Shanker, 2000)'s.

their realizations is an important issue here, and is also feasible (see (Kinyon and Prolo, 2002)).

References

Anne Abeillé and Marie-Helene Candito. 2000. Ftag: A lexicalized Tree Adjoining Grammar for French. In Abeillé and Rambow (Abeillé and Rambow, 2000), pages 305–329.

Anne Abeillé and Owen Rambow, editors. 2000. Tree Adjoining Grammars: formalisms, linguistic analysis and processing. CSLI, Stanford, CA, USA.

Anne Abeillé. 2004. A lexicalist and construction-based approach to coordinations. In Stefan Mller, editor, Proceedings of the 10th International Conference on HPSG (HPSG'03), Michigan State University, Michigan, USA. Available at: http://cslipublications.stanford.edu/HPSG/4.

Tilman Becker. 1993. HyTAG: A new Type of Tree Adjoining Grammars for Hybrid Syntactic Representation of Free Word Order Lang uages. Ph.D. thesis, Universität des Saarlandes.

Ann Bies, Mark Ferguson, Karen Katz, and Robert MacIntyre. 1995. Bracketing guidelines for the Penn Treebank II style Penn Treebank Project.

Marie-Helene Candito. 1998. Building parallel LTAG for french and italian. In Proceedings of the 36th Annual Meeting of the Association for Computational Linguistics and 16th International Conference on Computational Linguistics, pages 211–217, Montreal, Canada.

John Chen and K. Vijay-Shanker. 2000. Automated extraction of TAGs from the Penn Treebank. In Proceedings of the 6th International Workshop on Parsing Technologies, Trento, Italy.

David Chiang. 2000. Statistical parsing with an automatically-extracted Tree Adjoining Grammar. In Proceedings of the 38th Annual Meeting of the Association for Computational Linguistics, Hong Kong, China.

N. Chomsky. 1957. Syntactic Structures. Mouton, The Hague.

L. Clément and A. Kinyon. 2003. Generating parallel multilingual LFG-TAG grammars using a MetaGrammar. In Proceedings of the 41st Annual Meeting of the Association for Computational Linguistics, Sapporo, Japan.

Robert Frank. 2002. Phrase Structure Composition and Syntactic Dependencies. MIT Press, Cambridge, MA, USA.

Rebecca Hwa. 1999. Supervised Grammar Induction Using Training Data with Limited Constituent Information. In Proceedings of 37th Annual Meeting of the Association for Computational Linguistics (ACL '99), pages 20–26, College Park, MD, USA.

Aravind K. Joshi and Yves Schabes. 1997. Tree-Adjoining Grammars. In A. Salomaa and G. Rozenberg, editors, Handbook of Formal Languages, volume 3, pages 69–123. Springer-Verlag, Berlin.

Aravind K. Joshi. 2001. The XTAG project at Penn. In Proceedings of the 7th International Workshop on Parsing Technologies (IWPT-2001), Beijing, China. Invited speaker.

Alexandra Kinyon and Carlos A. Prolo. 2002. Identifying verb arguments and their syntactic function in the Penn Treebank. In Proceedings of the Third International Conference on Language Resources and Evaluation (LREC), pages 1982–87, Las Palmas, Spain.

Alexandra Kinyon. 2000. Hypertags. In Proceedings of the 18th International Conference on Computational Linguistics (COLING'2000), Saarbrücken, Germany.

Anthony S. Kroch and Aravind K. Joshi. 1985. The linguistic relevance Tree Adjoining Grammar. Technical Report MS-CIS-85-16, University of Pennsylvania.

Sususmu Kuno. 1987. Functional Grammar. University of Chicago Press, Chicago, Il, USA.

Mitchell Marcus, Grace Kim, Mary Ann Marcinkiewicz, Robert MacIntyre, Ann Bies, Mark Ferguson, Karen Katz, and Britta Schasberger. 1994. The Penn Treebank: Annotating predicate argument structure. In Proceedings of the 1994 Human Language Technology Workshop.

Carlos A. Prolo. 2002. Coping with problems in grammars automatically extracted from treebanks. In Proceedings of the Workshop on Grammar Engineering and Evaluation, pages 36–42, Taipei, Taiwan.

Ivan Sag. 2003. Coordination and underspecification. In Jongbok Kim and Stephen Wechsler, editors, Proceedings of the 9th International Conference on HPSG (HPSG'02), Kyung-Hee University, Seoul, Korea. Available at: http://cslipublications.stanford.edu/HPSG/3/hpsg02.htm.

Fei Xia, Chung-Hye Han, Martha Palmer, and Aravind Joshi. 2001. Automatically Extracting and Comparing Lexicalized Grammars for Different Languages. In Proc. of the Seventeenth International Joint Conference on Artificial Intelligence (IJCAI-2001), Seattle, Washington.

Fei Xia. 2001. Investigating the Relationship between Grammars and Treebanks for Natural Languages. Ph.D. thesis, Department of Computer and Information Science, University of Pennsylvania.

The XTAG Research Group. 2001. A Lexicalized Tree Adjoining Grammar for English. Technical Report IRCS 01-03, University of Pennsylvania.

Parsing TAG with Abstract Categorial Grammar

Sylvain Salvati
National Institute of Informatics
2-1-2 Hitotsubashi, Chiyoda-ku,
Tokyo 101-8430, JAPAN
salvati@nii.ac.jp

Abstract

This paper presents informally an Earley algorithm for TAG which behaves as the algorithm given by (Schabes and Joshi, 1988). This algorithm is a specialization to TAG of a more general algorithm dedicated to second order ACGs. As second order ACGs allows to encode Linear Context Free Rewriting Systems (LCFRS) (de Groote and Pogodalla, 2004), the presentation of this algorithm gives a rough presentation of the formal tools which can be used to design efficient algorithms for LCFRS. Furthermore, as these tools allow to parse linear λ-terms, they can be used as a basis for developping algorithms for generation.

1 Introduction

The algorithm we present is a specialization to TAGs of a more general one dedicated to second order Abstract Categorial Grammars (ACGs) (de Groote, 2001). Our aim is to give here an informal presentation of tools that can be used to design efficient parsing algorithms for formalisms more expressive than TAG. Therefore, we only give a representation of TAGs with linear λ-terms together with simple derivation rules; we do not give in complete details the technical relation with ACGs. For some more information about ACGs and their relation to TAGs, one may read (de Groote, 2001) and (de Groote, 2002).

The advantage of using ACG is that they are defined with very few primitives, but can encode many formalisms. Thus they are well suited to study from a general perspective a full class of formalisms. In particular, a special class of ACGs (second order ACGs) embeds LCFRS (de Groote and Pogodalla, 2004), *i.e.* mildly context sensitive languages. Therefore, the study of second order ACGs leads to insights on mildly context sensitive languages. Having a general framework to describe parsing algorithms for mildly context sensitive languages may give some help to transfer some interesting parsing technique from one formalism to another. It can be, for example, a good mean to obtain prefix-valid algorithms, LC algorithms, LR algorithms... for the full class of mildly context sensitive languages.

The class of languages described by second order ACGs is wider than mildly context sensitive languages. They can encode tree languages, and more generally languages of linear λ-terms. As Montague style semantics (Montague, 1974) is based on λ-calculus, being able to parse linear λ-term is a first step towards generation algorithms seen as parsing algorithm. Furthermore, since this parsing algorithm is a generalization of algorithms *à la Earley* for CFGs and TAGs, the more general algorithm that can be used for generation (when semantic formulae are linear) can be considered as efficient.

The paper is organized as follows: section two gives basic defintions and tools concerning the linear λ-calculus. Section three explains how the indices usually used by parsers are represented for the linear λ-calculus. Section four gives a rough explaination of the encoding of TAGs within a compiled representation of second order ACGs. Section five explains the parsing algorithm and we conclude with section six.

2 The linear λ-calculus

We begin by giving a brief definition of linear types and linear λ-terms together with some stan-

Proceedings of the 8th International Workshop on Tree Adjoining Grammar and Related Formalisms, pages 141–146,
Sydney, July 2006.

dard notations. We assume that the reader is familiar with the usual notions related to λ-calculus (β-conversion, free variables, capture-avoiding substitutions...); for more details about λ-calculus, one may consult (Barendregt, 1984).

Definition 1 *The set of linear types, $\mathcal{T}$, is the smallest set containing $\{*\}$ and such that if $\alpha, \beta \in \mathcal{T}$ then $(\alpha \multimap \beta) \in \mathcal{T}$.*

Given a type $(\alpha_1 \multimap (\cdots(\alpha_n \multimap *)\cdots))$, we write it $(\alpha_1, \ldots, \alpha_n) \multimap *$.

Definition 2 *Given a infinite enumerable set of variables, $\mathcal{X}$, and an alphabet Σ, we define the set of linear λ-terms of type $\alpha \in \mathcal{T}$, Λ^α, as the smallest set satisfying the following properties:*

1. $x \in \mathcal{X} \Rightarrow x^\alpha \in \Lambda^\alpha$
2. $t \in \Lambda^\alpha \wedge x^\beta \in FV(t) \Rightarrow \lambda x^\beta.t \in \Lambda^{\beta\multimap\alpha}$
3. $a \in \Sigma \Rightarrow a \in \Lambda^{*\multimap*}$
4. $t_1 \in \Lambda^{\beta\multimap\alpha} \wedge t_2 \in \Lambda^\beta \wedge FV(t_1) \cap FV(t_2) \Rightarrow (t_1 t_2) \in \Lambda^\alpha$

In general, we write $\lambda x_1 \ldots x_n.t$ for $\lambda x_1. \ldots \lambda x_n.t$ and we write $t_0 t_1 \ldots t_n$ for $(\ldots(t_0 t_1)\ldots t_n)$. Strings are represented by closed linear λ-terms of type $str = * \multimap *$. Given a string $abcde$, it is represented by the following linear λ-term: $\lambda y^*.a(b(c(d(e\,y^*))))$; $/w/$ represents the set of terms which are β-convertible to the λ-term representing the string w. Concatenation is represented by $+ = \lambda x_1^{str} x_2^{str} y^*.x_1^{str}(x_2^{str} y^*)$, and $(+w_1)w_2$ will be written $w_1 + w_2$. The concatenation is moreover associative, we may thus write $w_1 + \cdots + w_n$.

For the description of our algorithm, we rely on contexts:

Definition 3 *A context is a λ-term with a hole. Contexts are defined by the following grammar:*

$$\mathbf{C} = [] \mid \Lambda\mathbf{C} \mid \mathbf{C}\Lambda \mid \lambda\mathcal{V}.\mathbf{C}$$

The insertion of a term within a context is done the obvious way. One has nevertheless to remark that when a term t is inserted in a context $C[]$, the context $C[]$ can bind variables free in t. For example, if $C[] = \lambda x.[]$ and $t = x$ then $C[t] = \lambda x.x$ and x which was free in t is not free anymore in $C[t]$.

3 Indices as syntactic descriptions

Usually the items of Earley algorithms use indices to represent positions in the input string. The algorithm we describe is a particular instance of a more general one which parses linear λ-terms rather than strings. In that case, one cannot describe in a simple way positions by means of indices. Instead of indices, positions in a term t will be represented with *zippers* ((Huet, 1997)), *i.e.* a pair $(C[], v)$ of a context and a term such that $C[v] = t$. Figure 1 explicits the correspondence between indices and zippers via an example.

The items of Earley algorithms for TAGs use pairs of indices to describe portions of the input string. In our algorithm, this role is played by linear types built upon zippers; the parsing process can be seen as a type-checking process in a particular type system. We will not present this system here, but we will give a flavor of the meaning of those types called *syntactic descriptions* (Salvati, 2006). In order to represent the portion of a string between the indices i and j, we use the zippers $(C_i[], v_i)$ and $(C_j[], v_j)$ which respectively represent the position i and j in the string. The portion of string is represented by the syntactic description $(C_j[], v_j) \multimap (C_i[], v_i)$; this syntactic description can be used to type functions which take v_j as argument and return v_i as a result. For example, given the syntactic description: $(\lambda x.a(b(c[])), d(e\,x)) \multimap (\lambda x.a[], b(c(d(e\,x))))$, it represents the set of functions that result in terms that are β-convertible to $b(c(d(e\,x)))$ when they take $d(e\,x)$ as an argument; this set is exactly $/bc/$. Our algorithm uses representations of string contexts with syntactic descriptions such as $\mathbf{d} = ((C_1[], v_1) \multimap (C_2[], v_2)) \multimap (C_3[], v_3) \multimap (C_4[], v_4)$ (in the following we write $((C_1[], v_1) \multimap (C_2[], v_2), (C_3[], v_3)) \multimap (C_4[], v_4)$ for such syntactic descriptions). Assume that $(C_1[], v_1) \multimap (C_2[], v_2)$ represents $/bc/$ and that $(C_3[], v_3) \multimap (C_4[], v_4)$ represents $/abcde/$, then $\mathbf{d}$ describes the terms which give a result in $/abcde/$ when they are applied to an element of $/bc/$. Thus, $\mathbf{d}$ describes the set of terms β-convertible to $\lambda fy.a(f(d(e\,y)))$, the set of terms representing the string context $a[\,]de$.

Some of the syntactic descriptions we use may contain *variables* denoting *non-specified syntactic descriptions* that may be instanciated during parsing. In particular, the syntactic description variable F will always be used as a non-specified syn-

0	$(\lambda x.[], a(b(c(d(e\,x)))))$	1	$(\lambda x.a[], b(c(d(e\,x))))$
2	$(\lambda x.a(b[]), c(d(e\,x)))$	3	$(\lambda x.a(b(c[])), d(e\,x))$
4	$(\lambda x.a(b(c(d[]), e\,x)$	5	$(\lambda x.a(b(c(d(e[])))), x)$

$_0a_1b_2c_3d_4e_5$

Figure 1: Correspondence indices/zippers for the string *abcde*

tactic description representing strings (*i.e.* F may only be substituted by a syntactic description of the form $(C_1[], v_1) \multimap (C_2[], v_2)$), such syntactic descriptions will represent the foot of an auxiliary tree. We will also use Y to represent a non-specifed point in the input sentence (*i.e.* Y may only be substituted by syntactic descriptions of the form $(C[], v)$), such syntactic descriptions will represent the end of an elementary tree.

As syntactic desccriptions are types for the linear λ-calculus, we introduce the notion of typing context for syntactic descriptions.

Definition 4 *A typing context* Γ *(context for short), is a set of pairs of the form* $x : d$ *where* x *is a variable and* d *is a syntactic description such that* $x : d \in \Gamma$ *and* $x : e \in \Gamma$ *iff* $d = e$.

If $x : d \in \Gamma$*, then we say that* x *is declared with type* d *in* Γ.

Typing contexts Γ must not be confused with contexts $C[]$. If a typing context Γ is the set $\{x_1 : d_1; \ldots; x_n : d_n\}$ then we will write if by $x_1 : d_1, \ldots, x_n : d_n$. In the present paper, typing contexts may declare at most two variables.

4 Representing TAG with second order ACGs

We cannot give here a detailed definition of second order ACGs here. We therefore directly explain how to transform TAGs into lexical entries representing a second order ACG that can be directly used by the algorithm.

We represent a TAG $\mathbf{G}$ by a *set of lexical entries* $\mathcal{L}_{\mathbf{G}}$. *Lexical entries* are triples (Γ, t, α) where Γ is a typing context, t is a linear λ-term and α is either N_a, N_s or $N_a.1$ if N is a non-terminal of the considered TAG. Without loss of generality, we consider that the adjunction at an interior node of an elementary tree is either mandatory or forbidden[1]. We adopt the convention of representing adjunction nodes labeled with N by the variable $x_{N_a}^{str \multimap str}$, the substitution nodes labeled with $N\downarrow$ by the variable $x_{N_s}^{str}$, the foot node of an auxiliary tree labeled with N^* by the variable $f_{N_a.1}^{str}$ and the variable y^* will represent the end of strings. When necessary, in order to respect the linearity constraints of the λ-terms, indices are used to distinguish those variables. This convention being settled, the type annotation on variables is not necessary anymore, thus we will write x_{N_a}, x_{N_s}, $f_{N_a.1}$ and y. To translate the TAG, we use the function ϕ defined by figure 2. Given an initial tree T whose root is labeled by N and t the normal form of $\phi(T)$, $(, t, N_s)$[2] is the lexical entry associated to T; if T is an auxiliary tree whose root is labeled by N and t is the normal form of $\phi(T)$ then $(, \lambda f_{N_a.1}.t, N_a)$[2] is the lexical entry associated to T. A TAG $\mathbf{G}$ is represented by $\mathcal{L}_{\mathbf{G}}$ the smallest set verifying:

1. if T is an elementary tree of $\mathbf{G}$ then the lexical entry associated to T is in $\mathcal{L}_{\mathbf{G}}$.

2. if $(, t, \alpha) \in \mathcal{L}_{\mathbf{G}}$, with α equals to N_a or N_s, and $t = C[x_{N_a} t_1 t_2]$ then $(\Gamma, t_1, N_a.1) \in \mathcal{L}_{\mathbf{G}}$ where $\Gamma = f_{M_a.1} : F$ if $f_{M_a.1} \in FV(t_1)$ otherwise Γ is the empty typing context.

Given a term t such that $x_\alpha \in FV(t)$, and $(\Gamma, t', \alpha) \in \mathcal{L}_{\mathbf{G}}$, then we say that t is rewritten as $t[x_\alpha := t']$, $t \Rightarrow t[x_\alpha := t']$. Furthermore if x_α is the leftmost variable we write $t \Rightarrow_l t[x_\alpha := t']$. It is easy to check that if $t \overset{*}{\Rightarrow} t'$ with $FV(t') = \emptyset$, then $t \overset{*}{\Rightarrow}_l t'$. A string w is generated by a $\mathcal{L}_{\mathbf{G}}$ whenever $x_{S_s} \overset{*}{\Rightarrow} t$ and $t \in /w/$ (S being the start symbol of $\mathbf{G}$). Straightforwardly, the set of strings generated by $\mathcal{L}_{\mathbf{G}}$ is exactly the language of $\mathbf{G}$.

5 The algorithm

As we want to emphasize the fact that the algorithm we propose borrows much to type checking, we use sequents in the items the algorithm manipulates. Sequents are objects of the form $\Gamma \vdash t : \mathbf{d}$

[1] We do not treat here the case of optional adjunction, but our method can be straightforwardly extended to cope with it, following ideas from (de Groote, 2002). It only modifies the way we encode a TAG with a set of lexical entries, the algorithm remains unchanged.

[2] In that case the typing context is empty.

$\phi\begin{pmatrix} & N & \\ & \diagup \quad \diagdown & \\ T_1 & \ldots & T_n \end{pmatrix}$	$\longrightarrow$	$\lambda y.x_{N_a}(\phi(T_1) + \cdots + \phi(T_n))y$	x_{N_a} and y are fresh
$\phi\begin{pmatrix} & N_{NA} & \\ & \diagup \quad \diagdown & \\ T_1 & \ldots & T_n \end{pmatrix}$	$\longrightarrow$	$\phi(T_1) + \cdots + \phi(T_n)$	
$\phi(N^*)$	$\longrightarrow$	$\lambda y.x_{N_a}(\lambda y.f_{N.1}y)y$	
$\phi(N^*_{NA})$	$\longrightarrow$	$\lambda y.f_{N.1}y$	
$\phi(N\downarrow)$	$\longrightarrow$	$\lambda y.x_{N_s}y$	
$\phi(a)$	$\longrightarrow$	$\lambda y.ay$	
$\phi(\epsilon)$	$\longrightarrow$	$\lambda y.y$	

Figure 2: Translating TAG into ACG: definition of ϕ

where Γ is a typing context, t is a linear λ-term, and $\mathbf{d}$ is a syntactic description.

The algorithm uses two kinds of items; either items of the form $(\alpha; \Gamma \vdash t : \mathbf{d}; L)$ (where L is a list of sequents, the subgoals, here L contains either zero or one element) or items of the form $[N_a.1; \Gamma; t; (C_1[], v_1) \multimap (C_2[], v_2)]$. All the possible instances of the items are given by figure 3. The algorithm is a recognizer but can easily be extended into a parser[3]. It fills iteratively a chart until a fixed-point is reached. Elements are added to the chart by means of inference rules given by figure 4, in a deductive parsing fashion (Shieber et al., 1995). Inference rules contain two parts: the first part is a set of premises which state conditions on elements that are already in the chart. The second part gives the new element to add to the chart if it is not already present. For the more general algorithm, the rules are not much more numerous as they can be abstracted into more general schemes.

An item of the form $(\alpha; \Gamma_1 \vdash t_1 : \mathbf{d}; \Gamma_2 \vdash t_2 : (C_1[], v_1))$ verifies:

1. $(\Gamma'_1, t_1, \alpha) \in \mathcal{L}_{\mathbf{G}}$ where $\Gamma'_1 = f_{N_a.1} : F$ if $\Gamma_1 = f_{N_a.1} : \mathbf{e}$ or $\Gamma'_1 = \Gamma_1$ otherwise.

2. there is a context $C[]$ such that $t_1 = C[t_2]$ and if $\mathbf{d}$ is of the form $(\mathbf{d}_1, \ldots, \mathbf{d}_n) \multimap (C_2[], v_2)$ (n must be 1, or 2) then $C[y] \overset{*}{\Rightarrow}_l t'$ so that t' is described by $(C_1[], v_1) \multimap (C_2[], v_2)$.

3. if $\Gamma_1 = f_{N_a.1} : (C_3[], v_3) \multimap (C_4[], v_4)$ or if $\mathbf{d} = ((C_3[], v_3) \multimap (C_4[], v_4), Y) \multimap (C_2[], v_2)$ and $t_1 = \lambda f_{N_a.1} y.v$ then $f_{N_a.1} \Rightarrow_l t''$ and t'' is described by $(C_3[], v_3) \multimap (C_4[], v_4)$

An item of the form $(\alpha; \Gamma \vdash t : \mathbf{d};)$ verifies:

1. $(\Gamma', t, \alpha) \in \mathcal{L}_{\mathbf{G}}$ where $\Gamma' = f_{N_a.1} : F$ if $\Gamma = f_{N_a.1} : \mathbf{e}$ or $\Gamma' = \Gamma$ otherwise

2. $\mathbf{d}$ does not contain non-specified syntactic descriptions[4].

3. $t \overset{*}{\Rightarrow}_l t'$ and t' is described by $\mathbf{d}$ ($\mathbf{d}$ may either represent a string context or a string).

4. if $\Gamma = f_{N_a.1} : (C_3[], v_3) \multimap (C_4[], v_4)$ or if $\mathbf{d} = ((C_3[], v_3) \multimap (C_4[], v_4), (C_1[], v_1)) \multimap (C_2[], v_2)$ and $t_1 = \lambda f_{N_a.1} y.t'$ then $f_{M_a.1} \overset{*}{\Rightarrow}_l t''$ and t'' is described by $(C_3[], v_3) \multimap (C_4[], v_4)$

Finally an item of the form $[N_a.1; \Gamma; t; (C_1[], v_1) \multimap (C_2[], v_2)]$ implies the existence of t', $(C_3[], v_3)$ and $(C_4[], v_4)$ such that $(N_a; \vdash t' : ((C_3[], v_3) \multimap (C_4[], v_4), (C_1[], v_1)) \multimap (C_2[], v_2);)$ and $(N_a.1; \Gamma \vdash t : (C_3[], v_3) \multimap (C_4[], v_4));)$ are in the chart.

An input $\lambda y.C[y]$ is recognized iff when the fixed-point is reached, the chart contains an item of the form $(S_s; \ \vdash t : (\lambda y.C[], y) \multimap (\lambda y.[], C[y]);)$ (where S is the start symbol of the TAG $\mathbf{G}$.

[3]Actually, if it is extended into a parser, it will ouput the shared forest of the derivation trees; (de Groote, 2002) explains how to obtain the derived trees from the derivation trees in the framework of ACGs

[4]There is no occurence of F or Y in $\mathbf{d}$.

General items
$(N_a\ ;\ \vdash \lambda f_{N_a.1} y.t_1 : (F, Y) \multimap (C_1[], v_1)\ ;\ f_{N_a.1} : F, y : Y \vdash t_2 : (C_2[], v_2))$
$(N_a\ ;\ \vdash \lambda f_{N_a.1} y.t : ((C_1[], v_1) \multimap (C_2[], v_2), Y) \multimap (C_3[], v_3)\ ;\ y : Y \vdash t_2 : (C_4[], v_4))$
$(N_a\ ;\ \vdash \lambda f_{N_a.1} y.t : ((C_1[], v_1) \multimap (C_2[], v_2), (C_3[], v_3)) \multimap (C_4[], v_4)\ ;\ )$
$(\alpha\ ;\ \vdash \lambda y.t_1 : Y \multimap (C_1[], v_1)\ ;\ y : Y \vdash t_2 : (C_2[], v_2))$
$(\alpha\ ;\ \vdash \lambda y.t : (C_1[], v_1) \multimap (C_2[], v_2)\ ;\ )$
$(N_a.1\ ;\ f_{M_a.1} : F \vdash \lambda y.t : Y \multimap (C[], v)\ ;\ f_{M_a.1} : F, y : Y \vdash t_2 : (C_2[], v_2)$
$(N_a.1\ ;\ f_{M_a.1} : (C_1[], v_1) \multimap (C_2[], v_2) \vdash \lambda y.t : Y \multimap (C_3[], v_3)\ ;\ y : Y \vdash t_2 : (C_4[], v_4))$
$(N_a.1\ ;\ f_{M_a.1} : (C_1[], v_1) \multimap (C_2[], v_2) \vdash \lambda y.t : (C_3[], v_3) \multimap (C_4[], v_4)\ ;\ )$
Wrapped subtrees
$[N_a.1\ ;\ \ ;\ t\ ;\ (C_1[], v_1) \multimap (C_2[], v_2)]$
$[N_a.1\ ;\ f_{M_a.1} : (C_1[], v_1) \multimap (C_2[], v_2)\ ;\ t\ ;\ (C_3[], v_3) \multimap (C_4[], v_4)]$

Figure 3: Possible items

6 Conclusion and perspective

In this paper, we have illustrated the use for TAGs of general and abstract tools, syntactic descriptions, which can be used to parse linear λ-terms. Even though ACGs are very general in their definition, the algorithm we describe shows that this generality is not a source of unefficiency. Indeed, this algorithm, a special instance of a general one which can parse any second order ACG and it behaves exactly the same way as the algorithm given by (Schabes and Joshi, 1988) so that it parses a second order ACG encoding a TAG in $\mathcal{O}(n^6)$.

The technique used enables to see generation as parsing. In the framework of second order ACG, the logical formulae on which generation is performed are bound to be obtained from semantic recipies coded with linear λ-terms and are therefore not really adapted to Montague semantics. Nevertheless, syntactic descriptions can be extended with intersection types (Dezani-Ciancaglini et al., 2005) in order to cope with simply typed λ-calculus. With this extension, it seems possible to extend the algorithm for second order ACGs so that it can deal with simply typed λ-terms and without loosing its efficiency in the linear case.

References

Henk P. Barendregt. 1984. *The Lambda Calculus: Its Syntax and Semantics*, volume 103. Studies in Logic and the Foundations of Mathematics, North-Holland Amsterdam. revised edition.

Philippe de Groote and Sylvain Pogodalla. 2004. On the expressive power of abstract categorial grammars: Representing context-free formalisms. *Journal of Logic, Language and Information*, 13(4):421–438.

Philippe de Groote. 2001. Towards abstract categorial grammars. In Association for Computational Linguistic, editor, *Proceedings 39th Annual Meeting and 10th Conference of the European Chapter*, pages 148–155. Morgan Kaufmann Publishers.

Philippe de Groote. 2002. Tree-adjoining grammars as abstract categorial grammars. *TAG+6, Proceedings of the sixth International Workshop on Tree Adjoining Grammars and Related Frameworks*, pages 145–150.

Mariangiola Dezani-Ciancaglini, Furio Honsell, and Yoko Motohama. 2005. Compositional Characterization of λ-terms using Intersection Types. *Theoret. Comput. Sci.*, 340(3):459–495.

Gérard Huet. 1997. The zipper. *Journal of Functional Programming*, 7(5):549–554.

Richard Montague. 1974. *Formal Philosophy: Selected Papers of Richard Montague*. Yale University Press, New Haven, CT.

Sylvain Salvati. 2006. Syntactic descriptions: a type system for solving matching equations in the linear λ-calculus. In *to be published in the proceedings of the 17th International Conference on Rewriting Techniques and Applications*.

Yves Schabes and Aravind K. Joshi. 1988. An earley-type parsing algorithm for tree adjoining grammars. In *Proceedings of the 26th annual meeting on Association for Computational Linguistics*, pages 258–269, Morristown, NJ, USA. Association for Computational Linguistics.

Stuart M. Shieber, Yves Schabes, and Fernando C. N. Pereira. 1995. Principles and implementation of deductive parsing. *Journal of Logic Programming*, 24(1–2):3–36, July–August. Also available as cmp-lg/9404008.

The initializer

$$\frac{(\lambda y.t, S_s) \in \mathcal{L}_{\mathbf{G}}}{(S_s;\ \vdash \lambda y.t : Y \multimap (\lambda y.[], u); y : Y \vdash t : (\lambda y.[], u))}$$

The scanner

$$\frac{(\alpha; \Gamma_1 \vdash t_1 : \mathbf{d}; \Gamma_2 \vdash at_2 : (C[], av))}{(\alpha; \Gamma_1 \vdash t_1 : \mathbf{d}; \Gamma_2 \vdash t_2 : (C[a[]], v))} \quad \frac{(\alpha; \Gamma \vdash t : \mathbf{d}; y : Y \vdash y : (C[], v)) \quad \sigma = [Y := (C[], v)]}{(\alpha; \Gamma \vdash t : \mathbf{d}.\sigma;)}$$

The predictor

$$\frac{(\alpha; \Gamma_1 \vdash t_1 : \mathbf{d}; \Gamma_2 \vdash x_{N_a} t_2 t_3 : (C[], v)) \quad (\,, \lambda f_{N_a.1} y.t, N_a) \in \mathcal{L}_{\mathbf{G}}}{(N_a;\ \vdash \lambda f_{N_a.1} y.t : (F, Y) \multimap (C[], v); f_{N_a.1} : F, y : Y \vdash t : (C[], v))}$$

$$\frac{(\alpha; \Gamma_1 \vdash t_1 : \mathbf{d}; \Gamma_2 \vdash x_{N_s} t_2 : (C[], v)) \quad (\,, \lambda y.t, N_s) \in \mathcal{L}_{\mathbf{G}}}{(N_s;\ \vdash \lambda y.t : Y \multimap (C[], v); y : Y \vdash t : (C[], v))}$$

$$\frac{\begin{array}{l}(\alpha; \Gamma_1 \vdash t_1 : \mathbf{d}; \Gamma_2 \vdash f_{N_a.1} t_2 : (C_2[], v_2)) \\ (\Gamma_3, \lambda y.t_3, N_a.1) \in \mathcal{L}_{\mathbf{G}}\end{array}}{(N_a.1; \Gamma_3 \vdash \lambda y.t_3 : Y \multimap (C_2[], v_2); \Gamma_3, y : Y \vdash t_3 : (C_2[], v_2))}$$

The completer

$$\frac{\begin{array}{l}(N_a;\ \vdash t_1 : ((C_1[], v_1) \multimap (C_2[], v_2), (C_3[], v_3)) \multimap (C_4[], v_4);) \\ (N_a.1; \Gamma_2; t_2 : (C_1[], v_1) \multimap (C_2[], v_2);)\end{array}}{[N_a.1; \Gamma_2; t_2; (C_3[], v_3) \multimap (C_4[], v_4)]}$$

$$\frac{\begin{array}{l}(\alpha; \Gamma_1 \vdash t_1 : \mathbf{d}; y : Y, \Gamma_2' \vdash x_{N_a} t_2 t_3 : (C_1[], v_1)) \\ [N_a.1; \Gamma_2; t_2; (C_2[], v_2) \multimap (C_1[], v_1)] \\ \text{if } \Gamma_2 = f_{M_a.1} : \mathbf{f} \text{ then } \sigma = [F := \mathbf{f}] \text{ else } \sigma = Id\end{array}}{(\alpha; \Gamma_1.\sigma \vdash t_1 : \mathbf{d}.\sigma; \Gamma_2 \vdash t_3 : (C_2[], v_2))}$$

$$\frac{\begin{array}{l}(\alpha; \Gamma_1 \vdash t_1 : \mathbf{d}; f_{N_a.1} : F, y : Y \vdash f_{N_a.1} t_2 : (C_1[], v_1)) \\ (N_a.1; \Gamma_2 \vdash t_2 : (C_2[], v_2) \multimap (C_1[], v_1);) \\ \sigma = [F := (C_2[], v_2) \multimap (C_1[], v_1)]\end{array}}{(\alpha; \Gamma_1.\sigma \vdash t_1 : \mathbf{d}.\sigma; y : Y \vdash t_2 : (C_2[], v_2))}$$

$$\frac{\begin{array}{l}(\alpha; \Gamma_1 \vdash t_1 : d; \Gamma_2 \vdash x_{N_s} t_2 : (C_1[], v_1)) \\ (N_s;\ \vdash t_2 : (C_2[], v_2) \multimap (C_1[], v_1);)\end{array}}{(\alpha; \Gamma_1 \vdash t_1 : d; \Gamma_2 \vdash t_2 : (C_2[], v_2))}$$

Figure 4: The rules of the algorithm

Modeling and Analysis of Elliptic Coordination by Dynamic Exploitation of Derivation Forests in LTAG parsing

Djamé Seddah (1) & Benoît Sagot (2)
(1) NCLT - Dublin City University - Ireland
djame.seddah@computing.dcu.ie
(2) Projet ATOLL - INRIA - France
benoit.sagot@inria.fr

Abstract

In this paper, we introduce a generic approach to elliptic coordination modeling through the parsing of Ltag grammars. We show that erased lexical items can be replaced during parsing by informations gathered in the other member of the coordinate structure and used as a guide at the derivation level. Moreover, we show how this approach can be indeed implemented as a light extension of the LTAG formalism throuh a so-called "fusion" operation and by the use of tree schemata during parsing in order to obtain a dependency graph.

1 Introduction

The main goal of this research is to provide a way of solving elliptic coordination through the use of Derivation Forests. The use of this device implies that the resolution mechanism depends on syntactic information, therefore we will not deal with anaphoric resolutions and scope modifier problems. We show how to generate a derivation forest described by a set of context free rules (similar to (Vijay-Shanker and Weir, 1993)) augmented by a stack of current adjunctions when a rule describes a spine traversal. We first briefly discuss the linguistic motivations behind the resolution mechanism we propose, then introduce the **fusion** operation and show how it can be compared to the analysis of (Dalrymple et al., 1991) and (Steedman, 1990) and we show how it differs from (Sarkar and Joshi, 1996). We assume that the reader is familiar with the Lexicalized Tree Adjoining Grammars formalism ((Joshi and Schabes, 1992)).

2 Linguistic Motivations : a parallelism of Derivation

The LTAG formalism provides a derivation tree which is strictly the history of the operations needed to build a constituent structure, the derived tree. In order to be fully appropriate for semantic inference [1], the derivation tree should display every syntactico-semantic argument and therefore should be a graph. However to obtain this kind of dependency structure when it is not possible to rely on lexical information, as opposed to (Seddah and Gaiffe, 2005a), is significantly more complicated. An example of this is provided by elliptic coordination.

Consider the sentences Figure 3. They all can be analyzed as coordinations of S categories[2] with one side lacking one mandatory argument. In (4), one could argue for VP coordination, because the two predicates share the same continuum (same subcategorization frame and semantic space). However the S hypothesis is more generalizable and supports more easily the analysis of coordination of unlike categories ("John is a republican and proud of it" becomes "John$_i$ is$_j$ a republican and ε_i ε_j proud of it").

The main difficulty is to separate the cases when a true co-indexation occurs ((2) and (4)) from the cases of a partial duplication (in (1), the predicate is not shared and its feature structures could differ on aspects, tense or number[3]). In an elliptic construction, some words are unrealized. Therefore, their associated syntactic structures are also non-realized, at least to some extent. However, our aim is to get, as a result of the parsing process, the full constituency and dependency structures of the sentence, including erased semantic items (or units) and their (empty) syntactic positions. Since their syntactic realizations have been erased, the construction of the dependency structure can not

[1] As elementary trees are lexicalized and must have a minimal semantic meaning (Abeillé, 1991), the derivation tree can be seen as a dependency tree with respect to the restrictions defined by (Rambow and Joshi, 1994) and (Candito and Kahane, 1998) to cite a few.

[2] P for Phrase in french, in Figures given in annex

[3] see "John loves$_i$ Mary and children$_i$ their gameboy"

Proceedings of the 8th International Workshop on Tree Adjoining Grammar and Related Formalisms, pages 147–152,
Sydney, July 2006.

be anchored to lexical items. Instead, it has to be anchored on non-realized lexical items and guided by the dependency structure of the reference phrase. Indeed, it is because of the parallelism between the reference phrase and the elliptical phrase that an ellipsis can be interpreted.

3 The Fusion Operation

In this research, we assume that every coordinator, which occurs in elided sentences, anchors an initial tree α_{conj} rooted by P and with two substitution nodes of category P (Figure 1). The fu-

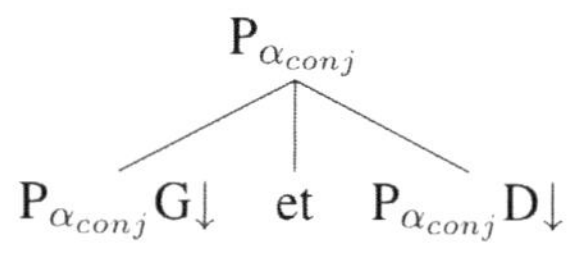

FIG. 1 – Initial Tree α_{conj}

sion operation replaces the missing derivation of any side of the coordinator by the corresponding ones from the other side. It shall be noted that the fusion provide proper node sharing when it is syntactically decidable (cf. 6.4). The implementation relies on the use of non lexicalized trees (*ie tree schemes*) called *ghost trees*. Their purpose is to be the support for partial derivations which will be used to rebuild the derivation walk in the elided part. We call the partial derivations *ghost derivations*. The incomplete derivations from the tree γ are shown as a broken tree in Figure 2. The ghost derivations are induced by the inclusion of the *ghost tree* α' which must be the scheme of the tree α. When the two derivation structures from γ and α' are processed by the fusion operation, a complete derivation structure is obtained.

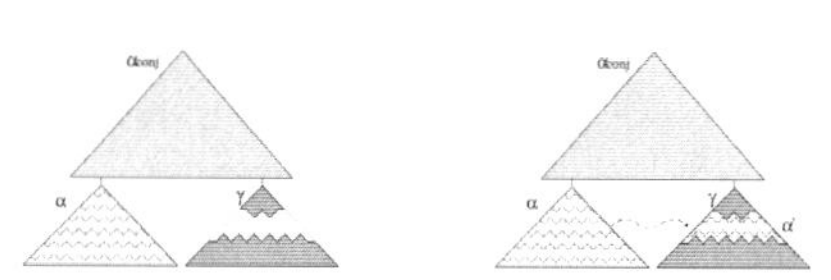

Derivations before the Fusion   After the Fusion

FIG. 2 – Derivation sketch of the Fusion Operation

4 examples anylysis

Let us go back to the following sentences :

(1) Jean aime$_i$ Marie et Paul ε_i Virginie
John loves Mary and Paul Virginia
(2) Paul$_i$ aime Virginie et ε_i déteste Marie
Paul loves Virginia and hates Mary

Obviously (1) can have as a logical formula : $aime'(jean', Marie') \wedge aime'(paul', virginie')$ whereas (2) is rewritten by $eat(paul', apple') \wedge buy'(Paul', cherries')$. The question is to differentiate the two occurrence of $aime'$ in (1) from the $paul'$ ones. Of course, the second should be noted as a sharing of the same argument when the first is a copy of the predicate $aime'$. Therefore in order to represent the sharing, we will use the same node in the dependency graph while a ghosted node (noted by ghost(γ) in our figures) will be used in the other case. This leads to the analysis figure 4. The level of what exactly should be copied, speaking of level of information, is outside the scope of this paper, but our intuition is that a state between a pure anchored tree and an tree schemata is probably the correct answer. As we said, aspect, tense and in most case diathesis for [4] are shared, as it is showed by the following sentences :

(3)*Paul killed John and Bill by Rodger
(4)*Paul ate apple and Mary will pears

As opposed to (4), we believe "Paul ate apples and Mary will do pears" to be correct but in this case, we do not strictly have an ellipsis but a semi-modal verb which is susbsumed by its co-referent. Although our proposition focuses on syntax-semantic interface, mainly missing syntactic arguments.

5 Ghost Trees and Logical Abstractions

Looking either at the approach proposed by (Dalrymple et al., 1991) or (Steedman, 1990) for the treatment of sentences with gaps, we note that in both cases[5] one wants to abstract the realized element in one side of the coordination in order to instantiate it in the other conjunct using the coordinator as the pivot of this process. In our analysis, this is exactly the role of *ghost trees* to support such abstraction (talking either about High Order Variable or λ-abstraction). In this regard, the fusion operation has only to check that the derivations induced by the *ghost tree* superimpose well with the derivations of the realized side.

This is where our approach differs strongly from (Sarkar and Joshi, 1996). Using the fusion operation involves inserting partial derivations, which are linked to already existing ones (the realized derivation), into the shared forest whereas using

[4] w.r.t to the examples of (Dalrymple et al., 1991), i.e "It is possible that this result can be derived (..) but I know of no theory that does so."

[5] Footnote n°3, page 5 for (Dalrymple et al., 1991), and pages 41-42 for (Steedman, 1990).

the *conjoin* operation defined in (Sarkar and Joshi, 1996) involves merging nodes from different trees while the tree anchored by a coordinator acts similarly to an auxiliary tree with two foot nodes. This may cause difficulties to derive the now dag into a linear string. In our approach, we use empty lexical items in order to leave traces in the derivation forest and to have syntacticly motivated derived tree (cf fig. 5) if we extract only the regular LTAG "derivation item" from the forest.

6 LTAG implementation

6.1 Working on shared forest

A *shared forest* is a structure which combines all the information coming from derivation trees and from derived trees. Following (Vijay-Shanker and Weir, 1993; Lang, 1991), each tree anchored by the elements of the input sentence is described by a set of rewriting rules. We use the fact that each rule which validates a derivation can infer a derivation item and has access to the whole chart in order to prepare the inference process. The goal is to use the shared forest as a guide for synchronizing the derivation structures from both parts of the coordinator.

This forest is represented by a context free grammar augmented by a stack containing the current adjunctions (Seddah and Gaiffe, 2005a), which looks like a Linear Indexed Grammar (Aho, 1968).

Each part of a rule corresponds to an item *à la* Cock Kasami Younger described by (Shieber et al., 1995), whose form is $< N, POS, I, J, STACK >$ with N a node of an elementary tree, POS the situation relative to an adjunction (marked $\top$ if an adjunction is still possible, $\bot$ otherwise). This is marked on figure 5 with a bold dot in high position, $\top$, or a bold dot in low position, $\bot$). I and J are the start and end indices of the string dominated by the N node. $STACK$ is the stack containing all the call of the subtrees which has started an adjunction et which must be recognized by the foot recognition rules. We used S as the starting symbol of the grammar and n is the length of the initial string. Only the rules which prove a derivation are shown in figure 6.

The form of a derivation item is $\boxed{Name :< Node_{\gamma_{to}}, \gamma_{from}, \gamma_{to}, Type, \gamma_{ghost} >}$ where $Name$ is the derivation, typed $Type$[6], of the tree γ_{from} to the node $Node$ of γ_{to}.[7]

6.2 Overview of the process

We refer to a *ghost derivation* as any derivation which occurs in a tree anchored by an empty element, and *ghost tree* as a tree anchored by this empty element. As we can see in figure 5, we assume that the proper ghost tree has been selected. So the problem remains to know which structure we have to use in order to synchronize our derivation process.

Elliptic substitution of an initial ghost tree on a tree α_{conj} : Given a tree α_{conj} (see Fig. 1) anchored by a coordinator and an initial tree α_1 of root P to be substituted in the leftmost P node of α_{conj}. Then the rule corresponding to the traversal of the Leftmost P node would be $\boxed{P_{\alpha_{conj}G}(\top, i, j, -, -) \longrightarrow P_{\alpha_1}(\top, i, j, -, -)}$. So if this rule is validated, then we infer a derivation item called $\boxed{\text{D1} :< P_{\alpha_{conj}G}, \alpha_1, \alpha_{conj}, \text{subst}, - >}$.

Now, let us assume that the node situated to the right of the coordinating conjunction dominates a phrase whose verb has been erased (as in *et Paul _ Virginie*) and that there exists a tree of Root P with two argument positions (a quasi tree like N0VN1 in LTAG literature for example). This ghost tree is anchored by an empty element and is called α_{ghost}. We have a rule, called *Call-subst-ghost*, describing the traversal of this node : $\boxed{P_{\alpha_{conj}D}(\top, j+1, n, -, -) \longrightarrow P_{\alpha_{ghost}}(\top, j+1, n, -, -)}$.
For the sake of readability, let us call $D1'$ the pseudo-derivation of call-subst-ghost : $\boxed{D1' :< P_{\alpha_{conj}D}, \boxed{?}, \alpha_{conj}, subst, \alpha_{ghost} >}$, where the non-instantiated variable, $\boxed{?}$, indicates the missing information in the synchronized tree. If our hypothesis is correct, this tree will be anchored by the anchor of α_1. So we have to prepare this anchoring by performing a synchronization with existing derivations. This leads us to infer a ghost substitution derivation of the tree α_1 on the node $P_{\alpha_{conj}D}$. The inference rule which produces the

[6] which can be an adjunction ($type = adj$), a substitution ($subst$), an axiom (ax), an anchor which is usually an implicit derivation in an LTAG derivation tree ($anch$) or a "ghosted" one (adj_g,$subst_g$,$anch_g$)

[7] γ_{ghost} is here to store the name of the 'ghost tree' if the Node belongs to one or – otherwise.

item called ghost(α_1) on Figure 5, is therefore :

$$\frac{D1' :< P_{\alpha_{conj}D}, \boxed{?}, \alpha_{conj}, subst, \alpha_{ghost} > \quad D1 :< P_{\alpha_{conj}R}, \alpha_1, \alpha_{conj}, subst, - >}{Ghost - D1 :< P_{\alpha_{conj}R}, \alpha_1, \alpha_{conj}, subst_g, \alpha_{ghost} >}$$

The process which is almost the same for the remaining derivations, is described section 6.4.

6.3 Ghost derivation and Item retrieving

In the last section we have described a ghost derivation as a derivation which deals with a tree anchored by an empty element, either it is the source tree or the destination tree. In fact we need to keep marks on the shared forest between what we are really traversing during the parsing process and what we are synchronizing, that is why we need to have access to all the needed informations. But the only rule which really knows which tree will be either co-indexed or duplicated is the rule describing the substitution of the realized tree. So, we have to get this information by accessing the corresponding derivation item. If we are in a two phase generation process of a shared forest[8] we can generate simultaneously the substitution rules for the leftmost and rightmost nodes of the tree anchored by a coordination and then we can easily get the right synchronized derivation from the start. Here we have to fetch from the chart this item using unification variables through the path of the derivations leading to it.

Let us call "climbing" the process of going from a leaf node N of a tree γ to the node belonging to the tree anchored by a coordinator (α_{conj}) and which dominates this node. This "climbing" gives us a list of linked derivations (ie. $[< \gamma_x(N), \gamma_y, \gamma_x, Type, IsGhost >, < \gamma_z(N), \gamma_x, \gamma_z, Type_1, IsGhost_1 >, ..]$ where $\gamma(N)$ is the node of the tree γ where the derivation takes place[9]). The last returned item is the one who has an exact counterpart in the other conjunct, and which is easy to recover as shown by the inference rule in the previous section. Given this item, we start the opposite process, called "descent", which use the available data gathered by the climbing (the derivation starting nodes, the argumental position marked by an index on nodes in TAG grammars..) to follow a parallel path. Our algorithm can be considered as taking the two resulting lists as a parameter to produce the correct derivation item. If we apply a two step generation process (shared forest generation then extraction), the "descent" and the "climbing" phase can be done in parallel in the same time efficient way than(2005a).

6.4 Description of inference rules

In this section we will describe all of the inferences relative to the derivation in the right part, resp. left, of the coordination, seen in figure 5.

In the remainder of this paper, we describe the inference rules involved in so called predicative derivations (substitutions and ghost substitutions). Indeed, the status of adjunction is ambiguous. In the general case, when an adjunct is present on one side only of the conjunct, there are two possible readings : one reading with an erased (co-indexed) modifier on the other side, and one reading with no such modifier at all on this other side. In the reading with erasing, there is an additionnal question, which occurs in the substitution case as well : in the derivation structure, shall we co-index the erased node with its reference node, or shall we perform a (partial) copy, hence creating two (partially co-indexed) nodes ? The answer to this question is non-trivial, and an appropriate heuristics is needed. A first guess could be the following : any fully erased node (which spans an empty range) is fully co-indexed, any partially erased node is copied (with partial co-indexation). In particular, erased verbs are always copied, since they can not occur without non-erased arguments (or modifiers).

Elliptic substitution of an initial tree α on a ghost tree γ_{ghost} : If a tree α substituted in a node N_i of a ghost tree γ_{ghost} (ie. Derivation g-Der2' on figure 5), where i is the traditional index of an argumental position (N_0,N_1...) of this tree; and if there exists a ghost derivation of a substitution of the tree γ_{ghost} into a coordination tree α_{conj} (Der. g-Der1) and therefore if this ghost derivation pertains to a tree α_X where a substitution derivation exists node N_i,(Der. Der2) then we infer a ghost derivation indicating the substitution of α on the forwarded tree α_X through the node N_i of the ghost tree γ_{ghost} (Der. Ghost-Der2).

[8] The first phase is the generation of the set of rules, (Vijay-Shanker and Weir, 1993), and the second one is the forest traversal (Lang, 1992). See (Seddah and Gaiffe, 2005b) for a way to generate a shared derivation forest where each derivation rule infers its own derivation item, directly prepared during the generation phase.

[9] The form of a derivation item is defined section 6.1

$$\frac{\begin{array}{c}\text{g-Der2'}:< N_{i_\alpha}, \alpha, \boxed{?}, subst_g, \gamma_{ghost} > \\ \text{g-Der1}:< P_{\alpha_{conj}D}, \alpha_X, \alpha_{conj}, subst_g, \gamma_{ghost} \\ \text{Der2}:< N_{i_{\alpha_X}}, -, \alpha_X, subst, - >\end{array}}{\text{ghost-Der2}:< N_{i_\alpha}, \alpha, ghost(\alpha_X), subst_g, \gamma_{ghost} >}$$

This is the mechanism seen in the analysis of "Jean aime Marie et Pierre Virginie" to provide the derivation tree.

Elliptic substitution of a initial ghost tree α_{ghost} on a tree γ substituted on an tree α_{conj} : We are here on a kind of opposite situation, we have a realized subtree which lacks one of its argument such as *Jean$_i$ dormit puis ϵ_i mourut* (John$_i$ slept then ϵ_i died). So we have to first let a mark in the shared forest, then fetch the tree substituted on the left part of the coordination, and get the tree which has substituted on its ith node, then we will be able to infer the proper substitution. We want to create a real link, because as opposed to the last case, it's really a link, so the resulting structure would be a graph with two links out of the tree anchored by *Jean*, one to *[dormir]* (to sleep) and one to *[mourir]* (to die).

If a ghost tree α_{ghost} substituted on a node N_i of a tree α (Der. g-Der1'), if this tree α has been substituted on a substitution node,P_{conjD}, in the rightmost part of a tree α_{conj}, (Der. Der1) anchored by a coordinating conjunction, if the leftmost part node, P_{conjL}, of α_{conj} received a substitution of a tree α_s, (Der. Der2) and if this tree has a substitution of a tree α_{final} on its ith node, (Der. Der3) then we infer an item indicating a derivation between the tree α_{final} and the tree α on its node N_i, (Der. g-Der1)[10].

$$\frac{\begin{array}{c}\text{g-Der1'}:< N_{i_{\alpha_{ghost}}}, \boxed{?}, \alpha, subst_g, \alpha_{ghost} > \\ \text{Der1}:< P_{\alpha_{conj}D}, \alpha, \alpha_{conj}, subst, - > \\ \text{Der2}:< P_{\alpha_{conj}L}, \alpha_s, \alpha_{conj}, subst, - > \\ \text{Der3}:< N_{i_{\alpha_s}}, \alpha_{final}, \alpha_s, subst, - >\end{array}}{\text{g-Der1}:< N_{i_\alpha}, \alpha_{final}, \alpha, subst, \alpha_{ghost} >}$$

7 Conclusion

We presented a general framework to model and to analyze elliptic constructions using simple mechanisms namely partial sharing and partial duplication through the use of a shared derivation forest in the LTAG framework. The main drawback of this approach is the use of tree schemata as part of parsing process because the anchoring process must have a extremely good precision choose algorithm when selecting the relevant trees. For the best of our knowledge it is one of the first time that merging tree schemata, shared forest walking and graph induction, i.e., working with three different levels of abstraction, is proposed. The mechanism we presented is powerful enough to model much more than the ellipsis of verbal heads and/or some of their arguments. To model elliptic coordinations for a given langage, the introduction of a specific *saturation* feature may be needed to prevent overgeneration (as we presented in (Seddah and Sagot, 2006)). But the same mechanism can be used to go beyond standard elliptic coordinations. Indeed, the use of strongly structured anchors (e.g., with a distinction between the morphological lemma and the lexeme) could allow a fine-grained specification of partial value sharing phenomena (e.g. zeugmas). Apart from an actual large scale implementation of our approach (both in grammars and parsers), future work includes applying the technique described here to such more complex phenomena.

[10]This mechanism without any restriction in the general case, can lead to a exponential complexity w.r.t to the length of the sentence.

References

Anne Abeillé. 1991. *Une grammaire lexicalisée d'arbres adjoints pour le français.* Ph.D. thesis, Paris 7.

Alfred V. Aho. 1968. Indexed grammars-an extension of context-free grammars. *J. ACM*, 15(4) :647–671.

Marie-Hél'ene Candito and Sylvain Kahane. 1998. Can the TAG derivation tree represent a semantic graph ? In *Proceedings TAG+4, Philadelphie*, pages 21–24.

Mary Dalrymple, Stuart M. Shieber, and Fernando C. N. Pereira. 1991. Ellipsis and higher-order unification. *Linguistics and Philosophy*, 14(4) :399–452.

Aravind K. Joshi and Yves Schabes. 1992. Tree Adjoining Grammars and lexicalized grammars. In Maurice Nivat and Andreas Podelski, editors, *Tree automata and languages*. Elsevier Science.

Bernard Lang. 1991. Towards a Uniform Formal Framework for Parsing. In M. Tomita, editor, *Current Issues in Parsing Technology*. Kluwer Academic Publishers.

Bernard Lang. 1992. Recognition can be harder than parsing. In *Proceeding of the Second TAG Workshop*.

Owen Rambow and Aravind K. Joshi. 1994. *A Formal Look at Dependency Grammar and Phrase Structure Grammars, with Special consideration of Word Order Phenomena.* Leo Wanner, Pinter London, 94.

Anoop Sarkar and Aravind Joshi. 1996. Coordination in tree adjoining grammars : Formalization and implementation. In *COLING'96, Copenhagen*, pages 610–615.

Djamé Seddah and Bertrand Gaiffe. 2005a. How to build argumental graphs using TAG shared forest : a view from control verbs problematic. In *Proc. of the 5th International Conference on the Logical Aspect of Computional Linguistic - LACL'05, Bordeaux, France*, Apr.

Djamé Seddah and Bertrand Gaiffe. 2005b. Using both derivation tree and derived tree to get dependency graph in derivation forest. In *Proc. of the 6th International Workshop on Computational Semantics - IWCS-6, Tilburg, The Netherlands*, Jan.

Djamé Seddah and Benoît Sagot. 2006. Modélisation et analyse des coordinations elliptiques via l'exploitation dynamique des forêts de dérivation. In *Proc. of Traitement automatique des Langues Naturelle - TALN 06 - louveau, Belgium*, Apr.

Stuart Shieber, Yves Schabes, and Fernando Pereira. 1995. Principles and implementation of deductive parsing. *Journal of Logic Programming*, 24 :3–36.

Marc Steedman. 1990. Gapping as constituant coordination. *Linguistic and Philosophy*, 13 :207–264.

K. Vijay-Shanker and D. Weir. 1993. The use of shared forests in tree adjoining grammar parsing. In *EACL '93*, pages 384–393.

8 Figures

1) Jean aime$_i$ Marie et Paul ε_i Virginie *John loves Mary and Paul Virginia* Predicate elision
2) Paul$_i$ mange une pomme et ε_i achète des cerises *Paul eats an apple and buys cherries* Right subject elision
3) Marie cuit ε_i et Pierre vend des crêpes$_i$ *Mary cooks and Peter sells pancakes* Left object elision
4)Marie$_i$ cuit ε_j et ε_i vend des crêpes$_j$ *Mary cooks and sells pancakes* Left object and right subject elision

FIG. 3 – Exemples of elliptic constructions

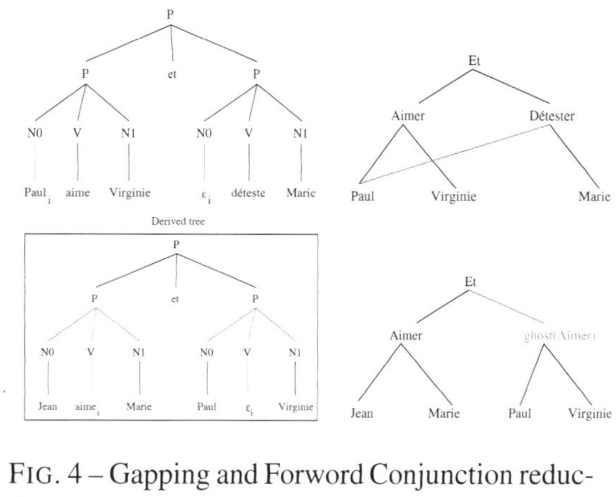

FIG. 4 – Gapping and Forword Conjunction reduction

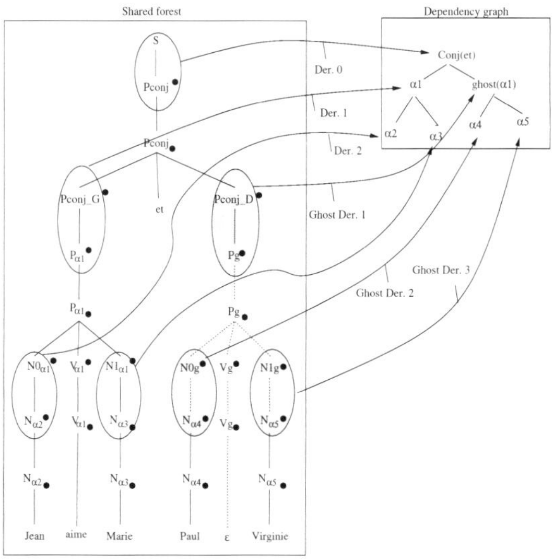

FIG. 5 – Shared forest and relative dependancy graph for "Jean aime Marie et Paul Virginie"(John loves Mary and Paul Virginie)

call transition	rules
Call subst	$< \bot, N_\gamma, i, j, -, -, R, Stack > \rightarrow$ $< \top, N_\alpha, i, j, -, -, R, Stack >$
Call adj	$< \top, N_\gamma, i, j, -, -, R, Stack > \rightarrow$ $< \top, N_\beta, i, j, -, -, R, [N_\gamma \| Stack] >$
Call axiom	S $\rightarrow$ $< \top, N_\alpha, 0, n, -, -, \emptyset, \emptyset >$
Call no subs	$< \bot, N_\gamma, i, j, -, -, R, Stack > \rightarrow$ true
Call foot	$< \bot, *N_\beta, i, j, -, -, R, [N_\gamma \| Stack] > \rightarrow$ $< \top, N_\gamma, i, j, -, -, R, [Stack] >$

The "Call subst" rule is the rule which starts the recognition of a substitution of the initial tree α on the node N of the tree γ between the indices i and j. "Call adj" starts the recognition of the adjunction of the auxiliary tree β on the node N of an elementary tree γ between i and j. "Call axiom" starts the recognition α of an elementary tree spawning the whole string. "Call no subs" starts the recognition of a node N of a elementary tree γ dominating the empty node between the indices i and j. "Call foot" starts the recognition of a subtree dominated by the node N_γ between the indices i and j, the node N_gamma was the start of the adjunction of the auxiliary tree β and $*N_\beta$ its foot node.
In order to avoid the "call adj" rule to be over generating, we control the size of the stack by the number of possible adjunctions at a given state : if the automata has no cycle and if each state of the automata goes forward (j always superior to i), the number of possible adjunctions on a spine (the path between the root of an auxiliary tree and its foot) is bounded by the length of the string to be analyzed.

FIG. 6 – Shared forest derivation inference rules

'Single Cycle' Languages: Empirical Evidence for TAG-Adjoining

Arthur Stepanov
Institute of Linguistics
University of Potsdam
P.O. Box 601553, D-14415 Potsdam, Germany
artorius7@gmail.com

Abstract

Russian and Polish lack 'unbounded' syntactic dependencies that fall into the primary empirical domain of TAG-Adjoining, namely, long-distance movement/filler-gap dependencies across a tensed clause boundary. A theory that incorporates Adjoining as a recursive structure building device provides a novel and straightforward account of this gap, whereas existing theories of syntactic locality, e.g. of the standard Minimalist kind, face difficulties explaining the phenomenon. These languages thus supply direct linguistic evidence for Adjoining.

1 Introduction

Frank (2002), elaborating on earlier work (Kroch, 1987) shows that incorporating TAG-Adjoining into a theory of Universal Grammar of the Minimalist kind (Chomsky, 1995; Chomsky, 2000) yields a number of important empirical advantages. In particular, Adjoining provides a simple and elegant solution for the long-standing and difficult problem in modern syntactic theory concerning a proper formulation of the recursive, or 'successive-cyclic', character of unbounded long movement in examples such as (1) where the wh-phrase stops by each intermediate CP ('Comp').

(1) $[_{CP}$ Who$_1$ does Peter think $[_{CP}$ t_1 (that) Mary saw t_1]]?

According to Frank (2002), there is no long movement per se in (1); rather, only a local wh-movement takes place within the embedded clause (2-a), and the matrix part (2-b) is later 'interpolated' by Adjoining at the C' node.

(2) a. $[_{CP}$ Who$_1$ $[_{C'}$ Mary saw t_1]]
b. $[_{C'}$ does Peter think]

Other long-distance dependencies, such as long 'subject raising' (e.g. *John seems to be likely to be smart*) are treated along similar lines.

Long-distance dependencies (LDD) thus reduce to local dependencies within an elementary tree (in the sense of TAG) coupled with the recursive mechanism of 'interpolating' additional structural chunk(s) by Adjoining. It follows that if the recursive engine in the form of Adjoining were rendered inoperative in some language, LDDs that are built with Adjoining will not be possible in that language. In this study, we investigate Russian and Polish and argue that those are indeed languages that meet that expectation.

2 Data

A systematization of the relevant data leads to the following descriptive generalization: movement/filler-gap dependencies of any kind in Russian and Polish are strictly confined to a single Tense domain, roughly, C(omplementizer) P(hrase) in the standardly assumed clause structure.

Consider first the case of A′-movement. It is well known that Russian lacks standard long-distance wh-movement out of finite (tensed) clauses of the type in (1) (Comrie (1972), among others). Russian also lacks other long-distance A'-dependencies such as Topicalization (Müller and Sternefeld, 1993). This is shown in (3).

(3) a. ?*Kogo ty sčitaeš' čto Maša ljubit?
Whom-acc you believe that Masha loves

Proceedings of the 8th International Workshop on Tree Adjoining Grammar and Related Formalisms, pages 153–158, Sydney, July 2006. ©2006 Association for Computational Linguistics

b. ?*etu knigu Ivan sčitaet čto emu
this book Ivan believes that him
dal Maksim
gave Maksim

Aside from finite clauses, wh-movement is possible out of control infinitival as well as out of subjunctive complements:

(4) Kogo Ivan xočet priglasit' na
Whom Ivan wants to-invite to
večerinku?
party

(5) Kogo Ivan xotel čtoby my priglasili?
Whom Ivan wanted that-sbj we invited

Control infinitivals in Russian have been independently shown to be domains smaller than CP, namely, VPs (Babby, 1998), unlike in English where they are analyzed as either CPs or TPs, depending on a theory.[1] Subjunctive clauses present a well known 'restructuring' context. In many languages, they trigger 'clause union' and allow otherwise clause-bound processes, e.g. clitic climbing. In Russian, subjunctive clauses display the obviation effect with respect to Condition B whereby the embedded subject must have a reference disjoint with that of the matrix subject, typical of a clause-bound process:

(6) *Ivan$_i$ xočet čtoby on$_i$ uexal
Ivan wants that-subjnct he left

Given this and other local effects, subjunctives in Russian and other languages have been argued to involve a 'domain extension' process (not very well understood in a derivational theory) collapsing matrix and embedded clauses into a single Tense domain ((Picallo, 1984; Progovac, 1993; Terzi, 1992) among others).

The precise nature of the single Tense domain restriction in Russian has remained largely unclear. A number of technical solutions were proposed in the Government and Binding and Minimalist frameworks in the form of various constraints on extraction and additional barriers (Müller, 1995; Zaenen, 1983; Pesetsky, 1982; Stepanov, 2001; Koster, 1978). However, the question why Russian and Polish should differ from English in this manner continues to be subject to much discussion.

LDDs are also missing in the context of so called A-movement. Long subject raising is unavailable in Russian (even though predicates with 'raising' semantics are available), unlike in English, cf. (7):[2]

(7) *Ivan kažetsja byt' bol'nym
Ivan seems to-be sick

On the standard view in transformational theory (Chomsky, 1981) both subject raising and object raising, or Exceptional Case Marking (ECM), cases are explained by the same principles. In this respect, it is not surprising that Russian lacks infinitival ECM contexts as well (Brecht, 1974; Lasnik, 1998):

(8) *Ivan sčitaet Mariju byt' umnoj
Ivan considers Mary to-be smart

Aspectual, or 'phase' verbs (*begin, continue*) have sometimes been argued to involve long (cross-clausal) raising (Perlmutter, 1970). A number of empirical diagnostics applied to Russian clearly demonstrate the monoclausal (single Tense) character of these constructions in this language (Stepanov, 2006). For instance, assuming that sentential adverbs such as *possibly* modify the Tense (TP) domain (Watanabe, 1993), in a truly biclausal configuration a lower TP adverb could in principle have a narrower scope with respect to the matrix verb. However, with Russian aspectuals the situation is different. In (9) *na sledujuščej nedele* necessarily modifies the entire sentence, along with *vozmožno*:

(9) On vozmožno prodolžit na
He possibly will-continue on
sledujuščej nedele čitat' knigu
next week to-read book

Other potential candidates for cross-clausal LDD in Russian such as epistemic modal constructions have also been argued to involve a single Tense domain (Schoorlemmer, 1994). In effect, the current literature on Russian syntax reveals no clear cases of LDD spanning more than one Tense domain, and those contexts that have been assumed

[1] Babby's relevant argument draws on the assumption that the silent PRO subject has null dative case in Russian. Thus a contrastive reflexive doubling the PRO subject appears in dative case in non-obligatory control sentences, but must appear in nominative in obligatory control cases. Babby argues that the latter involves no PRO at all, just a bare VP.

[2] The 'small clause' version of (7) (without *byt'*) is allowed. Small clause sentences also involve a single Tense domain (Stowell, 1981)

to do that (often on analogy with other languages), on closer introspection show the single Tense behavior, such as those above.

A similar state of affairs was found in Polish, where the lack of LDD in the domain of A′-movement out of finite clauses is well documented (see (Giejgo, 1981; Zabrocki, 1981; Witkos, 1981) for A′-movement cases, and (Zabrocki, 1981) for A-movement cases).

One may entertain two analytical strategies in handling the Russian/Polish facts. One is to look for separate analyses of the lack of long A'- and A-dependencies. We believe such an approach would miss an important generalization concerning the across-the-board character of local movement dependencies in these languages. A more intriguing and fruitful possibility to explore is that Russian and Polish only allow dependencies confined, roughly speaking, to a single CP. We call such languages 'single cycle' languages, in contrast to the more familiar, 'successive cyclic' language type (English). The question to be addressed now is: what is responsible for the 'single cycle' property?

3 The traditional approach

The standard approach in transformational syntactic theory since Chomsky (1965) and to this day (Chomsky, 2001) maintains that syntactic movement dependencies are a priori unconstrained by the size of the structure over which they are formed; in fact, in this approach there are no a priori restrictions on structure building at all. The structure building operation 'Merge' applies recursively until the material available for sentence building (lexical items, previously built chunks of structure) is exhausted. This approach has an inherent difficulty handling the Russian/Polish facts since it is not clear what would prevent a dependency to stretch as long as the size of the structure permits, in some languages but not others.[3] The usual strategy in this case would be to impose additional constraints on movement in 'single cycle' languages which do not apply in languages like English. This may be satisfactory at some level of analysis, but involves a real complication in this theory. A more attractive possibility, we believe, would be to have this constraint follow from the architecture of the theory itself. TAG provides just the right platform to make this explicit.

4 A TAG solution

We explore the linguistic version of TAG in Frank (2002) which bears close resemblance to the mainstream Minimalist model. In this version of TAG syntactic movement is naturally limited by the size of maximal structural domains built by Merge - *elementary trees*. Crucially, all movement takes place within elementary trees, *before* these trees are joined together into a complex structure by designated operations - Substitution and Adjoining.[4] The recursive character of LDDs ('successive cyclicity') is seen in this system as a consequence of recursion in structure building at particular structural nodes, such as C′ or T′ (in the sense of X-bar theory). In particular, the recursive aspect of LDD is captured via the structure building operation Adjoining which interposes additional structure in between the head and the tail of a local dependency at a recursive node within a given elementary tree (see Section 1).

Notably, in virtually all cases of LDDs considered in Frank's study the additional structure operated by Adjoining constituted a Tensed domain. This approach suggests a natural direction to pursue with respect to 'single cycle' languages that can be summarized in (10):

(10) *Proposal*
TAG-Adjoining is inoperative in 'single cycle' languages.

If Adjoining is unavailable, there is no way to combine two elementary trees as in (2). (10) straightforwardly accounts for the fact that Russian and Polish feature neither A- nor A'-LDD, that is, the type of constructions in which recursive ('successive cyclic') movement is involved. This proposal makes no recourse to additional theoretical constructs as the traditional approaches but makes use of the existing machinery of TAG which provides a simple and accurate description of the phenomenon.

In effect, (10) implies that a source of parametric variation lies in the phrase structural component, to which Adjoining naturally belongs. The

[3]The controversy in formulating the 'successive cyclic' character of LDDs in English and other languages, mentioned in Section 1 is part of that difficulty.

[4]Substitution connects the root node of one elementary tree in an empty slot in another elementary tree, similarly to a Generalized Transformation of Chomsky (1955/75) or Chomsky (1995), Ch.3.

idea of phrase structure as a locus of parametric variation, and implications for child language acquisition and learnability, have been explored in detail in Lebeaux (1988/2000), a precursor to standard Minimalism. We believe it is possible to frame (10) in the general scheme of Lebeaux's parametric model.

5 Parametric and acquisitional aspects

Lebeaux (1988/2000) proposes that particular grammars are hierarchically ordered by their complexity: a grammar G_0 that features operations O_1 and O_2 properly contain a grammar G_1 that features only O_1. Considering the operations Adjoin-α and Conjoin-α, Lebeaux represents the relevant parametric space as in (11), where arrows are to be read as addition of an operation to the grammar, and parenthesis as 'invisibility' for the learner.

(11) $$G_0 \; ((\xrightarrow{\text{Adjoin-}\alpha} G_1) \xrightarrow{\text{Conjoin-}\alpha} G_2)$$

Different parametric options correspond to different sets of erased parentheses (outermost first). Furthermore, Lebeaux proposes that the parametric sequence (11) actually mirrors (in his terms, is 'congruent to') the time course of children's grammatical development. That is, in the course of language development children proceed from less to more computationally complex grammars, along the lines of (11).

Frank (1998) takes up the developmental portion of Lebeaux's congruency thesis in the context of TAG-Adjoining, suggesting that the developmental sequence for English speaking children proceeds from the grammar without Adjoining to a grammar with Adjoining. Viewed in this manner, the proposal explains, among other things, why children learning English initially fail to construe even simple cases of long-distance wh-movement or subject to subject raising, while performing well on constructions with similar processing load that do not involve recursion. Representing Frank's proposal with Lebeaux type notation may look as in (12) (Merge and Move operate within an elementary tree; cf. above).

(12) $$...G_1{}^{Move,Merge} \xrightarrow{\text{Adjoining}} G_2$$

In the context of Lebeaux's congruency thesis, Frank's proposal begs a question as to whether there exist a parametric sequence that corresponds to the proposed developmental sequence. Frank does not attempt an answer. But now we are able to fill in this gap. Specifically, we now say that, indeed, the parametric sequence includes a computationally more complex grammar with Adjoining which properly contains the grammar without Adjoining, as represented in (13).

(13) $$...G_1{}^{Move,Merge}(\xrightarrow{\text{Adjoining}} G_2)$$

Here, one parametric option is G_1 (no parentheses erased) corresponding to 'single cycle' languages like Russian and Polish. The option erasing the parentheses in (13) results in languages with usual recursive LDDs (English etc). This is exactly as expected under the Congruency thesis. 'Single cycle' languages thus provide strong evidence for 1) the TAG operation Adjoining; 2) Lebeaux's congruency thesis; and 3) Frank's acquisitional sequence with respect to Adjoining.

6 Refining Adjoining

Auxiliary trees, utilized by Adjoining, come in two varieties, both of which adhere to a principal requirement: the 'root' and 'foot' node of such tree must be categorically identical (e.g. CP), in order for Adjoining to succeed. In one variety the root node directly dominates the foot node (14-a). This case corresponds to standard transformational adjunction. In the second variety there is structural material between the root and the foot nodes (14-b):

(14)

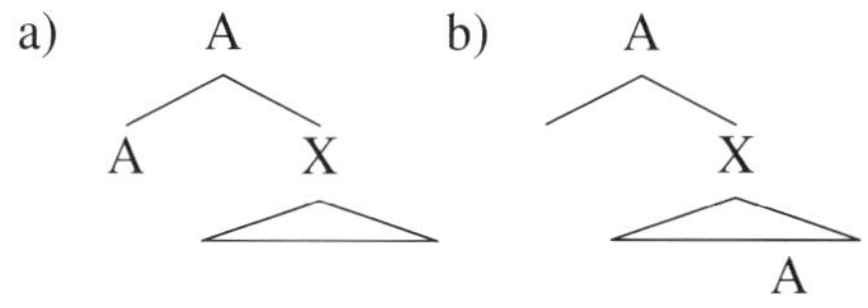

The recursive structures we are interested in involve only the 'interpolation' variety in (14-b). But (10) refers to the prohibition of Adjoining in general. That is, in the present form it is too powerful: it rules out not only 'interpolated' cases of Adjoining, but also regular cases of base-generated adjunction, e.g. VP or DP modifiers (adverbs or adjectives).

One direction that one might undertake in this regard is to relax (10) and allow Adjoining for particular nodes in Russian, while excluding it for others. This amounts, essentially, to specifying the list of recursive nodes for grammars of particular languages. In this manner, we automatically constrain the types of possible auxiliary trees, targeted by Adjoining. Such lists are commonly used in various formal versions of TAG (cf. (Abeillé and Rambow, 2000)). Our parametric variation could then be captured for instance as follows:

(15) English: Aux = {TP, CP, VP, DP}
Russian: Aux = {VP, DP}

Another, more interesting alternative, is to make a principled distinction between the two cases of Adjoining. In fact, there is a well established linguistically sound method of distinguishing the types of root and foot nodes in (14)a and (14)b. The method goes back to structural distinction between segments and full categories, along the lines of Chomsky (1986) (who, in turn, builds on the work of R. May). Namely, both nodes labeled A in (14)a are in fact segments of a single category A. In contrast, the nodes labeled A in (14)b are full categories (note that the 'listing' solution above ignores this state of affairs). It seems appropriate, therefore, to split Adjoining into two different operations, e.g. *Adjunction* (which coincides with the traditional transformational usage) for (14)a, and *Interpolation* for the case (14)a. The proposal in (10) then pertains to the latter, without loss of generality. Details of this alternative are discussed in Stepanov (2006).

7 Further issues

The proposal explored in (10) does not imply that the recursive component is completely excluded in 'single cycle' languages. Declarative sentences with one or more embedded tensed clauses are of course available. In the linguistic version of TAG adopted here, those are built by Substitution - at the CP node (for details, see Frank (2002). Furthermore, wh-extraction facts concerning control infinitivals and subjunctives and Russian and Polish suggest that certain recursive structural domains (e.g. VPs in control infinitivals) are built by Merge within a single elementary tree, and therefore, that not all prima facie LDDs are exclusively handled with Adjoining, in contrast to Frank (2002). In particular, Adjoining is responsible only for LDDs that involve more than one Tense domain, while all others are built with Merge within a single elementary tree, and are not, strictly speaking, LDDs at all as they do not display the 'successive cyclic' character.

This raises two further issues. One issue concerns a possible need to slightly modify the criteria of well-formedness of elementary trees formed by Merge as discussed by Frank (2002) to allow the above contexts. Another issue concerns making more precise the proper division of labor with respect to two types of LDDs. In a system such as Frank (2002) the distinction can be captured in terms of *selectional restrictions*, perhaps of semantic kind. Selection usually plays a crucial role in forming an elementary tree by Merge: in most recent transformational theories, selection directly determines a candidate for Merge. On the other hand, it is conceivable to suppose that Adjoining - the operation that interpolates one elementary tree into another *after* both have already been built by Merge - has little to do with selection. Therefore, dependencies that are formed via selection in direct or indirect manner, cannot be relegated to Adjoining. Further aspects of this suggestion remain to be explored.

8 Conclusion

Integration of TAG mechanisms into the mainstream linguistic theory leads to a significant widening of its empirical coverage in various domains. As shown in previous work, a major strength of the TAG formalism lies in its great potential to capture facts concerning strict locality of syntactic dependencies in natural language. The present study applies the TAG machinery in the domain of well known but ill explained phenomenon of radical across-the-board locality of syntactic dependencies in two Slavic languages, Russian and Polish. We have shown that making use of the TAG operation Adjoining leads to a simple and straightforward account of this phenomenon, while the standard (pre-)Minimalist model of syntax faces conceptual difficulties in this regard. We also provided independent support for the thesis of congruency of the parametric and acquisitional sequences with respect to Adjoining (Lebeaux, 1988/2000; Frank, 1998) and suggested ways of refining Adjoining in light of the new empirical data.

Acknowledgments

I am grateful to Robert Frank, Jens Michaelis, Penka Stateva and three anonymous referees for helpful suggestions.

References

Anne Abeillé and Owen Rambow (eds). 1986. *Tree Adjoining Grammars: Formalisms, linguistic analysis and processing*. MIT Press, Cambridge, MA.

Leonard Babby. 1998. Subject control as direct predication: Evidence from Russian. In *Formal Approaches to Slavic Linguistics: The Connecticut Meeting*, 17-37. Michigan Slavic Publications.

Richard Brecht. 1974. Tense and infinitive complements in Russian, Latin and English. In *Slavic transformational syntax*, ed. Richard D. Brecht and Catherine Chvany, 193-218. Michigan Slavic Materials, University of Michigan.

Noam Chomsky. 1955/1975. *The logical structure of linguistic theory*. Plenum, New York.

Noam Chomsky. 1965. *Aspects of the theory of syntax*. MIT Press, Cambridge, MA.

Noam Chomsky. 1981. *Lectures on government and binding*. Foris, Doredrecht.

Noam Chomsky. 1986. *Barriers*. MIT Press, Cambridge, MA.

Noam Chomsky. 1995. *Minimalist program*. MIT Press, Cambridge, MA.

Noam Chomsky. 2000. Minimalist inquiries: The Framework. In *Step by step: Essays in honor of Howard Lasnik*, ed. Roger Martin, David Michaels and Juan Uriagereka, 89-155. MIT Press, Cambridge, MA.

Noam Chomsky. 2001. Derivation by phase. In *Ken Hale: A life in language*, ed. Michael Kenstowicz. MIT Press, Cambridge, MA.

Bernard Comrie. 1972. *Aspects of sentence complementation in Russian*, Ph.D. thesis. Cambridge University.

Robert Frank. 1998. Structural complexity and the time course of grammatical development. *Cognition*, 66:249-301.

Robert Frank. 2002. *Phrase structure composition and syntactic dependencies*. MIT Press, Cambridge, MA.

Janina Giejgo. 1981. *Movement rules in Polish syntax*, Ph.D. thesis. University College London.

Jan Koster. 1978. *Locality principles in syntax*. Foris, Doredrecht.

Anthony Kroch. 1987. Unbounded dependencies and subjacency in a tree adjoining grammar. In *Mathematics of language*, ed. Alexis Manaster-Ramer, 143-172. John Benjamins, Amsterdam.

Howard Lasnik. 1998. Exceptional Case Marking: Perspectives old and new. In *Proceedings of Formal Approaches to Slavic Linguistics 6*, 187-211. Michigan Slavic Publications, University of Michigan.

David Lebeaux. 1988. *Language acquisition and the form of the grammar*, Ph.D. thesis, University of Massachusetts. Published in 2000 by John Benjamins, Amsterdam.

Gereon Müller and Wolfgang Sternefeld. 1993. Improper movement and unambiguous binding *Linguistic Inquiry*, 24:461-507.

Gereon Müller. 1995. *A-bar syntax: A study of movement types*. Mouton de Gruyter.

David Perlmutter. 1970. On the two verbs 'begin'. In *Readings in English transformational grammar*, ed. R. Jacobs and P. Rosenbaum. Ginn, Waltham, MA.

David Pesetsky. 1982. *Paths and categories*, Ph.D. thesis. MIT.

M.C. Picallo. 1984. The Infl node and the null subject parameter. *Linguistic Inquiry*, 15:75-102.

Ljiljana Progovac. 1993. Locality and subjunctive-like complements in Serbo-Croatian. *Journal of Slavic Linguistics*, 1:116-144.

Maaike Schoorlemmer. 1994. Aspect and verbal complementation in Russian *Proceedings of the Ann Arbor Workshop on Formal Approaches in Slavic Linguistics*, 400-422. Michigan Slavic Publications.

Arthur Stepanov. 2001. *Cyclic domains in syntactic theory*, Ph.D. thesis. University of Connecticut.

Arthur Stepanov. 2006 (to appear). 'Single cycle' languages: Implications for cyclicity, recursion and acquisition. In *Linguistic Variation Yearbook 6*, ed. Johann Rooryck, Pierre Pica and Jeroen van Craenenbroeck. John Benjamins, Amsterdam.

Tim Stowell. 1981. *Origins of phrase structure*, Ph.D. thesis. MIT.

Arhonto Terzi. 1992. *PRO in finite clauses: A study of the inflectional heads of the Balkan languages*, Ph.D. thesis. City University of New York.

Akira Watanabe. 1993. *AGR-based Case theory and its interaction with the A′-system*, Ph.D. thesis. MIT.

Jacek Witkos. 1981. *Some aspects of phrasal movement in English and Polish*, Ph.D. thesis. Uniwersytet im. Adama Mickiewicza, Poznan.

Tadeusz Zabrocki. 1981. *Lexical rules of semantic interpretation*. Uniwersytet im. Adama Mickiewicza, Poznan.

Annie Zaenen. 1993. On syntactic binding. *Linguistic Inquiry*, 14:469-504.

Reconsidering Raising and Experiencers in English

Dennis Ryan Storoshenko
Department of Linguistics
Simon Fraser University
Burnaby, B.C., Canada
dstorosh@sfu.ca

Abstract

In this paper, structures involving the raising verb *seem*, are examined. Specifically, it is shown that previously-proposed elementary trees for *seem* with an experiencer argument are inadequate, based upon syntactic testing. In Storoshenko (2006), new articulated structures for the *seem* predicate are proposed, modelled upon the treatment of ditransitive verbs. This paper recapitulates and further motivates the ditransitive-style analysis, while illustrating its potential value in issues surrounding extraction and the raising construction in TAG.

1 Introduction

The raising predicate *seem* is often cited as one of the core examples in discussions of TAG's application to natural language syntax. Under a generative/minimalist account, a sentence such as (1a) will have the underlying structure in (1b):

(1) a. John seems to like coffee.

b. John_i seems [t_i to like coffee].

In TAG, the subject *John* remains local to the elementary tree headed by *like*, the elementary tree in which its theta role is assigned. The observed displacement effect is a result of the extension of the *like*-headed tree after the adjunction of an auxiliary tree headed by *seem* (Kroch and Joshi, 1985). In the more recent analysis of Frank (2002), a sentence such as (1a) is derived through the composition of the elementary trees of Figure 1 to derive the final tree in Figure 2.

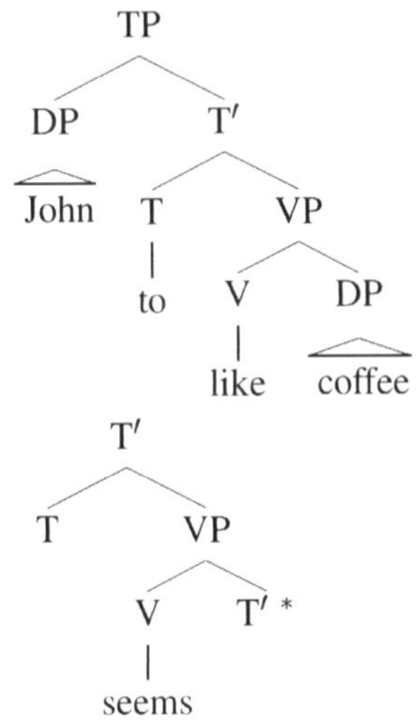

Figure 1: Elementary trees to derive *John seems to like coffee.*

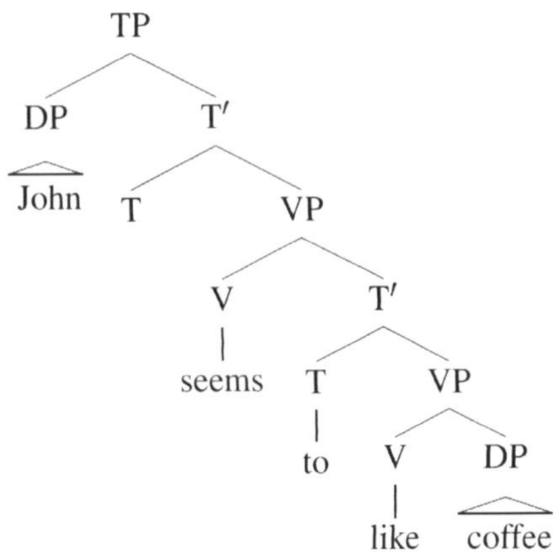

Figure 2: Derived tree for *John seems to like coffee.*

Proceedings of the 8th International Workshop on Tree Adjoining Grammar and Related Formalisms, pages 159–164,
Sydney, July 2006.

1.1 Defining the Problem

At issue in this paper will be the structure of sentences such as those in (2):

(2) a. John seems to me to like coffee.

b. John seems to like coffee to me.

Here, a prepositional phrase *to me* now appears in the clause; as illustrated, its position is variable. The individual introduced in this prepositional phrase is interpreted as being an experiencer of the verb *seem*, in no way dependent upon the embedded *like* predicate. As such, according to the Fundamental TAG Hypothesis (Frank, 2002), this experiencer must be composed as a part of the *seem* auxiliary tree. For discursive ease, the case in (2a) will be termed a medial experiencer, and the (2b) case will be a final experiencer. What is now required is an auxiliary tree for *seem* which retains the desired recursivity, and supports this experiencer in either possible position. Further syntactic diagnostics will be used to determine the necessary shape of such an auxiliary tree.

1.2 An Existing Account

In Frank (2002), a structure is given for this type of raising verb with an experiencer, as in Figure 3.

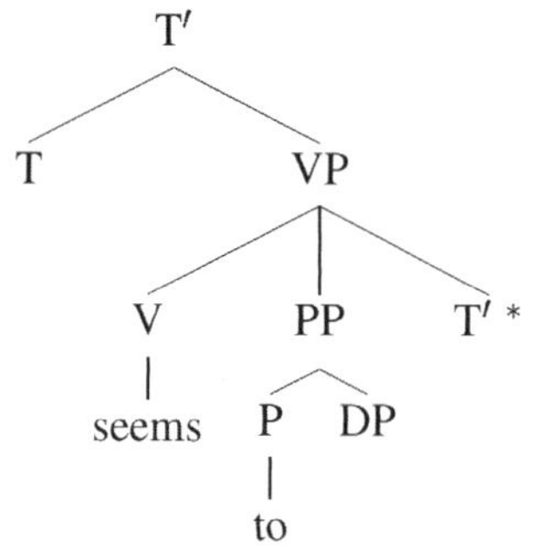

Figure 3: Auxiliary tree for *seem* with an experiencer (Frank, 2000)

This tree would adjoin into the T′ node of an infinitival clause tree, as in Figure 1, yielding the correct string order (after substitution of the frontier DP-experiencer), for a raising sentence with a medial experiencer (2a). Frank's discussion of this ternary structure is essentially limited to the well-formedness of its functional architecture, and the fact that a stipulation will need to be put in place to obviate the satisfaction of the T head's EPP feature by the experiencer. While a valid point, there are still two key unanswered questions with regards to this structure: first of all, are the complements of the verb straightforwardly interchangeable (to account for the variable position of the experiencer), and is there any evidence for or against the ternary branching structure? These questions emerge to be inter-related, and in exploring the consequences of the ternary structure, it will be shown that simple transposition of the verb's complements is not an option within a flat ternary structure.

2 Establishing Argumenthood

Before embarking upon a discussion of the consequences of Frank's ternary branching structure, a more straightforward solution must be considered. Instead of treating it as a part of the *seem*-headed tree, one could attempt to formulate an argument that the prepositional phrase bearing the experiencer is introduced as a syntactic adjunct. This could be conceivably be accomplished through the use of one of the two trees of Figure 4. These are adjunct auxiliary trees, recursive on VP, which would introduce an experiencer prepositional phrase at either the left or right periphery of the VP, respectively.

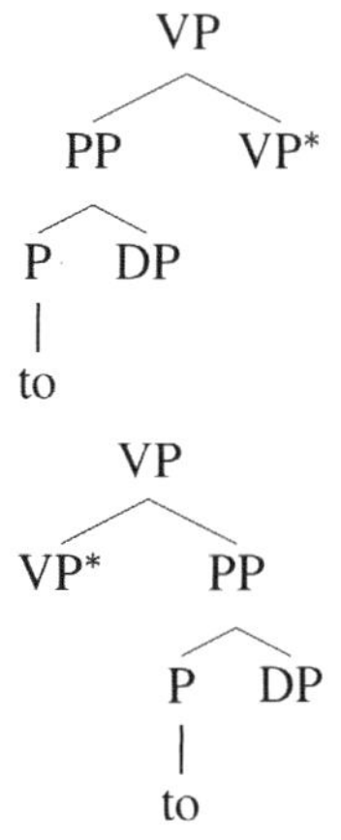

Figure 4: Possible adjunction structures for an experiencer prepositional phrase

While an anonymous reviewer points out that considering the experiencer to be an argument of *seem* is quite uncontroversial, there does appear to be some evidence that a prepositional phrase of this form, serving to introduce something akin to an experiencer, can exist independent of the predicate *seem*:

(3) a. ? John to me likes coffee.

b. John likes coffee to me.

While the first example here sounds quite marginal to the ears of most native speakers, the second sentence is perfectly acceptable, and is a likely paraphrase of a sentence such as *John seems/appears to like coffee to me*. This suggests at least the possibility that the prepositional phrase bearing the experiencer might be considered an adjunct[1].

However, in the case of a sentence such as (2a), it can be easily demonstrated that adjunction of the prepositional phrase as an independent auxiliary tree is not an option. Adjunction of the right-recursive VP tree of Figure 4 into the VP node of either tree of Figure 1 would, after all the trees were composed, yield one of the following string orders:

(4) a. * John seems to *to me* like coffee.

b. * John *to me* seems to like coffee.

As shown, there is no way to derive the medial experiencer string-order using a simple VP-adjunction tree. This provides clear evidence that the mechanics of TAG derivation force an analysis where at least the medial experiencer must enter the derivation as a part of the *seem* auxiliary, giving further thrust to the contention that the experiencer here is indeed an argument of *seem*.

In turning to the experiencer in final position, matters are less clear-cut, as there is a viable structure in which the prepositional phrase can adjoin to the *seem* auxiliary and appear at the end of the sentence, using the left-recursive tree of Figure 4. Recalling the examples of (3), it is possibly even more important to establish the argumenthood of this position, as there are strikingly similar sentences in which the equivalent prepositional phrase appears to be a *bona fide* adjunct. For the final experiencers of *seem*, evidence can be provided to show that the prepositional phrase is not opaque to extraction, and therefore not an adjunct:

(5) a. The woman whom$_i$ John seemed to like coffee to t$_i$ kept refilling his cup.

b. John seems to like coffee to the waitress. Her boss, too.

c. Who$_i$ is it that you saw the woman who seemed to like coffee to him$_i$?

[1]The possibility that sentences such as those in (3) are derived from a raising structure from which the raising predicate *seem* was subsequently elided can be easily dismissed. Aside from employing a host of tests to identify elision phenomena, one must simply observe that the verb *like* appears with fi nite tense, a distinct anomaly if one were to treat it as having been part of a raising structure.

In (5a), it is quite clear that the experiencer can be relativised out of the final position with no difficulty at all. Similarly, the stripping case in (5b), where it also seems to Mary's boss that John likes coffee, indicates that the experiencer *her boss* can be extraposed from the sentence final position, and the rest of the sentence stripped away. Finally, the use of a resumptive pronoun to repair the complex noun phrase constraint violation in (5c) provides further proof that the final-position prepositional phrase is not opaque to extraction. This is thus an argument position, part of the *seem*-headed auxiliary. As such, the question left at the end of Section 1 must now be answered: can the ternary-branching auxiliary tree account for independent syntactic observations related to this particular structure?

3 An Alternative View

At first glance, Frank's ternary branching structure is reminiscent of early accounts of ditransitive verbs. Such structures were famously argued against in Larson (1988), and subsequently reexamined in Harley (2002). In these treatments, a ternary structure is replaced with a VP-shell structure, as schematised in Figure 5.

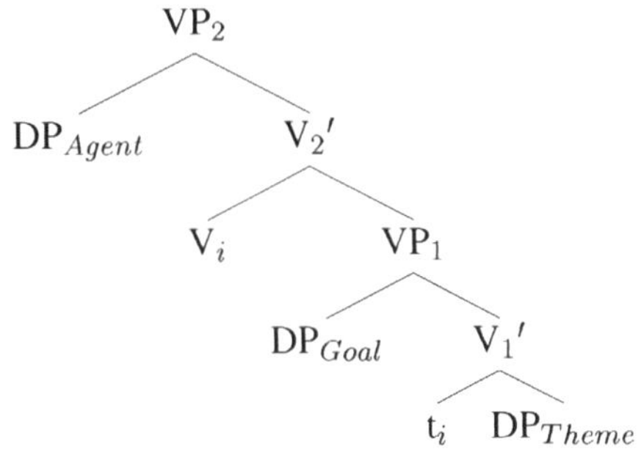

Figure 5: Schematic tree for a ditransitive verb phrase

In the lower VP, the goal and theme of a ditransitive verb are projected as the specifier and complement, respectively. The verb itself then raises to an upper VP, which supports the agent of the ditransitive predicate. The motivation for adopting this structure lay in the observation of c-command phenomena between the goal and theme positions. In a flat ternary structure, mutual c-command between these two positions would be expected, however Larson gives considerable data to argue that mutual c-command does not exist between these two positions.

In looking at the tree from Figure 3, it is clear that straightforward considerations of mutual c-command will not be informative, as one of the ternary branches of the *seem*-headed tree will contain the remainder of the embedded clause material which exists below the T′ adjunction site. However, what can be observed is whether or not a c-command relation exists between the experiencer of *seem* and the embedded clause theme. This will speak to the matter of the possible transposition of the VP complements: if they do indeed exist in a flat structure, then the experiencer should c-command the embedded clause theme from both the medial and final positions[2].

In Storoshenko (2006), it is argued that a *seem* auxiliary with an experiencer should be analysed with a similar VP-shell analysis. Among the evidence provided, three of Larson's c-command tests are employed to illustrate that the experiencer of *seem* does c-command the embedded clause object when in the medial position:

(6) a. John seems to nobody to like anything. (NPI Licensing)

b. John seems to every boy$_i$ to like him$_i$. (Bound Variable)

c. * What$_i$ does John seem to whom to like t$_i$? (Superiority)

For negative polarity licensing and bound variable readings to obtain in these cases, the experiencer must c-command the direct object. Similarly, the fact that extraction of the embedded clause theme (which would not in itself be the product of an ill-formed elementary tree), is ungrammatical here. This is a straightforward superiority violation, again illustrating that the experiencer c-commands the embedded theme.

The opposite is demonstrated to be the case where the experiencer is in the final position:

(7) a. * John seems to like anything to nobody.

b. John seems to like him$_{*i}$ to every boy$_i$.

c. What$_i$ does John seem to like t$_i$ to whom?

Here, the negative polarity item is not licensed, and a bound variable reading does not obtain. However, the embedded theme can be extracted in the case where the experiencer is in the final position. These results demonstrate that in the final position, the experiencer does not c-command the embedded object, contrary to what would be expected of a flat ternary structure like that of Figure 4. The experiencer must not be in a position where it c-commands the embedded clause material beneath T′ . The elementary trees for *seem* with an experiencer in medial and final position, respectively, are given in Figure 6.

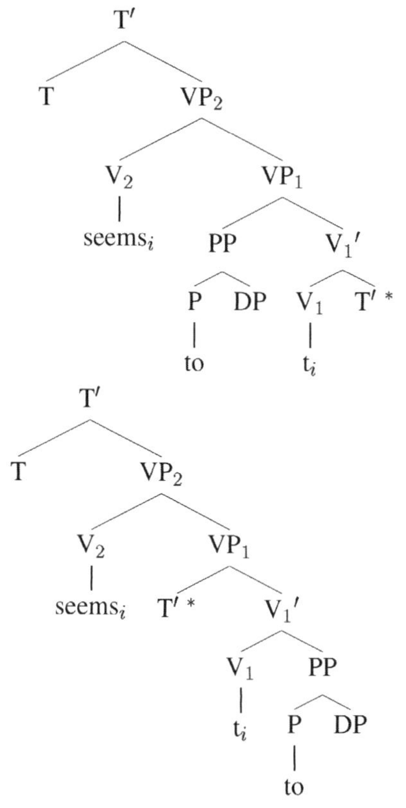

Figure 6: Two *seem*-headed trees with experiencers (Storoshenko 2006)

As in the case of the ditransitive structure of Figure 5, there is verb movement here. The lower VP supports the experiencer and the T′ foot node, essential if recursivity is to be maintained, while *seem* itself raises to an upper VP projection. Unlike the ditransitive case, *seem* projects no position for an agent argument, which retains Frank's argumentation for having an elementary tree rooted in

[2]The observed ability of an argument DP to c-command out of its PP in this type of structure is noted in Jackendoff (1990)

T′ . Crucially, this movement is licensed within TAG, as it remains local to this one elementary tree, and has no impact upon the recursive nature of the tree.

In terms of the relationship between the two experiencer positions, there are two possibilities, both of which have been explored in the parallel literature on ditransitives. In the pattern of Larson (1988), the two trees of Figure 6 would be derivationally related, one having been derived from the other. Countering this is the approach of Harley (2002), in which similar alternations are argued to be the result of lexically distinct (yet phonetically indistinguishable) predicates projecting different syntactic structures. The second argument is taken in Storoshenko (2006): there is no derivational relationship between the two trees Figure 6. Each is headed by a *seem* predicate which specifies whether the experiencer appears in the medial or final position.

Beyond c-command facts, there is additional evidence that such an articulated structure for *seem* may be required. An anonymous reviewer comments that the opening of potential adjunction sites is a common motivation for binarism over ternary structures in TAG-based syntax. In this case, neither the *seem*-headed tree of Figure 1 or 3 will account for the position of a VP-adjoined manner or temporal adjunct modifying the raising predicate:

(8) a. John seems *for all intents and purposes* to be a professor to me.
b. John seemed *for as long as we knew him* to like coffee.

Assuming these adjuncts to be introduced through elementary trees recursive on VP, only the presence of the lower VP node in the shell structure allows for an adjunction into the *seem* auxiliary which yields the correct string order. Indeed, (8b) may indicate that the shell structure is required even in cases where there is no experiencer.

4 Extending the Analysis

Thus far, this discussion has been limited to cases in which *seem* is adjoined into an infinitival clause. There are at least two other types of structure on which this analysis needs to be tested: those where *seem* adjoins into a small clause, and those where *seem* takes a finite clause complement:

(9) a. John seems happy.
b. It seems that John likes coffee.

In exploring these cases, a further challenge to the ditransitive-style analysis arises. While the experiencer is licit in both positions where the *seem*-headed tree is adjoined into an infinitival clause, apparent asymmetries can be noted in these other constructions, calling into question the broader applicability of the structures in Figure 6. Where the *seem* auxiliary has adjoined into a small clause, the experiencer is degraded in the position immediately following *seem*, and is more acceptable in the sentence-final position, as in (10). Conversely, in the finite complement case, the experiencer is marginal at best in the sentence-final position, illustrated in (11).

(10) a. ? John seems to me happy.
b. John seems happy to me.

(11) a. It seems to me that John likes coffee.
b. ? It seems that John likes coffee to me.

However, it has been pointed out (Tatjana Scheffler, p.c.) that considerations of phonetic weight may be at work in these cases. For the small clause cases, replacing the simple adjective with a more complex element yields a more comfortable sentence with the medial experiencer, and the experiencer in final position now seems more awkward:

(12) a. John seems to me competent enough to finish the task at hand.
b. John seems competent enough to finish the task at hand to me.

The same reversal can be observed with the finite clause cases where a heavier experiencer appears alongside the complement clause. The sentence final experiencer is made to seem much more natural than in the simpler case above:

(13) a. It seems to all of the cafe's customers that John likes coffee.
b. It seems that John likes coffee to all of the cafe's customers.

Taking this into consideration, these apparent variations are nothing more than red herrings, with the relative positioning of experiencer and embedded material demonstrating sensitivity to considerations of phonetic weight. Such considerations may determine which *seem*-headed auxiliary is the better choice for native speakers in a given context.

Furthermore, difficulties in the case of (11b) may be a function of ambiguity. An alternative derivation does exist in which the PP *to me* is not an argument of *seem*. Recalling the cases where a "pseudo-"experiencer appeared without an accompanying raising predicate, it is possible that the *to me* of (11b) and *to all the cafe's customers* of (13b) are adjuncts to the embedded clause VP, in the same pattern as (3b). Extraction tests along the lines of those employed earlier can be used to show that the experiencer can be an argument, but this still will not negate the fact that a derivation exists wherein it may simply be an adjunct.

5 Conclusion and Implications

With the elimination of challenges to this new analysis of *seem*, the conclusion is that the structures in Figure 6 are justified, and generalisable to many uses of the verb. Potential counterexamples are either functions of weight considerations, or interference from ambiguous analyses.

Having used extraction-based tests to reach this conclusion, it is worth noting that accounting for extraction from the *seem* auxiliary tree remains a problem for TAG (Frank, 2002). A *Wh*-question formed through the extraction of the experiencer argument would necessarily be extended all the way to CP, thus sacrificing recursivity. While this problem has not been solved here, the refinements to the structure of *seem* will contribute to future accounts. Specifically, any account of extraction which is sensitive to issues such as superiority or crossover will benefit from this analysis. Consider the sentences in (14):

(14) a. Bill seems to John_i to like him_i.
b. Bill seems to like him_{*i} to John_i.
c. To whom_i does Bill seem to like him_i?

In theory, either of (14a) or (14b) could represent the underlying structure of (14c). Binding, as shown in (14c), is possible for this question, though only the (14a) sentence shows equivalent binding. Extraction of the experiencer in the (14b) case would result in a weak-crossover violation, should the extracted experiencer bind the embedded object. This asymmetry between (14a) and (14b) would not be predicted by a ternary-branching analysis, but is captured by the structures in Figure 6. These sorts of alternations, and their implications, will need to be kept in mind as further work on extraction from raising predicates progresses.

References

Robert Frank. 2002. *Phrase Structure Composition and Syntactic Dependencies*. Cambridge, MA: MIT Press.

Heidi Harley. 2002. Possession and the double object construction. *Linguistic Variation Yearbook*, 2:29–68.

Ray Jackendoff. 1990. On Larson's treatment of the double object construction. *Linguistic Inquiry*, 21(3):427–465.

Anthony Kroch and Aravind Joshi. 1985. The linguistic relevance of Tree Adjoining Grammar. Technical Report MS-CS-85-16, Department of Computer and Information Sciences, University of Pennsylvania.

Richard Larson. 1988. On the double object construction. *Linguistic Inquiry*, 19(3):335–391.

Dennis Ryan Storoshenko. 2006. Seems like a double object. In *Proceedings of the 22nd NorthWest Linguistics Conference*.

Author Index